CLOSE WRITING

Duke University Press Durham and London 2026

ALICE BUTLER

close writing

Kathy Acker, Cookie Mueller, & Love-in-Pieces

*
*
*

Printed in the United States
of America on acid-free paper ∞

Project Editor: Livia Tenzer
Designed by A. Mattson Gallagher

Typeset in Garamond Premier
Pro, Ogg, and Fira Sans by
Westchester Publishing Services

Cover art: Hervé Guibert, *Les lettres de Mathieu*, 1984. Gelatin silver print. © Christine Guibert. Courtesy of the Estate of Hervé Guibert, Paris.

Publication of this book has been aided by a grant from the Wyeth Foundation for American Art Publication Fund of CAA.

Library of Congress
Cataloging-in-Publication Data

Names: Butler, Alice, [date] author
Title: Close writing : Kathy Acker, Cookie Mueller, and love-in-pieces / Alice Butler.
Other titles: Kathy Acker, Cookie Mueller, and love-in pieces
Description: Durham : Duke University Press, 2026. | Includes bibliographical references and index.

Identifiers: LCCN 2025033805 (print)
LCCN 2025033806 (ebook)
ISBN 9781478033240 paperback
ISBN 9781478029786 hardcover
ISBN 9781478061984 ebook

Subjects: LCSH: Acker, Kathy, 1948–1997—Criticism and interpretation | Mueller, Cookie—Criticism and interpretation | Women authors, American—Biography | Motion picture actors and actresses—United States—Biography | Writing and art—United States—History—20th century | Feminist theory—United States | Queer theory—United States

Classification: LCC PS3551.C44 Z557 2026 (print) | LCC PS3551.C44 (ebook) | DDC 809/.89287—dc23/eng/20251118

LC record available at
https://lccn.loc.gov/2025033805
LC ebook record available at
https://lccn.loc.gov/2025033806

Contents

Acknowledgments

Many correspondents and interlocutors inside and outside the pages of this book of enduring love letters have helped to grow, shape, challenge, and sustain it. All of them deserve my enduring thanks, which are enveloped here.

I must first thank Matias Viegener, the executor of the Kathy Acker estate and Acker's friend, and Max Mueller, the executor of the Cookie Mueller estate and Mueller's son, for understanding and supporting this project from when it first took seed in doctoral study; and for providing kind and thoughtful access to their intimate things in the spirit of close writing. I am forever grateful.

I also shared moving conversations with Acker's and Mueller's artistic, intellectual, and intimate companions during the early years of this research. Stories and ideas surfaced in these encounters and dialogues across time and space, which were meaningful and resourceful to me and my writing. It was the gift of exchange, and I am grateful to Eleanor Antin, Page duBois, Melvyn Freilicher, Chris Kraus, Del LaGrace Volcano, Jerome Rothenberg, and Diane Rothenberg for their generosity and openness. Some of these meetings took place before or after or in between visits to archives held within special collections and libraries across the United

States. The archivists, librarians, and archive/library assistants supported and expanded such research trips with their dexterity, knowledge, and care: appreciations (in a letter) to them. Special appreciation to Jonathan Miles and Rebecca Carson for sharing the scanned letters with me; and to Daniel Schulz at the Kathy Acker Reading Room in Cologne for generously sending catalogs, covers, and interior pages.

Before its expansion and development throughout the pandemic and after, the book first found form and tried out its epistolary touch during my time at the University of Manchester (funded by the Arts and Humanities Research Council). So much of this finding and trying is indebted to the vision, care, and ambition of Carol Mavor, who created the most inspiring and sensitive of learning environments and relations, who nurtured a dynamic between art history and creative writing in my work, and who challenged and supported me to discover close writing. She gave me permission: one generous act of many. Her words—spoken and written—have worked within me, my writing, this book.

I am grateful to Ian McGuire, Monica Pearl, and Luke Skrebowski for their brilliant feedback at key stages of the research and writing. John McAuliffe was a thoughtful and incisive reader whose questions breathed life into the book's becoming. Emma Wilson's sensitive, attentive, and capacious insights and readings have been inspiring and instrumental to the shaping of both my intellectual life and the forms and energies of this book. I am deeply appreciative of her support.

Collaborators, colleagues, editors, and students have sustained my thinking and writing. Catherine Grant, Kate Random Love, Sina Najafi, and Moran Sheleg have all been sensitive and generous editors, whose projects to which I have contributed have generated important developments in the methods of my writing-as-research. Nell Osborne and Hilary White nourished my readerly and writerly gestures. Fatema Abdoolcarim studied and taught beside me; she has been a dear friend and trusted reader. Jo Applin has been kind and curious in our conversations about Acker and Mueller; I'm so grateful for her encouragement and support in the years since my PhD. Thanks to David Peters Corbett, Tom Day, the Terra Foundation for American Art, and the Courtauld Centre for the Art of the Americas for supporting and funding the research project and events series "'What a Hazard a Letter Is': Correspondence in Feminist Art, Art Writing, and Art History, from Emily Dickinson to Now," which created much-needed writing time to work on the manuscript, expand my epistolary worlds, and connect with many writers, artists, and thinkers who are committed to methods and practices of correspondence (my special thanks goes to the series' brilliant speakers and participants). The reciprocal, archive-based praxis of Olivia McCall—a workshop participant in the event series—energized this project when it needed it. Kathleen Stewart, Erica Rand, and Monica Huerta read the manuscript with rigor, imagination, and care, helping it become a stronger book. The manuscript has been generously stewarded to publication by Courtney Berger, my editor at Duke University Press. I am grateful to Courtney for her enthusiasm and support for the project throughout the editorial process. Excellent readers were found; their detailed and thoughtful feedback also made it a stronger book. I am grateful to them for their close reading of close writing. My thanks, too, to Mattson Gallagher, Laura Jaramillo, Ryan Kendell, and Livia Tenzer for their assistance in steering the book into visual and material form.

The Health and Care Research Cluster at the Royal College of Art has been a source of intellectual nourishment and experimentation; so, too, the dazzling cohort of MFA students in the "poetics of care" elective. My thanks to staff and students and the points of slippage between us. Funding from the Research and Knowledge Exchange Office has been invaluable in realizing the visual ambitions of the book, along with a grant from the Wyeth Foundation for American Art Publication Fund of the College Art Association, which made reproducing the images possible. My thanks, again.

Along with Carol Mavor, Fatema Abdoolcarim and Rebecca Hurst invited me into their writing group in 2022. My letters have loved listening. Our Friday meetings on Zoom have brought friendship, connection, and joy, crafted through the sounds, impressions, and responses of their reading and writing. I am grateful to them for helping me finalize the form and reintroduce the ritual of a writing practice into my work.

Melayna Lamb has been there with love and solidarity throughout it all: my love and solidarity to Melayna in return.

Gemma Blackshaw is the dearest of dear correspondents, whose letters have shaped my own and whose companionship in classrooms, calls, all sorts of communications, including the page, has sustained me. Letters-within-letters for G.

Lastly, I post my enduring thanks to beloved friends and family, with whom I have walked, talked, written alongside, and been inspired by; their encouragement and support have kept me writing. Charlotte, Trish, and Stuart Butler are held close in these pages. My partner, Josh

Malby, has nurtured the foundations and architectures of this writing—embodied, spatial, emotional, material—in the deepest of ways, so much more than he will have realized. I am grateful for the spaces he has held and made for me, including my favorite pink desk, from where these letters begin.

Prologue

BELOVED, SO BITTERSWEET

In the interval between reach and grasp, between glance and counterglance, between "I love you" and "I love you too," the absent presence of desire comes alive.

Anne Carson, *Eros the Bittersweet*

An Office of Undying Letters

If two women had not died—or if the post could still magically find them—their mailboxes would be full of love letters. Licked, sealed, enveloped. Successfully delivered to 600 West 163rd Street. Or safely received at 285 Bleecker Street. Both dead women lived, at times, in New York City. But knowing what we (think) we know (staying with the surface of things)—that the two women cannot receive or reply to such letters—it seems likely that these vulnerable missives failed, got delayed, or lost, destined for the Dead Letter Office (figure P.1). Or rather its ghosts: white women clerks inspecting stray mail.[1] Perhaps the handwriting on each envelope

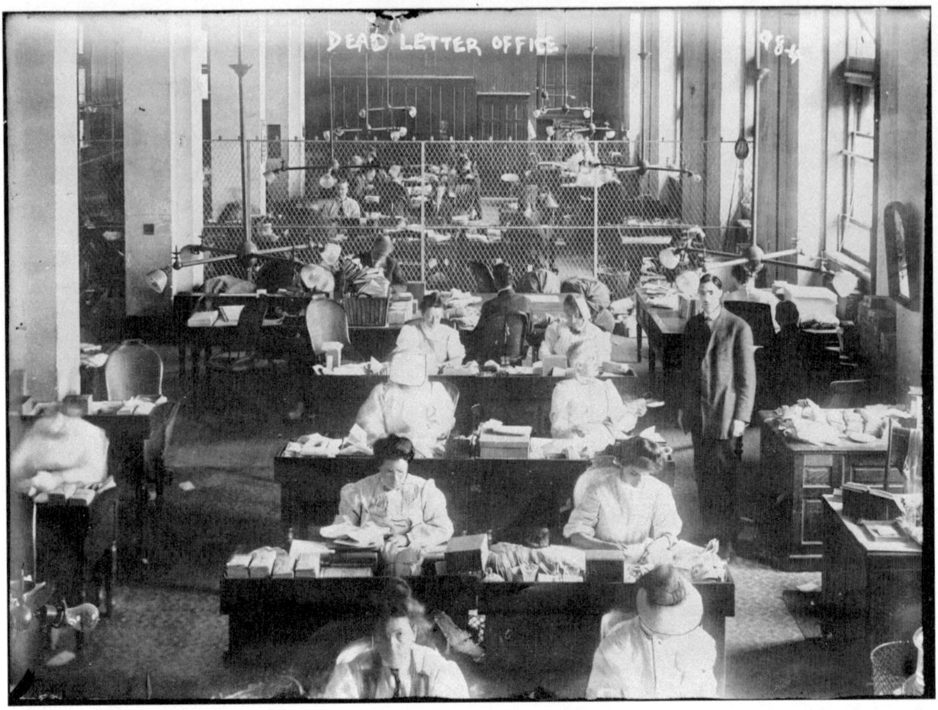

stray mail
letter detectives
the undying shadows

P.1 *Dead Letter Office*, glass negative, 12.7 × 17.8 cm. George Grantham Bain Collection, Library of Congress, Washington, DC.

was illegible, or communication channels got blocked, said these nimble letter detectives who examined the dead and undeliverable letters. Theirs was a type of skilled labor that was administration that was autopsy that was care.[2]

Unstable, precarious, purloined. *These* love letters move in the shadows.

I am consumed by the perversity of the impossible letter. Undeliverable.

Or undying.

* * *

Dear Cookie,

With flowers garlanded in your forever-blonde hair, scrap heaps of gold metals around your tiny wrists, bronze and pink beads draped at the neck, and gemstones on your clasped fingers: You picked out your favorite gold lamé dress to wear for the occasion. It was a farewell swamped in twinkling stars. It was a copper-silk sunset. A letter-in-a-bottle. It was an ending and a beginning.

It is hard to believe that your heart had stopped beating when your friend, Nan Goldin, took that candlelit, vanitas picture of you. I feel the warmth of your glow, like it was your Summer of Love in San Francisco all over again, or your first time on screen as an underground film actress just a few years after: those bronzed adolescent cheeks, the strange life in your still-life. I commence my correspondence here—in the middle of life and death: a sick time of suspension, a corpse-portrait of sleeping, dreaming, *writing* (your gathered pasts and presents)—to see how far and where your voltage burns. Still.

I fly to New York to feel close to you.
I fly to New York to feel close to your writing.
I fly to New York to feel close to the you that became your writing.

I search through manuscripts that did and did not make it: plays, short stories, art columns, an autobiographical novel. I spend time in the light and the dark. I dwell in the intimate inks of writing and image: midnight black, Cibachrome color, and mourning gray. It is never just one shade with you.

What was it like to write it, the closeness of pleasure and pain?

I hunt down ivory-satin wedding gowns and antique gold dresses in the cheap Downtown thrift stores of the city you call home. I feel your partial presence in my haunted palm. Loose threads spiral from the damaged seams, which I twist together with my fingertips, like the touch of this letter.

I pick up a shiny crimson dress cut from the same red satin entrails you sported at the Mudd Club. Then a denim jacket in the eighties indigo that sheltered your shoulders. To me this is buried treasure, but also a gift, like a message from you. Soon I realize all the blondes wandering these gentrified streets are wearing shiny crimson dresses and indigo denim jackets, too. Your generosity spreads wide. Your influence is contagious.

I spot the bright turquoise shine of your little last book in an East Village shop window. I carry my own loved copy (creased from years of contact, littered with messages in the margins) everywhere; all I need to do is open it, like an envelope, and I hear the candor of your voice so clearly. I hear you, speak with you, in the rustling, time-traveling intimacy of letter writing. I reply to the cares and pleasures and experiments-with-love of your pages, the ones that accumulated and accreted as a sickened but powerful effect of living and writing with AIDS toward the end of your not-too-late creative, embodied life. I fear what might happen to both our writing lives if I lose this jewel-sized paperback. Although, of course, in some ways, it's swallowed deep inside me; it's lodged there.

I knew you from the portraits first, but then I found words within them, as I also discovered the intimate rebellions of your life in writing, its utter refusal to conform, its beautiful practice of living and making and re-worlding and re-wilding, beyond the categories, to form twisted lines and vines and veins of loving and writing free. It was this desire that I recognized a glimmer of in myself, bringing me to your doorstep to release our shared stories in first-person mail, widening my capacity to love.

I gaze at the fourth-floor windows of your Bleecker Street apartment. A blind is half-drawn, and a light is on, its soft glow sneaks through the slats. A sash is shunted a little bit open to let in the crisp fall air, constant car horns on a loop. From outside to inside and inside to outside: I hear the clickety hops of shuffling footsteps, the soundtrack of your repaired spring-o-later heels, moving from typewriter to door. A torn-out manuscript page floats suspended, mid-flight: somewhere between sky and ground, you and me. Could it be you there, at home, with Max or Sharon or Vittorio or Nan, in the intimate throes of writing? Still?

But while I sense your abstract traces strangely alive all over the city, it is through witnessing the picture of you reclining in your gold and bronze and pink dashed casket, me cross-legged on a pitch-black museum floor, the sounds of Petula Clark's "Downtown" piercing through the space, my skin, my jet-lagged brain, that the love that I feel for you sparks as bitter-sweet. I cross time and space, from life into death, and back again. I feel my heart race too quickly. I struggle to breathe, unable to comprehend the injustice of you being physically gone.

And yet there are moments of connection, a bringing of life at the borderline, like the flicker of a lace glove on your wedding day: holding a ten-dollar note rolled up, ready to ingest a line of cocaine, bright like a strip light, becoming brighter again as a line of writing.

I see words in the crochet lattice of your antique glove: slipped inside the arm of your husband-to-be. He is held there, close to you, forever in your writing.

I cannot re-create that protected kind of closeness or love, for that was yours alone. But I am ready to take a risk, to gesture newly to love, to attempt to touch you and your stories back (of life and death, often both at once). My letters are falling (mid-flight, suspended): like the first snowfall of the year.

* * *

Dear Kathy,

The shirt was a smart choice. I'd be pretending if I wasn't enchanted, that I hadn't looked. In the sickened time of suspension—an in-between space where life and death move one across the other—you wore the finest polyester leopard-print mesh, lined in black satin, only one button fastened just above the navel to create a deep plunging V. The slippery shirt's undoneness encloses the viewer to stay with you there, at the intimate flesh, a form of accompaniment. From tight tummy to the shadowy beginnings of a scar: I begin to see your muscular, freckled mastectomized chest. Is that the dash of a drawing underneath? Soon I read the enfleshed line of writing; you marked it here and everywhere. There's a beautiful sense of ornament to the whole thing. Like ritual. I wonder if you went shopping for the shoot with a friend. This another kind of ritual.

And yet, with your peroxide-tinted shaved head downturned, those smudged kohl eyelids nearing closure, it's also a portrait of rest and sleep: the fray of living and dying. And writing, too? I dwell in the gauze of girl and boy. I stay with the enmeshed afterlife of image and writing, in this portrait named *RePose*. Taken by your close friend Del LaGrace Volcano, it would go alongside your illness essay published in the *Guardian*. Here, in "The Gift of Disease," you lacerated in words the personal and political circumstances of your breast cancer diagnosis, double mastectomy, and walking away from Western medicine, its many injustices. You turned to the possibilities of the imagination instead.

I follow your lead, twenty years after your devastating death at an alternative clinic in Tijuana, where you received palliative care. It was only thirty kilometers down the highway, and over the border, from the bed that had once been your writing desk, in the San Diego of your early twenties, many decades before.

I fly coast-to-coast to feel close to you.
I fly coast-to-coast to feel close to your writing.
I fly coast-to-coast to feel close to the you that became your writing.

While the tattoos may've got my attention when I, too, was a writer of "great expectations" (to purloin the title of your purloined punk novel), it's the quieter pictures of you I take with me: like *RePose*, or the state of recline captured in a friend's photograph of you dressed in a modest but artfully deconstructed tunic while daydreaming on your bed in your Lower East Side loft of the early 1980s. Your tufted head of hair sinks into an animal-print cushion propped up against your too-full library of books. A sense of synchronicity takes over, strangely spectral, when I find myself repeating this pose in the recurring jet-lagged dawn of early morning, as I lie strewn across the sheets of my sublet apartment (a few blocks over from yours): surrounded by your silver and pink paperbacks.

I read. I cite. I copy. I look. I touch. I sense. I write. It happens in the apartment, or the hotel, often while walking the city (was it you outside the Mudd Club struggling with too many books in your hand? For a second, I swore it was), sometimes sat on the subway's curved plastic seats, and always in the archive. I am experiencing a state of incorporation, as you incorporated the words of others—as well as yourself—in enchanting, illegitimate acts of licentiousness and renewal. Could I assume permission in no permission? Even your friends at the San Francisco memorial dipped their fingers into the beaux arts vase holding your ashes and *licked*, before your cremains got taken with the tides of the Pacific. It was a scattering that echoed the dispersal of your manuscripts: from the numerous notebooks in New York, to the papers at Duke, to the correspondences opened in California.

I skulk the aisles and passageways of the Geisel Library in San Diego, sense the shadows of your scribbles in the edges of the printed word. I scratch my finger on the staples of your handmade chapbooks. I listen to the open mouth of your letters to friends and lovers making room for the paradoxes of feeling. I talk with your friends who received them. I feel your partial presence in an imagined piece of paper retold as a story: the mailing list the performance artist gave to you so you could send your writing out. I travel from the university to the coast to summon a shared map of checkpoints. I run across the beach to end each day in your footprints.

I rest and catch my breath as the La Jolla waves lap and cool my feet. These are the same seas that took your ashes into their mouth. It's a swirling that sparks as beautifully but painfully bittersweet.

I am beginning to sense a voice on the page that is not just mine (could it be ours?), like the combined ink of two love letters caught in the rain, or the swirling foams of physical traces. It's the intimate stuff of your life in writing that has brought it to the surface. As I open ring-bound notebooks, diaries, envelopes, and photographs, where you were trying to figure it out (your creative and sexual and sensual life), not finished, not resolved (there are no neat conclusions), another kind of opening occurs. It's in those vulnerable pages that I touched my relationship to writing.

Too young for the memorials that happened all over the world, these daydreaming letters are all I have to say hello and goodbye—to stay with the ornament and quiet of you: your infectious contradictions—each letter as charged as a first-time meeting. Fragments of the personal have entered my writing. Quite simply, and I know I am not the first to write to you, but I could not have done it without you.

Fleeing, Flying, Longing, Love-Letter Writing

I grasp for their inked, jeweled fingers: *almost* touching, their bodies in pieces—their lives *in and as writing*.

ACKER, KATHY (née Weill Alexander, first name Karen), was born April 18, 1947, on New York's Upper East Side, an area that can be traced to the Manhatta of Lenape lands before their tribes were forcibly removed. Kathy's biological father, a German-Jewish businessman from Buffalo, New York, had abandoned her mother, Claire Weill, of Austrian-Jewish heritage, when Claire was just three months pregnant. A new husband in Albert Alexander came into the fold, becoming the infant's stepfather; a half-sister, Wendy, soon followed. But Wendy is not present in an early black-and-white photograph cut with shearing scissors of a young girl then named Karen, aged three. Karen wears a double-breasted woolen jacket. She shuffles inquisitively closer to the camera, her mouth partly open as she tries for new words, soft brown curls grazing her cheek. Soon after the picture was taken, she attended a private girls' school in an illustrious neighborhood, which was "unofficially known as the only 'white glove' Upper East Side" institution "that was widely open to Jews" (or was accessible to any white student whose family could afford the tuition).[3] She was a voracious reader. She was a "pirate" who ran away, "into the world of books."[4] And here she stayed: into adolescence. In an essay on her favorite writer of childhood, Colette (its typescript pages protected within an envelope scrawled with the French novelist's name), she would describe living a "double life, a life in the parent/school I had to inhabit and a life in the art world about which I could not talk."[5] She had an older filmmaker boyfriend when she was aged sixteen. She met poets and artists. This was her adolescent "forbidden world."[6]

The 1964 yearbook committee characterized her thus: "Whatever she is, she's different. She's more intellectual than many of her class; she reads more; and she acts more avant-garde. She practices a studied nonchalance, taking things in her stride, letting trivial matters in one ear and out the other."[7]

MUELLER, COOKIE. In Baltimore, a city that resides on the unceded lands of Indigenous Piscataway and Susquehannock peoples, she was born—on March 2, 1949—after her older sister and brother. She was officially named the somewhat demure Dorothy Karen, but as she remembers the mythic beginnings of what became her life in "My Bio—Notes on an American Childhood," "Somehow I got the name Cookie before I could walk. It didn't matter to me, they could call me whatever they wanted."[8] She is sweetly "Cookie" in a photograph of her taken in school, as she pirouettes on tippy toes in a sequin-splashed ballerina tutu. She danced, she read, she wrote, she wandered into the woods, as a young girl. She suffered unimaginable loss when her brother died after climbing a tree. Then, aged fifteen, she began escaping, like a daily ritual, the white middle-class home in which she grew. "I was always leaving," she would write, much later, "standing on the porch saying goodbye to the older couple in the living room."[9] New familial shapes would follow—in San Francisco, Provincetown, Positano, and New York City.

On graduating from high school in 1967, she was awarded the prize for "most expressive."[10]

Fleeing and flying, they longed to become writers. *Like little birds testing their wings.*

Almost Touching

Sometimes their paths physically crossed, like on Valentine's Day, 1980, when they performed alongside one another at the Mudd Club: the Downtown New York venue on White Street that was once a textile warehouse. Acker read aloud letters addressed to ex-boyfriends, and Mueller played the part of an ex-boyfriend in drag, for her friend Gary Indiana.

But it is more likely that they *almost touched*, too, as they shared the same publishers, the same pages, the same places, the same photographic portraitists (Robert Mapplethorpe, Marcus Leatherdale) the same people (friends and lovers, even the same hidden name in Karen), while never inhabiting the known boundaries of a close relationship.[11] Instead, proximity was conjured in echoes and traces and thumbprints, not always legible lines of contact, but palpable all the same, like the sensorial hum of an affective plane, from which my own correspondence is energized. And so, I speculate: that the spectral mutters of Kathy Acker reading her writing aloud for the first time at the St. Mark's Poetry Project in 1971 could also be heard nearly two decades later, at Cookie Mueller's funeral. Beneath those same vaulted ceilings, her friends said goodbye to her body but not her pieces. Their words filled and crossed and combined through the air.

It's possible, too, that Acker attended the 1990 launch of Mueller's small-in-scale but vast-in-spirit book, *Walking Through Clear Water in a Pool Painted Black*, which was published by Semiotext(e)'s Native Agents series, in painful, posthumous proximity to her AIDS-related death, the night of November 10, 1989. Kathy's hot-pink paperback of short pieces came out in the same series, which was founded by the then filmmaker, and later Native Agents author, Chris Kraus, just a year after Mueller's own compilation was published. Reflecting back on the series in a 2014 essay, Kraus describes how she soon realized that these works "had something in common": "*Yes* they were all written by women—*yes* they were all written in the first person—and like practically all books and films of their time, they included writing about sex."[12] Theirs is an "active, public 'I,'" a performative "I," who moves "through the text and the world."[13]

An Afterlife in Pieces

I have touched my beloveds' bittersweet pieces. In the archive, on the street, while *dreaming*—this is how they have come to me, and I have come to *love* them. I have absorbed reflections and refractions, pieces of text and textile, swatches of writing, and traces of voice. I have assembled their pieces into unfinished portraits. I am haunted by the piecemeal afterlives of my beloveds, flowing outward, sideways, refusing the conventions of the catalog or container. This is the capacious world in which my love for them has grown and flourished, in spite of the spatial, temporal, and physical distance between us. Closeness is conjured in flashes of contact, a fleeting feeling, the scribbling of correspondence.

In "Cookie," whose body is only familiar to me in the afterlives of her objects (an attachment that is a fantasy but that is also felt as *real*), I have also felt, physically and affectively, the pulse of her body through her fragments, the feverish part-objects of her writing: ring-bound and blue-lined notebook pages freckled with forget-me-not notations; friends' phone numbers so she could stay "in touch," or get her writing out; clothing designs near desiring drawings; drafts of pieces that emerged beyond her private envelopes (and pieces that did not); handwritten renditions of her own fantasy letters of healing sketched in a rush; doodled lines becoming figurative drawings (of her husband, Vittorio Scarpati); newspaper cuttings kept, folded, stacked, covers printed with headlines, horrible but true: "Die young, stay pretty";[14] incomplete copies of her "Art and About" columns for *Details* magazine and clippings that declare suspension;

fragments of her columns, sketches for stories, and stories repeated; drafts annotated and redacted; mountains of manuscripts; résumés when she needed more work; letters received and sent (intimate and administrative [and both]); hundreds and hundreds of *lists*. (She, like I, like Eve Kosofsky Sedgwick, takes pleasure in "the additive mode."[15])

I have fixated on the *c* to the twinned *o*'s to the *k* and the dotted *i* ending in the smile of an *e* of her signature, scrawled in biro on her manuscripts. Her name sings through time when I utter it. I have copied down her phone numbers and addresses (surreptitiously gleaned from the margins of her manuscripts). I have absorbed the specter of her in my writing, corresponding without a need for a conventional reply—just to talk or write—through and with the pieces of her life and text, including private and public correspondence.

She entered my life as "holographic projections" in printed pages bearing her name, in the photographs caressed in the archive not officially her own, or bad-quality portraits found online.[16] She's almost present, too, in the clothes I pull over my skin, those secondhand lace garments, or frayed, "too-full" denim jackets. In the ambient, amber-lit pictures taken of her by her close friend Nan Goldin (who was Nancy before leaving home), she is the sweetest morsel of a name on a tongue; she is *Cookie Laughing, New York City* (1985). In a different way (I know I could never, should never, claim that closeness), she is "Cookie" to me, too: I hold her in my open mouth.

Sometimes, encounters between her and me are momentary and brief, like the receiving of a letter—a voice, a sound—sent from the past. I hear her so clearly in the intensity of that contact, although the sharpness fades at the edges. She re-surfaced once at the surface of the page: the see-through paper upon which the details of her memorial at the Downtown venue MK were printed. Originally sent to the people with whom she was intimate, that is, "familiar," I held it delicately at the fingertips: life and death meeting at the transparence of its boundary.

My world vibrates with Cookie's body in pieces. Three short words written by her hand for the poet Richard Hell could be mine for her. "*Hi—I miss you.*"[17] Each sentence that I form in my mouth is spiked by this bittersweetness: the pain and pleasure of saying hello and goodbye in one epistolary gesture. I can taste it on my tongue. Eros, writes Anne Carson, is shaped by such emotional paradoxes, as the lover wants what she "does not have," sustained in ambivalent orbits, the energies of love and hate, presence and absence circling her.[18] She is hungry (*I am hungry*) for the body of her (*or my*) absent beloved. The distance between lover and beloved is what keeps desire alive, electrifies it. It keeps the desire of this writing alive, too. As Carson explains, "A space must be maintained or desire ends. . . . The reach of desire is defined in action: beautiful (in its object), foiled (in its attempt), endless (in time)."[19]

Kathy crawls and scuttles in the crevices and shadows of my life, too. She is the Black Tarantula, the pseudonym she used to author her early chapbooks sent through the mail or to sign off letters with a spider symbol drawing. She is the mysterious correspondent with an "enemy list."[20] She is this disguise, a game of literary hide-and-seek, which foreshadows the pose, the gesture, the cutaway Lycra leotard, performed and worn in a Robert Mapplethorpe portrait. She is the library she ate up as a young writer studying Classics. She is her copy of Virgil's *Bucolics and Georgics*, its solidified lines of Latin interrupted and smeared by ink-spilled insertions. She is the thousands of books she wanted to be available for public use after her death. She is archived in an answering machine message. She is wound in a tape reel or pixelated by VHS. She is an assemblage of fairytale-gothic tattoos. She is a wardrobe of designer clothes stored away in boxes. She is a Vivienne Westwood pirate jacket hanging on a wooden hanger. She is an astrological chart, or a natal chart mapped by Scary Spice. She is the Kathy Acker described by the friends of hers I've met, as well as the author absorbed in essays about her life and work. She is the stack of silver paperbacks strewn across my desk, infiltrated with felt-tipped lines and penciled annotations (messages of correspondence) across the years of my loving her. She once made contact with Virgil, as I've made contact with *pieces* of her: love letters; friend letters (sent and received); diaries and notebooks; published and unpublished part-objects (the books featuring her name and face, and the books in which she featured); videos; invitation cards; proofs; photographs.

She *is* her writing matter: It's where she viscerally realized, abstracted, her body, memories, and desire. When I cradle her correspondences in my palm, her childlike handwriting touches mine. My own desire to know or love her in writing swells with the turn of each typescript page, the obsessive handling of diaries, notebooks, and novels-in-notebooks. I peel away handwritten fragments collaged onto proofs and pages to uncover the physical processes of her writings, their intimacies with visual art; these are the pieces with which she made and re-made herself and writing body. I peel away at her pieces to pick closer to her life-in-writing.

She is and is not only, or never entirely, all of these *things*. She is a body in pieces. Only partial, never whole: *like Cookie*. In the archive, on the street, while *dreaming*—this is how they have come to me, and I have come to *love* them.

It is how they have come to me in their writings, too. Here they pieced together *in closeness* autobiographical episodes, bygone memories from childhood and adolescence, the ambivalent angles of their social, sexual, and sick lives. Their author portraits—of Cookie wearing black jersey in the shadows, or Kathy greased in punk leather and piercings—illustrate the glossy back covers of their Semiotext(e) paperbacks. My proximity to them through these pictures, the penetrating gaze held by their kohl-rimmed eyes, is unstable, as it was in the books' pages in which they mediated, abstracted, flayed, and picked apart the visceral substances and textures of their embodied lives.

I reach. I reach. I reach. I desire to get close, closer, closer still. But it will always be the boundary, the blanketing of absence that is interlaced within and around their bodies in pieces, which motivates my love for them in writing: "the boundary of flesh and self between you and me."[21]

When Carson describes in *Eros the Bittersweet* that it is the realization of the edge, the separating seam between lover and beloved, which defines and energizes the experience of desiring, loving, reaching, and imagining what or who could be, or could *never* be, pleasured and *touched*, she does so by turning back to the ancient poet Sappho—and the adjective coined by Sappho, *glukupikron*, with which the essay begins. Bitter-sweet, sweet-bitter: "There may be various relations between the two savors," begins Carson, later elaborating that, "like Sappho's adjective *glukupikron*, the moment of desire is one that defies proper edge, being a compound of opposites forced together at pressure."[22] Sappho sketched the conflicting forces of love as "bittersweet" in Fragment 130, which Jonathan Goldberg has read as a queer "divided, doubled, self-contradictory state."[23] It is a piecemeal state that emerges in my beloveds' written pieces, too, across the intermeshed spaces of the private and public in which their work materialized.

Goldberg calls Carson's book "about eros" a book also "about Sappho," "about the language for eros she created," which conjoined loving and writing into the same fabric of experience. Writing-as-loving and loving-as-writing is sapphic, argues Goldberg; it is the condition of being sapphic, which is not as universalized, or as ungendered and unsexed, as it first appears in Carson's book.[24] Reading Carson closely, Goldberg notes the gendering of the lover as the poet as Sappho as *her* when Carson revisits Fragment 31 in an essay fragment titled "What Does the Lover Want from Love?" It is that wanting which maintains the reach, the pulse, the lines of the network electrifying desire: "Having would annihilate eros."[25]

And eros, claims Goldberg, originates in the female poet writing to her same-sex beloved, like my sapphic letters to the dead; like Acker's erotic epistles to her friend, Terence Sellers, that she signed off in bold felt-tip "I MISS YOU I LOVE YOU";[26] or even like Mueller's anecdotal description in the portrait piece "Tattooed Friends" of the intimate attachments sewn together by inking your best friend's flesh, a letter laid over the skin.[27] All of us—Kathy, Cookie, Sappho, and *Me*, born years, decades, or centuries apart—use the first person "I." We learn and *love* from our bodies: in all their mess and multiplicity, in all their broken pieces. In loving my beloved writers in short bursts and broken lines—letters, messages, postscripts, pieces, which "create in the elusive, illusive fragmentary net of words the absent one, the desired one"—I, too, have felt the "disorder in the body in love . . . a body in pieces, disjointed, a broken set of organs, limbs, bodily functions."[28]

I endure disturbed nights in bed, consumed by the words to reply. I experience sudden menstruations, convinced it is our cycles aligning with the moon.

Fragment 31 is one dismembered part among many broken lines, shattered shards, absorbed citations in later authors' works, bits and pieces "painstakingly reconstructed from ancient papyri exhumed from Egyptian sands," and then re-read, translated, translated again (their sapphic desire and queer eroticism often erased), through which Sappho—in all her multiple configurations, echoing the first names with which I address the overlapping lives and texts of my alliterating beloved (from now on, always: *Dear Kathy; Dear Cookie*)—has come to us, too.[29] She is, as Page duBois writes in *Sappho Is Burning*, "not a person" whom we can ever truly know; she is "not even a character in a drama or a fiction, but a set of texts gathered in her name."[30] She is, like the queerness of the bittersweet desire she writes, an assemblage, a patchwork of pieces, wherein the voice that speaks blurs with the poet herself, creating a destabilizing slippage between life and fiction. As duBois announces, "We know her work only in fragments," before questioning how historians might begin to approach and access Sappho's poetry when so much of it, so much of *her*, has been rendered unknowable and indistinct.[31]

Thinking with Sappho (figure and verse) as a body in pieces, duBois invites a relationship to the past and its fragments that does not focus on "the restoration of lost wholes, or even on the tragic impossibility of the reconstitution," but recognizes instead its always partial, contingent nature.[32] DuBois describes this dialectic, between the postmodern thinker and its fragmentary objects, as being similar to the "disparate collection of body parts" that combine in the domain of the Lacanian symbolic, wherein the subject "alternates between a fictional 'I' and an invented memory, a phantasy, of a time before the capture of this 'I.'"[33] Suggesting that the desire to mend the past, to cohere it, to repair or clean up the "tears, frangible edges, erasures, abrasions," neglects the *processes* of historiography, duBois instead proposes that we "read what we have," to dream and desire and speculate these fragments *reparatively* anew.[34]

This mode of repair, which pleasures the partial rather than the whole, motivates my writing. I reach, *across absence*, for the bittersweet pieces of Kathy and Cookie, their (oft-misunderstood) lives and writings and part-objects and pictures. I am committed to reinvigorating their bodies in pieces, but in a way that I hope goes deeper than simply bringing their figures out of the dark and into the light. I look for the gray tones in between—by writing to and beside them, beginning with the dead letter. This book is a project of paying close attention; it depends on reparative gestures to do so. Such an approach has emerged with the recognition of what Kathy and Cookie—their lives and deaths; their expanded autofictional archives of paper ephemera, publications, photography, clothing, correspondence, books; their bodies in pieces; their afterlife—deserve and need. To be close like this invites me to slip between life and text, just like they did. I reject the urge to either mythologize like a biographer or analyze like a critic; instead, I do both (they always did *both*). I do both to unravel the formal and political textures of their performing, fictionalizing, and materializing of lived experiences in writing. Underpinned by a practice of reparativity, the book is interwoven with a three-way intervention: to reignite (rather than make whole) pieces of Kathy and Cookie by illuminating the radical complexities of their lives *in* and *as* writing; to show how such writing used interdisciplinary practices between art, literature, and performance; and to propose and perform a queer feminist methodology that feels and writes closely to them. Writing from love, as

Hélène Cixous would say, it asks how taking risks with form can engender new ways of taking risks with content, in a way that attends to the mess, the complexity, the vitality, of our subjects' lives and works.[35]

I cannot let my beloveds' bittersweet bodies in pieces go, decades after their deaths. I write *to* them and *with* them—closely, affectively, passionately, erotically, even *perversely*.[36] I do this to touch and breathe new life into their lives and texts, to explore their entangling, across word and image, and to newly attend to the complex feminist effects of such crossings in what I call their *close writing*. I match close writing with close writing, a reply to sender. I do this *for* them: the *risk* of writing reparative love.

This act of correspondence echoes Eve Kosofsky Sedgwick's loving-at-a-memorial-distance of the art critic Craig Owens, following his death from AIDS-related illness on July 4, 1990. As a "strange—*not* to say rare—form of love," it flourished across the "love of part-objects, snatches of print, glimpses and touches of a largely unfamiliar body."[37] Her eros writing was "sent out" at a time of devastating, deepening precarity, pain, and loss for the most vulnerable, shamed, and stigmatized in society, which included queer and trans people, sex workers, and IV drug users (as the "queer paradigm" of the epidemic depended on, with its homophobic, racist, and fundamentally biomedical, discriminatory narratives of risk-taking sexually deviant behaviors).[38] It also included Latinx and Black communities enduring unequal conditions "embodied as ill-health and vulnerability to disease"—what Adam Geary has termed in specific relation to anti-Blackness, "the violent intimacy of the racist state."[39] Writing near this context, there was much at stake for Sedgwick to turn "to love" in critical writing.

She addresses the "nauseatingly familiar blankness" she feels upon the death of her writer-beloved, that "someone whom so many of us saw as so self-evidently treasurable, could be in a society that so failed to treasure him . . . a society that found it (to put it no more strongly than this) so possible, so little painful to let Craig die."[40] Sedgwick challenges the pain, the hurt, the devastation of *a* death (although her attention is both singular and collective) wrought by pervasive and repetitive societal oppressions aimed at queer subjects, and responds not with what she would later describe as the paranoid impulse to anticipate, to know, to expose oppression to be true, but with the affective pleasure of a reparative reading.[41] This is an alternative critical position to the paranoid—one that does not deny the "reality or gravity of enmity or oppression" but instead undertakes a "different range of affects, ambitions, and risks" as a means of survival and love—which was theorized in two versions of the essay "Paranoid Reading and Reparative Reading," published in 1997 and 2003.[42] Departing from Melanie Klein's depressive position, described by Sedgwick as an "anxiety-mitigating achievement," whereby the infant or adult is able to "use one's own resources to assemble or 'repair' the murderous part-objects into something like a whole," though "*not necessarily like any pre-existing whole*," the reparative reading position seeks and sustains pleasure and plenitude as political energies and resources of resistance.[43]

As a mode of repair, I am indebted to its always partial, performative, and in-process effects. Rather than seeking full restoration of my beloveds' lives, bodies, and texts, this version of the reparative that I develop as close writing acknowledges cuts, tears, abrasions, fragments; it writes *with* them in a speculative afterlife, as a pleasure-glimpsing position and practice of love-as-attention-as-care. "The body beckons us," as Peggy Phelan writes in *Mourning Sex*—grappling with the corporeal myths and meditations that framed the overlapping emergencies of HIV/AIDS—and yet always "resists our attempts to remake it."[44] My performative writing also dwells in the paradoxical lure of this "resistant beckoning," recognizing that the "affective outline of what we've lost might bring us closer to the bodies we want still to touch than the restored illustration can."[45]

Similarly, in "Memorial for Craig Owens," Sedgwick was embodying and practicing the absent-present performativity of the reparative frame, as she recuperates within the short text a personal experience of writing (an essay inspired by "a couple of cryptic paragraphs of Craig's") that is also an experience of reading, or rather a felt fantasy of him reading her.[46] It is the "fun of imagining sending" the part-finished essay to him, which motivates her to write, binding writing up with reading, with influence and love, akin to epistolary exchange.[47] This fantasy is a source of "pleasure" for Sedgwick the writer, with her beloved's "magical . . . enigmatic, magnetic" words becoming "permanently lodged" in her heart, like the Kleinian printed part-objects with which she comes to love him, as noted in the second sentence, and with which their relation is nourished and sustained.[48] The adjectives Sedgwick uses to describe her beloved's writing suggest the alchemical, the otherworldly, the cosmic: forces and flows of energy that engulf her, merging language with body, subject with object. Toward the end of the memorial, Sedgwick mourns the loss of this binding. Her grief is entangled with the process of writing, with the felt loss of exchange and comment and echo and citation that animated their connecting worlds, and electrified Sedgwick's desire for him, the author (she affectionately calls him by his first name "Craig," too). In many ways, the relation she mourns continues to unfold following his death, becomes dangerously but resourcefully illicit, across the piece's three short paragraphs that were first spoken and then printed—another part-object.

How can writing lovingly to another writer after their death be both dangerous *and* resourceful? Jane Gallop notes in Sedgwick's queer theoretical memorial the affirmation of "stigmatized desire in the face of AIDS and death" and the crucial articulation, "at one and the same time" of both "desire and loss, both radical perversity and grief."[49] This, argues Gallop, energized queer theory in the early 1990s, as the connection between "mourning and theoretical insight," which Jacques Derrida had contemporaneously described as "indecent," became politically necessary: a source of reparative resistance for the dead and for the living and for so many living precariously in between.[50] The radical perversity imagined in Sedgwick's memorial extends to the web of erotic relations that brings writers into close, intimate, and thrilling proximity.

I am indecently familiar in my letters and letter-essays, collecting love-in-pieces and pieces of my love, written beside my bittersweet beloveds' own bittersweet pieces. As a reparative reader and writer, I take this risk for *them*, my absent beloveds: two sick women, as the contemporary artist Johanna Hedva would call them, suffering diseases and disorders that have come to them (but are not part of them), resistant to the forces of the "Western medical-insurance industrial complex" that thinks it understands them.[51] For Cookie, it was HIV/AIDS; for Kathy—and for Sedgwick—it was cancer that began in the breast. Sedgwick identified as queer *across* the lines of gender when her experience of being diagnosed with breast cancer brought her closer to the devastating effects of the AIDS epidemic felt by her closest friends. She writes about, and *through*, this identification in "White Glasses," an essay that anticipates becoming an obituary for her friend Michael Lynch, and also in her essay on reparative reading, wherein she describes, from a position of lived experience shared with friends like Michael, the "brutal foreshortening of so many queer life spans" as changing the paranoid stiffness and regularity of generational narratives.[52] Other relations are possible, suggests Sedgwick, producing lines of contact and love that track forward and back and *sideways*. To rethink erotic relations across time on behalf of the sick woman writer foreshortened is a necessary act of love, attention, and care, pointing to another of this book's motives—rooted in the urge to alleviate absence by paying attention to method, feeling, and writing (*what I can give you*). The sick woman calls for such reparative risks to be taken, and so I spill love letters to them: a way to illuminate, care for, and touch the wild and radical complexities of their lives in and as writing, their *close writing*.

I feel myself falling.

*
*
*

Introduction

A WRITER'S LOVE

Because I write for, I write from, I start writing from: Love. I write out of love. Writing, loving: inseparable. Writing is a gesture of love. *The Gesture.*

Hélène Cixous, "Coming to Writing"

I want the you no one else can see, the you so close the third person never need apply.

Maggie Nelson, *The Argonauts*

A note slipped under a door or a crumpled message passed from cell to cell, hand to hand is called a kite—words travel even when we can't.

Saidiya Hartman, *Wayward Lives Beautiful Experiments*

The Envelope (*You*: My First Love)

Etched into the pale interior of my right arm, close to the sweaty crease of my elbow, from which my stronger forearm extends, and then the hand I write with (letters, notes, *pieces*), is a small tattoo of an envelope. It's roughly the same size as a first- or second-class stamp, a simple line drawing. It encases bare, hidden-from-the-sun pale skin with its jet-black marks: a lightly tufted carpet of blonde, downy hairs. Comprising horizontal, vertical, and diagonal dashes, the symbol depicts a strangely anonymous verso of a sealed envelope, hiding the unwritten touch of desire in the secretive flaps, folds, seams, and seals. The desire to touch is palpable, if not clearly legible. *Who goes there?* There is no address to whom it might be sent, or where it might be returned to, if it gets delayed and lost. But if I look closely enough, their names coagulate at the surface of the cut. *Beloved.*

Prior to getting this "mail art," my body had never been inked. But after returning from six weeks in New York, where I'd touched my beloveds' bittersweet pieces and touched them with draft letters back, I had my heart set on imaging, on the surface of my skin, how our writings met. And yet I panicked about the thought of the needle, the shame of exposing this romance that bordered on obsession, as if I was writing/possessing their name on my flesh like a lover (*yes, that is me*). It took the breathing person I loved and lived with to surprise me with a tattoo appointment at a parlor in Brighton, a few streets back from the beach on which we met, near the pier on which one half of my epistolary beloved once walked, for me to finally get inked.

The tattoo is for them both, a permanent mark of how much their lives in and as writing have touched me. I feel them forever: at the envelope of my body, the boundary, where our pieces merge. Their words have touched my relationship to love: the difficulty to express it, inhabit all its broken pieces. After it was drawn, my secret envelope glowed bright pink, and now I'm blushing once more, the rising pulse of the personal. It bubbles and steams at the paper's folds.

(Almost) Pink Steam

Rather than send me a birthday card, a friend left a love letter at my door instead, a month after I was scored with epistolary lines. The letter was housed within an envelope, despite the fact I was then living on a forty-foot narrowboat that cruised the canals of London and was without an official address. She surreptitiously created her own postal network, so the letter wouldn't get lost. It was a gesture that gestured toward, with affective love and corporeal attention, the epistolary symbol printed on my body.

To write a friend a love letter is to feel the effects of what Dodie Bellamy calls her 2004 collection of essays, *Pink Steam*. The cover is hot pink, with a typeface that looks as if it has been cut from an eighties horror movie. Printed at its center is a singular almond-shaped eye in yellow; its curved lines and gloopy flicks of mascara clustered at the lashes suggest it to be part of a feminine face, the desire of a female gaze. Despite a long history of gendering with color—which Thomas Gainsborough captured when he painted a full-length portrait of a blushing boy wearing salmon-pink silks that ripple like the muscular tissues studied by the boy's anatomist grandfather (*The Pink Boy*, 1782)—Jane Gallop prefers to think of pink as "*the* color of sexual difference," a "blatant little-girl color." This association is expressed in her own essay on love letters that addresses the subjects of Flemish seventeenth-century painting (to which Gainsborough also turned) alongside an epistolary essay from 1977 by the French writer Annie Leclerc.[1] But before Gallop's close reading of suggestive ripples gets her there, she considers the penetration of French theory into American academia, which made an anthology such as the 1982 *Writing and Sexual Difference* possible, with a cover, dipped in "mauve . . . [a]lmost pink," that suggestively implies how pinkish tones unfairly (and phallocentrically) carry the "burden of sexual difference."[2] Pink is unseemly, explicitly girlish, which Bellamy (knowingly) mimics and plays with in *Pink Steam*, as she offers up intimate, adolescent-style letters and diaries as essays. Within them, she pushes pinkness to a state of girl gore that flirts with the blush of shame, with making it public, these vulnerable states of bodily abjection.

In the first-person piece "Barbie's Dream House," for example, Bellamy imagines "walking through Barbie's living room feeling off-kilter," its "cheap cardboard walls . . . those of postwar prefab housing."[3] In Bellamy's psychedelic queer reading, she begins to see "adolescent sexual secrets burst[ing] through cardboard dimensionality," which echoes her own autoerotic experience—of never owning a Barbie but touching one: "I . . . pulled down the top of her swimsuit and rubbed her rock hard breasts with my thumb," writes Bellamy.[4] Noting the "creamy angularity of Barbie's body" as manufactured in 1962, Bellamy alludes to what Erica Rand critically examines in *Barbie's Queer Accessories* (1995): that "'white' Barbie" has been made the "standard," the desirable norm, by racial capitalism, even when diversity is superficially displayed; or queer usages, subversions, and reinterpretations of the doll (like Bellamy's) seek to unsettle the heterosexist dominance of her surround.[5]

Magenta pink (named "Barbie Pink" by Pantone) was also chosen as the background for the poster publicizing John Waters's 1974

Baltimore-set film *Female Trouble*, which stars beloved Cookie, her friend Mink Stole, and a companion to them both, the drag star Divine, as three delinquent schoolgirls in an American high school.[6] Their eyes are heavily smoked, and their backcombed hair is monstrously big, to the extent that their white middle-class girlishness is gory and frightening. Pink, then, when cleverly parodied, can trash and transgress social norms—school, family, class, gender—and critically race. And, so, perhaps it is useful to think of pink as a range, as tinted with ambivalence, which Gallop also does when she recognizes how the book's cover is "not quite pink" but more like mauve: "a stylish, sophisticated version of that color, one that bespeaks not the messy, carnal world of the nursery but high culture, high feminine culture."[7] Neither Cookie as Concetta nor Bellamy in *Pink Steam* is seeking that sort of sophistication, but there is a use to thinking of pink as a palette, like femininity itself, and also like the love letter, the ways it can ooze girlishness and boyishness, embarrassment and exposure, innocence and lawlessness, unseriousness and critique, or, as Bellamy describes it in another epistolary performance (a book of blog posts to an ex-lover), "oppositional weakness."[8] She muses on the term's meaning: "an in-your-face owning of one's vulnerability and fucked-upness to the point of embarrassing and offending tight-asses is a powerful feminist strategy. Writing is tough work, I don't see how anyone can really write from a position of weakness. Sometimes I may start out in that position, but the act of commandeering words flips me into a position of power."[9] Could the love letter be pink, or could it be mauve, or could it be a shade in between? Could this edgewise pigment be a spatial territory to occupy in love-letter writing, where, as Eve Kosofsky Sedgwick would say, "strong *and* weak theory . . . interdigitate"?[10]

Nowhere in the book does Bellamy define pink steam as a term for her own oppositional/weak writing; we just have the blurb on the back to help us: "Pink steam rises from the vats of melting goo in the Vincent Price 3D horror classic, *House of Wax*. Railroad buffs know 'pink steam' as the first blast from a newly christened steam engine, which appears pink as it spews out rust."[11] Rising, melting, blasting, spewing—pink steam is a substance that travels, changes shape and consistency. It recalls the abjection of a gooey bodily fluid. Could pink steam (I picture sticky, hot vapor; or a young girl's blushed cheek; or a sickly menstruation; or the infected blood of the "gay" disease that killed Cookie Mueller) be the subversive substance of the love letter *as* essay? By turns messy, explicit, emotional, desiring, overloaded, innocent, sexual, sensual, critical? Should I call it *almost-pink steam*?

"Almost" implies being near to something but not quite *it*—or being multiple things at once. Likewise, Gallop attends to the ways Leclerc's essay contains slippages, from the private, feminized space of letter writing, to the public (and more "masculine") domain of an "essay published in a book."[12] As Gallop writes—inspired by Leclerc's queer address to her lover, and also Mary Cassatt's depiction in *The Letter* (1890–91; plate 1) of a woman with skin as "smooth as the paper," handling, licking, and kissing the seal of another (address-less) envelope in "direct oral contact": "Love letters have always been written from the body, in connection with love. Leclerc wants all writing to have that connection; she wants love to enter into general circulation, inscribed knowledge, rather than remaining private and secret." Impassioned, Gallop continues further: "We women must continue to write from our loving bodies, but we must break 'discretion' and 'intimacy' and 'risk that subversion' in public, in print, in general circulation. . . . Leclerc brings the love letter out of the closet and into the public domain."[13] Following Gallop's correspondence with Leclerc's essay—which inhabits its own erotic correspondence with the working-class maid in Vermeer's interior painting who waits in the background while her mistress pens a letter—the homosocial letters I write to my beloved, whom I feel as both proximate and distant, risk the projection of desire and love in critical writing. As a space of almostness, it holds dozens of shifting, paradoxical pieces, by turns close and far away, private and public, hetero and homosexual, alive and dead. To be almost real, and almost fiction, to know and to never-know at once: This is the fragile state of displacement from which my letters grow.

Sent out into the atmosphere, almost-pink steam moves through time, space, and bodies, holding distant writers together in similarity and difference. Bellamy's essay "Delinquent," which takes the form of a letter written by Bellamy to our shared beloved, Kathy Acker, buzzes with this stuff. The first time I read it, I ate up Bellamy's use of the past tense—"Kathy *worshiped* the girls who were bad" and "I wish you *had* met her"—rather than her occasional use of the present.[14] I fell for the neatness of the life narrative, immediately assumed that Bellamy's epistolary essay had been written in late 1997, in the aftermath of Kathy's death from cancer. I saw an echo between Bellamy's epistolary gesture and Kathy's earlier, "almost" attempt at expressing grief publicly in the form of a love letter, which she considered doing for her friend Robert Mapplethorpe, after the photographer's death from AIDS-related illness.[15]

My assumption that Bellamy's piece was trying to touch the dead in epistolary writing came despite this letter-essay first appearing in 1994, with its unlicensed quoting from the unpublished manuscript of Kathy's novel-in-progress at the time, *My Mother: Demonology*.[16] This novel also features abject letters of love, as Kathy reimagines the erotic and emotional correspondence sent between the French writers Colette Peignot (pen name: Laure) and Georges Bataille. "Dear B," writes Kathy *as* Laure, "All my emotions, fantasies, imaginings, desires are reality because I must have a life that matters, that is emotional."[17] In epistolary, interdisciplinary novels like these, Kathy critically reimagined the much-historicized, often-pathologized conflation of women with weak, private, domestic love letters.

We might think of Samuel Richardson's characterization of Clarissa in his titular, serialized novel of 1748, or Vermeer's earlier domestic visions of women sat at wooden desks, draped in silks and furs, and daydreaming of their epistolary beloved, as indicative of this Eurocentric historical stereotype that is entangled within imperialist, colonialist, capitalist, and patriarchal regimes of power.

So, I made a mistake in my casual assumption that Bellamy's love letter is also an elegy, but might there be a use to my blunder that's "sexy, creative, even cognitively powerful," as Joseph Litvak once told Sedgwick in a "personal communication" (the epistolary impulse resurfacing again in critical gestures), which she later draws on in her essay on reparative reading?[18] Inspired by my error, I entrust the affective, attentive, desiring, erotic, loving, fantastical, and speculative energies of the love letter, as a way to *almost* touch, *nearly* get inside, get *closer* to, the bodies of my beloveds, the vitalities and complexities, even perversities, of their close writing. My own close writing beats with a never-ending correspondence, akin to Carolyn Dinshaw's vision of queer affective communities touching "across time."[19] This "queer historical touch," writes Dinshaw (in close contact with Roland Barthes), involves "partial, affective connection," rather than a full embrace.[20] It is all the more erotic for denying the complete, final grasp of a body. I empathize. Close writing is an attempt to draw *closer*, without fully healing, the severed line separating life and death, the present and the past.

The Author Is Dead (But I *Love* the Author), or, From Close Reading to Close Writing

In the essay "Sedgwick's Perverse Close Reading and the Question of an Erotic Ethics," Meridith Kruse is curious as to how methods of close reading, like the ones her former teacher Jane Gallop had taught her, could be "erotic and ethical at the same time."[21] Kruse remembers Gallop's "2007 seminar on Sedgwick" and her invitations to the class to "slow down and savor the queer details," to "linger over the features of an unusual image," to "trace the way a minor phrase or odd word shifted in significance."[22] In many ways, this echoes the attentive, accumulating style of critical reading, involving "looking at what is actually on the page, reading the text itself, rather than some idea 'behind the text,'" which Gallop described as an ethical practice in an essay published seven years earlier.[23] Here Gallop argues that when close reading "pays attention to elements in the text which, although marginal, are nonetheless emphatic, prominent," the surprise of finding them can facilitate a closer, more ethical, awareness of difference and "specificity."[24] It can help us to listen "to the other," suggests Gallop, the voice and desire, for example, of the queer working-class correspondent who desires from the margins of a painting.[25] And yet, in spite of the fact that Kruse's description of Gallop's close-reading classroom is charged with an erotic, bodily atmosphere (savoring, lingering, tracing: I feel their bodies moving together), the author comes up against a paradox when they read Gallop's earlier essay—which considers the desiring projections of the reader (be they seeking to love *or* to criticize) as totalizing and dangerous—finding within that text an "undoing" of passion entirely.[26]

This is, of course, a reversal of the dynamics Maggie Nelson writes of in *The Argonauts*, when the author encounters Gallop—whom Nelson "liked" for her "heady, disobedient books on Lacan"—coming up against the art historian Rosalind Krauss in a research seminar.[27] After Gallop showed a slide show of naked photographs of herself and her son, taken by her husband named Dick, Krauss "excoriated Gallop for taking her own personal situation as subject matter," without any appreciation of Gallop's in-process, accumulating ideas about the maternal and photographic representation.[28] Krauss is shown to be the paranoid scholar, acting "as though Gallop should be ashamed for trotting out naked pictures of herself and her son in the bathtub, contaminating serious academic space with her pudgy body and unresolved, self-involved thinking (even though Gallop had been perfecting such contamination for years)."[29] And, so, perhaps Gallop's practice of close reading is muddier, more contaminated (full of almost-pink steam)—in the ways it sensualizes, even spoils, critical acts with scenes, spaces, and affects of love and eroticism—than Kruse's analysis first implies. Could it be closer to Sedgwick's passionate, perverse, obsessive, overidentifying style of close reading than Gallop recognized it to be in 2000, when she equated close reading with the dispassionate, but certainly important, ethics of listening to others? Interestingly, Nelson brings both thinkers into her loving orbit in *The Argonauts* (as I bring all three of them), paying as much attention to the ways their intimate work entered their intimate lives, as the work itself, with life and work exchanges being central to her understanding of queer *practice*. Of Sedgwick, Nelson writes, "Such were Sedgwick's identifications and interests; she was nothing if not honest. And in person she exuded a sexuality and charisma that was much more powerful, particular, and compelling than the poles of masculinity and femininity could ever allow—one that had to do with being fat, freckled, prone to blushing, bedecked in textiles, generous, uncannily sweet, almost sadistically intelligent, and, by the time I met her, terminally ill."[30] Like many of Sedgwick's own writings that directly name the friends, associates, and citational bodies of combined presence and absence who sustain her theory and give her pleasure, Nelson does not withhold the facts of her lived proximity to her charismatic and sick teacher. She appears to be writing alongside Sedgwick, who, according to Kruse, was committed to the idea that "projecting one's own desires and expectations onto a text is not unethical; rather, it serves as a valuable survival tactic to counter cultural erasure," which includes the silencing of sickened bodies.[31]

I, too, am inspired by Sedgwick's close-reading methods for what they can *do*: from the making of "invisible possibilities and desires visible," to smuggling "queer representation in where it must be smuggled," to investing our "mysterious, excessive, or oblique" objects of attachment with "fascination and love."[32] These urges, both "formalist" *and* "passional," are put forward in the introduction to "Queer and Now," which (*almost*) begins the 1993 essay collection *Tendencies*.[33] Reading from the first person and "against the grain," identifying with the text or object or author viscerally, "becoming a perverse reader": These positions are inextricably bound up with the ethics of her intellectual project, of realizing the full and complex possibilities and solidarities of queer experience, its lived entanglement with reading and writing, as is expressed in the intimate, close readerly absorption of life, text, and body that defines "Memorial for Craig Owens," Sedgwick's work of creativity, grief, and "fairly strange" love-at-a-distance-through-words.[34]

If we read closely elsewhere—in the 2011 book by Gallop, *The Deaths of the Author: Reading and Writing in Time*, which followed the seminar on Sedgwick and features close readings of the theorist's essays—it is possible to pick up on a similar tendency throbbing throughout Gallop's work. And yet the book was, she says, in its initial stages of planning, titled in a similar way to the earlier article: "The Ethics of Close Reading."[35] Gallop was inevitably drawn to the work of Emmanuel Levinas while researching this book-in-development and his theory of ethics based on one's intersubjective encounter with the other. As a result, when Gallop received a separate invitation to "write about Derrida's work and [her] work" (this article for *differences* was an early testing ground for her imagined book on the ethics of close reading, before it transformed into *The Deaths of the Author*), Gallop turned to the book she was surrounded by (ever the spatially oriented, *close* reader) and thus "decided to write about the only book by Derrida sitting on my desk at the time, his *Adieu à Emmanuel Lévinas*."[36] Published in France in 1997 and translated into English in 1999, this volume comprises two texts, Gallop tells us—a short piece, titled "Adieu," which was delivered at Levinas's funeral in 1995, and a much longer piece called "Le mot d'accueil" (translated as "A Word of Welcome") that opened a conference focused on the philosopher's work a year later.[37] A greeting combines with a farewell in this volume; the closeness of the two gestures comes into sharper focus.

(I remember an epistolary line to my beloved: *These daydreaming letters are all I have to say hello and goodbye*.)

In fact, the passing gesture of "Adieu"—the first text of Derrida's volume—contains within it the self-shattering intimacy of grieving someone just lost while also caring for them, talking to them, as if they're still alive. "I've feared having to say *Adieu* to Emmanuel Lévinas," Derrida writes (but he also spoke it, on the day of the funeral): "I knew that my voice would tremble at the moment of saying it, and especially saying it aloud, right here, before him, so closely to him . . . addressing *directly*, *straight on*, the one who, as we say, is no longer, is no longer living."[38] In direct and dazzling proximity, Derrida conjures contact with his friend, in a way that echoes Levinas's *Totality and Infinity: An Essay on Exteriority*, by rejecting binary thinking, the "traditional 'philosophical and religious' interpretation of death as either 'a passage into nothingness' or 'a passage to some other existence.'"[39] In Derrida's phrasing, "The greeting of the *à-Dieu* does not signal the end."[40] Through reading and writing *with them*, beside them, "the dead can speak."[41] In this way, I am reminded of Derrida's work on hospitality, and the arrival of an "invited guest, or an unexpected visitor . . . a living or dead thing," forcing an "insoluble antinomy" between the absolute law of hospitality and the conditional laws that bind it.[42] Indeed, within the second volume of *Adieu to Emmanuel Levinas*, titled "Word of Welcome," Derrida speaks *with* Levinas, finding within the textures of his thought an unnamed commitment to an ethics of hospitality, the "welcoming of the other."[43]

1 Gallop picks up on this as well, reading both texts of the volume
0 in close relation and in close relation to her own work. She writes with
Derrida:

> If we connect the two titles respectively between hospitality and death (the two themes of the book, I would say), we might see this double title pointing to a relation between hospitality and death. If I were still writing a book on the ethics of close reading, I would want to connect it to this ethics of hospitality toward the dead. I would certainly want to connect this hospitality toward the dead with Barthes's notion . . . that even though the author is dead there are nonetheless authors we "live with," authors we welcome into the texture of our life.[44]

To close-read, then, in this context, and as is felt in Sedgwick's memorial, is to care for the words of the dead, to absorb their words (hospitably) into our writing, our *text-ures*; it's to say welcome and farewell, all at once—which also sounds erotic. "These are theorists *I love* to read," Gallop writes, referring to Barthes, Derrida, Sedgwick, and Spivak, whose "lively" work sustains the close readings the book contains.[45] In the chapter on Barthes, Gallop encourages us to look sideways, away from the theoretical concept that gained currency due to the "elegant, memorable last clause" of a "little essay written in 1967" ("The birth of the reader must be at the cost of the death of the Author") and toward hints and glimpses of the author's piecemeal return that got written into his essays soon after.[46] As Gallop close-reads, addressing Barthes's 1971 *Sade, Fourier, Loyola*, the author's return is described as "friendly," and it occurs when we embrace "the pleasure of the Text."[47] This encounter is relational, synergetic. It draws out the kinships we can make in reading and writing. To some, "friendly" might suggest a dynamic of reserved withholding. But I am attracted to the word for its role in the homosocial network, how the figure of the friend is laced in erotic mystery, too, especially when transferred to this readerly encounter, full of desire if not exactly sexual. As a relation, it then gets even steamier in the 1973 book-length essay-in-pieces *The Pleasure of the Text*, which Gallop quotes from: "As institution, the author is dead: his person . . . has disappeared . . . but in the text, in a certain way, I *desire* the author."[48] In spite of the author's absence, there remain traces of fantasy in the reader/writer for them, like the perverse desire for split and fragmented body parts, akin to fetish objects.[49]

In *Becoming: The Photographs of Clementina, Viscountess Hawarden* (1999), Carol Mavor shares in some of Gallop's attachments, including Barthes and Sedgwick, as part of an intimate and self-proclaimed fetishizing, flirtatious address to a woman photographer "'just missed.'"[50] "[Clementina] Hawarden and her work will always remain young, a brief moment marked by death, absence of information, mature life, images of self, diaries," writes Mavor, in an articulation of an entangled life and practice that, while from a different century, resonates with my own beloveds' piecemeal corporealities, materialities, and temporalities.[51] Out of this chasm of "ghostly image[s]," the writer is bound to a state of longing akin to Barthes's sense of a trembling, desiring language.[52] As Mavor writes, "Although my fingertips have longed to touch the beaten hems of their skirts . . . their bodies and all that has touched them, I have only touched the precious edges of their pictures."[53] And yet, in touching images and materials *with words*, in combining close reading with close looking, in traversing the synergetic relations of animating the absent subject and becoming animated by it, Mavor comes into a space of reciprocal and critical pleasure, surfacing the long-erased secrets of the homoerotic energies and gestures of "sapphic love" that infuse Hawarden's photographic fragments depicting her adolescent daughters as sisters.[54] It is a project in flirting critique, argues Mavor, which, "as a game of suspension without the finale of seduction, keeps our subjects alive" (in elusive and desirable ways).[55] Led by this writerly form of sensual and flirtatious discovery, Mavor's work has helped me to find my fantasy sisters, by recognizing their desire and withholding. She has given me the permission to write and read *closer*, pulling me—with tenderness and daring, in dialogue with Sedgwick's sense of adolescence as a model for queer critique that is theorized within *Novel Gazing*'s introductory essay—into the risky and reparative (blissful, flirtatious) edges of close reading becoming close-writing practices.[56]

Interestingly, *Novel Gazing: Queer Readings in Fiction* (1997) is cradled by the tender touch of a Clementina Hawarden cover image, alluding to the intertextual and intimate atmospheres resonating in the work of both authors: of shared nineteenth-century citations and queer-feminist acts of revisionist re-reading,[57] transforming the close looking, close reading, and close writing of Victorian paintings, photographs, novels, and homosocial love letters.[58]

Indeed, for Sedgwick, it is the Victorian novel—"queer texts (or authors) and non-queer ones . . . female ones and male," as she puts it in the *Novel Gazing* introduction that articulates the sensual praxis of attending intimately to texts: with pleasure and in absorption of the "speculative . . .
1 methodologically adventurous" adolescent reader—that fills her world.[59]
2 Many of the essays in the collection strike up a readerly relationship with nineteenth-century figures (Marcel Proust, Henry James); others turn to "the age of AIDS" (in Toni Morrison's *Beloved*).[60] Such a cross-historical range is thought-provoking, as the propositions made by such texts also inform Sedgwick's opening call—which is mobilized and contextualized by the ethics and emotions of AIDS activism across the long 1980s into the 1990s, and also cites Proust—for the queer and critical practice of reparative reading, which is intertextual and affective in its close, "overattached" readerly and writerly identifications of "deroutinized . . . temporality."[61] Already this had been felt in the earlier "Memorial for Craig Owens," wherein the queer temporalities of sickness, death, reading, and writing are intimately drawn across the distances of time and space, the paradoxes of presence and absence. This is the pulse of when close reading—in all its textures and identifications—becomes *close writing* to critical and reparative effect.[62]

The Ambivalence of the Reparative Communion

I encounter similar "close" terms and temporalities in the Black feminist scholarship of Saidiya Hartman, while recognizing that there is in her work a specific encounter that grapples with the absences, the silences, the violent misrepresentations, registered in the historical archive of the racialized dead. Critically engaging the unbearable difficulties of ever being able to trace, represent, and recover the full lives and social deaths of enslaved, incarcerated, confined young Black girls and women, for Hartman, *to read* the historical archive *closely* is rather "to imagine what cannot be verified" within the textures of an "impossible *writing*," as she theorizes in the essay

"Venus in Two Acts."[63] It is a methodological gesture that combines fiction and history: a specific and necessary movement toward "redressing the violence that produced" precarious, captive, and enslaved Black lives during chattel slavery as "numbers, ciphers, and fragments of discourse."[64] Hartman's method, *critical fabulation*, seeks to register the gaps in the archive, particularly the absent autobiographical narratives of female captives who survived the Middle Passage, and speculate anew, *with care*—always negotiating, rather than smoothing over—the murderous violences that constructed the archive as a repository of disappearance for young Black women and girls.[65] In this practice, close reading is transformed as an act of attention that does not simply seek to recover, console, or even repair the absent "lives of the enslaved . . . the dead."[66] Instead, close reading for Hartman is reconfigured as a reparative method that depends on a paradoxical encounter with the archive's limits; its construction (history's construction) as fiction itself; the always-present impossibility of resuscitation. Writing imaginatively through narrative fiction, in and among archive traces, opens out a contingent set of possibilities for what else might have been said, or done, or desired, or *sensed*, in the past, the enduring present, and for a future otherwise. Close reading in Hartman's work stimulates the critical imagination of a *counter*-historical close writing.

In her *Wayward Lives Beautiful Experiments: Intimate Histories of Social Upheaval* (2019), Hartman develops this critical practice more explicitly into a language defined by *closeness in* and *as* storytelling, what Hartman terms *close narration*: a speculative, choral writing of multiple vantage points, wherein the voice of character and narrator collapse into one another, in the desire and effort to "inhabit the intimate dimensions" of her subjects' sensual lives.[67] Close narration also runs subversively counter to the vast, dispersed archives attached to "rent collectors; surveys and monographs of sociologists; trial transcripts; slum photographs; reports of vice investigators, social workers, and police officers; interviews with psychiatrists and psychologists; and prison case files," all of which sought to surveil, pathologize, discipline, and control young Black women and queer folk dreaming and practicing new forms of social life, love, and affiliation within turn-of-the-century urban enclosures in northern US cities.[68] The attention, the *care*, with which Hartman "elaborates, augments, transposes, and breaks open archival documents"—the intimate register from which her collaged, choral, close picture-of-moving-pictures emerges—has also been read as a gesture of love, *to* and *for* her "minor figures."[69] It is an affective investment that pulses through the shifts, processes, and compositions of writing, an enduring and necessary project given how far "Black women are treated with such little regard . . . in the world": their bodies, desires, lives, and literatures "dismissed and ignored," "belittled and mocked," rather than loved and cared for, *recognized*.[70] Nourishing Hartman's wayward writing of wayward practices are "utterances from the chorus," the "circle" of Black radical and feminist thinkers to whom she reads and writes alongside (in motion), whose work Hartman recognizes as also underpinned and sustained by love.[71] I read these citational slips of italicized lines in her book as indirect traces of love-letter writing: a close correspondence.

The love letter is both conceptual and material in Hartman's close-narrative writing of archival fullness. It is a writing tool *and* a research object. Many of the snapshot biographies that constitute its collective song are based on the case files of personal interviews, family histories, psychological and physical examinations, intelligence tests, social investigators' and probation officers' reports, personal correspondence, love letters, photographs, poems, and life writings attached to the New York State Reformatory for Women at Bedford Hills, where young Black women and girls were incarcerated for desiring to live differently—marked "as pathological and immoral, if not criminal."[72] These documents create the trails of traces that Hartman follows, then disturbs. Reading "against the grain," she writes, Hartman breaks "open the stories they told in order to narrate" her own, and get closer to the radical, riotous beauty in and of their waywardness, wherein this "collective endeavor to live free unfolds in the confines of the carceral landscape."[73] We learn of how the act of writing letters (to mothers, to friends, to companions, to lovers) came up against the institution's disciplinary racist forces—the controlling gaze of a matron reading and surveilling the girls' letters before being re-enveloped and sent—exerted in the name of social hygiene and "reform."[74]

And yet—recalling the fugitive letters written and sent by Harriet Jacobs from her tiny crawlspace attic enclosure, where she hid for seven years, enacting a written practice of correspondence from within her space of confinement to imagine and discover new forms of freedom, creativity, kinship, intellect, and love—Hartman catches "glimmer[s] of possibility . . . the ache of what might be," even in the files where letters are physically missing.[75] There is the surreptitious desire for intimacy, for contact, and also for writing itself, held in the punishable passing of notes to other girls in prison, as Mattie Nelson, one of Hartman's wayward figures, did (*or could have done*), before being sent to the Disciplinary Building in

1918 for "hiding stationery and stamps in her room." Hartman begins to imagine stories of sensual and creative life otherwise, between the lines, and amid the silences, working *with* and *against* the archive. "What stories were shared in all the letters lost and disappeared, the things whispered, and never disclosed?" she asks. "Is it possible to conjure the sentences and paragraphs and poems contained in that lost archive? Or find a way to Mattie's language of self-expression?"[76] For Hartman, the question holds a speculative, close reimagining of a life's desire.

Lines from prisoners' love letters also enter the counter-historical frame more tangibly, akin to a close writing of correspondence transcription, as in rioting refuser Loretta Michie's letter "to 'Devoted Pal'" that addresses the "sweetheart in my dreams I'm calling you."[77] But Hartman holds contingency in her grasp, through the narrative deliberations, questions, and pauses, the mixing of tenses and timelines, the improvisations of the writing (that recall the Bedford Hills rioters' collaborative energies), meaning that her minor figures desire and move, articulating wayward practices of radical love through fugitive letters, in a sensitive, carefully wrought relation to their right to opacity. This again echoes the fugitive register of desire, movement, and creative practice as situated within "impossible strictures of enclosure and confinement" signaled by Jacobs's "loophole of retreat," which Tina Campt, alongside Hartman and the artist Simone Leigh, has mobilized "in an effort to revalue black women's intellectual labor."[78] As a site of writing, the crawlspace reminds us of the resourceful strategies developed by Black women to narrativize their private worlds, and kindle intimate relations across textual forms, from within brutalized and suffocating spaces of enclosure. When *Incidents in the Life of a Slave Girl* was first published in 1861, Jacobs used the pseudonym "Linda Brent" to protect herself, family, and friends from punishment during the Antebellum period; it was addressed, as Ashon T. Crawley notes, "to white women to engage them in abolition work," signaling the degree to which white reading publics, even for a "proto-black feminist project," shaped the parameters and reception of the text.[79]

Hartman collages her love-letter traces as a speculative rendering of close still lives, of fugitive letters, of pseudonymous private texts, as moving pictures. This is a specific Black feminist method that mobilizes the archival tools, the storytelling contingencies, the cross-historical effects of close writing, in a particular way: an expansive "love letter to all those who had been harmed" in an age defined by state and sexual violence against young Black women and girls, involuntary servitude, ghettoization, segregation, anti-Black legislation, the shadows and afterlives of slavery—within and beyond the archive.[80]

Scholars such as Tavia Nyong'o have recognized the critical and conceptual linkages and tensions between the Black feminist thought of Hartman, queer of color critique, and Sedgwickian queer theory of affective tone and reach: bodies of work I, too, correspond with—letters, memorials, archives, close readings *with* and *to* the dead—as I trace close writing's particular elaboration and performance of the reparative position.[81] Nyong'o emphasizes that what motivates the impulse to "redress" or "repair" in Hartman's reparative practice of critical fabulation, for instance, is *ambivalence*: a freighted and careful grappling with the frictions and limits of historical rescue. In fact, José Esteban Muñoz's own ambivalently reparative reading of the controversial project that saw the editing, afterwording, and publication of the stories, journals, and notebooks of Gary Fisher, a minor, sick, unarchived, racialized figure, by his friend and former teacher, Eve Kosofsky Sedgwick, after Fisher's death from AIDS-related illness in 1994 (resulting in *Gary in Your Pocket: Stories and Notebooks of Gary Fisher*, 1996), provides Nyong'o with an example of this complex strand of queer optimism that troubled the "identitarian logics of the multicultural academy."[82] Muñoz deliberately locates this "rich, complicated, and sometimes troubling collaborative scene" within the context of a "sponsorship," indexing as it does a "history of African American cultural production that was not possible without a certain level of white patronage."[83] Muñoz also recognizes that such a history finds a difficult contour in Fisher's own writing of submissive desire that was "intricately linked" to an "experience of the self as a racialized sexual object."[84] "Reading Fisher," Muñoz writes, "is a challenge for those of us who toil in the archives of collective dispossession."[85]

But then from here, Muñoz pivots, reconsiders Fisher (his writing, his desire, his Blackness), reads him—*with* Sedgwick—another way, and not simply by foreclosing the realities of systemic racism that condition the "erotics of racial fetishism" the dialogic project plays out.[86] Instead, by turning (via Jean-Luc Nancy) to the sensed relations of this shared scene—wherein "Eve 'knows' . . . Gary" and "Gary 'knows' . . . Eve" through "trajectories and intersections between our senses of the world that make the world"—the reparative forces of *Gary in Your Pocket* emerge with Muñoz's gesture: a "sharing (out) of the unshareable."[87] This, argues Muñoz, helps us to return to the "strange optic allowed by their communion with each other," which existed and flourished *because of* awkward convergences they felt and wrote.[88] An affective relation surfaces that is the "experience of being-in-common-in-difference," that is rooted in a "vaster commons of the incommensurable," that is the excess (strange, intangible) *sense* of queerness.[89]

Occupying the ambivalence of the reparative communion, I, too, write *through* a sense of the incommensurable, to share what perhaps can never be shared. It is a strange optic. It troubles, but it is tender, also (potentially, perhaps) invasive. Or uneasy. In this orbit of likeness but not sameness, I ask what we, too, can glean about the difficult contours of Kathy and Cookie, through loving and communing and speculating and corresponding with them this way.

As a triangulated scene of association, affection, and attachment, which brings together the lives, bodies, works, and love letters of three white women writers, it could also be read as reproducing racialized dominances in art and literature. I am aware here of how whiteness, as Sara Ahmed argues, "orientates bodies in specific directions, affecting how they 'take up' space."[90] Perhaps this also includes the affectionate and desiring "taking up of texts": an example of what Ahmed understands as an "inheritance . . . of orientations."[91] In this understanding of inheritance, a problematic occurs within gestures of feminist research, as the reader absorbs "proximities (and hence orientations)" to certain objects (meaning physical things, but also "styles, capacities, aspirations, techniques, habits," and archives of *writings*), which shape "'what' we come into contact with," in a way that enables, but also delimits, the availability and "*reachability*" of certain objects, encompassing the texts we read and cite, *write to*.[92]

I acknowledge the project's entanglement within such lines of contact. In response, I question and surface how the structural forces of whiteness impacted my subjects' writing lives, alongside the contemporaneous creative labors of artists and writers of color, whose intersectional working lives intersected with Kathy's and Cookie's at varying degrees of proximity. Such relations also draw attention to racialized violences and the disorientations of social and aesthetic formations. Connections, tensions, differences, and ambiguities of contact and affection are unraveled—in ways that future work could further trace to critical effect in circular rather than triangular motions—in this reparative gesture of ambivalent communion.

Love Letters and Love-in-Pieces (Dwelling in My Pocket)

Neither only a memorial, nor a work of close narration, nor a posthumous stage: In *this* close-writing archive of affection and ambivalence, it is the queer feminist love letter that touches, smuggles, makes visible and palpable, despite (or because of?) the temporal distance that separates us, "the powerful, refractory, and exemplary" forces of my texts, who are also my beloved, who are their own close writing.[93] I receive their pieces like letters, to which I relate, reply, and respond, ask questions, and move dangerously and precariously closer, through the acts and affects of writing itself. Close writing is process; it captures the perpetual loops of correspondence. It is an elastic space that liberates critical scenes of interpretation, as the intimate enclosure of the letter gives me the courage and protection to say the (perverse? embarrassing? risky? overinvolved?) thing that *I think* my beloveds would want me to come out and say (saying *too much*) about their works enveloped in their lives and their lives enveloped in their works. Close writing breaches distance: It addresses authors as if they were kin, making space to be proximate with one another. It creates an atmosphere of electrical charge that is edgy. Close writing is attentive, like close reading, but it is not always duly precise, seeing the erotics of fantasy—the exposure of it onto the page, an un-closing—as another form of attention.

In the short letters I write *to* my beloveds, I am repeatedly "*thinking of you*." These pieces of exploratory love-letter writing—which are etched with the affective and bodily temporalities, materialities, and textualities of the private, almost-pink-steamed, handwritten missive—hold a waking "out of . . . forgetfulness," as Barthes describes the powerful effects of the familiar epistolary address in love-letter writing.[94] The fleeting absences of the beloved, suggests Barthes, electrify and solidify their return.[95] The writing of the love letter sustains the beloved in an erotic *relation*, bringing "together two images."[96] This networked loop involving flashes of presence and absence is "like desire," writes Barthes: "The love letter waits for an answer; it implicitly enjoins the other to reply."[97] I wait and wait and wait—in the devotional, undeliverable, unreturnable letters that reach and revive my beloveds in a different way, through the persistent writing of and through desire.

I think of Paul B. Preciado writing in *Artforum* after being sick with COVID-19; the short piece's haunting echoes with my own position of expressing love but forever living "with the impossible anticipation of a physical encounter," the tangible arrival of a letter "that would never take place."[98] Preciado's attempt to reach, *across distance*, for his ex-lover, also occurs in the postviral, delirious writing of a futile letter: "a poetic and desperate declaration of love . . . a shameful document for the one who had signed it."[99] The letter did not enter the postal network; he could not move beyond the sick scene of his quarantined confinement of care to send it. It found a more familiar, intimate home instead, close to his own feverish body: the bottom of his garbage bin. It is a seductive, spatial image, his love letter first housed within a "bright white envelope," then placed within a dark, cavernous passage of waste (his domestic Dead Letter Office), seemingly going nowhere.[100]

Preciado's is the letter that evades physical delivery, or the reception of what is materially legible, echoing Ocean Vuong's irreconcilable, never-to-be-read letter to his mother, a Vietnamese immigrant, whom he had once tried to teach how to read "the way" his "third grade" teacher had "taught" him. As he remembers of this reversal of pedagogical "hierarchies" traditionally inscribed onto the parent-child relationship: "After the stutters, the false starts, the words warped or locked in your throat, after failure, you slammed the book shut."[101] Vuong writes across this chasm, traversing the unpredictable, aching line of yearning: "I am writing to reach you—even if each word I put down is one word further from where you are."[102] I hear the frequency of this ache. However undeliverable, or unreceivable, Vuong's or Preciado's or my own letters might be, new paths (not necessarily chronological) can still stretch out, through the feeling processes of writing.

I, too, am interested in the love letter—be it to someone dead or alive, deliverable or not; be it to a person, or species, or idea, or feeling, or thing—as shaped by a desiring relation that is always marked by distance, by lag, by missing messages and missing bodies (sapphic-style), as if the love letter is always (ambiguously) a part, section, or fragment of something else. Indeed, Anne Carson recognizes in *Eros the Bittersweet* how in "numerous epistolary scenarios to be found in ancient novels," "Letters stand oblique to the action" and the lover's strategies are "obstructed by an absent presence."[103] Written or received, the love letter, therefore, is always partial, constructed of divergent pieces and paradoxes, including the poles of proximity and distance, as the love letter travels across time, space, bodies, and readers.

Moreover, when loving means writing means *waiting* (as Carson also writes, "The experience of eros is a study in the ambiguities of time. Lovers are always waiting. They hate to wait; they love to wait"), the love-letter writer experiences pleasure and pain at once (another almost-pink-steamed paradox).[104] And it was Carson again who recognized Sappho to be the first poet to conceive of such splitting, whereby love involves a kind of emotional and bodily fracture, with the lover navigating conflicting affects—pieces of sweet and pieces of bitter—that rub one against the other.[105] This ambiguous state is intensified through the composition of close writing's partialized love letters, as the form becomes a reparative means of "coming to terms with," as Page duBois writes of the historical positioning demanded by Sappho's archived body in pieces, the poetic traces of which emanate with self-seeing, unshamed, disordered bodies in love.[106] It is a state, position, and form that facilitates a piecemeal broaching of the breach (temporal, spatial, physical) separating and connecting my fragmentary beloved and me.

To think of love's configuration is to think of those unsealed edges, which echo the wasted materialities of Sappho's own ancient poetic pieces, or the spare, lightweight sheathes of cloudy papers that form Theresa Hak Kyung Cha's 1977–78 mail art and performance project *Audience Distant Relative* (figure I.1). In this iterative work in pieces, Cha explores the contingency of correspondence, its fragility to refract, to never *quite* reach. Her empty envelopes (printed with words becoming concrete poems: "audience distant relative"; "lettersenderreceiver"; "messenger"; "echo"; "object/subject"; and "between delivery") do not meet the closure of the (material, linguistic) seal; they remain adrift in a space of belated in-betweenness, which is particularly significant for Korean American diasporic identities and social bonds. Could the "irresolvable problem of distance" at the heart of the second-person address in letter writing—which Cha addresses directly in the 1977 live performance of this work, when she articulates, "You are the audience / you are my distant audience / i address you / as i would a distant relative / seen only heard only through someone else's description"—make a different kind of contact and community formation happen, that loves with the dispersal of *traces* rather than intelligible wholes?[107] Materially and figuratively suggestive of this characterization, the contemporary poets Ada Limón and Natalie Diaz have more recently described their poem-letters exploring abstractions of kinship, heritage, and belonging as "envelopes of air."[108]

The unending letters, asides, messages, fantasies, and postscripts interlaced throughout this close writing listen to the idea that the love letter is messy like love itself; both the feeling and its writing are made of affective,

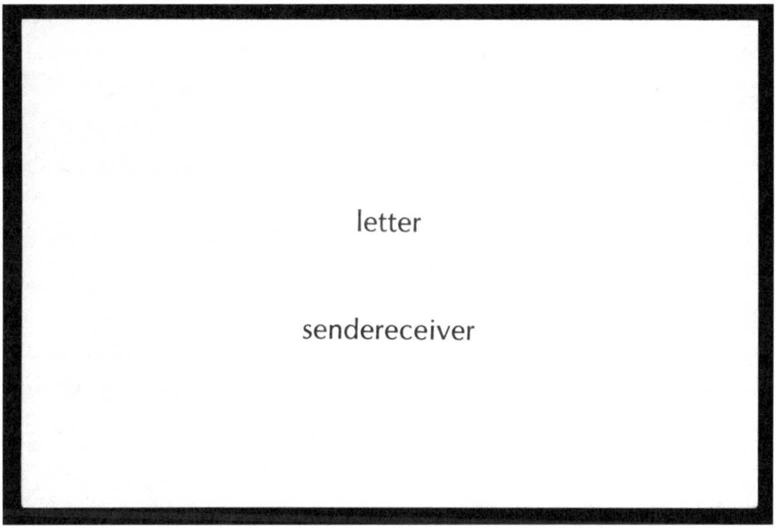

an empty envelope of air
(printed with words
becoming concrete poems)

I.1. Theresa Hak Kyung Cha, *Audience Distant Relative*, 1977–78. Black ink on six white envelopes; 6 ¼ × 9 ½ in. University of California, Berkeley Art Museum and Pacific Film Archive; Gift of the Theresa Hak Kyung Cha Memorial Foundation.

bodily, durational, linguistic, and material pieces and shards. These are *my* relational *love-in-pieces*; these pieces are *me*, which I share with my beloveds. Through these nonlinear pieces, written in an ever-changing personal present tense, and sometimes retrospectively (or nostalgically; it is a long love story in letters), I love them, think of them, seek to know and understand them (never "own" them), while reckoning with the impossibility of ever knowing them *completely*. I am *always waiting* for their return, if only in short glimpses.

Like Emily Dickinson making thrifty use of envelopes as tactile and domestic materials for her penciled poetry, the love of this writing arrives obliquely: at odd temporal angles formed by scattered shapes. Strange mergings of past and present occur that are physical and affective, akin to Sedgwick and Michael Lynch's tender caressing of Dickinson's gravestone, which became the black-and-white photographic-collage frontispiece that begins *Tendencies*—dedicated "in memory," and "with love," to her fellow Dickinson devotee.[109] "We are both obsessed with Emily Dickinson," Sedgwick writes in "White Glasses," manifesting in the queer collecting of "tokens, readings, pilgrimages, impersonations," which could be seen to embody the desire of an epistolary response *to* one of their "lesbian ego ideals."[110]

Dickinson's "envelope poems," as they have come to be known, are letters-in-miniature. They are poem drafts. They are, in a way, a series of preliminary sketches for something fuller, more "epic" to come. But it did not come in her lifetime. Instead, Dickinson lingered forever in this intimate zone of unfinished pieces, perhaps preferring not to "officially" publish her writing. She sent it in the post instead, circulated it among friends and associates, hidden within letters "that were often indistinguishable from poetry."[111] Lined by wrinkles, spotted by ink stains, smudged by a lip, these are fragile paper-things that recall the touch and smells of a previous owner, which in this case happens to be two, as Dickinson unfolded, smoothed out, ripped, cut, and manipulated with delicate abstractions of form, the epistolary materials she first received, then wrote on, or we might say replied *to*, in her distinctive, spaced-out pencil script. She was, as Jan Bervin writes, "reading and responding to her materials, angling the page to write in concert with the light rule and laid lines of the paper, using internal surface divisions, such as overlapping planes of paper, to compose in a number of directional fields."[112] She wrote into the space of the envelope visually, made space anew. And so, as well as pieces of poetry, or little bits of letter, these objects should be "understood as visual productions," as Susan Howe writes; they hold multiple disciplines and practices—the *artistic* and the *lived*—in their capacious, sprawling reach.[113]

I like the word "piece" as a writing descriptor because it is malleable and stretchy, which extends, as it did for Dickinson, into my love-letter practice of braided pieces traversing poetry and prose, art and literature, creative and critical writing, which is intercut with the influence of Carol Mavor's own writing—visual, intimate, spare; sewn and unsewn—on and beside Dickinson's sketched poems.[114]

I hold my beloveds close in this process, caressing their words and pieces in my pocket, occasionally pulling them out from inside, up to the surface and into the air. Dickinson's envelope obsession was matched by a love of pockets, to which she would secretly store her materials of and for writing close to the outline of her flesh: slips, scraps, envelopes, letters, pencil, thread. Only a few items of Dickinson's clothing remain, one of which is a demure, inexpensive house dress typical of late 1870s and early 1880s New England fashions: "cotton piqué, loose fitting with no waistline, featuring a box-pleated flounce at the bottom, twelve mother-of-pearl buttons, a flat collar, and a pocket on the right hip."[115] I think of that right hip pocket edged with a scalloped lace trim—its intimacy with the body's sweat and smells; its location within the private-domestic; its capacity to care for things, while also inviting erotic play with them, too—as a close-to-flesh, tactile dwelling for my own *love-in-pieces*.

Similarly sensorial, my "writer's love"—its partialized love-in-pieces—has grown with *archival touch*.[116] Within research repositories of varying degrees of order and strategies of assembly, located within cities across the United States, the body has touched material has touched affect. I thumbed the transparent invitation to Cookie's memorial at the venue MK, felt death between thumb and forefinger as I clutched and creased the see-through paper. I feverishly turned the fever-suffocated pages of Kathy's ring-bound notebooks. I began with the version at 8 x 10 inches, the size of a picture frame, which she marked with her address in blue fountain pen, could not decide if it was a "diary" or "poems" (plate 2).[117] I held Cookie's fragile postcards in my hands, trying desperately to not smudge the marble print (plate 3). I unfolded from envelopes the typed and handwritten letters they pocket. I caressed fraying manuscripts of fading typewriter ink, dog-eared at the annotated edges. I stroked the lists in CVs. I pressed the play button to hear them read aloud. I grasped my beloveds' worn pieces of presence and absence and "erotic crypticness," as Mavor describes the scattered archives of Sappho's poetry.[118] In such meetings, a cross-historical relation of love flourished at fragmented sites of text and texture: sites that Kate Eichhorn suggests are important for queer feminist writers, artists, and activists in that they open out "the possibility of being in time and in history differently," staging reengagements with feminist pasts that seek to imagine "other ways to live in the present."[119]

From the one-time touch of the recipient, through the posthumous touch of the researcher, to the belated touch of the close writer: Letters are contagious in their complex appeals to the tactile sense. And so, even if archival research is mostly tactile—although the polymorphous pandemic era has shifted sensory interactions into digitally haptic domains—it's doubly so with the strange temporality of close writing. As Jean Luc-Nancy's epithet provokes, "*Touching*—happens in writing all the time."[120] Touch in close writing is physical and emotional; it is by getting corporeally close to their writing objects that I am "touched," or *invaded* (because love is also a "microbial intruder," as the poet Daisy Lafarge has written).[121] Through this touch, I *fall*, into the textures of my love-in-pieces, *trying* to touch them back.

I steal pieces of my beloved, *with love*. Their pieces merge with my looped and threaded pieces, in letters "small enough to fit in your pocket."[122]

Maggie Nelson's *The Argonauts* conjures a similar image in its piecemeal materiality and visual layout. I picture slips of paper: handled, folded, scored at the seam, then stitched back together. Dickinson's envelopes also recall the dashed lines found on the flimsy paper pattern for a dress. However, when looking for a citational model, Nelson turned to Barthes's *A Lover's Discourse*, as swatches of quotation get closely woven into her personal writing in an echo of the French writer's fragmentary pages. These inked "figures" bring her company, kinship, hope for survival and love, amid oppressive threats to queer intimacies. Theory sustains life, and life sustains theory; reading meshes with experience: Both are to do *with love*.

Love flies in *The Argonauts*; it has multiple wings—romantic, familial, political, *written*—that spread out across multiple genres: pieces of essay, memoir, autofiction, queer theory, and love letter. The first paragraph is dated "October, 2007," and it begins with the most euphoric of epistolary denouements: "The words *I love you* come tumbling out of my mouth in an incantation the first time you fuck me in the ass, my face smashed against the cement floor of your dank and charming bachelor pad."[123] Nelson speaks directly to her lived beloved, in a writing of visceral contact, as forceful and loving as the anal sex it describes. She "smashes" us into their moment, between "I" and "you," because, as Barthes writes, "*I-love-you* has no 'elsewhere' . . . no distance, no distortion will split the sign."[124] Nelson creates the closest of spaces for her love projection: Subject, object, and reader become entangled—*beside one another*—as one body.

While Barthes's discussion of the "I love you" phrase in *Roland Barthes by Roland Barthes* is referenced just a few pages after Nelson's incantation, there are other figures in *The Argonauts* with whom she writes "beside," with love—this another kind of writer's love—to explore the queer possibilities of sex, family, survival, and *writing*.[125] Sara Ahmed, Judith Butler, Anne Carson, Eileen Myles, and Eve Kosofsky Sedgwick are just some of the names she gets close to (their names listed affectionately in the margins—spatially and emotionally *close*). Nelson does not specifically reference Sedgwick's discussion of "beside" as a critical practice (which is stitched into *Touching Feeling*), but it beats throughout the relational, reparative energies and spatial, affective proximities of her writing.[126] Indeed, when Nelson calls on Sedgwick's work on reparative reading (which the discussion of "beside" both extends and prefaces, "beside" being an alternative to paranoid critical practices of *beneath*, *behind*, and *beyond*, which conversely seek a climactic "drama of exposure"), it generates the effect of an echo, two writers in epistolary contact.[127] *The Argonauts*, with its affectionate desire to write with those whom Nelson loves in life and language—stitching their words of desire, connection, sex, and politics into her personal flow—is surely what Sedgwick had in mind when she explained the queer potential of reparative work.

Hence, the reparative position enables the risk of writing openly and emotionally (across all the paradoxes of feeling), even when it "feels . . . like a bad idea," as Nelson describes of her own work.[128] To write with love has always been dumped into the category of "bad idea" for most critics and scholars, but in *The Argonauts* such desire is inseparable from the broader arguments it's making about gender, sexuality, and representation: the freedom to write (in close dialogue with Sedgwick's 1987 essay "A Poem Is Being Written," which links poetry with spanking with "female anal eroticism"), an incantation as naked as "I am not interested in a hermeneutics, or an erotics, or a metaphorics of my anus, I am interested in ass-fucking."[129] It's as if she's emotionally involved with "Eve" *and* Harry—the person whom she fucks. Thus, *The Argonauts* not only opens up the complexities of sexual desire and the ways we write it; it also shows the complex emotional, often erotic involvement it's possible to have with the people whom we love and read, the figures she calls "the many gendered-mothers of my heart."[130] Nelson writes against the paranoid voice of criticism and against the policing of desire; for her, the two intentions are knotted as one, in her "wild theory" *of love*.[131]

Nelson's desire to be close to Harry, as it's posed within the terms of an epistolary address, describes the relational writer's love that nourishes this close writing: "I want the you no one else can see, the you so close the third person never need apply."[132]

(*I pocket this slip*.)

"Love-in-pieces" in this book—as an enveloped, partialized form and force field—is spun with the affects and attachments of a writer's love. I dream and write and love beside my writer-beloveds, feel them closely in my pocket. I piece letters together—an impulse to repair—to love and care for their bodies in pieces, across life and text and scattered archives, across the pieces of their close writing. These are the "fragments and part-objects" I encounter or create, as a "reparatively positioned" close reader and close writer.[133] In piecemeal, private, public, and unpublished close writings, which mined epistolary and autobiographical materials, Kathy and Cookie always pocketed (like adolescent shoplifters) more than one genre or discipline. I attend to this undisciplined approach by *responding to* it in a similar way, inhabiting the unresolved, tentative, and speculative tendencies of the torn piece, rather than the finished letter. Writer's love is a project of endurance. I hold back from reassembling their bodies in pieces when the cuts and violences of their lives in and as writing are so central to their understanding. A different shape emerges that listens to the breaks, the absent space around the pieces we have left. These letters shift across time and space and come in short, grasping bursts with the closing in of a pandemic; they have no fixed route mapped out for them.[134]

Encompassing dual senses (aesthetic and affective) of writerly form and writerly love, I use "love-in-pieces" as a method to address, almost touch, get closer to and care for the similarly cross-genre and cross-disciplinary effects of my beloveds' close writing, which was tested and performed in their partialized, piece-by-piece archives becoming *diary pieces*, a *novel-in-pieces*, and *letter pieces* (each explored in the book's three full-length but patchwork chapters). Love-in-pieces is a state of slippage, enfolding love as a feeling, love as a historical relation between writers, and love as a piecemeal, epistolary, undisciplined literary form (that expands on histories and practices of the love letter in queer feminist lives and works, which I have addressed in this section)—all slipped inside its pocketed vessel. And form and content get close within it: "Love-in-pieces" gathers multiple genres and forms to speak *to* a chaotic, messy, paradoxical, enduring, never-finished cross-historical experience of writing love, of feeling love *in* and *with* writing. As the third correspondent and character in the love triangle, love-in-pieces is my offering, my output: reparative pieces rather than paranoid wholes. Kathy, Cookie, and Me. To commit to this unfinished task is to write through the bittersweet, ambiguous, partialized, transitional, erotic, afflicted, and fragmented spaces of writerly love across time, the breach between life and death, the *and*.

The Intimate Slippages of Close Writing

Energized by the formal and affective method of love-in-pieces, close writing stakes its claim as a queer feminist methodology that offers a way of reading and writing differently and makes possible reparative engagements, newly touching what is risky, sexual, sensual, and surprising about the works and lives of my beloved, including the formal and political possibilities, the queer feminist effects, of their own close writing. I propose that we need approaches like this to remind us of the textures of thought—and otherwise readings—that come through the textures, affects, processes, experiments, and embodiments of writing itself. This is writing as feminist praxis, practice, and research, writing that does not, as Lauren Berlant describes in an interview on their collaborative project with Kathleen Stewart, "separate the tone of the action-voice from the ambition for knowledge production."[135] In so doing, I absorb the epistolary materials of my beloved into my writing, a way to think beside them. Their tools meet other tools in my "feminist toolbox" (to cite Sara Ahmed), which expands as I read, as I *write*, gathering fellow correspondents across the spaces of art, literature, and theory: Ahmed, Berlant, Stewart; also, Anne Boyer, Tina Campt, Alexis Pauline Gumbs, Saidiya Hartman, Johanna Hedva, Quinn Latimer, Carol Mavor, Maggie Nelson, Eve Sedgwick, Julietta Singh, authors to whom I continually return, or feel nearby, at the skin of the page.[136]

Love manifests in this book as a writing practice-oriented methodology that highlights the bodily and affective materialities of the pieces that make my beloveds' interdisciplinary close-writing archive. By writing, looking, feeling, and loving (*in/as pieces*) closely, I move closer to the intimate matter they transcribed and transformed in art and writing: how far they mined the visceral substances of their intimate lives to shift the boundaries of sexual desire, the sick body, and love, and subvert and challenge the sexed, classed, and gendered limitations placed on them, from the misogynistic attitudes of the 1970s conceptual art world in America, to the stigmatizing absence of treatment, education, and support for high-risk groups during the American AIDS epidemic in the 1980s. "Close writing"—the book and the term—is an interdisciplinary intervention into the existing scholarship on the two writers. Showing how their discipline and genre-shifting pieces provided new understandings of what it means to desire and love, *in* and *through* and *with* the sick body, "close writing" revitalizes the queer feminist politics of their lives in and as writing—which frayed the edges separating fiction and lived experience, past and present temporalities, visual and literary modes. Our close writings slip and collapse into one another.

Never have their entangled lives, works, and archives received such close and dialogic attention, in synchronicity, affinity, and correspondence, and through this interdisciplinary lens. To highlight the hybrid crossings at work in close writing—between the visual, the material, the performative, and the literary—I inhabit a position that is figured in close proximity to Kathy's early works, which meshed private and public documents in response to conceptual and feminist art practices: from her diary experiments in the 1970s, to her self-published chapbooks, to her 1980s novels combining stolen life writings and literary texts. The focus of this research emerged from daily, desiring encounters in the archives of Acker's notebooks and papers, at New York University and Duke University, over a six-week period. In this regard, this study builds on the archive-rich research of literary scholar Georgina Colby, theorist McKenzie Wark, and writerly biographers Jason McBride and Chris Kraus.[137] While Wark attends to the philosophical transness of Kathy as a "low theorist" via a textured "web" of archived citations, in a differential swerve from these methods of critical surface and dance, I harness the depth of close reading made possible with close writing.[138] It is a mode of close archival attention that also determines my critical objects. Indeed, while Colby focuses on unpublished poetry materials in the archive, drawing links between these early 1970s experiments and the work of the L-A-N-G-U-A-G-E poets, I turn more explicitly—as Kraus also does in *After Kathy Acker*—to the unpublished diaries and private notebooks that preceded Kathy's first self-published chapbook *Politics* (1972), newly positioning these earliest pieces in an often-ambivalent correspondence with conceptual art, experimental poetry, and feminist art practices. I am grateful to Kraus for the archival drive of her literary-biographical work and for the passion, commitment, and sheer breadth of McBride's life-writing research, which I broaden and deepen here, in dialogue with theoretical debates and concepts coming from multiple disciplines: feminist and queer theory, performance studies, critical theory, art and literary history, and philosophy.

My interest in the visual and performance aspects of Kathy's close-writing practice also aligns with Courtney Foster's proposition that in *The Childlike Life of the Black Tarantula by the Black Tarantula* the author invented a mode of "performative reading" in response to developments in 1970s performance art.[139] But for the most part, and following a conference on Kathy's work held at New York University's Fales Library five years after her death in 2002, which then became the 2006 essay collection *Lust for Life: On the Writings of Kathy Acker*, critical scholarship has tended to come from exclusively literary circles, focusing on Kathy's avant-garde aesthetics in the context of postmodern theories and punk poetics.[140] Beyond recognizing that Kathy experimented with modes such as *autoplagiarism*, wherein the author recounts "one's own life as if it, too, were a stolen text"—also *allobiography*, "the writing of one's life *as other*"—I ask why there has been a reluctance to address the particular, transgressive role of the autobiographical "matter" that informs and nourishes, to the extent it is often transcribed and reworked *into*, her interdisciplinary close writings.[141] In some ways, the intimate perspectives engineered in the hybrid works of Kraus, McBride, and Wark have loosened this censoring; I take this project up and advance it, as I meet close writing with close writing: a creative-critical reply that revitalizes the queer feminist complexities and narratives of sex, sickness, and love that animate Acker's interdisciplinary (diary, letter) *pieces*.[142]

Cookie Mueller, meanwhile, is more familiar to art and film historians as a portrait sitter for the photographer Nan Goldin (flickering as an image in slideshow versions of *The Ballad of Sexual Dependency*) or as an underground "sort-of-famous" film actress affiliated with John Waters (flickering as an image in low-budget movies like the 1970 *Multiple Maniacs*, which was her first big-screen role: won after her ticket stub was drawn in a door prize).[143] In this Baltimore-set B-movie about the gigantic and glamorous Lady Divine's "Cavalcade of Perversion"—a traveling and thieving "freakshow," featuring a trash troupe of misfits' wild and grotesque acts, desires, fantasies, and manias—Cookie plays the owner's hippie daughter, also named Cookie. Becoming a firm member of Waters's Dreamlander crew, parts in the so-called trash trilogy of films followed: *Pink Flamingos* (1972) sees diva Divine resolving to fight off the attempts of two kidnapping sociopaths to retain the notoriously criminal title of "Filthiest Person Alive" before an infamously scatological end (while Cookie plays the part of a spy who is abused by a delinquent armed with live, then decapitated chickens); *Female Trouble* (1974) revolves around the criminal activities and fame-hungry trash-beauty enterprises of a pregnant high school student turned mother, Dawn Davenport (played by Divine), alongside her delinquent friends Concetta (played by Cookie) and Chicklette (played by Susan Howe); lastly, *Desperate Living* (1977) follows the exiled life of a suburban housewife (Peggy) and her lesbian lover (Grizelda) following the murder of Peggy's husband, as the couple join a shantytown of social misfits (including Cookie's part as a one-armed lesbian named Flipper) ruled over by a tyrannical queen.[144] On the surface or in the frame, Cookie is all image and style (still and moving and anachronistically clothed; enchanting, original, infectious, resplendent), despite the autobiographical art writing she performed and published, which included pieces recording her countercultural life in film and fashion. Rather than the movies themselves, glossed briefly here as an instructional guide, it is Cookie's autofictional remembrance of certain filmic episodes that I prioritize, within and against the "look" of her, in my intimate address of analysis and attachment: soon-to-come snapshots of close writings *to* her own.

Some of Cookie's close writings "made it" within her lifetime; others, tragically, did not. I recuperate her in these pages as an important artist-writer whose autofictional close-writing archives (across images, letters, manuscripts, chapbooks, paperbacks, performances) offer vital resources in reimagining the representation, the voice, the desire, the community, and the care of the sick body with AIDS. By bringing Cookie's close writing into an interdisciplinary conversation that explores interactions between images and words—in correspondence with Kathy's own intermedia piecemeal experiments—I deepen the critical engagements provided by similar feminist projects that have revisited, often from a personal lens, the journals, events, and publishers with which *both of my beloveds*—never before brought together side-by-side—were involved with.[145] I also broaden the literary scope offered by Jennifer Cooke on "the new audacity" in contemporary feminist life writing and by Kaye Mitchell on the feminist effects of inhabiting a negative affect like shame in experimental autofiction.[146] This book builds on such explorations, offering an original, energizing, interdisciplinary term through which to think beside such work by women—work that sits between art and literature, fiction and criticism, autobiography and performance.

Furthermore, while there has been, in recent years, renewed critical interest in the visual and literary productions of Downtown New York artists with whom Cookie was writing in close proximity *to* across the late 1970s and 1980s (such as Jean-Michel Basquiat, Keith Haring, Jack Smith, and David Wojnarowicz), and in the aesthetic field of AIDS visual representation more broadly, her rich and distinctive writing—which emerged *near* artistic practice and scenes of the visual—has not been foregrounded in histories of Downtown aesthetics. A comprehensive, scholarly study of her genre-crossing fiction and art writing has not yet been written, although I hope this book, together with a recently expanded edition of her writings, will correct such cultural neglect, encouraging further complex and interdisciplinary readings of her writing as well as her image, which avoid the dangerous tendency to separate and police the boundaries between them.[147]

Love Triangles

Offering a radical mode of making reparative contact between feminist writers, I use close writing as a tool to (almost) touch, explore, write, and breathe life (momentarily, partially) into Kathy Acker and Cookie Mueller—two magnetic but indefinable figures and writers who left the world too soon. This is not a memoir; it is a relational, critical gathering, collapsing subject and object. Resonances, affinities, and synchronicities between my two subjects, across the aesthetic and the lived, across art and writing—from the friends and acquaintances they shared in Downtown circles, to scenes of possible commingling, to queer feminist provocations shared and animated in their close writings of autofictional performance and disclosure—reverberate across these pages, sometimes loudly, but more often quietly, like the hardened hum of chronic illness and end-of-life care, which both writers wrote through near the ends of their lives. It is a love story of more-than-one-story, characterized by embodied experiments and speculations in sexuality, sickness, intimacy, and care.

Held within those two alliterating names is the closeness of body and text. They were casual friends (published by the same presses; they also read at the same clubs and contributed to the same films), but I'm bringing them closer together—drawing out their shared political commitments to rewriting the sick body and its desires, the intimacies and care networks they crafted—in this strange, writerly love triangle. I remember how, in her essay-of-fragments *Eros the Bittersweet* (1986), Anne Carson even goes as far as to call erotic desire itself "a three-part structure": "three points of transformation on a circuit of possible relationship, electrified by desire so that they touch not touching."[148] I think of the friendships I had at school, always three: casting in while casting out, in tense lines of contact; always seeking the approval of the intruder; always unsure of whose turn it was to be her. It would be awkward to hold hands all together. Two was safer, but less exciting.

I wonder, then, if this love triangle is also kept alive erotically, sustained reparatively, by the other "lovers" and intimates of Kathy and Cookie who have written on and about them, too, over the course of my own loving writing. For example, Wark's erotic study of Kathy's low theory praxis expressed in gender and sexual multiplicities begins with the author recounting the visceral fusion of their own bodies and words. The "gift" Wark received from her lover/beloved? "A body that writes is a body that fucks."[149] McBride's biography "on the radical life and work of Kathy Acker" also begins with a fleshy, if less sexual, encounter at a public reading; he confesses to being completely "bewitched by her."[150] And Chloé Griffin's oral history, *Edgewise: A Picture of Cookie Mueller* (2014), no doubt a labor of love in its admirable endeavor to archive the beautiful imagination and spirit of her subject by talking at length with those closest to her, is described by its author as an act of "communing": "I saw something in Cookie that I desired in myself."[151] So much of the storytelling (its snapshots, anecdotes, and details) in this book would not have been possible without Griffin's formidable and tender historical project in life-writing collage and collective chorus-making.

As an affective, networked, and citational kind of fandom, the feeling that Cookie and Kathy are "my beloveds," then, is strangely shareable, rather than sacredly singular. As the contemporary artist Celia Paul writes, in her own book of fantasy love letters to the modernist portrait painter Gwen John, "Jealousy heightens love"; it asks for *more*: endless replies.[152] In recent years, a plethora of biographies, novels, and book-length essays have emerged, inspired by—or in kinship with (real or imagined or both)—my beloveds' wild lives, texts, theories, and practices. In addition to Griffin's *Edgewise*, McBride's *Eat Your Mind* (2022), and the life-writing intimacies of Semiotext(e) affiliates Chris Kraus, Dodie Bellamy, and Eileen Myles, there's been Douglas Martin's lyric essay *Acker* (2017), Linda Stupart's Acker-ghosted experimental novel *Virus* (2016), and Olivia Laing's novel *Crudo* (2018), which meshes the autobiography of the author with Kathy Acker's own life and writing. These antecedent works of attachment have been important and influential to my distinct theorization and performance of close writing as a mode of creative critique that enlivens my beloveds' bodies in pieces; their partialized archives; their piecemeal, intergenre, intermedia works; and their own expansive and infectious close writing.

Love for my beloveds is contagious, infecting the space around the triangle itself, marked by "affective entanglements and encounters, by echoes, citations, mutterings, and silences: words said, left unsaid, confusing who said what," which are felt in the choral epigraphs that begin each chapter of this book.[153] It is an erotic shape of multiple relational lines that has also structured the citational correspondence practice of Tina Campt, when she "hear[s]" the work of Saidiya Hartman, Christina Sharpe, and Denise Ferreira da Silva (three points), in concert with a triangulated grouping of Black contemporary artists whose multimedia work resonates with and responds to past images in fugitive gestures of "visual frequency."[154]

First, I felt protective, so close that I felt uneasy about another writer also being close, within this triangular orbit that attends to word and image together. But my beloveds' lives and works defy such a possessive engagement; they seek—they celebrate—multiplicity instead, relations outside of familiar, familial patterns, in correspondences that travel between past and present. As Wark notes "in passing" of her and Kathy's position on such things: "We shared a dislike for both writers and scholars who treat some body, or some body of work, as if they owned it."[155] The power of my beloveds' close writing also comes from its seductive status as an invitation to be responded *to*—from more than one correspondent. In this way, the "writer's love triangle" that has made this book is kept going by the spiraling effects of more triangles multiplying, as if an expanding envelope formed from equilateral parts.[156] This is "love-in-the-background," the reparative force of choral competition. I see those frictions as nourishing for (post) critical acts that break and remake, for the continued revitalization of Kathy Acker and Cookie Mueller, and for the ways their close writing also transformed configurations of love. I do not think I could have touched it, had I not written them endless, enduring letters that listen and respond and fantasize anew. Through this epistolary queer feminist method that breaches the distances of time and space; that gets intimate with visuality, materiality, and textuality at once; that applies archival, historical, and theoretical close reading *in* close writing: This book of blurred love-in-pieces acquires an accreting and original power and communion that dwells in the afterlives of its subjects, enriching, expanding, and energizing the narratives by which they have been read, framed, "known." Close writing reckons with the precipice of never knowing them completely; love draws its breath here: the edge.

As the third point of the love triangle, I send love letters to the dead, which *touch not touching*. However much there are others in the background, this triangular orbit is *ours* in *this* writing, a relationship I feel to be real. It is a heady, hot, sticky space from which to write, calling to mind the early adjectival meanings of "close" as confined, concealed, fastened, secret, before it shifted to its allusions to nearness, proximity, and intimacy.[157] I do not claim to be "the same" as the two points of the triangle whom I love, absorbing the contagious influence of their writing in my own. I do not claim—cannot claim, would never claim—the trauma, sickness, suffering, and loss they endured. Nor do I absorb the specific scenes of their "wild" undisciplined lives of desire *as* and *into* my own. (Such scenes fed and sustained their lived and literary praxes *as* [to cite Jack Halberstam] queer "wild thinkers."[158]) My love for them doesn't rest on identifications drawn from biography-infused likenesses that are in any way "exact"; it draws its breath instead from a particular connection that is sustained by our shared, embodied relationship to, and discovery of, close writing.

Addressed to Kathy and Cookie, my love-in-pieces offers a subversive means through which to create careful discussions about their works and lives. I risk the embarrassment of such a wild gesture in order to get close to the nakedness of their wild writing: to care for the boldness and braveness with which they put their emotional, sexual, bodily lives to paper, sculpting different "ways of being that resist expert knowledge," which "fail to resolve into identity forms" rendered legible or coherent within conventional social structures organized around work, reproduction, and the nuclear family home.[159] From wild locales beyond these recognizable axes, they provocatively wrote what was personal in *their* close writing: How could I *not* write them letter pieces in response?

You helped me come to (close) writing.

Cookie's short stories and art criticism, documenting weird and wonderful and *wild* life events (from burning a friend's house down in British Columbia to performing a violent sex scene bloodied by the presence of chickens in *Pink Flamingos*), were published in the chapbooks and magazines of New York's Downtown scene and collected later in two posthumous collections, *Walking Through Clear Water in a Pool Painted Black*

(1990) and *Ask Dr. Mueller: The Writings of Cookie Mueller* (1997), following her death from AIDS-related illness on November 10, 1989. Kathy also wrote closely to the stuff of her own life, collaging pages from her diaries in her first self-published chapbooks, and appropriating correspondence sent to friends and lovers as raw material for performances and novels. In 1974, for example, she wrote a strange letter to the artist Alan Sondheim, asking him to collaborate on an epistolary art project that would explore the mutual desire they shared for one another after a brief meeting in New York. "How close can I get to someone?" she wonders. "Will we become each other?"[160] It is an intellectual question, and an erotic seduction, where desire, identification, and writing get messy and confused—just like they do in my own close writing through the forms and affects of its love-in-pieces. Inasmuch as Kathy's and Cookie's writings *flirt with* the autobiographical (get *close to*, but not right next to, hence inconclusive: displaced) in diaries and notebooks, almost novels, and epistolary pieces—the forms of their own close writing—they invite this kind of contact.

Pieces of Diary, Novel, Letter (I Collect Close Writing)

The three-part structure of this book arises from close, erotic encounters with my beloveds' own close writing that traverses published and unpublished contexts and materials, collapsing archive into art into writing into performance. These encounters manifest as letters, essays, letter pieces, essay pieces, asides, messages, P.S. additions, and notes in parentheses: the formal objects of my love-in-pieces, which sustain the reparative desires of my close writing. Through this, I attentively reach for, and *collect*, the never-before-felt forms of my beloveds' close writing: *diary piece*, *novel-in-pieces*, *letter piece*. I collect epistolary materials like an adolescent in love. Seeking ephemeral, interdisciplinary, sometimes-secret-or-small pieces that lie on the edges of what is labeled as "finished" in the hierarchies of cultural production, my practice is spun with the wild desires of a "low theorist."[161] Such a position echoes the "low theory sort of philosopher" characterization Wark has also recalled in Kathy: "a philosophy whose skill is threading words together as its own kind of more carnal love."[162] Similarly, it is through the threads and affections of close writing that *I flirt* with improper conduct in knowledge making.[163]

Endless collecting, flirting, love-letter writing: These "unfinished" activities that are also lived practices recall the undisciplined attentions of adolescence. I adopt this creative-critical practice to enter my beloveds' worlds and writings, which are *pliably* and *perversely* adolescent: in narrative content, in spirit, in style (the literary and the sartorial). I tap in to their adolescent "genres of the middle"—diaries that could be prose fictions that could be experimental poems that could be conceptual artworks; autobiographical stories that could be works of fiction or nonfiction (or both) that could be the parts of a novel that could be a series of anecdotes; letters and epistolary pieces that could be documents of performance art that could be intimate archives that could be art writings.[164] Close writing, like adolescence, occupies the messy middle ground of genre and discipline. Kathy was out of her teens when she committed herself fully to the practice of writing beyond academic assignments in Classical Literature. Cookie, also, was getting closer to thirty when she landed in New York with the adolescent hope of becoming a professional writer. Neither were typical "adolescents" if we think of adolescence as a fixed age category. But as wild thinkers, low theorists, reparative close writers, they, too, were somehow always, fluidly, nonhierarchically "adolescent" in the ways they resisted finalized outcomes, traditional family units, and resolved subject and aesthetic positions, including ideals of the "well" body. In the introduction to an interview with Kathy published in *Artforum* in 1994, Laurence Rickels also finds in her work a passion for adolescence: "not as the phase or phrase everyone has to get beyond rather than stuck on, but as a channel that is always there, ready to be tuned or turned into."[165]

In chapter 1, "The Diary Piece: The Line, the Cut, the Blur of Two Lives, or, Kathy Acker's Bad Sex Blur," I pick at the scrappy pages of where she first "tuned in": the piecemeal diaries, notebooks, and diaristic chapbooks that she filled up with personal explorations "4 hours a day every day" during the early 1970s, first while living and working in New York City, then later in Southern California. This expansive and partialized diaristic archive—the feverish outputs of her extended adolescence in her early twenties—contains the visceral and messy *material* forms of her automatic, autoerotic close conceptual writing. I emphasize that the slippages across form, genre, and discipline that occur within these inked, typed, and performed diary pieces—as Kathy wrote *within* and *against* the fields of conceptual art, feminist art, experimental poetry, and prose; *in between* private and public domains—change our understanding of those art and literary histories, while making possible a different kind of blurring, too. Following the bad sex–oriented work of Jennifer Doyle, I argue that, within these diary experiments, Kathy opened out the ambivalent, paradoxical, shifting, and *sapphic* blur of female sexual desire, its perverse loose ends, its "sick" spaces and embodied states, its plural forms and affects, and its complex shapes, *at home and at work*.[166] This is an important feminist contribution, offering a vision of sex and sexual desire that does not silence or shame its violent, uncomfortable angles, recognizing instead how those angles can bring pleasure, excitement, curiosity, and knowledge.

Narrative threads, not necessarily linear, begin to twist outward from the throat of the text, like the spiral of glass language that spills from the open mouth of an adolescent Francesca Woodman communing and communicating crystallized speech (in her photograph *Self-Portrait Talking to Vince*, 1977).[167] The conceptual figure of the adolescent—her wayward desires and tendency toward wayward writerly forms; her crossings of all kinds of category (sexed, gendered, aesthetic; healthy versus sick)—returns in chapter 2, as an association between the two writers (Kathy and Cookie) is drawn across these first two monographic, archive-incorporative, materially attentive chapters, which connect sickness and adolescence as correspondent states: intimate, vulnerable, resistant. Offering risky and reparative visions of pleasure, the body, and time, their autofictional close writings challenge pathologizing narratives and power structures. From the autoerotic drive of Kathy's partialized diary pieces sketching the ambivalence of sexual desire comes the restless, never-full desire felt and depicted in the similarly sapphic and scrappy materials, narratives, and forms of Cookie's "unfinished" manuscripts: the traces of her sickened-by-AIDS "adolescent" productions. Accompanying the reader throughout all of this, too, is Me, or rather the echoes of their close writing through my own, beating, reverberating, in self-directed curiosity and bittersweet pleasure. Like them, my form is my content.

In chapter 2, "The Novel-in-Pieces: 'Like Little Birds Testing Their Wings,' or, Cookie Mueller's Adolescent Reverie," I feel my way—physically, affectively, and attentively—through Cookie's archival, unpublished, and published pieces: lists, letters, personal documents, chapbooks, notebook pages, autobiographical stories in journals and collections, and an unfinished novel. I propose, via Jack Halberstam on queer failure, that the scrappy, unfinished materialities of her work and archive offer their own queer possibilities, political imaginations, and temporal resources, revising narratives of the sick, pathologized body and its care networks and disordering the capitalist wellness of chronological time.[168] By encountering the scattered, speculative, genre-defying parts of what I term her novel-in-pieces, I touch on the reparative *adolescent* energies of her retrospective close writing. Here, in short, distracted, unfinished pieces of writing, she restored the transgressive marks left in her perverse adolescence—incorporating the adolescent's never-full desire for freedom, for bad taste, for pleasure, for the paradoxical bittersweet—when the mortal frame of her sick time pressed hard on her body: vulnerable *and* resistant. To nostalgically *become* a "perpetual subject-adolescent" *in writing* this way, I argue—drawing on the adolescent-attentive work of Julia Kristeva, Carol Mavor, Eve Kosofsky Sedgwick, and Joseph Litvak—is nourishing, intimate, and political.[169] She remembers the queer adolescent energies, desires, and temporalities of her past and turns them into lifelines in her sick present, staking her claim that freedom for her, as a woman writer with AIDS, is also unfinished.

The triangular orbit of this book's loving beat is echoed in the book's tripartite shape. In the third chapter, "The Letter Piece: Around Valentine's Day, 1980, or, Lovesick Perversions in Correspondence," my beloveds come into closer contact across three scrolling parts. This extended chapter is drawn from association across selves, lives, texts, companions, collaborators, characters, dreams, and intimate reoccurrences; the slippery appearances of masturbator, masochist, kleptomaniac, and hospitalized "hysteric" that feature in chapters 1 and 2 return in a choral fashion in chapter 3, extending the book's interrelated examinations—in and through the epistolary—of sickness, adolescence, pleasure, and care: the vitalities and precarities of life and death. From chapter 2's focus on Cookie's AIDS writing to the coupled assessment of both writers' animations of lovesickness in close writing amid HIV/AIDS contexts that is the form and content of chapter 3, the mortal shroud of chronic, incurable illness cloaks the writing most intensely across these chapters, before the postscript turns to the ghostly envelopes of their afterlives.

Chapter 3, "The Letter Piece: Around Valentine's Day, 1980, or, Lovesick Perversions in Correspondence," begins with a portrait of Cookie, dressed as a writer-friend's ex-boyfriend, from an epistolary performance at New York's Mudd Club on February 14, 1980. Kathy Acker and Gary Indiana played love-letter writers and Cookie was the love-letter object. Departing from José Esteban Muñoz's understanding of "ephemera *as* evidence," I propose that this part-object picture of Cookie is an invitation to dream, gossip, and speculate new possibilities about, but also for, with, and especially *around* the original event, in a way that dates it and also departs from it, circling it, stretching ideas and texts and events beyond it, which have an affinity with one another.[170] This stance makes it possible to reconsider the Mudd Club performance as an entry point into recognizing the critical effects of the love letter in both of my beloveds' close-writing archives, *singularly together*. I write between, across, and toward them, to show how both writers transformed the tradition of the love letter etched into histories of women's writing—they let it be *perverse*; they let it be *sick*—to transform and repair our narratives of love and the affective relations of affinity. The private-blurring-with-public form of the letter piece makes such transformations possible; it is where love, sickness, perversion, and writing coalesce. Together but apart, my beloveds cared for the often-hidden, always-plural perversities and pleasures of lovesickness (meaning *loving*, and *writing*, *in* and *with* sickness) in its multiple, complex iterations, encompassing delirium, disorder, and disease: voices of the vulnerable, the masochistic, the pathologized (from erotomaniac to kleptomaniac), the chronically, incurably ill. The figure of the love/sick woman writer channels the pleasures of perversion as a critical tool, a means to alleviate or subvert the haunting repetition of hystericizing, pathologizing discourse against sick, gendered, and racialized bodies in the 1980s. I write beside the lovesick; I unravel a secretive and reparative love plot that lies beyond the intimate public's coupled normative shape; its lines have already begun to be drawn.

I give you the pieces of this writer's love.

P.S. I feel on the edge when I write you letters, as if my skin has been etched with a needle, oozing particles of almost pink. I feel weak. And then I feel powerful, as the incantation of *I love you* blushes the page.

ONE

The Diary Piece

THE LINE, THE CUT, THE BLUR OF TWO LIVES, OR, KATHY ACKER'S BAD SEX BLUR

Kathy was doing what people in the poetry world called "writing." . . . And it made a baggy loose space, a trans form where poets could meet everybody. Which was poetry's project then.

Eileen Myles, "Dear Reader: Eileen Myles on Kathy Acker"

Conceptual Blood

As I enter the writing of this letter, I enter the writing of you. Our bodies blur. Words, too. I'm delirious in letters, as you are in diaries, where dreams become desire. Coming to writing. You and me. I dream and desire and touch those first inked gestures, released with all the relief of an orgasm—the difficulty of getting there—in staggering stops and starts. Like writing. Desire rubs up closely against the angles of feeling. I picture your room in Washington Heights, the sharp needle of the island, a precipice. The edge of the city, and the edge of yourself—the edge of writing it—mess, heartache, desire, and pain. To me, it is fearless.

How did you enter; how did you jump? I feel giddy, unstable, shattered into pieces by risk, when I scribe my love in shards of glass, risking rejection and exposure.

The sunshine of San Diego must've seemed a long way away when Kathy moved back to her native New York in spring 1970. She came back with her boyfriend, Len Neufeld, because she wanted to be close to writers.[1] The poet Jerome Rothenberg, and his anthropologist wife, Diane, lived downstairs on the fifth floor in thrillingly intimate proximity.[2] But for the most part, they were in a poetry dead zone, nearly ten miles north of the St. Mark's Poetry Project, in Washington Heights. A broken subway ride separated her from the poetry readings she craved. Stranded at the city's edge—*before* David Wojnarowicz would wander the nearby piers taking photographs of ghostly figures masked as outlaw poets; *before* Chantal Akerman would also move about unseen in a decaying city far from the place she called "home"; *before* Cookie chronicled the trials and tribulations of Manhattan life—Kathy might as well have been drowning in water.[3] The city's stagnating economy was closing in, pressing on the streets she sometimes walked, which overflowed, alongside crumbling apartment blocks.

Were there mountains of garbage at your young, tired feet?

Sickness blighted her first months back in the big city: Pelvic inflammatory disease—a bacterial infection of the female reproductive organs that would be, for Kathy, persistent and chronic—destroyed her. And so, at 600 West 163rd Street, squeezed between the Hudson and Harlem Rivers—the destitute blocks of the South Bronx just beyond its watery strip—Kathy came to the brutal realization that *sex has its bad side*.[4]

This shadows the form and content of her daily notebook writing. She was writing "4 hours a day every day," devouring endless ring-bound diaries with personal explorations (figure 1.1).[5] Kathy licked pages with blue and black ink. She often wrote in bed, which was also, often, her sickbed. Kathy's diaristic writing was like drawing; it was girlish doodles, letters-as-circles, abstract marks: the wandering attentions of adolescence returning.[6] This is the intimate stuff of her close "conceptual" writing.

I long to feel the surfaces you wrote on, with, inside, and beside; I itch to rub the cracked plaster of your walls, of your apartment and body; I yearn to cross your threshold with this writing that is dreaming that is waking that is touching. I desire the pieces of you that don't line up; keep me guessing. Your shadows evade my full "grasp." But you are here with me,

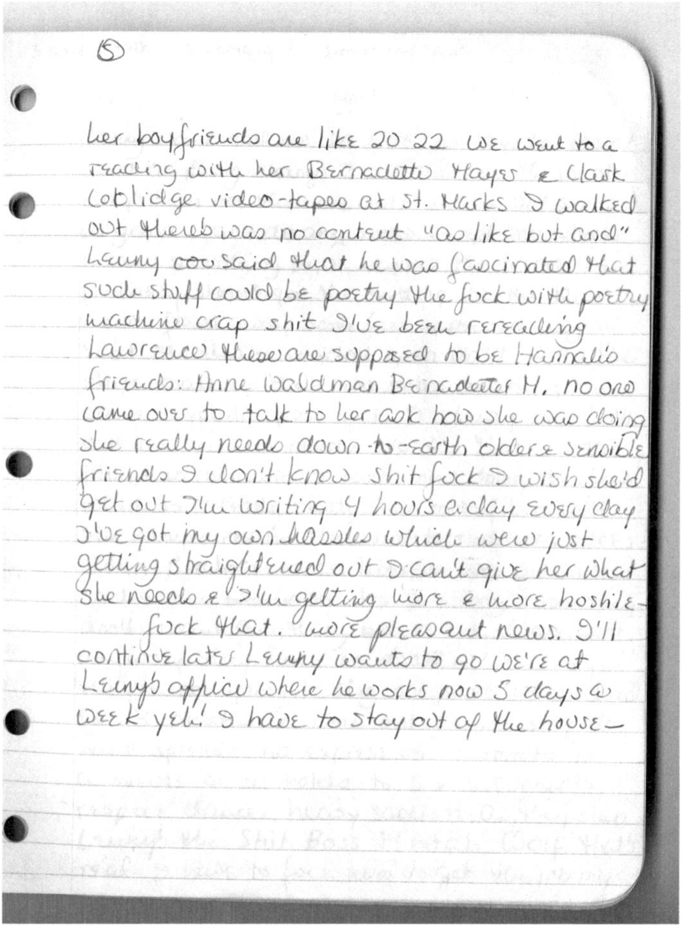

(5)

her boyfriends are like 20 22 we went to a
reading with her Bernadette Mayer & Clark
Coolidge video-tapes at St. Marks I walked
out there was no content "as like but and"
Lenny cou said that he was fascinated that
such stuff could be poetry the fuck with poetry
machine crap shit I've been rereading
Lawrence these are supposed to be Hannah's
friends: Anne Waldman Bernadette M, no one
came over to talk to her ask how she was doing
she really needs down-to-earth older & sensible
friends I don't know shit fuck I wish she'd
get out I'm writing 4 hours a day every day
I've got my own hassles which were just
getting straightened out I can't give her what
she needs & I'm getting more & more hostile-
fuck that. more pleasant news. I'll
continue later Lenny wants to go we're at
Lenny's office where he works now 5 days a
week yeh! I have to stay out of the house—

a page licked blue

1.1 Kathy Acker, page from "Poems/Diary" notebook, undated (ca. 1971). Fales Library and Special Collections, New York University Libraries, KAN, B3, F14. Courtesy of the Kathy Acker Estate.

right now, if only momentarily. I see bloodstains etched into the cotton like autumn leaves; faded walls that hint at the deepness of a nighttime black; used packets of medicine thrown about the room in pain. I caress crumple-fucked bedsheets (are those bodies or words hidden in the tide of their creases?). I fixate on the single pillow to share. I wonder how you slept peacefully, or if you sometimes slept and felt alone, in pain. I listen closely to the sounds of a typewriter. Or is it a cockroach darting? I stumble on dozens and dozens of ring-bound notebooks at my feet; books everywhere, spread-eagled open on the floor—face down, page up—asking to be penetrated. Torn pages, like cuts to the flesh: pleasure and pain coagulating. Blood seeps, like irrepressible ink. I like the like of correspondence. I submit to you, as you give yourself to the desire in dreams. Possession. I like the company of correspondence. It is enveloping, a coming together of more-than-one. I feel closer to you as I caress these words with my fingertips, scrawling through the weight of a bandaged bruise, the breaking of blood below the surface. My flesh was cut open two days ago so it could be inserted with an implant of hormonal contraception. As the days collapse from one to the next, I have sex in the hours before and after my writing you, touching you, no borders between us. No child to pull me away from you. The spaces of home and work have blurred with this virus—like it did for you. Your sick objects haunt my sickened letters. Shared thumbprints. I trace the lines of this love.

Within these notebooks, Kathy appropriated conceptual art methods based on duration to produce a close writing of diaries, involving an exhaustive display of detail regarding her emotional-embodied-sexual life. She explored desire, sickness, emotion, and writing, in fragmentary free-form passages that appeared to come out of her breathlessly, a particularly visceral form of automated writing that bordered on autoerotic. As Kathy affirms in an early diary, "I don't have any privacy if it keeps up I'm going to go batty I need to be left alone I've got to masturbate stay in touch with my daily fantasies I've got a constant storyline inside my head."[7] Exploring the material connections between masturbation, orgasm, reading, and writing as nonmimetic, nonlinear spaces of fantasy, dream, and wonder would be picked up and played with (by herself, and by others) in a repetitive, autoerotic fashion over the course of her life and practice. From the scrap of the analogue to the slip of the digital, her autoerotic appetite in and through writing took in diaries, essays, interviews, novels, CDs, and (as explored in chapter 3) love letters.[8] In this, as McKenzie Wark writes, "Acker finds another language, a mythic language of the body, of its metamorphosis."[9] And before her public image and infamous novels worked her masturbating-writing into myth, she tried it all out in the scrappy, preliminary, intimate environments of the diary page contextualized by the space of the bedroom.

It is autumn now, and discarded face masks smeared with foundation fight for air among fallen copper leaves. I'm back to showering at strange times of day to cleanse my body of mildew, to wipe it free of the time that sticks to it. I'm writing to you in short bursts because it is all the sick day allows for. I think about the boundaryless time of your mythic language, a relationship to writing we share. Is this how you ink-scratched your sick life, your sex life, the close edges between them? Is this how you slipped between it all, the plural pages of your body? So many letters I have smeared quickly, not sent, or un-sent, in autoerotic pleasure. This is the desire, if not the reality, to make surrogate, belated contact. Or is the desire a kind of reality, too? To be belated is to be overtaken by night, the pressure of time: a swallowing. I take you—or is it that you take me (?)—with this belated touch.

Kathy wondered what this autobiographical form might uncover, writing, in 1971, "I'm getting fucked up by a sense of worthiness how well I'm writing the main thing is to get down to the reality."[10] And within the same volume: "This writing is getting to be like junk. I'm going crazy doing it more I decided to write so much a day have to write so that I keep in touch with my feelings not to overwrite."[11] She fulfills that promise in diary upon diary, where the sense of grammar is rejected, to make space for expressions of desire, consciousness, the body—sloppily etched out as intimate junk. Full of tics and uncertainties, her writing is raw, as she keeps in touch with the aliveness of her feelings, *through methods of conceptual art*.[12] As Kate Zambreno writes of Kathy's work, "Sometimes she taps into a vein of deep feeling. She's conceptual, but not bloodless."[13]

The deeply political and feminist nuance of this paradox, as it is activated in Kathy's early 1970s diaristic experimentations of multiform, private-public activity—comprising notebooks, intimate journals, self-published chapbooks, performances, and mail-art serialized xerox novels—is the focus of this chapter's unfolding correspondences, spatial scenes, and artistic networks. As Kathy traveled restlessly in repetitious cycles from New York to San Diego and back again, she gathered a constellation of cross-disciplinary influences from across the *blurred* spaces of conceptual art, experimental poetry, and feminist art practice (Bernadette Mayer and Eleanor Antin were close friends and artistic-intellectual companions, whose work is closely examined here in ambivalent affinity with Adrian Piper). She both admired and resisted, or diverged from, such influences, expanding art and literary historical narratives, in a distinct, embodied project of endurance that scratches at the sick, messy, emotional, violent, contradictory, and ambivalent angles and affects of female sexual desire, its slippery intimacy with sexualized labor, across blurred artistic forms and materialities. Slipping across the blur of art and life objects in close writing, I argue for the queer feminist politics of Kathy's theoretical *and* artistic bad sex experiments, the reparative embrace of the "blur."

Years after the autoerotic production of the full-of-blood notebooks, Kathy enshrined the importance of aesthetic influence in an autobiographical essay: "I was taught by the Conceptualists that all that matters, in art, in the making of art, is the intention, intentionality."[14] She became a child of conceptual art when she escaped from the economic privilege of her "57th Street" prison, to the golden shores of La Jolla, near San Diego.[15] There she finished her BA in English—which she'd started at Brandeis University near Boston earlier in the decade—at the University of California San Diego (UCSD) in the world-shattering month of May '68. Kathy, though, wasn't directly political in an activist sense, as she would defensively recall in a conversation with Sylvère Lotringer: "When I was in the university at San Diego I was SDS [Students for a Democratic Society], but the student left was very elitist."[16] And much earlier, in a 1972 diary positioned temporally and subjectively closer to the student scene, she also flatly describes being absent from embodied gatherings urging sociopolitical change: "I don't go to demonstrations or political meetings."[17] As Jason McBride puts it, "The barricades she went to were in her brain."[18]

If this stance of peripheral retreat from left-wing activism was somewhat of a pose, still it stands in stark contrast to the activities and autobiography of another Brandeis-cum-UCSD alumni, the Black Marxist-feminist philosopher Angela Davis. In a later 1986 interview that coincided with the publication of *Don Quixote*, Kathy would claim to have "lived with Angela Davis for a while," instrumentalizing her spatial proximity *to* Davis to legitimize her interest in African narrative and literary forms.[19] But to suggest they were "roommates" is exaggeratedly inexact; it is a fictional flourish to the truth that calls to mind another detail that persists in Kathy's determined, performative mythologizing of her intellectual beginnings. The tracks she made to the West Coast, she would say, in interviews upon interviews, were because the Frankfurt School philosopher Herbert Marcuse had also moved there after he lost his tenured position at Brandeis over a series of political wranglings. This was the same Marcuse whom Davis had "mustered up enough courage to put in a request for an interview with," to help her "draw up a bibliography on basic works in philosophy" while in her senior year at Brandeis.[20] For Davis, this meeting initiated—as she describes in her autobiography in a section titled "Waters"—"stimulating weekly discussions" that amounted to an intellectual coming into critical theory.[21] Meanwhile, according to Chris Kraus, neither Kathy nor Bob Acker "attended Marcuse's classes or knew him at all"; "if anything, they and their friends" in the Art Department "were at odds with him."[22] But still, Kathy put a claim on high theory; she pulled it inside out with gossip. She put a claim on Angela Davis, too; she imagined them adjacent—in an utterance that brings to light my close writer's unshakable tendency to autofictionalize with bodies of theory. For when the dates of their travels get etched into timelines, the tightness of the "living with" narrative begins to unravel.

When Kathy started her undergraduate studies at the progressive but overwhelmingly white Brandeis University—which had been "named after a Jewish Supreme Court justice in the immediate aftermath in World War II" and was "committed both to social justice and to the welfare of the Jewish community"—it seems likely that Davis would have already been in Biarritz, where she spent a year abroad on the Hamilton College Junior Year in France, a scholarship extension from Brandeis she had to fight hard to get.[23] For Davis, her first two years at Brandeis involved feelings of alienation, anger, and discomfort at this "virtually all-white college campus," which gradually morphed into increased confidence, tenacity, and recognition of the white cohort's commitment to defend and distinguish themselves from "the Slave master and the Southern segregationist" in the absence of doing anything "concrete to fight racism."[24] When Davis reached the French coastal resort town—where the imperialist Napoleon III, whose reign instigated the increased colonization of West Africa by the French, had commissioned a grand summer residence on the shoreline in 1854 to give the place a patina of whiteness and wealth—the young student of French literature felt "old familiar feelings of disorientation" being "rekindled," unsettling repetitions of her experiences at Brandeis, which had followed a segregated childhood.[25]

Hers was a southern hometown (Birmingham, Alabama) that she would later recall in interviews antithetical to autofiction as being soundtracked by the sounds of bombs detonating "in her neighborhood during the violent years of white resistance to integration": this the sonic force of extending and maintaining orientations of whiteness.[26] It is such orientations that no doubt naturalized, as Davis describes in her autobiography, the envy she felt as a child: the desire, as Alice Kaplan puts it, "to be white—the equivalent of wanting to be your own worst enemy."[27] Such orientations would've made Brandeis a vastly different place to arrive as a young white student from the Upper East Side (Kathy Acker's painful, privileged home). And in France, a country where Davis had recognized "a drama of migration, the pressure cooker of racial intolerance coupled with economic misery," Davis felt these racialized and racist orientations again as "deeply personal" grief and pain.[28] On September 16, 1963, Davis picked up a copy of the *Herald Tribune* to discover that "four fourteen-year-old Birmingham girls, friends and neighbors, died instantly in the bombing of the 16th Street Baptist Church."[29] The "group of typically American students" with whom Davis found herself in close proximity to—and who would have been "lily-white" without her "presence"—met her grief with "closed" faces.[30] "They knew nothing of racism," Davis writes. "The only way they knew how to relate to me at that moment was to console me as if friends had just been killed in a plane crash," instead of as the victims of murder to which "the whole society was guilty."[31] In protest, Davis makes their names known: "Carole Robertson. Cynthia Wesley. Addie Mae Collins. Denise McNair"—a slow, still, poetic gesture that refuses the "logical, inevitable" structural racism and violent forces of white supremacy that brought about the "savage dismembering of four little girls."[32] The power of Davis's autobiographical, political writing comes from the sharp, candid turns she makes, from the micro to the macro, the intimate to the collective, the tender to the violent, in tone, language, and nonevent.[33]

Saidiya Hartman's italicized recitation published in *Artforum* in July 2020 echoes after: "*Breonna Taylor's murderers have still not been charged*."[34] It reminds us, as Davis also did, of what Hartman has described in *Lose Your Mother* as the "afterlife of slavery," wherein "black lives are still imperiled and devalued by a racial calculus and a political arithmetic that were entrenched centuries ago."[35] Hartman argues that what is needed is "a radical divestment in the project of whiteness and a redistribution of wealth and resources. It requires abolition, the abolition of the carceral world, the abolition of capitalism."[36] She invokes a "movement unfolding for decades" that has long been making this demand, which builds on the work of Angela Davis and others.[37]

Who was Davis to Kathy Acker? A roommate? A senior student? A rival for Marcuse's academic affections? An affection of her own? An entanglement of all these relations? In surfacing their *almost* coming into contact—down the corridors of the university, or across the imagined, shared pages of French writers Alain Robbe-Grillet, Jean Genet, and Arthur Rimbaud, their books borrowed from the same library—I intend to illuminate the orientations of whiteness that shaped the structures of their intellectual worlds differently, which brought the objects and rituals of fiction, fantasy, and nonattendance at political meetings closer to Kathy, while making the mobilization of *dis*orientation essential to Davis and her understanding of a Communist, abolitionist Black Liberation Movement.

They shared citational objects, even if they shared them via incongruent access points. In the fall of 1964, Robbe-Grillet gave a lecture at Brandeis on the revolutionary effects of what he termed the antiplot, anticharacter "New Novel." Davis would go on to write her dissertation thesis on Robbe-Grillet's "Phenomenological Attitude," while the philosophy of conceptual writing the author theorized and performed there would be reinterpreted by Kathy in San Diego—stimulated by the practitioners she was more intimately and intellectually involved with.[38]

She learned from her teacher; she loved him as a friend; she trespassed the poetry classes of David Antin after she graduated. Antin was a luminous ray of light in Kathy's big brown eyes. She eagerly apprenticed herself to him, an education that she describes in the essay "A Few Notes on Two of My Books." "I wanted to be a writer," she recalls, "but I couldn't find my own voice. . . . Why did I have to find my own voice and where was it?"[39] As an experimental poet and recognized art critic, Antin gave her permission to do it differently: "Just writing."[40] This cross-disciplinary way of doing things was echoed in Antin's two jobs at UCSD; he was a curator of art, and teacher of poetry, in the Art Department.[41] Through these correspondent activities, Antin introduced Kathy to "the early conceptual artists, Dan Graham and Joseph Kosuth," as well as conceptual writing procedures that overlapped with the anti-anthropomorphic character of the French Nouveau Roman.[42] Forget finding your own voice, Antin said. Steal from the library instead: plagiarize, collage, construct; treat writing as *work*. Kathy listened intently: "Intentionality is all."[43]

Kathy's close writing coincided with Antin's early "talk poems" that blurred the lines between experimental poetry, performance, and conceptual art, through a process of improvisation (Antin's "intention"). As a critical position, it energized cross-disciplinary approaches, with the fluid medium and material of the *work* (*language*) shared and exchanged between artists and poets. Jackson Mac Low's collaged, chance-inflected poems used found text like a conceptual artist, and they often became material for artworks and live performances—as Kathy would also later experiment with when she embodied her diaries with voice in spoken readings. Mac Low was a fan of Kathy's cross-disciplinary pieces, comforting her in a letter sent in 1973 when she wasn't receiving praise for her early "Black Tarantula" chapbooks: "I'm no kinda critic but I've been moved by them in all sorts of ways."[44] Is that a double entendre? Mac Low had a crush on Kathy, made more dramatic when their respective lovers (by this point her historian husband had been traded for a doctoral student in linguistics named Len Neufeld) fucked as well.

Bernadette Mayer was a mutual friend on the scene, who spilled to Mac Low about the chapbooks' bad press, and who also fused the fields of conceptual art and experimental poetry in the magazine she edited with Vito Acconci, *0 to 9* (1967–69). It spliced together visual and verbal experiments, forms discharged from discipline, as Clark Coolidge, Dan Graham, Sol LeWitt, Dick Higgins, Rosemary Mayer, Adrian Piper, Yvonne Rainer, Hannah Weiner, and Kathy's neighbor (with whom she was briefly infatuated), Jerome Rothenberg, fondled closely within its pages. For the fifth issue of the magazine, published in 1969, Acconci transported the final words from other contributors' pieces to the bottom right-hand corner of the page, generating an experimental poem that functioned as a conceptual artwork. Encroaching upon Sol LeWitt's *Sentences on Conceptual Art*, for example, he moved the word "art" to make "moving art/—V.H.A.," a pithy aphorism suggestive of the magazine's kinetic vibrations in genre and discipline.[45]

But Kathy's intentional improv was sicker and sexier than Antin's or Acconci's. She confesses within a later notebook to having a huge crush on the poet-turned-artist Dan Graham, whom she meets through Antin and his wife, the feminist artist Eleanor Antin. His "work I like & influences my work," she notes, entangling desire and writing in a confused mashup of life and art that is etched throughout her conceptually wired close writing.[46] Graham adopted operational tools to produce his self-reflexive conceptual art, as in the 1966–67 *Schema*, which used the form, structure, and context of magazine pages to model a series of "poems"—published in the magazine from which it culled its information—that were open-ended by virtue of their endless inputs. Graham's early work, summed up in his *Schema*, embodies the characteristics of conceptual art set out by LeWitt in his earlier *Paragraphs on Conceptual Art*, published in *Artforum* in June 1967. Famously stating "The idea becomes a machine that makes the art," LeWitt's artwork-text (also staged within the administrative surround of a magazine, far from the gallery white cube) is peppered with phrases that emphasize the intellectual, the "emotionally dry," the verbal, and the preparatory.[47] Working against previous obsessions with craftsmanship and ornament (and the market value that this implies), conceptual art ran into language instead. "In this context," Liz Kotz writes, "language is increasingly understood not just as a material but as a kind of 'site,'" a space from which to work, to build: language as architecture, rather than self-expression.[48]

This has become the dominant narrative of conceptual art, further demonstrated by Alexander Alberro's discussion of Dan Graham's schematic language as "impersonal." As Alberro writes, "By rejecting all manual intrusion on the part of the artist, relying instead on an a priori scheme that generates itself once placed in a magazine context, Graham's *Schema* also effected the total depersonalization of the work. As the system of a self-perpetuating structure, the artist virtually disappears behind the structure's self-generation."[49] But does Graham's reliance on a self-generating language depersonalize the work, or simply shift where selfhood and authorship is inscribed? Could the artist's "virtual" disappearance suggest instead a *flickering*—a nearly but not quite—in which the subject is imprinted in structures, rather than brushstrokes? As Peter Osborne contends in his post-conceptual philosophy of contemporary art, a work like LeWitt's *Sentences on Conceptual Art* (1969) might appear to root for antisubjectivist practices, but those roots aren't wholly secure, as the "productive infinity of the subject has merely been withdrawn from the realization of the work back into its *idea*."[50]

Eve Meltzer also grabs at the promise of the "virtual," seeking to dispel the myth that conceptual art was completely deprived of affect in its artworks based on language and systems. But rather than come out with the visceral specificity that stains Kathy's close writing of scrupulous sexual details, Meltzer draws on Jean-François Lyotard's term *intensities* as a way to describe the "free-floating and impersonal" emotions that circulate through conceptual artworks.[51] Even Mary Kelly's 1973 Super-8 film, *Antepartum*, which shows the artist stroking her pregnant belly over and over again, is loaded with a "recursive, suspended" sort of presence: the baby about to be born, the virtual baby, the not-quite baby.[52] Why this hesitation in calling conceptual art *personal*?

You scribbled your address on the inside cover of a ring-bound notebook, veiling and unveiling your visceral insides. It is a lipstick watermark. A mouth parted. An unsealed envelope. A first-person smear. Did you do this on purpose, so I could send you a reply? So bodily is your notebook writing: It wants to be touched again. Here it is, Kathy. My kiss. My stain. X. I hope it reaches you.

For Meltzer reading Mary Kelly—an artist known first for framing her baby's poo rags as art in an epic work of many parts, *Post-Partum Document* (1973–79), than this work's complex reading of Jacques Lacan—this skirting of the personal address could be a means to reverse the disparaging reputation of women's art in the 1970s as self-involved and diaristic, a verdict that the men of the period never received, even when they masturbated live, as Acconci did in the 1972 performance *Seedbed*. This was "me as a generalized person," said Acconci: "When I see a lot of work that women have done with diary-like self ideas, the difference between that kind of biographical self and the kind I was using are [*sic*] really vast."[53] Jane Blocker quotes this passage in *What the Body Cost: Desire, History and Performance*, to then follow it up with a question I must also ask in response to Kathy's inked bodies of artistic, sexual, physical, and emotional work: "Women's performances were more often seen as personal, narcissistic, specific, base, tedious, transient, noncommodifiable, and intransitive. What is the body if not these things? What is it if not personal?"[54]

Blocker's provocation has helped me to scratch at the impersonal reputation of conceptual art. I've turned to women artists who made specific, base, and tedious diaries, as conceptual experiments in subjectivity, desire, language, and embodiment. Kathy's close writing "bleeds" this way, all over the clean, general, "structural" subjectivity of the virtual self in conceptual art. Shockingly specific to her own life, these "sloppy account[s]" comprised the diary forms of her conceptual methodology, an intellectual and artistic exercise that probed the line between fiction and reality: "Does language correspond to reality? Can you get to reality (that's the goal, there's a reality despite me) by using the language in a certain way? Yes (because I'm a poet). Don't separate from sensual reality (diary). In what way? Describe? Find out about the language? A mixture?"[55] While she worked to specific rules in her sensual investigations, she wasn't completely alone (but did it feel like it? Stranded Uptown in that crummy apartment, body arched over your notebook in pain?) in placing the personal and bodily affects and relations of the diary at the center of her conceptual art practice that evolved across performance, poetry, prose, and the visual object; her work was an intimate precursor to the genre and discipline-crossing space of contemporary "art writing." Following the interventions of Jayne Wark in her essay "Conceptual Art and Feminism"—in which she recognizes, via the work of Martha Rosler, Adrian Piper, Eleanor Antin, and Martha Wilson, the "vital interaction between precepts of Conceptual art and emerging feminist efforts to challenge prevailing values and authorities within and beyond the art world"—I am redrawing the lines, forms, and narrative spaces of conceptual art from a feminist perspective: a political tracing of the intimate body, the sensual and sick reality.[56] For women artists and writers feeling their ways through and against the particular limitations placed on their lives "in" and "as" work, it became absolutely "necessary," a means of speaking, surviving, and connecting, "to move outside the abstract, self-reflexive, and disembodied investigations" that had defined conceptual art.[57] The diary offered a visual and verbal form to explore, filter, and mediate the violent angles of their censored circumstances, within and across the complex intersections of aesthetic, domestic, and corporeal spaces, and traversing private and public sites.

Indeed, for Piper and other women artists of color whose bodies are "*not* extended by the spaces" they inhabit but are instead "stopped," disoriented by institutional habits and structural injustices through which whiteness "holds" in the art world, the personal was not and could never be translated into a homogenous female experience.[58] In Piper's *Talking to Myself: The Ongoing Autobiography of an Art Object*, which was published as a delicate cream chapbook in 1974, the artist recalls the politically volatile events of spring 1970—"1) The invasion of Cambodia; 2) The Women's Movement; 3) Kent State and Jackson State; 4) The closing of CCNY, where I was in my first term as a philosophy major, during the student rebellion"—as instigating a shift in her practice toward performance and performance writing that centralized her own body and lived experience of it (the art object in becoming) in critical relation to social forms and structures.[59] In newly engaging with what was sociopolitically at stake in and not outside of her practice, she writes, "I did a lot of thinking about my position as an artist, a woman, and a black."[60]

Such a reflective mode, however, did not suddenly produce frank scenes of revelation or exposure, even when the materiality of the work

was drawn from the artist's closest environment: the visceral events, rituals, and happenings of the body. Presented in a grid format, *Concrete Documentation Infinity Piece* (1970), for example—which comprises fifty-seven framed pages of dense, handwritten diary entries alongside collaged black-and-white portraits the artist took of herself in the mirror, with the image annexing the script from the top right-hand corner of the *almost* sheer graph paper—provides a complex interpretation of the diaristic mode that gives *and* withholds, that abstracts, that refuses the totalizing and pathologizing effects of visibility for Black women. The work's performative and intensely embodied commitment to the personal diary as an art object (a form of "object maintenance" she calls it) begins with a series of
5 rules and abstract restraints that include the demand to "write everything
4 I do"; to take "Temp & weight on rising & going to bed"; to "Picture once a day"; to omit the "subject"; to disavow more-than-one verb in each sentence and restrict excessive sensory information.[61] Intersecting with Kathy's own rules not to "overwrite," Piper's writerly system distills and exhausts the daily movements and functions of the body into a clinical rendering—"Woke up at 5:30 A.M. Peed. Went back to bed"—that is microscopic in its detail, discipline, and attention, with the effect that the personal narrative is difficult to fully grasp or see, dissolving into granular operations, ritualistic descriptions of eating and excreting, and an impenetrable field of repeated abstract writing.[62] Piper's inked cursive is held formally within the interior grids of the graph paper, each line of looped letters positioned just below its previous, close but never quite touching, creating a thickly packed mist of dense, disciplined, textual form that is echoed in the giving and withholding dark grain of the photographs. I suggest that Piper diarized this particularly disorienting way—harnessing *restraint* in an early configuration of what Hartman would theorize as the Black feminist method of critical fabulation that depends on "narrative restraint, the refusal to fill in the gaps" (such as the first person "I," or a verb)—as a means of claiming space for the Black female body and subject *in opacity*, challenging and revising the sexist and racist codes and structures by which such bodies and subjects were in 1970, and continue to be, *consumed*.[63]

The cross-disciplinary work of Kathy's close friend Eleanor Antin, a poet-turned-conceptual-artist, implements a similar aesthetic and temporal register to ask what consuming differently—by which I mean *anorecticly* (also, *always*, performatively)—could enact for complex and agentic forms of gendered and corporeal representation. This is most vividly explored in *CARVING: A Traditional Sculpture* (1972), wherein the artist transformed the experience of gradual weight loss into visceral and candid corporeal "information," via 148 black-and-white photographs taken over thirty-seven days from four repeated angles (figure 1.2). Herein Antin critically appropriated the homogenizing narratives and processes used by the "traditional" sculptors and canonical male "Masters" of Ancient Greece—processes oriented toward extending constructions of white feminine beauty—as she worked on and with her white body, carving it like stone or ceramic, a pliable material. In the photographs, flesh falls away daily, in subtle and magical ways, through a lived dieting performance that cuttingly examines, by way of subtle embodiment (impossible to achieve in a clearly "visible" way), the effects of a capitalist beauty industry built on Western body ideals. If conceptual art was all about the dematerialization of the art object, as Lucy Lippard and John Chandler described it in their famous 1968 essay, "The Dematerialization of Art," then this photographic-performance work, which included text, showed how this anti-object impulse could also speak to feminist intentions, with its upfront display of the artist's disappearing naked body, as a photographed "virtual" sculpture. The cross-disciplinary attitude of the work is intimately tied to its idea, a blurring between sculpture, conceptual art, and performance that frightened the curators of New York's Whitney Biennial into rejecting Antin's proposal to exhibit it there.

Corporeal information emerged as the material for Antin's personal and conceptual artwork at a time in which she was "very sensitive in those days about being excluded from the 'boy's club.'" "That's what I called the small group of conceptual artists who were travelling around," she says, "having a ball in Europe and being written about all over the place, while I felt insulted and injured in San Diego."[64] Leaving behind the New York avant-garde scene she had squirreled for blood samples for her *Blood of a Poet Box* (1965–68), she landed in California with her husband, David, and their one-year-old-son, Blaise, in June 1968. And it was there, feeling the coast as an edge, that she experienced the brutally gendered effects of censorship, as she was marginalized for making work that was considered *too* conceptual, excessively lifelike, sloppily "un-sculptural." Kathy brought the artist company and comfort and creative exchange when in San Diego, while the younger writer continued to absorb and learn about feminism, performance, and the miracles of mail art (its blurred edges) from the work that was taking place around her. It was an intimate and creative partnership that extended into solidarity and care when the critics came for Kathy. Antin wrote to her friend so tenderly, but fiercely, in a letter:

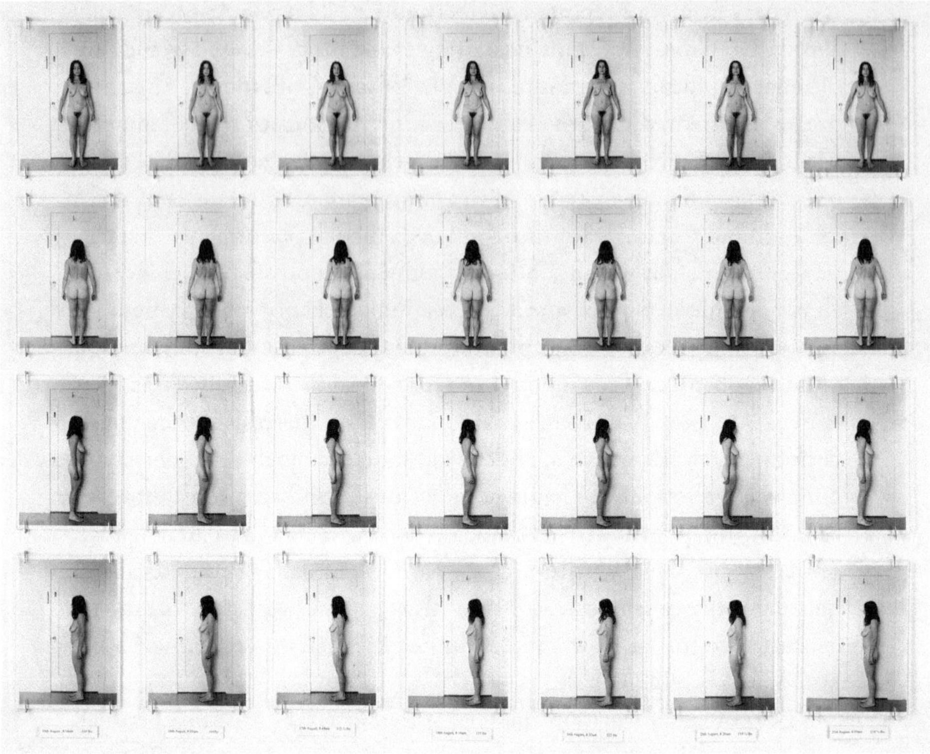

pliable and daily materials

1.2. Eleanor Antin, *CARVING: A Traditional Sculpture*, 1972. 148 gelatin silver prints and text panel, each photograph: 17.7 × 12.7 cm; text panel: 39.4 × 26 cm; installed: 79.4 × 518.2 cm; 79.4 × 518.2 cm. Art Institute of Chicago. © Eleanor Antin. Courtesy of the artist and Richard Saltoun Gallery, London.

"They're the New York art scene? . . . I'll revenge both of us, all of us. Don't let them worry you with their pettiness and old-fashioned ideas. I forbid my Kathy from worrying one inch about those creeps."[65]

In London, my teacher, whom I learn from and love as a friend, who just missed you in California, brings me closer to your own friend who became your teacher (and the King of Solana Beach). *She* brings me closer to you. Her big smile broadens when I mention your name, eating you up as we pick at morsels of breakfast (fried eggs) at lunchtime. Like you, she is small, but magnificent, stately; she continues to speak New York. I can see why you loved her. And I sense that everybody loved you, too. It is contagious; it endures (this love, this influence), even while it lands different in my distant hand. The love I speak is one of materials, the fingertips; it fizzes in words. Talking to her, about you, in recollections conjuring spatial proximities (parts, not wholes) makes me feel at times like an intruder, oddly out of place. But somehow it is different in words. I am less shy in letters. Was that how you felt in diaries? The artist writes to me (an email) in the days after our meeting—news of a photographic discovery: you in black-and-white, aged twenty or so. The picture file never surfaces, but you materialize differently between us (a splutter, a splinter, an imagined snapshot) in this exchange. It feels like gossip. Which feels like love. I search the network, arms outstretched, groping for the "you" in plain white t-shirts before you became the ornamental figure, the writer, the body, the name, the myth, we assume ourselves to know. I ache for the abject adolescence of you: when poems and passages cluttered your busy notebooks, when you tried it all out, indecisively, when art and life got blurry.

Despite being "somewhat pissed about the show" because of the lateness of the invitation, an earlier work of Antin's—*Portraits of Eight New York Women* (1971)—was included in Lucy Lippard's *c.7,500* traveling exhibition in 1973, the last in a series of conceptual art exhibitions that featured only women artists and included Adrian Piper's 1974 artist book crossed with autobiography, *Talking to Myself*.[66] Bernadette Mayer—as an editor of Piper; a receiver of Kathy's epistolary affections; a feminist protagonist of "conceptual closeness"—was also featured, via her 1972 work *Memory*. First exhibited at Holly Solomon's 98 Greene Street loft in February that year, it would've been a must-see for Kathy, despite its Downtown location. She had been catching the effects of Mayer's kaleidoscopic diary processes, penning in one of the diaries: "B. Mayer's work list of daily events facts (whatever 'facts') means."[67]

Mayer made these lists-cum-poems at 74 Grand Street. Like it was for Kathy, she interrupted the dividing lines between work and home, and lived experience trickled into the obsessive textures and images of her writing and making, as she, too, set about to "record special states of consciousness" in "neurotic" amounts of detail.[68] Friends on the St. Mark's poetry scene, their diaries mediated the personal—a "close" but not exact proximity—as one of Mayer's own scribbled pages indicate, with its instructions to use "cut ups" or "a strict form and/or try to destroy it" (figure 1.3).[69] And how *close* this is to Kathy's own self-reflexive annota-
5 tions, sketched upon leaves wrapped pink: "This diary is (about) the de-
8 struction of myself everyone else I know as the destruction is taking place from day-to-day" (figure 1.4).[70]

Choosing another "strict" schema for *Memory*, Mayer documented and distilled her daily happenings into pieces, as she shot a roll of 35-mm film a day across the month of July 1971 and arranged these enigmatic photographic fragments sequentially on the wall. As an epic horizontal grid, it was formally reminiscent of *Concrete Documentation Infinity Piece* and *CARVING*. Mayer also recorded a stream-of-consciousness, seven-hour narration, which used the "pictures as points of focus, one by one, and as taking off points for digression, filling in the spaces in between" to form a fragmentary prose of scattered notation.[71] It's an overwhelming, exhausting accumulation of intimate data that has been abstracted to obsessive levels of detail.

Memory begins inside. An opal-white sink in domestic shadows contains an embroidered cream blouse within dirty water. Lower East Side tenements dusted blue follow. Then, a portrait of the artist clutching her camera. Smoky scenes of Manhattan at dusk get cut with blurred pictures of banal domesticity get cut with cloudy skies get cut with sleepy afternoons (each day is a different color). The narration got transcribed as a book in 1975, within which it's possible to trace the slow pile-up of scenes, the language used to describe them as dense and strange as the photographs. It's a thickly woven quilt of objects, conversations, and feelings. Mayer maps the difficulty of writing this way, of writing through past images: "I've no idea what happened really happened this day not yet."[72] But while the "endurance" held within *Memory* (for writer and reader) is also contained in the schizo-detail of Kathy's close writing, the reader is tested in a different way by Kathy's urge to talk and "improv" sexually.[73]

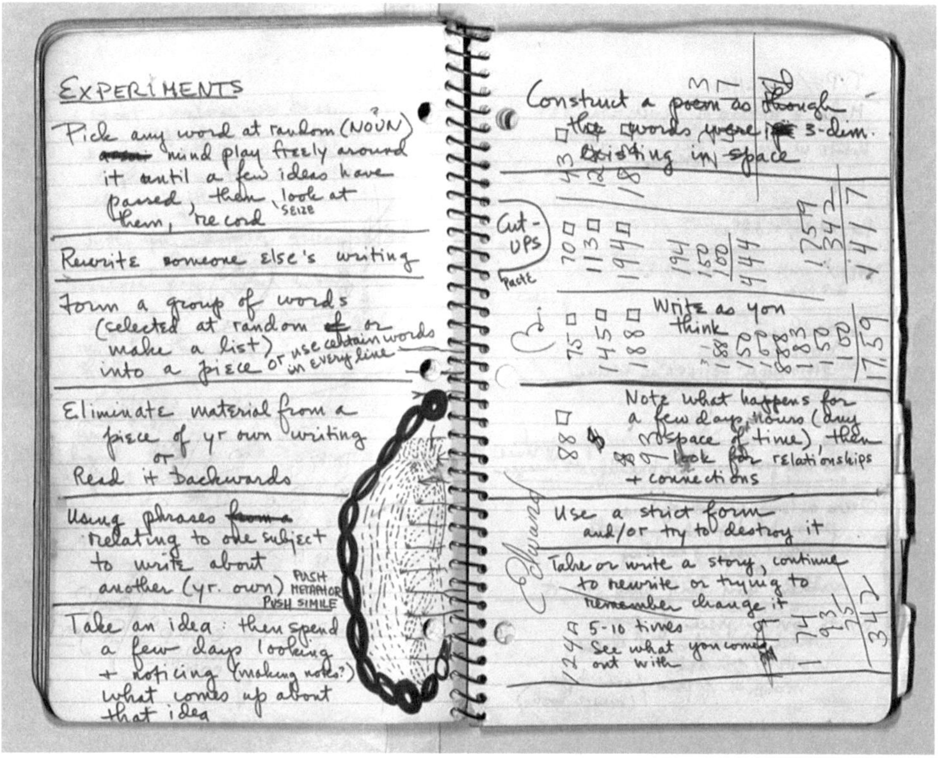

a scribbled page
instructions

1.3. Bernadette Mayer, notebook, pages with "EXPERIMENTS," October 1971. University of California San Diego Special Collections, BMP, B37, F6. Courtesy of the Bernadette Mayer Estate.

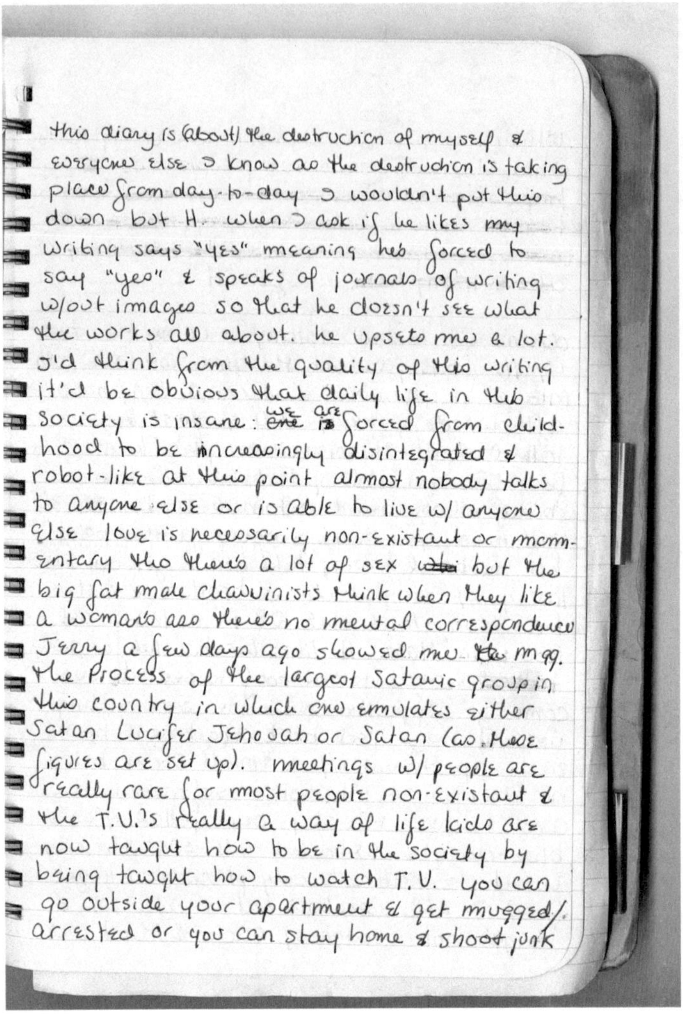
this diary is (about) the destruction of myself &
everyone else I know as the destruction is taking
place from day-to-day I wouldn't put this
down but H. when I ask if he likes my
writing says "yes" meaning he's forced to
say "yes" & speaks of journals of writing
w/out images so that he doesn't see what
the works all about. he upsets me a lot.
I'd think from the quality of this writing
it'd be obvious that daily life in this
society is insane: we are forced from child-
hood to be increasingly disintegrated &
robot-like at this point almost nobody talks
to anyone else or is able to live w/ anyone
else love is necessarily non-existant or momm-
entary tho there's a lot of sex but the
big fat male chauvinists think when they like
a woman's ass there's no mental correspondence
Jerry a few days ago showed me mag.
The Process of the largest Satanic group in
this country in which one emulates either
Satan Lucifer Jehovah or Satan (as these
figures are set up). meetings w/ people are
really rare for most people non-existant &
the T.V.'s really a way of life kids are
now taught how to be in the society by
being taught how to watch T.V. you can
go outside your apartment & get mugged/
arrested or you can stay home & shoot junk

self-reflexive annotations
leaves wrapped pink

1.4. Kathy Acker, page from "Dreams in Night for the Painters of Decadence & for Harriet Golden" notebook, undated (ca. 1972). Fales Library and Special Collections, New York University Libraries, KAN, B1, F11. Courtesy of the Kathy Acker Estate.

"You and & E. Antin [are] my female stars," Kathy splurged to Mayer in a letter sent in 1974.[74] And in 1976, she'd cite Adrian Piper—though does not directly name her as an influence—as connected to a group of "art world women" whose investment in "changing themselves, changing parts of themselves" intersected with her own autobiographical destructions of the early 1970s.[75] But while *Memory*, *CARVING*, and *Concrete Documentation Infinity Piece* occupy a conceptual space "close" to the visceral textures, affects, and rituals of their own lives, the architecture of their grids could be seen as a barrier to the erotic pleasures of the unclean. Although it is arguable that for Piper, vis-à-vis Ahmed's work on "whiteness as a phenomenological issue," a certain mode of the sexual was not, or at least not without extreme risk, a reachable object available to her as a racialized subject.[76]

In Kathy's close writing, there is a specific *blurring* at work that extends from its cross-disciplinary form (where the distinctions between artistic categories and literary genres, across art, writing, and performance—traversing poetry and prose—are obscured) to its bodily, sloppy, sexual unfoldings. Indeed, the etymology of "blur" as a verb is to "blot out by smearing ink over"—reminding us that the act of blurring is intimately connected to the act of writing, to bodily and abject interventions, as ink flows into other sticky fluids that smear, stain, and blemish, threatening erasure, confusion, even illegibility.[77] To write with the blur is to walk the fragile line between exposure and disappearance, risking a "moral stain" (according to the meaning of "blur" as a noun in the 1540s).[78] Kathy shamelessly unleashes this stain in her handwritten, antigrid but not-without-restraint smearings that explore the emotional mess, psychic fragility, and shifting fragments of sexual desire, felt in this ceaseless clause: "I want to see someone only to fall in love or to fuck I know that fucking or getting from talking to fucking is usually of me impossible because of my shyness & my fear of going from one place to another."[79] To immerse oneself in the frenetic blur of her passages—crossing between pleasure and pain, fucking and feeling—is to experience the destabilizing force of her sexual, specific close writing.

Cast adrift from home, I find solace in you. I follow the angles of your annotations, the fever of your crossings, the silence of a torn sheet. I absorb the time you must've spent within those lined leaves, getting deeper within the contours of yourself, the edges of your desire. I turn the pages of you quickly and feel our bodies entangle. From writer to reader: the blur of correspondence. Bubbles rising to meet foam at the mouth. It has nowhere else to go but language: notes and late-night messages to bodies I am dreaming of—separated by oceans and time. Unfixed by the headiness of an island city, where bodies move closely in hives, I miss the person I love and live with, while sweating at the shoulders of strangers in transit. There is distance in this kind of intimacy, and there is a gravitational pull in the gaps. I miss his warm hand on my stomach saying hello to the morning light. But I miss you every minute of every day, however impossible that sounds.

Sex Objects

On May 7, 1971, Kathy embodied her diarized blur with the liveness of voice, bringing the skin separating life and fiction closer together, at the St. Mark's Poetry Project open mic night. The women of the audience lavished praise on her, and Kathy got giddy with excitement. To connect this way, via the blurring of the lived and intimate body into the distributable work, was an important part of her intention, as she wrote in her diary: "to make this poem not only my blood but my work I have to angelicly constantly publicly read this aloud publish it make myself known and heard."[80] In her self-conscious and conceptual close writing, Kathy combined intimacies and publicities in a blurring of private and public worlds.

This was further performed in the notebooks' embodied materiality. In the archive, it is a visceral encounter: There are fuzzy felt-tipped titles slashed through the front covers at odd angles; words scattered in the margins that bark at the meaty stuff of her adolescent recto-writing; crossings out that speak of fierce intent; collaged cuttings pasted over existing pieces of writing; numbered pages; and sections marked "PRIVATE" (however much she strayed from such containment). The flux and fever of Kathy's energetic writing body is interwoven into these material interventions, which together imply a larger project beyond these atomized, preparatory pieces. "DON'T WRITE MUCH UNTIL THE ABOVE GETS TYPED," she warned herself, in big bold handwriting.[81] Her diaries are dotted with speedy annotations such as these that hint at her conceptual processes: from automatic writing, to transcription, to live reading and self-publication. For while not all the notebooks got spliced within the 1972 self-published chapbook *Politics*, or read aloud at St. Mark's, the diary as a conceptual art form was the vehicle for her close-writing practice at this time, and so I cross between all bodies of work, what I newly term her cross-disciplinary *diary pieces*, in *this* close writing.

I travel to New York to place my body close to your traces, to touch the materiality of your writing, to map out the spatial movements of your writing body. Every day I walk from my sublet apartment on the Lower East Side, down Rivington, Allen, East Houston; then all the way up the Bowery, past the club CBGB's, now John Varvatos, a menswear clothing shop. I hallucinate your presence in shadows, your threadbare clothing. I daydream about your adolescence on the Upper East Side and wander aimlessly around the park, where the leaves are turning yellow to amber to bronze. I see, almost touch, that gold-leafed door handle: the privilege, wealth, neglect; well-stocked libraries of feelings and words. Teardrops in the swell of the pages. Boyfriends, girlfriends, in-between friends: Can anything consume you like language?

Now, the virus locks me in letters.

Like it was for the conceptual feminist artist Lee Lozano, who also opted for the noun "piece" to reference her anti-object artmaking (from the conversations that formed *Dialogue Piece* [1969] to the disappearing act in *General Strike Piece* [begun in 1969], all drafted in notebooks first), this conjunction captures the ephemeral temporalities, experimental distractions, fragmentary dispersals, tactile energies, and bodily passions of her "never finished" close writing that groped for the "intentionality" of conceptual practices, blurring life into writing into art. This work listens to and moves with the shifting, contradictory, and violent shards of her emotional, sick, and sexual life. She shatters herself, an act of self-destructive but incredible aesthetic and intellectual will, into an infinite number of sharp pieces. Indeed, while other women writers have edited and published their diaries (one of which my beloved devoured: "reading Anais *[sic]* Nin's diary nothing else"), Kathy's diary pieces "perform" the unexpurgated.[82] Transforming the legacies of women's diary writing, historically made dirty by Victorian scribes (like the maid-of-all-work, Hannah Cullwick, who unleashed on the page erotic fantasies about her master-husband in her distinctive rural twang), Kathy extends the possibilities afforded by the diary in her close writing, using time-based rules to write restlessly, about and through, the violent and emotional pieces of her shifting sexual desire.[83]

Maybe I should've kept a diary aged twenty-one. Could it have helped me to realize, like these lines do now, the erotic shape and shade (blurry, gray) of what I really wanted? Today's sky (blurry, gray) *is* desire, its unpredictable particles.

In later interviews, Kathy would refer to this practice—an entangling of poetry, prose, and conceptual art that was inspired by the formal experiments of William Burroughs and David Antin—as one of the main reasons for her felt alienation from the St. Mark's poetry scene. For while admiring the work of Mayer, who taught poetry workshops at the Project, Kathy felt uneasy about the generalizing haze of its abstractions, hurling within a diary piece of 1971 (titled "Poems/Diary"): "Bernadette Mayer & Clark Coolidge video-tapes at St. Mark's I walked out there was 'as like but and' Lenny said he was fascinated that such stuff could be poetry the fuck with poetry machine crap shit."[84] On the flip side, Kathy's diary pieces overflowed with content, sexual content, communicated in aggressive, angular, and also abstract ways. For even when St. Mark's poets like Alice Notley and Joe Brainard also risked self-exposure in epistolary pieces—as in Brainard's illustrated *Bolinas Journal* (1971) (a book that Kathy was gifted by a poet-boyfriend)—rarely do they plunge deep into the splintering affects of sex, its cruel contexts. Containing notational diary entries documenting a trip to a literary enclave in Northern California and the fleeting relationships he forms there, Brainard showed the queerness of desire in his journal, writing honestly and amusingly about the awkwardness of his social and sexual encounters, in confessions like the following: "I sometimes wonder if *wanting* to fall in love isn't just as important as *who* you fall in love with. (Just as important, I mean, towards helping it happen.) And perhaps even more so. I don't know. To tell you the truth—I'll consider myself lucky just to get a little sex out of him."[85] But this writing—unlike in Kathy's—appears to occur within an innocent, protected bubble of nonviolence.

She loved to make a drama of this difference, between her work and the majority of the St. Mark's poets, in autobiographical essays: "The poets who were my age at that time didn't terribly like me, perhaps because the content of my writing was . . . full of a certain kind of sexuality, sexual perspective, which being feminine and political, is upsetting, that is anti–status quo. The status quo being male."[86] Her edgewise position evolved from questions of discipline, feminism, and sexuality; through these correspondent poles, she challenged forms, bodies, and values. And she was spatially on the edge, too: writing away from the hotbed of poetry (but she made one of her own at West 163rd Street) and working in a live sex show off Times Square to pay the bills. Times Square was the epicenter of the growing sex trade wherein the industries of pornography and sex work were brought into the economic (/misogynistic) clutches of late capitalism. Kathy saw her paid participation in it as a sort of break from the labors of capitalist time, as she wrote on one of her more optimistic days, "Working in a live sex show for bread it gives me 6 days of leisure don't have to fuck the boss."[87] She asserted in a 1976 interview at a New York restaurant that "it was work," that it was "always work," but that she was also "into it"—at least at times. "I don't draw hard categories," she says.[88]

Your lived commitment to the blur.

The live sex show was called Fun City, and Kathy worked there on Sundays, performing improvised routines with her boyfriend, Len Neufeld, that brought surreal sexual fantasies to simulated life. With a recently shaved head that must've scared the hippies of St. Mark's, Kathy played the part of Joan of Arc in one of their routines, transporting her far away from the grit of her difficult reality. She told Sylvère Lotringer two decades later that this experience had politicized her: "I had two lives, the poetry [scene] and the sex-show. I was in it only six months but it pretty radically changed my view of the world. . . . The 42nd Street experience made me learn about street politics. You see people from the bottom up, and sexual behavior, especially sex minus relationship—which is what happens in 42nd Street—is definitely bottom. Then you see it in a different way, especially power relationships in society."[89] This postmodernist concern with the interrelation of sex and power was foregrounded in her diary pieces, to the extent that the "two lives" she was living began to blur and overlap, as the paid sex work, and the work of writing it—gathering the pieces of her sexual, affective, and embodied life and labor—came into closer proximity.

As Kathy focuses on the grimy experiences of her sex work, as well as the contradictory desires that animate her sexual experiences at home, an unsettling paradox between pleasure and pain emerges. Like Jennifer Doyle's archive of "sex objects," Kathy's diary pieces dig deep into the "everydayness of sexual subjectivity" across both spaces, letting "boredom," "misunderstanding," and "humiliation" into the fold of desire, and the close embrace of her writing.[90] For example, in one of her first diary pieces from 1971, Kathy expels in boundless close writing the negative affects that animate her sex work: "For the first ten minutes I felt as if I wasn't me," she writes. "I was going through mechanical changes & actions I got scared I'd flip in front of the audience."[91] She captures the disorientation, embarrassment, vulnerability, and fear that comes with working her body this way: affects that then pour, seep, and blur into the suffocating shroud of her close writing that moves rapidly "home." Here the discomfort of being left out of a threesome ("I didn't want to watch watching Lenny fuck someone & not being involved would blow me") or the frank need for "anyone reasonable to fuck" her expresses the unwritten edges of sexual desire, where things get hazy and masochistic, where pleasure and pain blur.[92] It is a materialization of the political, sexual, and gender revolutions, transformations, and transitions made possible by what Wark describes as Kathy's "practice of masochism, not as theater but as a phenomenology."[93]

This approach not only drove a wedge between her work and the poets at St. Mark's: It also indicated a more provocative, intersectional, even queer, reading of feminist politics (closer to Doyle's proposition), which attends to the multiplicities of desire and embodiment in all its "sick" or "perverse" forms. As Kathy herself claims in her close writing, "I'm not going to get along w/the women in women's lib or in any other movement who have the portraits of a good person or a bad person set & force me to be someone else."[94] Echoing this sentiment, Doyle's particular use of the term *bad sex*, first applied to the "bad girl" art of Tracey Emin, has helped me to touch the queer feminist politics of Kathy's early 1970s close writing: the reparative "openings" (like the cleft of this erotic envelope stuffed with letter pieces) her blurrings and breakages can afford.[95] In this essay, Doyle describes the necessity of driving "a wedge into discourse on women and sexual history in which negative, disabling, unpleasurable, humiliating, abjecting sexual experiences might be projected into a space defined by something more complex than a contractual consent/nonconsent model of sexual encounters."[96]

This important theorization confuses the binary poles of good and bad that have so traditionally defined sexual experience, by bringing into play negative affects—from boredom to vulnerability to shame—that can elicit unexpected types of sexual pleasure. Following Doyle's work, I argue that it is through the blurring, layering, and cutting of bad sex scenes in her diary pieces that Kathy reassembles the meanings and manifestations of female sexual desire. And in so doing, Kathy—with a brutal buzz cut, handling a notebook in bed (maybe even masturbating with it?)—also muddies the asexual and impersonal narratives of conceptual art, including the feminist approaches she was temporally, spatially, affectively, and aesthetically *closer* to.

As she wrote on a bad morning (I can almost feel the cold of that lonely apartment; the brutal shafts of light) after some bad sex: "I wasn't willing to fuck him whenever he really wanted me he wasn't upset when I couldn't fuck because I had PID because I was actually still available he woke me up around 6.00 or 7.00 wanted to fuck I was hurting but I fucked because I was scared to hurt L."[97] In disorienting run-on sentences that smudge from one to the next, the desire in Kathy's bad sex life does not rest still. Amid physical sickness, and emotional pain, desire *returns*—however bad or violent or messy it may seem. It is a document that cuts close to those moments in our sexual lives we have likely rendered as difficult, a space in between the clarity of "yes" and "no," commingling states of health and sickness, of pleasure and pain, which is intensified by the form of her close writing, its determined, dense, and difficult textures. Held within this textual blur are the gray moments of sex and sexual life: the indecisive blanks and vulnerable decisions, which cause desire to spiral, unravel, and fray.

Sticking with the sexual politics of the blur, never does she do this in a way that feels like sex policing, wherein bad sex is always bad for you, an experience from which to be separated.[98] The desire imagined in Kathy's bad sex narratives is more complex, as she opens up the possibility that sex which causes pain, boredom, and/or abjection, among other negative feelings, can bring surprising moments of excitement and knowledge. As Doyle argues: "States like self-abandonment, submission, objectification—the experience of being made the object of another's pleasure—are not only exciting and fun . . . but important, even necessary, to experiences of sexual pleasure."[99] This is demonstrated in another of Kathy's diary pieces, wherein she writes herself as an abject, but curious, "thing," within close writing that bores and excites at once with its uncensored, autoerotic flow (figure 1.5):

> we went to bed, the phone rang for R., L & I got on the bed kissed, L. ate me for a few minutes it was OK we starting fucking, R. was watching I waved to him and turned away my head, he wasn't talking very much, later he told us that Taylor was telling about a heavy sex experience, I turned my head around and saw him watching, I turned my head away, R. said yes I have to go came over to the bed, I said to L. let's stop for a minute I had come twice I didn't want R. to feel left out, for the last two days L. has been hardly deigning to know him,

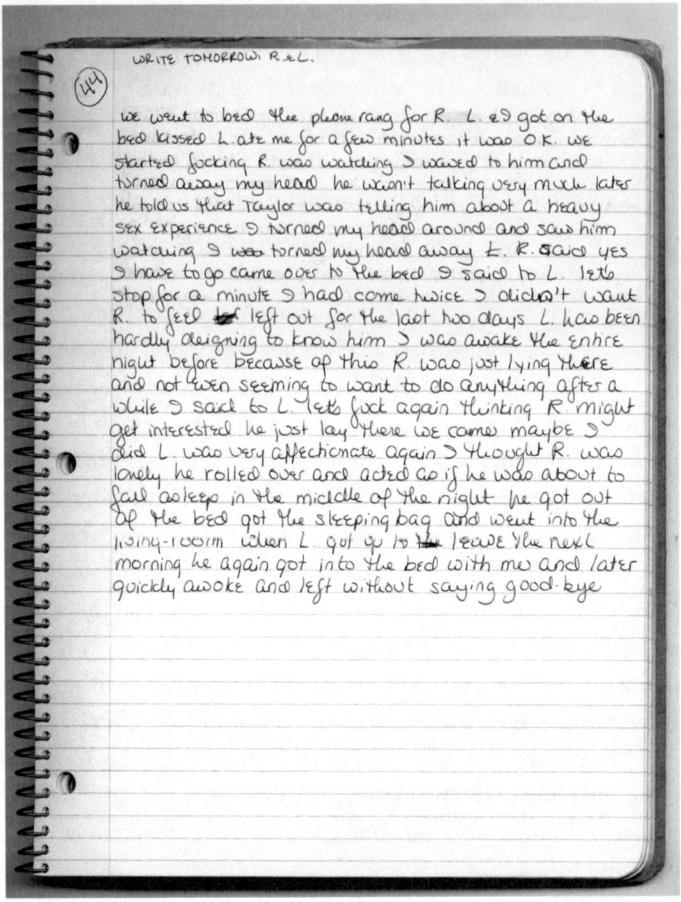
WRITE TOMORROW: R&L.

44

we went to bed the phone rang for R. L. & I got on the bed kissed L. ate me for a few minutes it was O.K. we started fucking R. was watching I waved to him and turned away my head he wasn't talking very much later he told us that Taylor was telling him about a heavy sex experience I turned my head around and saw him watching I was turned my head away L. R. said yes I have to go came over to the bed I said to L. let's stop for a minute I had come twice I didn't want R. to feel left out for the last two days L. has been hardly deigning to know him I was awake the entire night before because of this R. was just lying there and not even seeming to want to do anything after a while I said to L. let's fuck again thinking R. might get interested he just lay there we came maybe I did L. was very affectionate again I thought R. was lonely he rolled over and acted as if he was about to fall asleep in the middle of the night he got out of the bed got the sleeping bag and went into the living-room when L. got up to leave the next morning he again got into the bed with me and later quickly awoke and left without saying good-bye

a diary piece
autoerotic flow

1.5. Kathy Acker, page from "Ex-Libris: Morda/Diary Poems Dreams right after: what I can remember" notebook, March 9, 1971. Fales Library and Special Collections, New York University Libraries, KAN, B1, F12. Courtesy of the Kathy Acker Estate.

> I was awake the entire night before because of this, R. was just lying there and not even seeing to want to do anything after a while, I said to L. let's fuck again thinking R. might get interested, he just lay there we came maybe I did[100]

It is a passage of unbearable closeness, where bodies trespass, one upon another, where feelings combine with desires, where confusion reigns. I, too, get buzzed from the pour of her language, its incessant verbs: no space to pause, or breathe. As Kathy lists their movements, her writing feels as kinetic as the mechanical sex it describes, in which Kathy fucks and is fucked, from subject to object and back again, in a series of robotic actions. She kisses; is eaten; waves to a voyeur, or maybe it's just a friend; comes twice, but then only *maybe* came in climax. Her writing, as well, refuses to come, with its insistent atomizing of actions and emotions, as pleasure gets fuzzy with the banality of it all and its narrative refusal. The cold mechanics of the telephone interrupt proceedings, reminding us that these bodies are domestic objects, vulnerable to abjection: She turns her "head and saw him watching." She is caught exposed, potentially embarrassed, a confused, desiring thing—because while bad sex can be fraught in Kathy's diary pieces, it can be intriguing, too.

But, of course, there are scenes and encounters emerging from social processes wherein the objectification is so violent that it's not coherently erotic for *all* bad sex participants, in a smooth way, *all of the time*, as when Kathy describes "the reality" of the sex show in a diary piece: "I have to show my cunt to stay alive."[101] This exclamation points to the complexities and risks of her material conditions during this period, as she experienced the financial and emotional rejection of her family when she needed money for medical care during a flare-up of chronic pain. "They pissed on me when I was sick," she describes in a diary piece.[102] And with few resources at her disposal, still she wanted time for writing, willed to avoid all kinds of administrative employment. As Kraus writes, "The two months she'd spent as a file clerk for Texaco between her freshman and sophomore years at Brandeis convinced her that she wasn't well suited to 'robot' employment."[103] This, ironically, contradicts Sol LeWitt's manifestoing that the conceptual artist "functions merely as a clerk cataloguing the results of his premise."[104]

It was Florence Weill, Kathy's affluent Uptown grandmother, who paid for the two years of her tuition fees at Brandeis. And in early 1981—nearly ten years after the six months of sex work, wherein she had been earning

"$120 a night for performing six shows, twenty or thirty minutes each time"—Kathy received a substantial inheritance from Florence's estate, following her grandmother's death.[105] Like the tuition fees that got invisibly banked on her behalf and enabled her to reject a summer job, this money transformed her writing life, alleviating the burden of finding regular employment. Florence, the third daughter of well-off Austrian-Jewish immigrants, was "known as the most driven, astute, and financially ambitious of her extended clan," as Kraus describes after conversations with Kathy's cousin, Pooh Kaye.[106] Kathy's 1988 novel *Empire of the Senseless* begins with an autofictional description, "My Grandmother," collapsing subject and object: "She's my father's mother. He came out of her. And she came out of a German-Jewish family which was real wealthy. But when she was still a kid, cause of all the pre-Nazi nationalistic shit murkiness in Germany . . . her family had to leave. . . . Wealth was the price and cost of political escape."[107] Florence married "well" when she married Alexander Weill, who owned and later sold a successful glove-manufacturing business. Both inheritances were combined in Kathy's package: a lump sum of $100,000 with the remaining funds placed in fifteen-year residual trusts. Kathy also chose a pair of "white silk upholstered chairs" when "Florence's furniture, jewelry, and personal effects were divided between her two granddaughters."[108] These were the material objects Kathy inherited on the surface, and without denying the transmissive effects of intergenerational trauma for the Jewish diaspora in twentieth-century America (Ellen G. Friedman has written of the "Jewish voice" and "sense of homelessness . . . the frenetic wandering travel that mark" Kathy's texts), it is arguable that the unmarked structures of whiteness, as Ahmed notes, put "certain things within reach" as well: an education without financial burden; a less restricted creative practice; work that she could write around; a transitory job at a sex show that she both liked because it took her "as far as imaginable from her Upper East Side private school childhood" and didn't always like "because it's degrading."[109]

LeWitt, born into a family of Jewish immigrants from Russia, may have aligned the artist with clerk, echoed again in Seth Siegelaub's presentation of the exhibition *January 5–31, 1969* as a catalog resting on a desk, with a secretary behind that desk, poised to answer the telephone or grasp for the filing cabinet—but none of the white male participating artists in Siegelaub's conceptual show performed the role of secretary demanded by its administrative apparatus. In a black-and-white installation shot, it is a young woman named Adrian Piper—then an undergraduate student at

New York's School of Visual Arts—who dutifully inhabits the office furniture and performs the secretarial tasks that such objects invite. Within this environment, her body was no doubt forced to absorb the casual sexism and racism of an utterance that lingers in the air, or indifference to her presence. It was a paid role that she also took up beyond the aesthetic framework of this gallery setting—typing, filing, mailing, as a bookkeeper at Cameo employment agency—to financially sustain her emerging practice.[110] Siegelaub's photograph of Piper at work (she is not listed as a participating artist in the catalog, despite her essential role as a performer within it), an image that is seemingly taken from the threshold between corridor and office without Piper's acknowledgment or permission, brings into historical focus the secretarial worker as a racialized, gendered, and classed figure, an object of the capitalist gaze.[111]

"Objectness" in this context is always already socially inscribed onto certain bodies as a result of social forces and regulatory norms, as Doyle also implies in *Sex Objects* when she writes that "becoming object may not be sexy if objectness is always already thrust upon you" and as Hortense Spillers has argued in relation to what she terms *pornotroping*—a violent process that possesses, others, and objectifies the "captive" bodies of Black women and girls while making them sexually available through the turning of their bodies into thinglike flesh.[112] Amber Jamila Musser has more recently expanded Spillers's argument to ask what other sensualities, "selfhoods, intimacies, and knowledge systems" might emerge "from thinking with the flesh" and the racializing, ungendering effects of the pornotrope, without denying its deeply sedimented and continuing brutalities of dispossession.[113] Musser's work intersects—from a critical race perspective that thinks with queer feminist contemporary artworks by people of color—with the sexual politics of the paradoxical blur I am gesturing toward, holding "violence and possibility in the same frame."[114]

In her early 1970s diary pieces, Kathy recognizes the objectifying violence of sex-as-power, while she also boldly and bravely exposes, authors *anew*, the paradoxical pleasures of self-shattering: the erotic openings possible when such breakages can occur, demonstrated in the conflicting clauses of the following passage. As an anticipation of her later "lovesick" letter pieces, caressed in this book's closing coupled chapter, in this passage she reemerges as powerful in the act of writing it, the jealous and erotic extremes of her desire to possess and submit, all at once: "I'm very possessive & I can't handle my possessiveness any other way I want you completely you've got me completely well not when we're around someone else I have to hold myself up do you love me do you love me do you love me do you love me do you love me do you love me do you love me."[115] This is the exploratory drive of her boundless bad sex blur, in which she refuses the binary frame, the singular affect or cause, pushing into a space wherein, as Lauren Berlant also claims, "images of sex without optimism don't leave optimism behind."[116] In her bad sex desire to be "got," to be "held," to be "loved," Kathy—as character, author, and performer—actively *becomes* an object in her close writing of lived and aesthetic entangled forms. Life blurs into work blurs into practice in the diary pieces through which the hard categories of discipline and desire elude their finite edges, the lines policed.

7 It's my birthday: A green paperback arrives on my doorstep. I hazard that
2 you sent it. Encased in an envelope with a postage stamp that says "shipped" (across the Atlantic, its belated ocean time), it comes through my letterbox all slippery, like a fish underwater. Or like your mail-art novels. I receive the glassine-covered book like a letter, to be saved. Hungry to know the message, I unwrap the package (then pages) quickly; it's so small—a perfect first edition (beautiful emerald-green). It possesses me, as we possess each other. Smudging the line.

Cuts to the Skin

By the late spring of 1972, Kathy's relationship with Len Neufeld (the abstracted "L." or "Lenny" of her pieces: a character she both adores and fears) was severing. The edges it relied on became too sharp, as she scrawled in a fuchsia-pink notebook: "what's going thru my mind—breaking up/not breaking up w. L."[117] In another of her diaries she wonders what had drawn her to him, the shock of the truth forcing her to cross it out fiercely, but the childlike curves of her script are still visible: "I had been living w/L. only because I liked the situation he put me in."[118] And so how did *he*—flattened to an anonymous glyph—now view her? Like her ex-husband, Bob Acker, she thinks: "a goddamn whore."[119] The sunshine of San Diego—the glistening comfort of her close friends there: David, Eleanor, and Melvyn Freilicher—was calling once more.

She probably camped out in the Antins' spare room a few streets back from the beach. There she ransacked the New York notebooks, cut up her chosen pages, then typed them back together in a jerky arrangement.[120] This was *Politics* (1972), her first self-published work, and another diary piece, which further mediated the close-writing body through cutting, collaging, blurring. It was a simple production with no pictures, just the graphic rush of the typewriter repeated on offset printed pages, and two staples, probably punched by hand.

Traces of the author's body, its visceral encounters with writing, are stitched into the book's sloppy materiality, in a way that evokes the bodily actions of Yoko Ono's New York version of *Cut Piece* (1965). But while Ono invited audience members to cut off fragments of the fabric that clothed her body, Kathy traversed sadist and masochistic positions in her cut-up close writing that scraped at the skin of her pages, excerpting and layering passages that documented her experiences working at Fun City. (This composes the book's middle section, the longest part that was later published in Semiotext[e]'s 1991 edition *Hannibal Lecter, My Father*, as part of the imprint's Native Agents series of feminist autofiction.[121]) In this conceptual art process, breaks occur in the prose, like an open cut, or a mouth parted: pieces dislocated from a bodily "whole." Life writing blurs with dreams blurs with fiction, by way of her cut-up interventions.

I, too, cut love letters into pieces, like rough swatches of fabric, interwoven with feeling and fantasy, the lines of past and present, threads of you and me. It is an unraveling that begins with the blade, a cutting open: from which love spills. Intimate violence. Flashes of flesh. You imprint me.

William Burroughs was her role model for this project: "the only prose writer I could find," she claimed in interviews, "who was a conceptualist."[122] And so she "used *The Third Mind*"—a book-length collage of pieces that while not published in English until 1978 began to appear in parts, via other publications, between 1960 and 1973—"as experiments to teach myself how to write."[123] Here Burroughs reflects on the Dada origins of the literary cut-up and how Brion Gysin adapted modernist techniques, bringing painting and writing into conversation, when he "cut newspaper articles into sections and rearranged the sections *at random*" to produce, incidentally, "quite coherent and meaningful prose."[124] It was a methodology that mined randomness, accident, and antilyrical constructions to break the power lines of language and linear narrative, and unsettle the "real."

Kathy's adoption of the cut-up in *Politics* follows this violence in form, but it is emotionally and sexually violent, too. And so, while she may have been a Burroughs fangirl who blushed through interviews when talking about him, and with him (when she interviewed him at the October

Gallery in London in 1988 to coincide with a show of his infamous shotgun paintings, her round cheeks glowed peony-pink with embarrassment as he corrected her line of questions), she wasn't totally blinded by her love object. She could still criticize and contradict him, when "love and hate" are the "motive energies" of erotic desire, as Anne Carson writes in her study of the ancient Greek poet Sappho.[125] This conflict circumscribes the ways Kathy reads her favorite Burroughs novel, *The Wild Boys*, "seeing" "girls everywhere, girls being sexual, girls doing all and more than the boys I saw did when I used to sneak in my twenties down to the New York City wharves."[126] She brings girls' desiring voices into the fold, into the blur, as she also did in *Politics*, when she snuck about in her own diary words, aged only twenty-five.

While Alex Houen has argued that Kathy's relation to Burroughs existed in two parts, from her early adoration of his cut-ups, to her later departure from his work because of his attitudes to women, for me the dividing line is not so neat. A writer's love can be messy: pieced (and pierced) with love and hate. Her desire to "revive the body by potentiating new forms of gender and sexuality," as Houen argues in relation to Kathy's later work, was in fact an integral component of her earliest diary pieces, too, as she reimagined the forms and affects of the cut-up through a specifically sexual feminist lens.[127] This involved the excavation of her earlier sex-work writing, about the bad sex she experienced at home and the bad sex at Fun City she got paid for, where "the creeps males chauvinists rednecks pukes John Birchers worse liberals murderers we get in the audience . . . make everything dead with their eyes."[128]

Sometimes diary pages got lifted and placed in *Politics*, recontextualized by the cut but hardly changed at all, as when she declares in the 1971 diary and in *Politics*, "I need Bob's shit like a hole in my head."[129] (Bob is Bob Wolfe, the manager of Fun City, and a "hippie porn entrepreneur," in the words of Chris Kraus.[130]) And sometimes phrases became more forceful with the edit. "I'm sick of fucking and not knowing who I am"—hidden within an earlier diary passage—exposes itself in *Politics* as "I'm sick of fucking not knowing who I am," the final-line climax to the chapbook's "sex show" section.[131] The loss of a conjunctive turns an action into a feeling, an exclamation of shattering vulnerability, exhaustion, and loss. This is the force of Kathy's close writing: where distilled moments of direct emotion, combined with the pointed, paradoxical pieces of her bad sex desire, continue to seep through its conceptual cuts to create a performative closeness between writer and reader.

The power to say "I," but to be more than one "I," to blur between the lines of the "I's," to escape the policing of "I" via conceptual cut-up methods: This encapsulates so much of what is subversive about Kathy's diary pieces of this time, and which have an earlier antecedent than Burroughs, Ono, Mayer, Piper, or the Antins. Could the gesture of titling her diary pieces "Poems" be more than suggestive; could it be *sapphic*? Kraus writes that in spite of these works containing "no actual poetry" Kathy was still "a poet, in the sense of the word as she and her friends [namely David and Eleanor Antin] understood it."[132] Indeed, even when Kathy went on to commit herself to writing novels full time, David Antin maintained she was a poet, always, because "poetry is the language art."[133] And in the early years of her practice, informed no doubt by an impressive breadth of reading, her close (if awkward) interactions with experimental poets, and her hungry study of Classics, the confidence to call out divided desire in the first person is laced with traces of Sappho: figure and verse.[134] They are conjoined poetic bodies in pieces. Almost touching.

Like the disintegrating effects of writing love-in-pieces, as I encounter the afterlives of the pieces I have loved, Sappho's ancient poetry is materially fragmented, scattered across ruins and shards, luminous in their very incompleteness. "Preserved on papyrus" or "derived from citation in ancient authors," these pieces have been reconstructed, re-translated, devoured by the centuries of scholars who have followed in their wake.[135] And it is very likely Kathy—whose role as subject and object in her close writing echoes the metonymic force of the first name Sappho that holds poet, voice, and texts together as one—devoured them, too: "eating, incorporating . . . enchanted."[136]

Page duBois writes in *Sappho Is Burning* (a book that features in Kathy's personal library of 6,054 books, magazines, and pamphlets: now cared for by the Kathy Acker Reading Room at the University of Cologne, along with other writings on and by Sappho) that "Sappho and the poets who are her near contemporaries are among the first to inhabit fully the first person singular, to use the word 'I' to anchor their poetic speech."[137] It was an intimate address applied by Sappho in lyrical investigations of "erotic struggle," scenes and feelings spun with the fractious interplay of "pain as well as pleasure," wrought from the desiring paradox of "presence and absence" between lover/writer and subject/object.[138] This is the bittersweetness of love, first conceptualized by Sappho in Fragment 130 ("Eros once again limb-loosener whirls me / sweetbitter, impossible to fight off, creature stealing up"), and revisited by Carson in 1986, when she writes through Sappho to claim desire as an "ambivalent being, at once friend and enemy, who informs the erotic experience with emotional paradox."[139] Carson's essay (also in fragments) opens out the divisive, indecisive, contradictory, messy, plural, wayward, and oblique angles of desire.

For Jonathan Goldberg, the essay's philosophical reach for universal concepts instigated an initial pang of disappointment in him when reading it: Carson's "sidestepping of any discussion of gender and sexuality" specifically.[140] But as he begins to read Carson's text more closely, and the gendered Sappho enters the frame, Goldberg recognizes that Carson's understanding of "sapphic love," of "love *as* sapphic," is intimately connected to the body and desire of the writer (eros), to the female same-sex desire invoked in Sappho's poetry.[141] In my groping for Sappho as a way of getting closer to Kathy (a cross-temporal entanglement; much like ours, between I and you), I am scribing a new inscription of eros, where a woman's desire is *specifically* hers: bittersweet, plural (potentially queer), and always *written*: as it moves across the energies of presence and absence, love and hate, pleasure and pain; as it traverses the paradoxes of feeling in textual pieces. Hence, while my focus has been on the one hand "heterosexual," by returning to Sappho and Sappho's critics, in conversation with the queer work of Doyle, it is possible to illuminate the divisive forces and cuts of Kathy's first-person erotic writing: its unsettling refusal to desire in binary ways; its perverted, "sick" departure from normative straight couplings; its embrace of multiplicity and contradiction, all across pieces (with torn and enigmatic edges, like Sappho's) that reveal the blurred lines between poetry, prose, and conceptual art. In Kathy's bad sex blur, discipline and desire are equally (and politically) paradoxical. Form and content are thus motivated, as a feminist strategy, by the smearing effects of the blur.

Your name holds a constellation of infinite selves, texts, pieces. A celestial body of luminous matter. You sometimes feel light-years away. All I have left is writing, a brief act of consolation, to overcome you not being here, physically by my side. I touch not-touching. I live through bittersweetness.

The interdisciplinary diary piece *Politics* was materially fragmented like Sappho's corpus, and it also staged desire as cut, divided, recalling the ancient poet's contradictory confessions ("I'm in love! I'm not in love! I'm crazy! I'm not crazy!" is one of Sappho's boldly bittersweet fragments).[142] But the conflicts in Kathy's close writing are also specific to her own sexual life, often shockingly so, particularly in the ways her body is economized at home and at work: arousing unexpected exchanges of pleasure and pain, sensing agency and vulnerability at once, *unfixed*. In *Politics*, Kathy challenges further the separation between discomfort and desire, bringing them closer in her close writing of bad sex. She provocatively makes this public, performs it, when describing a sex-show performance with a coworker: "Mark's good at being aggressive a tinge of nastiness they're sadists a good fit I worked easily except for the sex I felt weird with Mark couldn't get into it and fake coming I was more interested in kissing him or looking at his body."[143]

Kathy can't flow; she's frozen like plastic, a fake "uncanny body" on the edge of the erotic action.[144] But in spite of her stillness, she's "a good fit" for Mark's sadistic streak. Like the masochist she first sketched in the diaries, this bad (fake) sex scene doesn't lack enjoyment or interest for Kathy, as she looks at him from the side, finding pleasure in objectification, becoming the subject of her own gaze.

The same feelings (and similar scenes) get thrown up at home, as the fierce splinters between texts and timeframes in *Politics* further blur the edges between home and work. Kathy quits her job at Fun City toward the end of this section in *Politics*, tells "Bob Wolf Big Shit Boss" that "there's broken glass in the bed it's raining through the roof on the floor where I have to dance and on the bed so I'm working all day in sopping wet clothes," in a scene that captures the gritty abjection of her situation, dense with tactile and visceral language.[145] Then, through the conceptual work of the cut-up, this soon slides into a domestic space that feels uncomfortable with detail, too, another threesome involving Reggie, Lenny, and Kathy:

> Lenny was sitting on Reggie's lap kissing him they went into the bedroom Lenny told me Reggie said he didn't want to be alone with Lenny anymore Lenny called me could I come into the bedroom I had to peel vegetables but it could wait Lenny was reading a Paul Bowles' story a guy is hot for his son finds out his son's homo and blows a gasket they both go off to Havana I was lying beside Reggie smelling his skin and barely touching him I got into it really hot so I got up to the kitchen masturbate in a little privacy they all came in why'd you get up so I told Lenny I was hot for Reggie so Lenny wouldn't think I was bored with his reading Reggie seemed hurt I was talking in a low voice to Lenny I explained he acted nice kissed me we were in bed Reggie fucking me so much[146]

Kathy might be the "wanted" one of the three this time, but the threat of boredom and hurt keeps the angles sharp. Kathy finds this abject space, of olfactory, "barely touching" desire erotic, and so she escapes to the kitchen to masturbate, a proximity that she must've known the other two would also find arousing. There is only a "*little* privacy" in the kitchen (a typically gendered space of care, cooking, and sacrifice; shaped by the sexual hunger of the male gaze), which Kathy briefly inhabits differently—showing and unshowing herself, delaying her domestic tasks, like a lived reworking of Acconci's contemporaneous *Seedbed*—in a state of self-pleasure before the others join her.

Within this threesome scene, sex manifests as a series of autoerotic
7 poses, gestures, and sensory experiences (smell, touch, hearing: the sound
8 of someone reading and speaking sex). Intercourse is delayed, suspended, rerouted into the mouth, rather than the genitals. Instead, sex becomes an exchange of gestures and words, as if a script to be performed, between more than two people. Even when the passage's final line suggests genital intercourse, it happens so quickly, almost banally, maybe even violently ("Reggie fucking me so much"), and the slippage between who desires who is so difficult to disentangle in the unedited blur of the writing, that sex continues to be represented as a constantly shifting space encompassing multiple participants, performances, scripts, gestures, and affects—far from the "'point' of heterosexual union."[147] In Sara Ahmed's queer theorization of perversion, "the straight line" of heterosexuality "would be that which moves *without any deviation*" toward sexual coupling, while "any acts that postpone" it are perverse.[148]

In many of Kathy's bad sex scenes it's the difficulty of the perverse love triangle that keeps the desire burning: a desire that shakes with risk and vulnerability. Carson also finds that shape within the fragments of Sappho: desire "*as* a three-part structure," whereby the three points on the circuit are "electrified by desire so that they touch not touching. Conjoined they are held apart."[149] It's this fragile tension that's always vulnerable to break, to pull apart, to fray, which shapes Kathy's bad sex blur.

For in the sapphic *Politics* of broken diary pieces, Kathy sketched the complex and paradoxical blur of female desire, its perverse loose ends, its plural forms and affects, its complex shapes, at home *and* at work. She provocatively brought two lives into closer proximity to perform the violent, unwritten edges of sexual desire, in pieces that blurred disciplines as a feminist strategy of illegibility-as-escape. Working on and with her own life and textual objects, *Politics* is an important flashpoint in her close writing. It supports a reparative unraveling of *desire and form.*

Opening the Blur

From illegible forms come other possibilities, new ways of understanding the difficult contours, contradictory impulses, negative affects, and complex social processes that shape and re-shape women's specific sexual lives. Kathy's close writing across the early 1970s diary pieces—a cross-disciplinary term that groups together the early diaries, the live readings, the transcriptions, the cut-ups, and the chapbooks, including the ones she would mail out in 1973 that became *The Childlike Life of the Black Tarantula*—has helped me to discover (*to touch*) the political openings such violent representations of bad sex and its forms can afford. I have opened the blur of bad sex, its emotional, sexual, sick, and perverse angles that confuse the categories of home and work, that show desire as divided, not whole; and which was authored, controlled, and *conceptualized* by Kathy in her feminist close writing, blurring plural lives into plural art forms. Here she broke the constructs of desire, subverted its narrative and voice, and challenged its policing across domestic, commercial, and aesthetic spaces, in deviant acts of sexual, bodily, and creative agency, which would find a new outlet, inspired by her friend Eleanor Antin, in the serial novels she sent through the post, authored by the anonymous Black Tarantula.

After hitching a ride from San Diego to New York with a young composer named Peter Gordon, Kathy soon squirreled him, for he was now her new boyfriend, into the secret, spider-webbed corners of the Washington Heights apartment she shared with Len. Then, when Peter headed back to Solana Beach via Los Angeles, she followed the tracks of the composer's trail and the "rush of correspondence" she had been tirelessly, desiringly sending him from afar.[150] In no time they were cohabiting; their apartment on Sierra Avenue—reassuringly close to the Antins' fold—became the new site of her daily notebook scrawl. There she made the autobiographical documents that would then be stolen, cut, and intercut into a new project involving first-person rewritings of mass-market biographies documenting the lives of nineteenth-century murderesses. She *became* them this way, like magic, as she also became William Butler Yeats and the Marquis de Sade in later chapbooks that year.[151] It was a type of aesthetic role-play, wherein she tested the limits of identity as schizophrenic—in an echo of Eleanor Antin's own becomings in the photographic-performance series *The King of Solana Beach* (1972). (In another solidarity-forming letter of support, Antin wrote to her friend: "I forbid my beloved Kathy from worrying one inch about these creeps. And the King is not used to being disobeyed."[152]) She was probing the self as always textual, interwoven, both fictive and real, which was felt in the David Antin–inspired compositional layering of stolen materials, with no clear dividing line between the cut-up passages of her own diary pieces (aside from the suggestive use of parentheses) and the works of others (on others' lives).

The tangible lines of her close-writing body blurred with these methods, as it did also in the unbroken syntax and dreamlike recuperation of memories and desire in the diaries and in *Politics* (even if these earlier works appear more directly positioned toward the autobiographical): a bittersweet merging of presence and absence that became even more electric, *erotic*, with the surreptitious strategy of postal distribution. First from Solana Beach, and then from hers and Peter Gordon's new place at 46 Belvedere Place, San Francisco, she sent her writing—which was drafted in cut-and-pasted, collaged notebooks first; then printed offset for cheap—to a network of artists and writers. She had an original rubber stamp made, which declared the author-correspondent to be "The Black Tarantula." This inked gesture of the hand decorated the envelopes that held her stapled compositions.

Many correspondents in the network replied in gossiping letters (and "there were actually people who were genuinely pissed off that she did that," that she "reach[ed] out and touch[ed] the inside of all these peoples' mailboxes," remembers Eileen Myles) back to this strange, sexual, sapphic figure.[153] Fielding Dawson, a Black Mountain poet, was enamored by the second chapbook, awkwardly titled "a point-to-point comparison between my life and the life of moll cutpurse, the queen-regent of misrule, the roaring girl, the benevolent tyrant of city thieves and city murderers, the bear lady." "Your voice is fresh and so new as to be a bright influence on anyone seriously involved in writing. . . . Your style of containing dialogue within the prose line is utterly refreshing, as is your humor and your divided self," he wrote to her on a return postcard, dated July 7, 1973.[154] Bernadette Mayer decided to offer a critique couched in a compliment when the second mail-art novel, *I Dreamt I Was a Nymphomaniac: Imagining*, got sent out the following year. "New book great but make em longer!" she replied on a pithy postcard sent from Anne Waldman's Downtown apartment at 33 St. Mark's.[155] Then, after the conceptual artist and theorist Sol LeWitt tipped off Kathy's work to Ted Castle and Leandro Katz of TVRT Press and offered to subsidize an official publication of *The Childlike Life*, a letter arrived on her doorstep, which doubled as an invitation to join (as Cookie Mueller would soon do, too), the energized and experimental post–fiscal crisis New York art world: "Since you began issuing 'The Childlike Life' we have read each installment of your writing with great interest and pleasure. . . . We would like to publish some of your work."[156]

This essay in pieces, which is also an essay of love, written in durational bursts like her own piecemeal writing, is my reply—my attempt to join and blur with her. Through it I have traced the role of conceptualism in her adolescent-tuned work: before the "official" publishers of the art world made contact; before she was sponsored and legitimized this way. *The Childlike Life* was an item of correspondence, but the earlier conceptual diary pieces—ephemeral, scrappy, always sexual (mostly "bad")—invite my epistolary touch as well: from the pieces of the archive to pieces of letter writing. Even when her close writing was formally blurry, involving pieces and influences from across the disciplines and genres of conceptual art, feminist art, poetry, and prose—never was it without "intentions," or even rules.

Each discipline had something to offer her, but each discipline was also marked by absence, absence of the personal, the violent, the sick, the perverse. And so never would she be confined to just one in her blurred practice of diary pieces, as she sought a mobile, even illegible close writing that traversed the spaces of art and life to hold bold revisions of sex and gender. At the complex site of her close writing, Kathy "deviated," turned away from, binary concepts of sexual desire, to expose, find freedom within, if only momentarily, its paradoxical energies and affects.

She is of the future in her queer multiplicities, publicly navigating negative affects in specifically sexual—that is, bad sexual—close writing. But she is also strangely of the past, too, in her conceptual, cut-up reworking of the sapphic piece. Kathy is a sex object, *torn to pieces*, disintegrating her life into writing. Her erotic body flashes brightly in description, in fluid lines, visceral textures, and broken cuts, appearing and disappearing (like a half-open envelope, spilling love letters), the irrepressible desire of the stain. The blur seeps, runs, overflows; it has smeared the edges of time . . . bringing me closer to you.

P.S. Your words make me want it; writing these letters makes me want it. Right cheek, then left. I scream. I ask for it, from a mouth parted, like this open envelope. I glow my head from behind, face glossed rose-pink, before retreating into the folds of the pillow, drowning in the blur: the meshwork of pleasure and pain. You have helped me to realize that other stories, forms, shapes, lives are possible. And it's only now, on this cold November morning shrouded in light gray skies the color of our sheets that I can come out and "say" it. You helped me find the opening. You helped me come to close writing. You changed my life, by letting it blur.

T
W
O

The Novel-in-Pieces

"LIKE LITTLE BIRDS TESTING THEIR WINGS," OR, COOKIE MUELLER'S ADOLESCENT REVERIE

Your rib cage lives on as a tree house for adolescent swallows
who if they've never had a chance to rebel, do now

Denise Duhamel, "Beauties Who Live Only for an Afternoon"

The Risk of Writing

I wake up early with sapphire skies: my first jetlagged day in the city. I wander the streets in suspension. I linger outside clothing boutiques in basements that are priced beyond our shared reach. I am waiting waiting waiting for you to return: a reflection or a shadow or the echo of a called-out name. "*Hi hon.*" Your stories give me the map. 101 Avenue A. I long for the door to open but it is too early (or too late), and so I press my ear against the roller shutter (sprayed with voices of protest) to hear the vibratory traces of your much-kissed lips kissing the mic once more. Stories of loving and dying, meeting the world. I meet you here, my host. I see and feel and hear and touch you closely by my side. I move with you through your city. I witness unhoused bodies in doorways, treated as waste, unwanted materials, soundtracked by the background noise of a siren, a kind of haunting, the sounds of a privatized medical emergency. I mourn the chronic cycles of greed and neglect. It's not even 9 a.m. (the time of "work," the time of suits, the time of extra-large caffeine containers to be held efficiently in one's hand). The library is not yet open. Books, as you know, like novel manuscripts, are slower to rise. And so, I keep walking—as I keep waiting, as I keep writing, for you—further west than Washington Square. I reach my destination: the flames of your railroad building, dashed in rust-red, desert-orange, magenta-pink—like a city sunset. Swallows circle above my head, in readiness for the day. The stench of cut meat rages below in the local butchers. I hold my breath, as your absence etches deep within. And yet, when I gaze up to your apartment, on the second, third, or fourth floor, I think I see you writing there, eating up your past as you let out your stories. The strange afterlife of you.

It was close to Christmas 1989 when Nan Goldin went to photograph her friend Cookie Mueller's empty apartment (plate 4). The funeral had taken place at St. Mark's Church—the Downtown literary mecca where Cookie had given readings at their annual New Year's Day Poetry marathons—a few weeks before. And it was on November 10, 1989, the same night the Berlin Wall crashed into pieces, that Cookie died of a cardiac arrest caused by AIDS, aged just forty. In the candle-lit photograph Goldin took of Cookie in her casket (it glows orange, pink, and yellow like a sunset, like an ending: a farewell that I hope will last a lifetime), she wears her favorite gold dress, flowers garlanded in her forever-blonde hair, and a scrap heap of gold metals around her tiny writer's wrists (plate 5). She is adorned in copper silks, bronze beads, with gemstones on her clasped fingers. Shimmering strands stick to her glowing skin. This haptic picture invites my close touch, my first and endless letter.

And with painted eyelids closed, head facing the sky, her reclining pose is suggestive of sleeping and dreaming, the lacework of her past haunting, knotting, and surfacing, even after her heart had stopped beating—threads and pieces that reemerged in her autobiographical close writing, published posthumously the following year. This funeral portrait taken by Cookie's close friend is entangled within a tradition of postmortem photography that expanded as a practice and marketable product in the West during the mid-nineteenth century, as prints of the deceased—dressed in middle-class lace and frills, flesh puffed, and faces painted, the embodied traces of sickness erased in the creation of racialized and classed forms of normativity—were framed and placed on mantelpieces, keepsakes to fetishize and remember lost loved ones, conjuring the comfort of an afterlife. “I used to think I wouldn’t lose anyone if I photographed them enough,” says Goldin, of her touching photographic gestures. “In fact they show me how much I’ve lost.”[1]

In 1922, Man Ray touched with his camera the contemplating closed eyes of Marcel Proust on his deathbed of creased white sheets, from which the novelist continued to sculpt his autobiographical production *In Search of Lost Time* (*À la recherche du temps perdu*) via struggling, spoken citations. Chronic asthma led to bronchitis and pneumonia, which led to him falling “permanently” asleep. When remembering and reenacting time past in her own close writing, this death portrait materializes in Cookie’s mind: a “sexy” visual likeness for her sick, “contagious” adolescent boyfriend.[2]

As conservative ideologies conflated sickness and sexual deviance during the AIDS epidemic of the 1980s, and as grief became rage—a tight wrapping of bodies (like Proust’s suffocating cotton sheets at his neck)—artists such as Goldin and David Wojnarowicz appropriated the form of the postmortem photograph to affirm the creative and intimate lives of their *artist-beloved*. Shaped by the close relation between the living and the dead, these photographs became objects of company, and *caress*, of reparative, radical care, in the stigmatizing absence of medical funding, research, and treatment for people living with AIDS (as the activist group ACT UP [AIDS Coalition to Unleash Power] declared, “Silence = Death”).[3] For when Wojnarowicz printed, in 1989, the close-up he captured of Peter Hujar’s open mouth and half-closed eyes (taken seconds after his friend’s last breath two years prior), the intimate proximity between subject and object overwhelms; it pricks the skin of the viewer with affective and embodied intensity, in a resolute declaration of love (figure 2.1).

Hujar’s body vibrates between life and death: the loosening of the flesh, the *fall*. If “sleep is a temporary death,” as writes Jean-Luc Nancy, might death (as represented by Goldin and Wojnarowicz) also be “necessarily temporary, for it lasts only as long as time lasts”?[4] Like a sunset on a clear day (marking the passing of time), Cookie’s casketed beauty is blinding, embodying the disembodied. Is this a portrait, or a still life, or is it both?

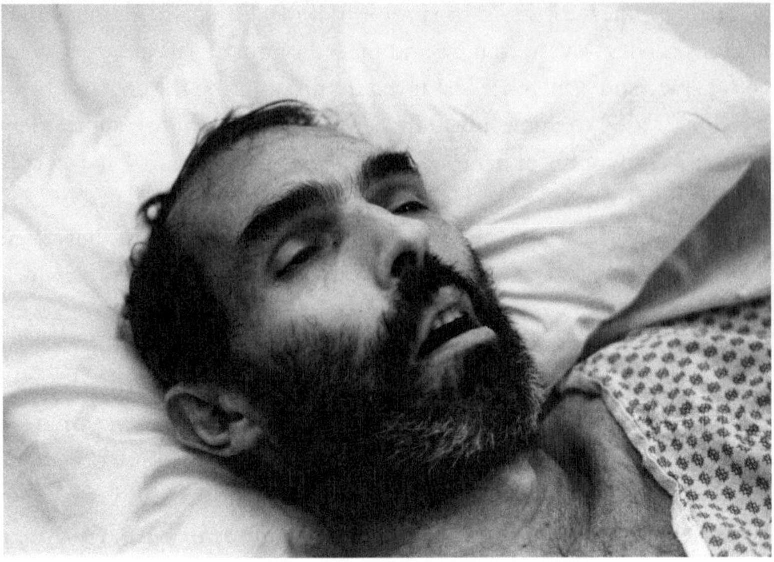

a postmortem photograph
(a declaration of love)

2.1. David Wojnarowicz, *Untitled* (detail), 1987. Gelatin silver print. © Estate of David Wojnarowicz. Courtesy of the Estate of David Wojnarowicz and P·P·O·W, New York.

I pick up these photographic pieces with my touching eyes, caress the afterlives of Cookie in the objects she loved. I conjure (out of love) close hospitality with the dead.

When I say goodbye, it is only a beginning.

In the festive photograph of Cookie's "vacant" living room (which is the final image in Goldin's photographic series *The Cookie Portfolio* [1991], posthumously paired with affectionate autograph captions), her golden corpse has departed the scene, leaving behind the eccentric detritus of her writer's life. It is somewhere between a portrait (with no body) and a still life, as the eclectic things she liked to collect become "hacked-off" surrogate pieces of her: vase, mask, lamp, raccoon.[5] And artwork on the walls: famous photographs that spell her name and picture, spectral reminders that cleave life and death apart, at the same time they bring us (however momentarily) closer together. In the central portrait by David Armstrong, Cookie stares out from a wall, her right arm resting provocatively behind her neck to show the pale insides of her limb. Forever held in Goldin's loving picture, it is a defiant assertion of presence in absence.

I absorb bittersweet traces of you. When I look at your striped silk couch, I think of you writing there—sprawled and splayed and frayed (and beautiful)—right up until the end. Is this the risk of your writing?

In the time-warped parlor that became a photographic postscript, Cookie did most of her writing: the short stories, the parts of a novel, the plays, the art columns for *Details* magazine, and the health columns for the *East Village Eye*. In the summer before her death, Cookie contributed one of her last pieces to *Details*, a tribute to her artist-husband Vittorio Scarpati's final project, wherein—severely sick with AIDS and hospitalized for over three months—he began drawing endless self-portraits on scrappy notebook pages. Cookie captures how Vittorio "rises above the woe" of the disease by making art shaped by the reparativity of ambivalence: "a visual narrative that told of deep despair, sadness and pain, *but also* hope, happiness and joy."[6] Sculpted from a close relation between writer-lover and artist-beloved that was intensified by the shared experience of diagnosis and disease, this column "risks" the writing of love (love is *risky* in the "objective" confines of art criticism; their infected bodies make their love high risk; to write it, publicize it, amid a conservative climate of discrimination and stigma is risky, *calls* for risk, when the risk of becoming even sicker to do so is real, the inevitability of death darkening each word) in this piece as a political, reparative act of solidarity, hospitality, and care. Reparative work, writes Eve Kosofsky Sedgwick (listening closely to the energies of AIDS activism), "undertakes a different range of affects, ambitions, and *risks*."[7] For Cookie, this manifested in the determined, affective writing *for* and *to* her loved ones, caring for the futurity of their lives and work, as well as her own (for her, life and writing were inseparable), in spite of (or even *because* of) the increasing weakness of her body.

Cookie's funeral was held just one day before the opening of Goldin's exhibition on the impact of AIDS on artistic practices, *Witnesses: Against Our Vanishing*. Held at New York's Artists Space, the exhibition catalog begins with a dedication, the losses Goldin and her friends have *witnessed*:
8 "Kenny Angelico, Keith Davis, Max diCorcia, Peter Hujar, Mark Morris-
8 roe, Vittorio Scarpati, Bibi Smith and everyone else we have lost to AIDS."[8]
If this small red booklet had been printed just days later, Cookie's name would be there. But her sick voice still pierces its pages, with the reprint of the epistolary piece "A Last Letter," published a year earlier in *City Lights Review*. While it was David Wojnarowicz's abject and breathless catalog essay that frightened the National Endowment of the Arts into "de-funding" the catalog (following a directive from Congress that prohibited the state funding of artistic material considered "obscene"), Cookie's shorter contribution also bravely made public the shocking truths of the epidemic, its politicized context, with a penetrating, painful simplicity that cuts close to the skin.

In Cookie's "high-risk" close writing, republished and redated as "1989" when placed at the end of the posthumous collection *Walking Through Clear Water in a Pool Painted Black*, she returns us to her loved ones that have *left*—to the closest people (the sickest people) to her:

> In 1982, my best friend died of AIDS. Since then there have been so many more friends I've lost. We all have. Through all of this I have come to realize that the most painful tragedy concerning AIDS death has to do with something much larger than the loss of human life itself. There is a deepening horror more grand than the world is yet aware. To see it we have to watch closely who is being stolen from us. Perhaps there is no hope left for the whole of humankind, not because of the nature of the epidemic but the nature of those it strikes.[9]

From the personal relation—the close proximity—comes the hopeless realization that the incalculable losses she and her artistic community are suffering are in some way designed; there is a purposeful, discriminatory "angle" to each "strike," each death. Cookie focalizes the violent brutalities of the epidemic beyond epidemiological discourse by first thinking with and from the first person, but not staying there; she hints at the crisis as *plural.*

Lorna Simpson brought text to photography to articulate the racialized complexities of the crisis in the 1989 work she made for the Art Against AIDS Project. *Untitled (A lie is not a shelter)* is also a focalized picture, depicting the torso of an anonymous Black woman in a white cotton sundress: a simple garment that was worn by enslaved women in the colonization of the Atlantic World, constructed from a cloth that, as Anna Arabindan-Kesson has traced through historical and contemporary artworks, "continues to exist in the present as an artifact charged with the traces of labor under slavery, the hardships of southern agriculture, the colonial expansion of Britain, and the endurance of Black Americans."[10] In Simpson's photographic depiction—a medium that transports us into loss by recording an object of the past as frozen in time, but also, as Tina Campt recognizes, a medium that has the paradoxical capacity to *hum* visually, aurally, and affectively *across* time and space—the afterlife of the cotton material is re-surfaced in a "fugitive register."[11] The depiction of the simple white dress in Simpson's work resonates, in material terms, with the ongoing durational contexts that make up what Saidiya Hartman terms the "afterlife of slavery": the systematic, structural, and continued threat to and devaluing of Black lives.[12] As Simpson's phototext work strategically confronts, such afterlives are felt in anti-Black prejudice, in paranoia, in generalized, discriminatory misunderstanding and lack of research on issues of AIDS transmission and treatment, at a time when infection rates were rising quickly among African American women and access to education and healthcare was limited.

As a composition, it is "up close" but not necessarily personal, as an abstract, monochrome arrangement of starched cloth on black skin ("the fetish object of racism") dominates the photographic field.[13] Across the picture's centralized, horizontal plane are a woman's folded limbs, which—as a gesture of active refusal, of resistance in opacity—challenge continuing forms of dispossession and "domination that inhabit our ways of looking," as Hartman has also described of the artist's work in a 1992 catalog essay. "Simpson interrupts and refigures the politics of visuality," writes Hartman, through which Black women have been constructed as "highly visible yet unrepresented."[14] Above and below this complex corporeal figuration is overlaid printed text in the form of slanting black type on white cloth: "a lie is not a shelter / discrimination is not protection / isolation is not a remedy / a promise is not a prophylactic."

Simpson's fugitive practice hums differentially beside Cookie's close writing to recite that there is not one "singular and authentic AIDS story." Instead, "crises" are "experienced in specific contexts" in a way that highlights how "the Acquired Immune Deficiency Syndrome is not merely a crisis in epidemiological terms," but rather it is the "uneven and varying spatialization and temporalization of *crises*."[15] And, so, while the dominant histories of AIDS have been "animated by gay white men: their stories, resources, archival holdings," there are diverse and complex lived experiences of the disease, the accounts and/or critical fabulations of Black gay men and women, other queer folk, trans women, gender-nonconforming people, houseless people, IV drug users, sex workers (many of whom were women of color), Haitian migrant working-class communities, and Latinx communities, that must be registered anew—challenging stigma, blame, erasure—in the afterlives of their remembering.[16] White supremacy, racism, sexism, misogyny, transphobia, and homophobia are intertwined social biases that affect "the health, wealth, and representation of people living with and impacted by HIV" in 1989—the year of *Witnesses*, also Simpson's work—and the endurance of *now*.[17]

Cindy Patton described the dangerous slippage between medical virus and systemic violence soon after, in 1992: "It is easy to start an AIDS panic. . . . [C]ultural narratives of perversion and contagion seem endlessly capable of turning apparently interpretation-proof facts into ammunition for panics and discrimination."[18] Medical research and treatments were thus held back, or slowed down, by government agencies suspicious of already marginalized high-risk groups; sex education was culled from schools and television sets; contemporary art and writing was censored as part of escalating "culture wars." When Cookie challenges this "deepening horror" in her close writing, she does so by offering an alternative (her writing *is* hope), by helping us to "see" the beautiful people near her, those who fought "the truancy of culture," those who also, in return, "tried to make us see."[19] I turn to her particular context, its multitextured afterlives, not to narrow the historical study of HIV/AIDS, or prioritize her sick moment, wherein the social orientations that structure whiteness no doubt brought certain objects nearer; rather, my proximate position is assumed to attend closely to the complexities, temporalities, pleasures, and pains of her writing *in* and *through* and *beyond* the lived experience of disease.

In this strange, sick time, the annotated, bended, and much-creased pages of the book that becomes a "book" after you leave become malleable extensions of my body. I am attached to this object. It is small yet magnetic. I carry it from the bedroom to the sofa to the desk. You transform states of sickness into events of beauty within the stories it contains; it is a project you give life to, over and over, again. *Still.* It sustains my replies. Still. Too late. I write impossible love out of necessity and difficulty, a meeting of pleasure and pain. I am angled on this edge.

In "A Last Letter," Cookie also transcribes and reenacts an epistle sent from her friend Gordon Stevenson, within which he emphasizes "freedom" as being the energy of the high-risker, the reason for their "punishment."[20] It was the last letter she received from him before he died: handwritten on his own "frayed" letterhead, decorated with a "big black heart, inscribed with the words Faith, Hope and Charity on a background of orange."[21] The crumpled materiality of this decorative letter could be felt to recall the messy pieces scribbled, scrawled, and sent in adolescence, as if pen pals in bedroomed confinement, rather than sick, hospitalized correspondents. *Like* an adolescent, the letter yearns for, *hopes* for, freedom, a reparative "paradise" to rest in—where a golden sunset does not signal the end.[22]

Across her close writing, which emerged in close, sick proximity to her diseased body and beloved, Cookie's desire for freedom scratched the surface of the page, a paradoxical, bittersweet thing of pain and beauty. Gordon sought the intimate context of the letter to voice it, and so does Cookie in the following epistolary address to more than one reader: "Fortunately I am not the first person to tell you that you will never die. You simply lose your body. You will be the same except you won't have to worry about rent or mortgages or fashionable clothes. You will be released from sexual obsessions. You will not have drug addictions. You will be free."[23]

Woven with the surprising threads of her dark humor (its paradoxical *bittersweetness*), this passage rewrites the morbid fate of high-risk bodies, by celebrating the necessity of freedom, another life—like the gold picture of a strangely youthful Cookie, glowing in her casket: dreaming and weaving and maybe even *writing*. Her repetitions sing like an elegy, but her words climax in hope (there is freedom in the paradox). Sliding between the first- and the second-person address, this fragment of close writing is shaped from, and speaks to, atomized and collective relations, becoming a manifesto of solidarity for the "perverse" members of the diverse HIV/AIDS community. For them she brings life curiously full circle.

For to fall and lose one's body brings about a magical return to a previous state of existence unshackled (for most, or for many) by concerns of survival, sickness, or sex, by the passing of time: the depleting clock of the body container. She's written an elegy, but also a *spell* (I weave the picture of you wearing a black cape over a leather dress into these words, this fantasy), an urgent incantation (as spectral as her beautiful corpse or her empty living room), which dreams and imagines a life "after" the disappearance of one's abject and alien materiality. Echoing the "liberatory archival traces of a queer past . . . the pleasures of looking back," which Fiona Anderson attends to and encourages in the context of Wojnarowicz's "nostalgic cruising sensibility," Cookie here longs for an alternate world otherwise, reaches for a time before the disease entrapped her and disciplined her body: a bringing of youth into death.[24] This is a devastating and painful premonition. Still, there is a glimpse of freedom to be found.

Juliet Jacques's 2017 short film *You Will Be Free*, comprising an oral and visual collage, also begins with this passage from Cookie, giving way to a meditation on afterlives and queer freedoms, the allure of childhood in dreams. Archive footage of an English summer, showing school kids competing on their annual sports day, gets spliced with archive footage from ACT UP demonstrations and horrifying, homophobic newspaper headlines haunted by the narrator's voice telling us that politicians thought AIDS was a "gift from God."[25] It's a film that beautifully combines sadness and rage, shifting scale and volume with emotion and intensity, much like Cookie's own small texts of paradoxical affects, which overwhelm bodies and hearts. She wrote emotional epics in miniature.

But while Jacques thinks about childhood, I absorb adolescence in Cookie's four short lines; the ecstatic joy of time, freedom, writing, and life moves there. As Carol Mavor notes in her 2007 book, *Reading Boyishly*, "The adolescent has life before him. . . . The adolescent has *time*."[26] History has told us that Cookie didn't have it on her side. But does she *make* it in writing? She knew that she needed to be more than a body, and so it's in writing that she carves a space in which to be free, releasing the specter of the adolescent "before" AIDS (but always in a wounded relationship to it) and setting her free to fly, desire, consume, and waste.[27] This is the "freedom one has to fight for," aged fourteen, says Adam Phillips, but the same applies to Cookie at age forty: "the freedom to sleep-walk; the freedom, that is to say, to do things in one's own way."[28] Cookie's elegy is a manifesto for life as well as death: It's a manifesto for writing through the *figure of the adolescent*.

But how are we to define this ambiguous subject known as the adolescent? How to define adolescence itself, when it overflows with contradictions, an awkward space in between childhood and adulthood, "smudged by sexuality, changing bodies and body fluids"?[29] It could be that the adolescent's very obliqueness was an initial barrier to her scientific "invention," as it was only at the turn of the century that psychologists began to speak of this transitional stage of development. Before this, concepts of the child or adult dominated social and economic discourse in the West, as modern capitalism relied on the logics of reproduction, on work, on the mother reproducing "the cult of the child." In 1904, as part of his "recapitulation theory," the psychologist Stanley G. Hall proposed that while adolescence is kickstarted by the beginnings of puberty, it can also proceed all the way through the early twenties, shaped by a period of "Sturm und Drang," or "storm and stress." According to Hall, "lack of emotional steadiness, violent impulses, unreasonable conduct" represent some of the defining behavioral and affective features of this messy time: the smudged adolescent subject position.[30]

Invested in the importance of recognizing the social, cultural, religious, and racial differences available to us in the "figure" of the adolescent, I bring the psychosexual characteristics theorized first by Hall (and later adapted by D. W. Winnicott, Julia Kristeva, and Adam Phillips) into specific representations and contexts familiar to Cookie's life, body, and times, and also her close writing, the blurred edges between them, as past memories resurfaced in dated autobiographical pieces. Cookie's subject position "*as* adolescent" was shaped by multiple and conflicting scenes, spaces, and states, which she traced and performed in her close writing: from growing up girlish within the confines of white, middle-class suburbia, then busting free from them (while experiencing certain objects within reach); to living through the social, medical, and political impacts of the 1960s that Winnicott argued "altered the whole climate for adolescents in adolescence"; to experiencing hippie, filmic, and artistic sites of experimentation; to becoming a mother to Max; to being sexually queer; to inhabiting drugs; to enduring the "boyish" reality of AIDS by living and loving in proximity to it.[31]

I stay with her in my reading of adolescence. *Beside*. The adolescent is *never full* in her desire to be free.

Memory: I'd waited a long time for his saliva, his way of saying yes. I wrapped my arms around his soft gray sweatshirt and savored the smell of stale cigarettes. I was fifteen, the age you were when you had two lovers. I brought his tongue closer to mine and felt my cheeks go red with embarrassment. That sticky feeling of not knowing, never knowing, if it's "right" or not. Like the stick of a love letter. I fill my mouth with your writing to catch some of your adolescent hunger, taking in good bits and bad bits, feeling the shame and pleasure of it all.

I Caress Her Scraps

Things have changed since I last wrote to you. I stay home, as we all stay home. Apart. Away from. Nowhere near. Paranoia fills the air. I can almost touch it, this enveloping threat of contagion. My best friend who lives a mile away sends me a postcard. My sister sends me flowers. I miss them both. Yet, the pain of this distance is oddly familiar, a space of unmet touching. I change the title of the book I am writing.

Toward the end of her life (reclining in gold, on that silk couch? You forever falling, into close writing: feeling pleasure alongside pain), Cookie was tweaking a manuscript that comprised a "compilation of autobiographical short stories," the stories "all true, sort of like episodes from a diary."[32] She sent it to Raymond Foye of Hanuman Books, and an alternative version to Chris Kraus, newly of Semiotext(e), who was poised to start a line in contemporary American fiction, mostly by women, mostly first-person—"deeply intellectual and rigorously subjective"—as a counterpoint to the books of French theory the press (founded by Sylvère Lotringer in 1973) had become known for.[33] Called Foreign Agents, these were the "little-black-books" authored exclusively by white European men—from Jean Baudrillard to Paul Virilio, and other "micropolitical" philosophers associated with the 1975 *Schizo-Culture* conference—that slipped into the pockets of New York City's avant-garde.[34] "They were a coveted design object," Kraus told me, over a transatlantic telephone call. "Everyone in the art world was reading them."[35] Lotringer was based in the French Department at Columbia University, but Semiotext(e) was, in spite of its academic credentials, unsupported by its affiliated institution. Being on the edge of the academy this way, Lotringer thought, helped the press to realize its aims of dismantling "repressive hierarchies" across art, culture, class, and pedagogy, until Kraus and her Native Agents authors intervened within that effort again, to explicitly critique the sexist restrictions placed on the form and content of the category known as "women's writing."[36]

Cookie's book *Walking Through Clear Water in a Pool Painted Black* was the first in Kraus's Native Agents series, with books by Ann Rower, Eileen Myles, and Kathy Acker continuing its explorations into the reinvention of feminist autofiction.[37] As a shared project in collapsed genre, the Native Agents books were written in the "vernacular manner of the Post New York School," reenacting the abject materialities of the authors' social, sexual, domestic, and creative lives. "A lot of Semiotext(e) fans were critical of it," remembered Kraus in our conversation. "They thought the seriousness of the Foreign Agents French theory books was being compromised by mouthy American women who just wanted to talk about themselves."[38] This failure among Semiotext(e) readers to recognize the interdisciplinarity of their writing—the playfulness, publicness, politics, and performativity of it—vindicated Kraus's project. She has written that Native Agents began "from a social situation, out of love, but also for vengeance against the status quo and what was, and was not, considered important" (in the hierarchies of cultural production).[39] And so, after hearing a sick Cookie read at the St. Mark's Poetry Project, "moved by her work and her situation," Kraus "realised that whatever cachet Semiotext(e) held at the time could be used to *help* Cookie Mueller."[40]

Cookie's little blue book launched at the New York venue Quick!, alongside Ann Rower's *If You're a Girl* (glossed bright pink, provocatively *unserious*), on March 21, 1990.[41] But Cookie missed it. In a repeat of *Witnesses* and many after, Sharon Niesp read in Cookie's place, with the punk musician turned poet and novelist Richard Hell. *Garden of Ashes*, which featured life stories, anecdotal pieces, and profiles of friends, also came out that year from Hanuman. Its small front cover features a hand-tinted color portrait of Cookie as a blonde bombshell, a lioness: a witch with a black ribbon choker, casting your spells.

Semiotext(e) picked up Cookie's manuscript when no one else would, though she got lucky with Hanuman later. "They wanted to change this or that, and she was in no condition to do that, and perhaps didn't want to," described Kraus in an essay published in 2014.[42] But what was Cookie's manuscript? A short story collection? An autobiographical novel? Or somewhere (*scrappily*) in between? On a handwritten sheet of paper, she calls it the "semiotext book quazi-auto-bio etc," suggesting that she hadn't quite worked it out yet either (figure 2.2).[43] Or perhaps didn't want to.

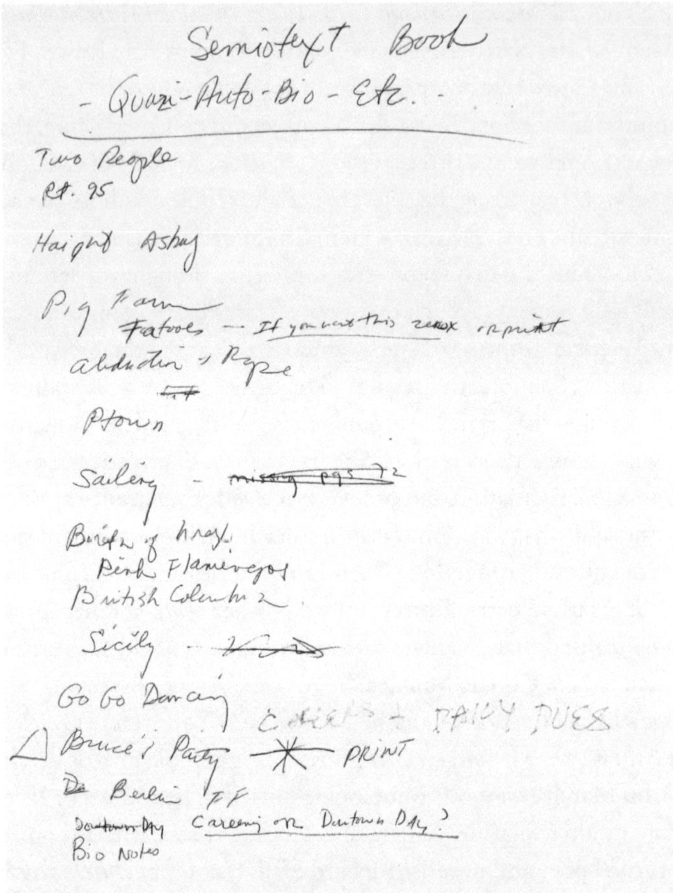

Semiotext Book
- Quazi-Auto-Bio - Etc. -

Two People
Rt. 95

Haight Ashbury

Pig Farm
Fatooes — If you want this xerox reprint
abduction + Rape

Ptown

Sailing

Birth of
Pink Flamingos
British Columbia

Sicily

Go Go Dancing

Bruce's Party — PRINT
Berlin FF
Careening on Downtown Day?
Bio Notes

a handwritten sheet

a working out

2.2. Cookie Mueller, handwritten list, undated. Fales Library and Special Collections, New York University Libraries, STHRA, BVII.1, F14. Courtesy of the Cookie Mueller Estate.

Did you want to?

Those ripped hyphens spasm and vibrate, another blurred line, a thread conjoining and separating multiple genres. This manuscript was materially and metaphorically frayed (echoing Gordon's last epistle, or your hand-stitched dresses), on the unfinished, ambiguous edge of autobiography—an edge that refused to settle into a familiar code, logic, or order. A hot rebel was her manuscript, just like the adolescents causing chaos (*affray*) within it, fraying things apart. As Winnicott proposed in the 1960s (the decade of Cookie's teens), "adolescent boys or girls" do not want to be "understood."[44] The form of Cookie's Semiotext(e) book, with its collected episodes from her past arranged chronologically—beginning with the Baltimore teenage years in the 1960s, through San Francisco acid trips; then childbirth, house fires, and go-go dancing in the 1970s; climaxing in showbiz parties on the Lower East Side in the 1980s, and finally the impact of AIDS—confuses the reader in a similar spirit of adolescent refusal. Scrappy like a short story collection, or like Kathy's diary pieces written in an early-twenties adolescent blur of ambivalent desires and sickened bodies, it has the emotional reach of an autobiographical novel, in spite of its youthful size.

Preparatory notes within her accreted archive indicate that Cookie was feverishly working toward this project, but there were others as well, like Hervé Guibert "coughing, typing" his essays, fictions, novels, diaries, or his similarly "in-between" diaristic novels, out.[45] Cookie, like the French writer, was full of sickened, unsilenced energy; but while Guibert (like Kathy again) "valued the diary, as genre . . . because it wrote time and wrote body accurately, wrote body as it actually occurred, nonmonumentally, *in* time," Cookie's life writing is retrospectively oriented, activating a belated version of time and memory.[46] She wrote endless lists detailing the stories written, and then rewritten, along the way in real time, in her commitment to compose and re-compose the pieces of her book. Are these the oblique doodles of an adolescent or the marks of an AIDS writer? (Or somewhere *in between*?) On pale to bright-pink sheets, with a blunt pencil (no time to sharpen), she rushed through page counts, played about with the order (plate 6), later instructing herself to place some "transitional piece[s]," not yet done (and not *unlike* the "transitional object" that Winnicott abstracted as the comfort blanket or piece of cloth [even a fragile, handwritten page] that an infant handles, becomes attached to, in the effort to relieve pain and separation from the mother), in between the completed texts.[47] The transitional piece is a lifeline, a caregiver, even a transitory creative practice: a fantasy for something *more to come*. And so are Cookie's lists, her counting of pages, which, while producing her sick body in their fidgety pour, also reveal the agency of her writerly desires, the will to cancel out her impending disappearance.

It is strange, haunting, how AIDS can bring Cookie closer to adolescence, through these notes of "unfinished" activity. But how "adolescent" it is to leave projects unfinished, when boredom gets in the way, or time gets wasted. Mavor picks apart the melancholic prick of the paradox: "The adolescent wastes time. . . . Yet, when one is old, one panics at the thought of wasting time."[48] Of course, the wasted time the AIDS writer must navigate—make art *through*—is not a chosen path, when the sick temporality connected to the disease is the direct result of a system of social, sexual, racial, gendered, and ableist inequities, producing a physically wasted and vulnerable body, too. Such a temporal and physical collision is felt in the poems and book covers (printing early-teenage Francesca Woodman body portraits) of Tory Dent, reminding us of the wasted abject body of the sick in "Spared": "When will I know that I won't lie / with a tube in my throat, the weight I was at fourteen years old / the K.S. lesions, leeches fulminating my body."[49] Dent's medicalized body is also accompanied by a "voice" of a "benevolent caller" and the "hand" of a "bedside friend," plunging into the intimate depths of the sickened scene, which offers its own care networks beyond the institution and beyond the "well" progression of linear time.[50] For Dent's poem also affirms the "irrepressible" and "mysterious" rejuvenation and subversion of the "adolescent" body with AIDS.[51] Similarly paradoxical, in Cookie's manuscript two timeframes (the diseased and the adolescent) come into reparative contact, entangling the scraps of life and text. Perhaps, therefore (and as Kraus alludes), Cookie didn't want to change her manuscript; maybe she liked its scrappy, sloppy, piecemeal form, *because* it's adolescent.

I risk the prick of an undone staple when I caress your typed pages. When paper touches metal comes terracotta rust, caused by contact and time. It looks like decades-old blood, the traces of a thirteen-year-old's frightened but thrilling menstruation. You scrawled your editor's name and number in the margins, misspelled her name, like an adolescent.

Embroidered with penciled notes and numbers, Cookie's desire "to write" above all else is interwoven into the surface of her pages: She is at "the center of the action of speech . . . the *scriptor* inside the writing," as Roland Barthes describes in his essay on writing as an intransitive verb.[52] She's groping for the outer edges of her writing, feeling it, emotionally and physically, the scale she might reach. But the scrawls interrupting the unpublished space of her parchment (her close writing *skin*, an interface between body and writing) also embody the compulsion to scratch an intransitive itch. Cookie is restless, uncertain of where the limit (or the end) might lie, if such a thing exists at all. She bares her anxiety about completion in the cover letter that accompanied one version of her manuscript: "This manuscript needs a lot of work. Most importantly I think it badly needs those segues, from one story to the next. It has to flow, and it doesn't yet. It needs to slow down a bit, and shift moods, and be more reflective at times, which it isn't now. What's missing here also, are lots of chapters (short stories) the opening story isn't here yet. (Or maybe it is?)"[53]

Cookie's commentary marks her manuscript by what is missing, by the "work" that is to come, by the promise of connection and seamlessness, when her body was under pressure to survive, when her life was at stake (the *edge*). "Always writing, or trying to write," as Kate Zambreno writes of Guibert.[54] The restless desire for (*hope for*) a future life *in writing* is in conflict with the depleting time of sickness, which closed in on her body, a "hardening."[55] As the contemporary crip artist Johanna Hedva has written in the recent context of COVID-19, "For the sick person, or someone caring for the sick, time freezes, hardening around the body, locking everything into this new center of gravity. All that can be done is to wait. The future gets further and further away, and the present moment—the one soaked in illness—becomes huge and cruel. In illness, the now feels like a punishment."[56] Cookie's concern, therefore, that her manuscript needs "work"—also, *time*, time that was being kept from her: no longer fluid, but hard—is deeply, *painfully*, implicated in the experience of writing through and with illness, against the effects of the disease. This might sound like the opposite of the adolescent sleepwalking, but the sick time of Cookie's writing also necessitates the *return of adolescence*.

Cookie was worried her never-before-published-as-a-collection pieces (that blurred the line between chapter, fragment, short story, autobiography, and novel, as awkwardly liminal as adolescence itself) "read pretty fast, maybe too fast."[57] But what if the shortness of those texts was both a material consequence of her chronic sick time and an artistic protest against it, as she shaped adolescent pleasures *of time* in the broken, short, sick pieces of her close writing? It calls to mind Barthes's declaration that "a text on pleasure cannot be anything but *short*," while also being deeply felt within a sickened, durational context.[58] As Hedva explains in their 2016 essay-manifesto "Sick Woman Theory," "the word 'chronic' comes from the Greek 'chronos,' χρόνος, which means 'time' (think of 'chronology'). In certain contexts, it can mean a 'a lifetime.' So, a chronic illness is an illness that lasts a lifetime. In other words, it does not get better. There is no cure."[59]

Hélène Cixous captures what was at stake in this desire to write absolutely, however short, sick, or discontinuous the form: "Writing: a way of leaving no space for death, of pushing back forgetfulness, of never letting one be surprised by the abyss. Of never becoming resigned, consoled; never turning over in bed to face the wall and drift asleep again as if nothing had happened; as if nothing could happen."[60] Cixous's definition of writing as a force or energy that refuses the mortal, that delays the amnesiac, that staves off feelings of emptiness in the past or in the future, might first appear to contradict the figure of the adolescent drifting through the nights and the days theorized by Phillips and Mavor (who worries, but also *envies* [like Cookie, she recognizes the value of adolescence to life], that her "beautiful boys sleep too much . . . wander about aimlessly").[61] But in Cookie's close writing, the subject of writing and the autobiographical object of adolescence become entwined in her remembering (not forgetting) of bygone adolescent happenings, inscribed in her surplus of short-form pieces. Here she wards off death, leaves her life behind, gets closer to it. This is writing-as-happening: a sick-time alleviation. As the chronically ill Virginia Woolf also described in her diary, later used by Joyce Carol Oates to sign off her 1982 essay "Notes on Failure": "*This insatiable desire to write something before I die, this ravaging sense of the shortness and feverishness of life, make me cling . . . to my one another*."[62] For Cookie, her "one another" is a series of adolescent selves (full of insatiable desire), lodged, incorporated, and ingested, in the voice, narrative, and form of her close writing.

Memory: I begged my mother for bleach, one of those do-it-yourself caps. It was a weekend, no school. I wanted to be blonde so badly, but the needle she used was so sharp it scraped my scalp, made a cut. I screamed. Then my hair turned green. I screamed again. Your mother's remembered words come back to me: "'Whenever you're depressed, just change your hair color.'"[63] I wonder if you were always sad when you smothered those chemicals of light into your roots. Or maybe you just liked the way it looked. I guess it was probably both; adolescence works that way—aged fourteen or even forty.

Cookie's close-writing desire is hungry and hopeful, calling to mind Barthes's proposition that "*writing* presents itself as a Hope, the color of a Hope," and that this is especially felt with the "jubilatory reading that occurs in Adolescence."[64] It occurred for adolescent Cookie: She was, as Chloé Griffin notes in the introduction to *Edgewise*, "an avid reader with the teenage hope of becoming a writer."[65] And Cookie's later pieces, lists of pieces, or her lists in general are also shaded with this palette. For example, on the back page of a ring-bound notebook, she wrote a list for professional and personal improvement, detailing addictions to conquer and creations to achieve. She tells herself "no regret no guilt." She wills to stop smoking, doing dope, and drinking. But as I'm faced with your manuscripts, as I hold them in my hand, it's "number six" on the list that startles, an encounter that I didn't expect: the unfair reality that you didn't "have a novel written by 2 months time" (figure 2.3).[66]

It was the only form lacking from Cookie's writer's CV. She'd written stories, art criticism, health columns, plays, opinion pieces, and poems, featured in the pages of Downtown zines and journals like *Cuz*, *Just Another Asshole*, *BOMB*, *Top Stories*, and *Wild History*.[67] She gave voice to her life in her writings, turned the familiar magical and strange, and then voiced them again at live readings (at the Mudd Club, ABC No Rio, Neither Nor, Pyramid, Area, Studio 54, and the St. Mark's Poetry Project), each word curled at the tongue with a lisp.

I trace my finger along the fold of a xerox flyer inviting me to your reading with Ann Rower at the Public Theater, Sunday, October 17, 8 p.m. (figure 2.4). I am late. I am sorry. A dinosaur skeleton is dancing across the page with overlaid type: "Without a skeleton, you couldn't stand up / You could only lie on the ground / like a rag doll." The handwriting looks like yours. My eyes dart and dance with the curl of the C as it flows into two looping Os. I flail and flail and flail. I am your rag doll.

In performances, publications, photographs, and parties at her apartment on Bleecker, Cookie imaged and inked, with a flick of a fountain pen or an eyeliner stick, the scenography of the Downtown scene. She arrived in the city in 1976 from the Atlantic swells of hippie, on-the-tip-of-Cape-Cod Provincetown; she was just nineteen years old when she had moved

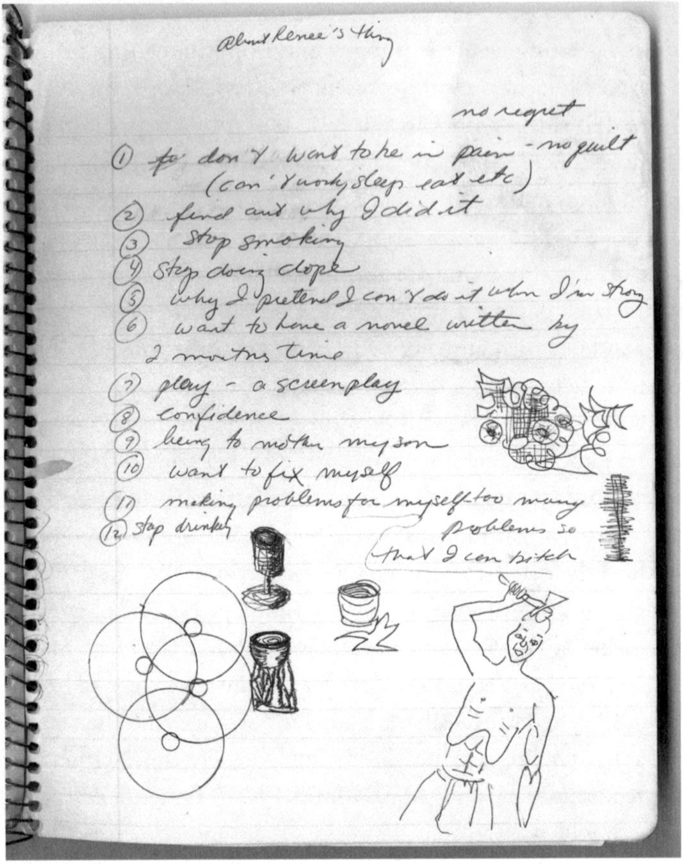
about Renee's thing
no regret
(1) don't want to be in pain - no guilt
(can't work, sleep, eat etc)
(2) find out why I did it
(3) stop smoking
(4) stop doing dope
(5) why I pretend I can't do it when I'm strong
(6) want to have a novel written by
2 months time
(7) play - a screenplay
(8) confidence
(9) being to mother my son
(10) want to fix myself
(11) making problems for myself too many
problems so
that I can bitch
(12) stop drinking

a list hidden on the back page
of a ring-bound notebook

2.3. Cookie Mueller, page from notebook, undated. Fales Library and Special Collections, New York University Libraries, STHRA, BVII.1, F17. Courtesy of the Cookie Mueller Estate.

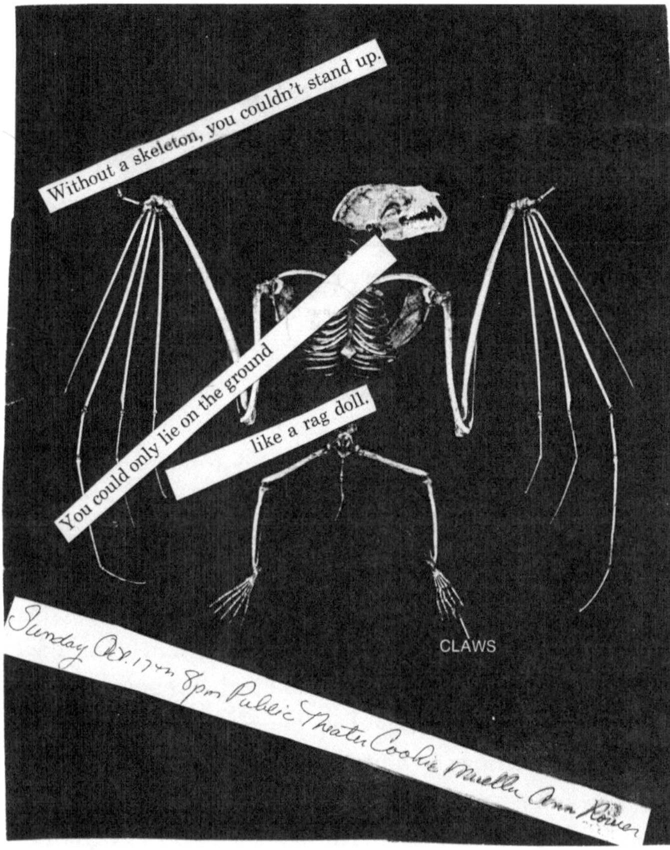

a xeroxed folded flyer
(folded to fly)

2.4. Cookie Mueller and Ann Rower, flyer for reading at the Public Theater, New York City, October 17, no year given (1982), 18.4 × 22.2 cm.

to the coast. There she became a daughter to drag queen Divine and later a mother to Max, making ends meet by sewing for others and stacking boxes in the local fish factory.

Cookie brought poetry to hedonism, bohemianism to glamour, when she blew into the city as a bad girl from the sea. In a newly born Manhattan—which was attractive to artists because it was cheap, the economic recession manifesting in burnt-out real estate and soiled avenues abandoned by the urban middle classes—Cookie began pounding its pavements. She soon go-go-danced in New Jersey to fund days spent writing and mothering. As she writes of this moonlighting labor in a piece retrospectively dated as 1978–79, "It wasn't something I especially wanted on my resume but I had been casting around, looking for work . . . something to pay the bills while I was making a start at designing clothes, searching film parts and writing. I was down to thirty-seven dollars. That kind of money doesn't go far in New York, especially when you have a kid."[68]

In a few years, her life in New York would become the vivid backdrop to the art columns she contributed to the avant-garde fashion magazine *Details* (for which she was paid a fee that almost sustained her lived and written stories). It was a job, also, that she often riffed on in her anecdotal pieces. In "Narcotics," for example, she remembers being bored at a "post art opening party" in SoHo, joking that "New York art climbers were there mingling and tittering and chit-chatting discreetly, the women in sensible low heels and expensive stockings with no runs . . . trying to make themselves look old."[69] She is different from these women; her garments and her writings are conversely tuned in to the countercultural verve of adolescence.

Cookie's life-in-work, therefore, suggests a hive of hybrid activities. Her printed résumés list parts in stage plays and underground performances (like the fated, mythic blondes Sharon Tate and Lady Godiva); voiceover gigs; published short stories and journalism; live readings of her writing (beginning at Joe Papp's Public Theater and then at New York nightclubs like Danceteria that housed DJs, bands, filmmakers, performers, artists, and writers); as well as infamous roles in experimental films and videos.[70] She was "Cookie," the promiscuous, primarily topless daughter of Lady Divine, in John Waters's raw and DIY *Multiple Maniacs*, a film that mocks bourgeois pretensions in its jerky portrayal of a carnival tent show ("the sleaziest show on earth") and blasphemous, criminal acts, becoming a monstrous theater of the absurd. Soon after, she was "Cookie" again in

Waters's filthy portrait of perversities, *Pink Flamingos*, this time playing a spy who gets lured into a bizarre, violent, and bloody sexual encounter with humans and animals that teases at the codes of consent. Later, she was the beehived, spit-curled schoolgirl "Concetta" in *Female Trouble*, Waters's grimy filmic tale of hitchhiking, sex, pregnancy, burglary, sex work, modeling, celebrity, and murder that parodies and pulverizes suburban moralities and sentiments. But, despite the range of this multimedia repertoire, there was no CV section, as this self-identifying "writer-actress" called it, worthy of the subheading "Novels."[71]

This was in spite of the fact that she wrote and produced one during puberty, aged somewhere between ten or thirteen, depending on the particular version of the piece describing its content, production, and distribution (there are many variations scattered across published and unpublished typescripts).[72] "My Bio—Notes on an American Childhood" paints it as a historical novel of ravenous scale, perhaps longer than was necessary:

> After facing death, I became a young novelist and wrote a book about the Jonestown Pennsylvania flood in 1830 something, where Clara Barton threw her weight around. I did research. Clara Barton was the American version of Florence Nightingale. She was a nurse in Gettysburg during the Civil War, just like Ms. Nightingale in the Crimean War . . . or some old war over there.
>
> On Barton's hemlines there were always blood stains and she carried morphine in her pockets. She wasn't as much of a tramp as Florence Nightingale, though, Nightingale spread syphilis to all the European soldiers, but Barton was probably an American pioneer celibate.
>
> The book was 321 pages long, and I finished it the day before my 11th birthday. I'd heard somewhere that the girl who wrote *Black Beauty* was 11, so I wanted to be the youngest novelist in the world.
>
> I didn't have any idea how to get the book published, so I typed it all up, stapled it together, cut up some beer case cardboard, covered this with white butcher paper and Saran wrap. Fashioned after any legitimate library book, I smuggled it into the library and put it on the shelves in the correct alphabetical order. I never saw the book again.
>
> I learned early that writing was hard on the body. Blood turns cold and circulation stops at the typewriter; the knee joints solidify into cement, the ass becomes one with the chair, but I kept writing.[73]

Curiously, a catastrophic encounter with a beehive (a seventeen-sting brush with death) had instigated Cookie's youthful novel-writing, echoing the mortal frame the elder writer is working near to in her return to adolescent times. While Cookie becomes the character in and of her own piecemeal close writing, in this early novel, she also made a pseudo-adolescent of its nurse protagonist. She blurred fiction and historical biography with fan-girl flair. Clara Barton's hemlines are bloody; her pockets are overflowing with narcotics; she's a body in a menstrual flood, as gory and girlish as the author who wrote her—first aged eleven, and then again in remembered reenactment.

The playful reference to Nightingale's scandalized, "sick" sexuality of pathologized desire and deviance also subverts historical and contemporary gender portraits, with Nightingale's high-risk, contagious body resonating with the vulnerable position of the sex worker during the AIDS epidemic. Indeed, Paul B. Preciado recently pointed out that as a sexually transmitted infection—viscerally entangled in the "European colonial enterprise" from the sixteenth century onward—syphilis "materialized in bodies the forms of repression and exclusion that dominated modernity."[74] For the body most violently controlled, stigmatized, and abjected was that of the prostitute: "a working and often racialized woman, a body outside the laws of home and marriage, who turned her sexuality into her means of production."[75] Knowing this, and turning to the ways it is the sick, sexed, and gendered body of Nightingale who is dangerous to European men (in spite of her whiteness and her familial wealth), could Cookie's resurrection (or "rehabilitation") of her signify a transgressive intervention? Could it be a necessary act of care for the political complexities of care? By connecting nurses, sex workers, people with AIDS, and adolescent novelists, Cookie breaks apart the discourse that seeks to criminalize them, a gathering of alike (but not the same) "nonsovereign," sick bodies. As Preciado elaborates, "In the late twentieth century, AIDS would be to heteronormative neoliberal society what syphilis had been to colonial capitalism during early modernity."[76] Cookie explores this association, linking adolescence with perverse sexuality in her belated, and politically radical, recontextualization of her own "deviant" historical novel.

The description of its scrappy composition, its covert distribution, and its DIY aesthetic is deviant, too. We learn how she crossed the biopolitical boundaries of library legitimacy (stepping on teachers' and adults' toes) and illicitly smuggled in her own "delegitimized" writing. Is this a vital source of adolescent indiscipline, leading Cookie to write about the novel *later*?

Cookie emphasizes that she "kept writing" after her early flirtations with the novel craft: from adolescence through to adulthood and the wilting knee joints of actual disease.[77] Like the military conflicts endured by Clara and Florence, AIDS is a "war zone" as well, "but it's a different battlefield," as Cookie writes in "A Last Letter."[78] In this piece, and in "My Bio," Cookie points to the disciplinary institutions that were central to Michel Foucault's theorization of biopower—the medical, educational, and military networks of surveillance and control that penetrate the body and bodies, and which Foucault felt acutely, but privately, in his own experience of the disease that his friend, Hervé Guibert, later autofictionalized in 1990 in *To the Friend Who Did Not Save My Life*, shocking the French press who thought it was cancer that had killed Foucault. Instead, he died of AIDS-related complications on June 25, 1984, at the Salpêtrière hospital in Paris—originally a women's asylum (that had informed Foucault's own history of madness), where hysterics had been marked, controlled, looked at, stigmatized, photographed a century earlier. Of Jean-Martin Charcot's muse-patients at the clinic displaying symptoms of hysteria, "Blanche" was an eighteen-year-old named Marie Wittman when she was admitted to the Salpêtrière, and "Augustine," or Louise Augustine Gleizes, was even younger, aged only fourteen when she arrived, fresh from a stay at the world's first children's hospital.[79] It seemed as if hysteria, as it was medicalized and mythologized, was also a disease of adolescent girls.

My beloved is a one-name muse, too; she received the name Cookie "before [she] could walk," as she begins "My Bio."[80] Her adolescent literary practice is haunted by hysteric traces, the student/patient subverting the power lines of school and medicine, like the hysteric performers before her, or like the AIDS writers that circle her writing *of* adolescent writing. For Cookie, adolescence, as a container of sickness, perversion, creativity, and care, becomes a space for resisting the violent exclusions implied by the immunological hierarchies Preciado recognizes (via the work of the philosopher Roberto Esposito) in all biopolitics. Preciado maintains that the management of epidemics, including syphilis and AIDS, as well as COVID-19, reveals the ways in which gendered and racialized marginalized groups are controlled as a means of ensuring the continued patriarchal-colonial dominance of the "immunized body."[81]

Skin sticky from the hot city fumy air, I went to the clinic last week. I was told to undress quickly before the speculum was quickly inserted into my vagina, to open its walls, and aid the brush into my cervix, collecting a sample of cells. It was just a routine procedure, near the end of a working day from home. But still, it felt like "female trouble," as you liked to say. I, like so many others, should've booked a smear test back in March, but then the virus came, and my flesh stuck to the living room walls, with drafts of letters scattered across the desk, spilling onto the floor.

Cookie's scrappy publication confirms what Barthes said in the final lectures he gave before he died, called *The Preparation of the Novel* (transcribed, translated, and published in English in 2011): that "the desire to write is, if not puerile, at any rate *adolescent*; it's been noted that the awakening of the literary 'vocation' more or less coincides with puberty."[82] Barthes recuperates adolescence in these lectures (and also in his lovesick letter to Guibert, which Guibert then published); he awakens its awakenings, at a time of intense melancholy and grief, following the death of his mother in 1977. Loss suffocated his writing, but splutters of something new (something *hopeful*) could be heard.

Over the course of these years—up until his death in 1980 (also at the Salpêtrière), one month after he collided with a laundry van while walking home on the streets of Paris—Barthes wrote his book on feeling, photography, and absence, *Camera Lucida*, as well as the spare and intimate fragments of his *Mourning Diary* (another posthumous publication). He was also—like his desired love object in Guibert, and his literary love in Proust—seeking to find the shape and scope of an autobiographical novel. Within the lecture transcriptions, Barthes summons adolescence with hope, that those youthful energies might persist and keep him writing in the long form. Up until this point, Barthes (like Cookie after her handmade novel) was a writer of short things—notes rather than novels. But in these lectures, also hinted at by Cookie's desperate desire for length, for living, for novel-writing, Barthes wonders how to navigate the "the conflict between the short form and the long form," how to forge ties, make narrative, an alternative relationship to writing that recalls the "bits of life."[83]

A red cardboard shirt box, pasted with the title VITA NOVA, was found after his death. Housed inside its neat angles was the archive of his unfinished novel, proof that he had been trying. Eight sheets of paper, a mixture of typewriter and graph, inked with his words and amended with marks in red and black pencil, amounted to his novel's preparatory pieces.

Within Cookie's archive, I've found stories upon stories, pieces meeting pieces, edits, notes, plans, and lists. Hidden inside one folder is an autobiographical novel in waiting. These manuscript leftovers and unfinished pieces hint at her novelistic desire (the adolescent's apprenticeship), scrappier than Barthes's immaculate box but haunted by loss all the same. Blanks give way to repetitions, as the same episodes resurface in manic edits, overlaid with annotations, crossings out, loops, and arrows. Contained by the pressure of her sick time, across these manuscripts I can feel her writing (intransitive) but also counting (intransitive): pages, chapters, *and* days left. Content fatigues itself, as her knee joints became cement.

Some pages are almost see-through, like the skin of a sick person, or a hole in time. One sheet is misspelt "Autobogrphical Novel," and it comprises a long list of her life's memories, with scrawled additions (figure 2.5). The beginning groups extreme traumas and ecstasies from childhood and adolescence: "brother dieing, car accident, family trips with mom, dad and judy, dad with stroke in Salisbury, drinking beer on the tracks, taking seconals." The middle is more glamorous: "parties, meet sharon, films, acting with greats, writing career." And the end is an ambiguous mixture of euphoria and loss: "marriage, heavy drug use, writing the drug play, last year in Italy, stay of my family, aids death of good friends" (figure 2.6).[84] Its multiple clauses are exhausting, as Cookie desperately archives her life in a list.

The virally numbered Box VII.1, Folder 13 holds an irregular mesh of manuscripts, but within it there are novel traces. "Chapter 1 Page 1" appears as a reworked version of "My Bio—Notes on an American Childhood," the story of Cookie's adolescent novel: "I started writing poetry while still in grade school so by the time I was thirteen or so, I was working on a few novels. One that I especially was obsessed with was the story of a nurse in the nineteenth century who wore hoop skirts in the fields of Gettysburg during the Civil War."[85] Cookie's "coming-to-writing" is more infantile than adolescent in this version (grade school being pre–high school), but she's a young adolescent when she gamely switches from "the *Note*, to the Novel."[86] Undecided, she's gorging on not one novel but many, a casual "few." Shared by Kathy in her diaristic excess, this is the attitude of the "never-finished" adolescent; it reemerges in Cookie's scrappy manuscript pieces that she thumbed out later in life, in *extended adolescence*.

The folder is full of first chapters like these, some as slight as a paragraph and others fatiguing at four pages. The tale of her handmade novel continues, though, with another perverse kind of fantasy: "The next time I went into the library it was gone. I was upset that it had disappeared for good in the months to come, but I passified [*sic*] myself with the thought that maybe someone was reading it dog-eared and it made them laugh

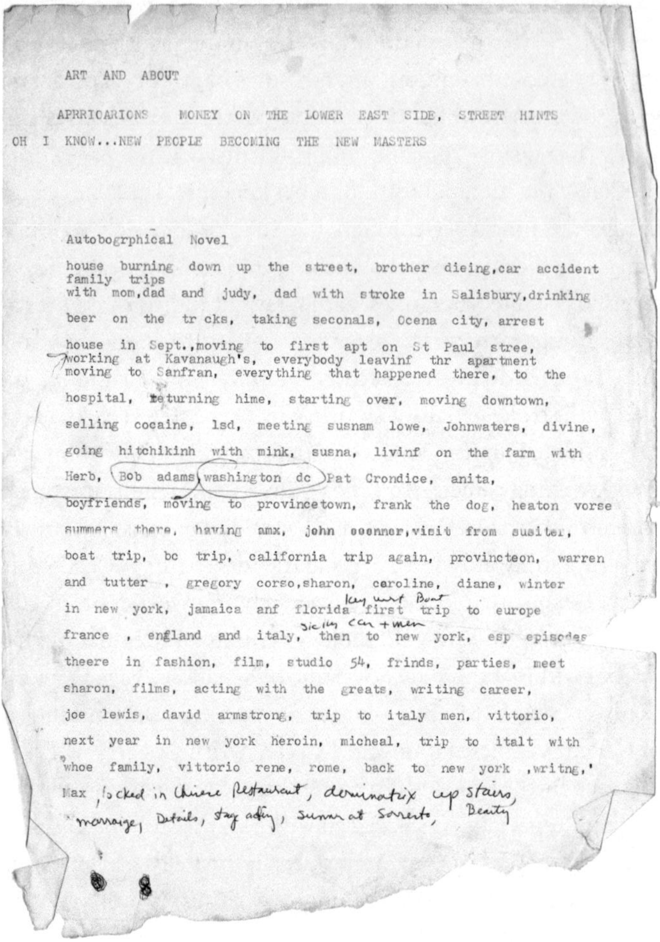

ART AND ABOUT

APRRIOARIONS MONEY ON THE LOWER EAST SIDE, STREET HINTS
OH I KNOW...NEW PEOPLE BECOMING THE NEW MASTERS

Autobogrphical Novel

house burning down up the street, brother dieing,car accident family trips
with mom,dad and judy, dad with stroke in Salisbury,drinking
beer on the tr cks, taking seconals, Ocena city, arrest
house in Sept.,moving to first apt on St Paul stree,
working at Kavanaugh's, everybody leavinf thr apartment
moving to Sanfran, everything that happened there, to the
hospital, returning hime, starting over, moving downtown,
selling cocaine, lsd, meeting susnam lowe, Johnwaters, divine,
going hitchikinh with mink, susna, livinf on the farm with
Herb, Bob adams washington dc Pat Crondice, anita,
boyfriends, moving to provincetown, frank the dog, heaton vorse
summers there, having amx, john eeenner,visit from susiter,
boat trip, bc trip, california trip again, provincteon, warren
and tutter , gregory corso,sharon, caroline, diane, winter
in new york, jamaica anf florida key west Boat first trip to europe
france , england and italy, Sicily Car + men then to new york, esp episodes
theere in fashion, film, studio 54, frinds, parties, meet
sharon, films, acting with the greats, writing career,
joe lewis, david armstrong, trip to italy men, vittorio,
next year in new york heroin, micheal, trip to italt with
whoe family, vittorio rene, rome, back to new york ,writng,'
Max, locked in Chinese Restaurant, dominatrix up stairs,
marriage, Details, stag acting, summer at Sorrento, Beauty

a see-through page
a misspelled sheet
typed lines of collected memories

2.5. Cookie Mueller, typed list for "Autobogrphical Novel," undated. Fales Library and Special Collections, New York University Libraries, STHRA, BVII.1, F18. Courtesy of the Cookie Mueller Estate.

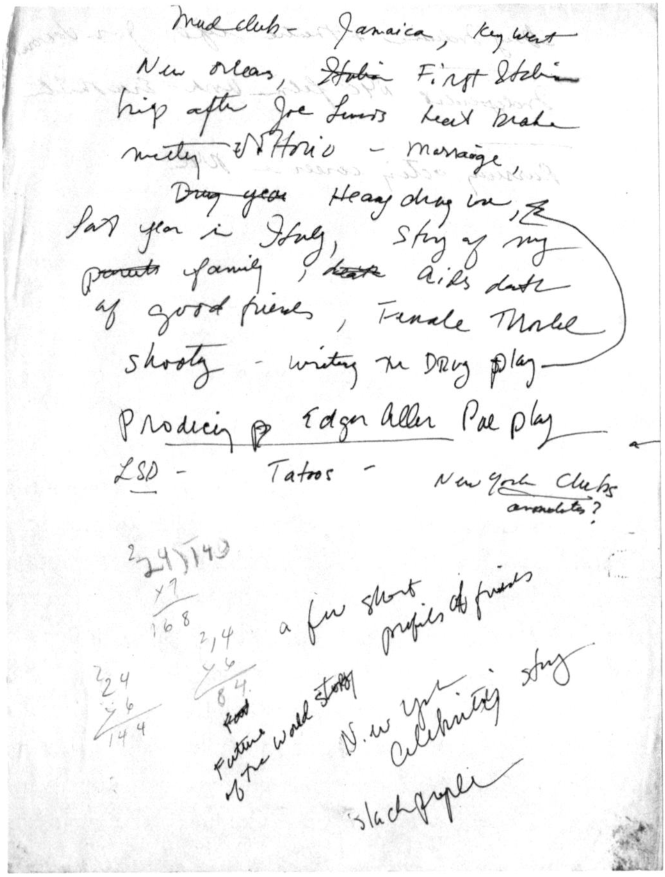

Mud club – Jamaica, Key West
New Orleans, ~~Italian~~ First Italian
trip after Joe Lewis's heart break
meeting Vittorio – marriage,
~~Drug year~~ Heavy drug use,
last year in Italy, story of my
~~parents~~ family, ~~death~~ aids death
of good friends, Female Model
shooting – writing the Drug play
Producing ~~p~~ Edgar Allen Poe play
LSD – Tatoos – New York Clubs
anecdotes?
a few short profiles of friends
~~food~~ Future of the world ~~story~~
New York celebrity story
black people

a scrawling end
a life in a list

2.6. Cookie Mueller, handwritten list for "Autobogrphical Novel," undated. Fales Library and Special Collections, New York University Libraries, STHRA, BVII.I, F18. Courtesy of the Cookie Mueller Estate.

and cry at the end or better still perhaps someone was masturbating to it, in their bathroom."[87] While the object of her creative achievement disappears (did someone steal it?), the manuscript has an erotic life in adolescent sexual fantasies, which the elder author re-lives in her close-writing remembrance. Her framing suggests a perverse fetish: a folded, torn, pleated, crumpled, handled thing; a tactile text; a stolen fragment (like the erotic fetishes claimed by the slippery hands of a kleptomaniac). For whom was Cookie writing, as an adolescent novelist and as a later "adolescent" writer? Who was (who *is*—tenses slip in Cookie's close writing) the typescript for? At the center of her dreaming-writing is an autoerotic reader, a suburban adolescent masturbating herself free, claiming perversion for herself—like the nineteenth-century "hysteric" kleptomaniacs before her, who were found to enjoy autoerotic sexual thrills from stealing consumer goods.

But while early psychiatric chronicles authored by the masculine, medicalizing gaze denied women the agency of perversion when they pilfered tactile things, Cookie shows the subversive angles of the adolescent's creative and erotic imagination.[88] Her willful and wayward fantasies permeate the material and metaphorical walls of the family home, barriers that are invoked by the image of the bathroom, a bodily space of imposed hygiene and order, as well as one of intimacy, closeness, and waste. As Sara Ahmed writes in her discussion of diversity work in the academic institution, walls become "barriers that we experience as physical; barriers that are physical." "A wall," Ahmed elaborates, "is what you come up against. It is a physical contact; a *visceral* encounter."[89] Cookie's wall is an institutionalized space of domestic, familial confinement, enclosing embodied actions of discipline and training that a masturbatory encounter with a stolen manuscript then comes up against, or rather *smears*, recalling similar interventions made by Kathy's autoerotic, automatic writings (form) sketched in the blur of visceral inks (material) and featuring masturbatory "adolescent" scenes (content). It is an intensely visceral encounter that is imagined by Cookie, becomes perversely queer, as the gender and sexual identity of the kleptomaniac reader seeking autoerotic pleasure refuses normative, knowable conventions. Preempting the opening scene of Brontez Purnell's 2017 film and the Visual AIDS commission *100 Boyfriends Mixtape (The Demo)*, wherein a queer person of color spills down the telephone a recent story of them shoplifting a new pair of Levi's and "liberating them from capitalism," the autoerotic love object of Cookie's close-written fantasy steals, reads, and masturbates as embodied, desiring, visceral acts of resistance, challenging a number of interconnected regulatory norms—educational, familial, legal, medical, sexual—that are entangled within the heterosexist-patriarchal discourses of late capitalism.[90]

Similarly, and just a year after the publication of *Walking Through Clear Water in a Pool Painted Black*, Eve Kosofsky Sedgwick published an essay, "Jane Austen and the Masturbating Girl," in the academic journal *Critical Inquiry* that returned the queer reader (indelibly marked by the impact of the AIDS epidemic—how far sex was silenced, perversion erased) to the adolescent queerness of the nineteenth-century female onanist and her solitary pleasures. Sedgwick close-reads the bedroom scenes of Jane Austen's *Sense and Sensibility*, focusing on the sixteen-year-old Marianne's "erotic identity" as "not in the first place exactly either a same-sex loving one or a cross-sex-loving one (though she loves both women and men), but rather the one that today no longer exists *as* an identity: that of the masturbating girl."[91] Sedgwick absorbs documents-within-documents within this essay, as an 1881 case history of a little girl masturbator—which was published within "Polysexuality," the 1981 special issue of Semiotext(e)'s titular journal that explored plural perversions—connects with Marianne's disorderly, desiring, undisciplined adolescent attentions.

For Cookie, writing within the sexually repressive regime that Sedgwick also attends to via a historically contingent perspective—a regime that policed and pathologized queer people, IV drug users, sex workers, Black communities, and other working-class, migrant communities of color, especially Haitians, in heterosexist and racist ways hauntingly familiar of nineteenth-century Western medicine—the figure of the masturbating girl offered "a reservoir of potentially utopian metaphors and energies of independence, self-possession, and a rapture that may owe relatively little to political or interpersonal abjection."[92] In Cookie's speculatively sexual fantasy of a manuscript's afterlife, which I find etched in another archival object, the autoerotic desire of the haptic reader has the potential to subvert and reorganize their "surround," the space, structures, and signifiers of the family home.[93] This masturbating reader, an elusive but powerful erotic identity that is imagined by Cookie, finds freedom in the messy and dog-eared edges, a world off-kilter, where wayward desires of reading, stealing, and touching discover an outlet in secret spaces usually kept under the influence of exterior control. Here it is possible to recode, as Sedgwick writes, the "hierarchically oppressive relations between genders and between sexualities."[94] Cookie, like Sedgwick, also connects adolescence with queerly oriented perversion, full of ambiguous gendering and a sexual identity that slips and slides between recognizable binary categories. It is a recoding of desire *as* perverse *via* adolescence that manifests in her manuscript fiction and her lived and embodied writing *of* it: from the scene of close, intimate, autoerotic reading to the similarly close, belated reenactments of close writing. I picture Cookie involving herself in the haptic typing and endless retyping of her manuscript pages, reenacting via hand and word the memories and pleasures of perverse adolescence.

I cut, I piece, I slip: our wandering hands. Pleasures meeting in purloined letters.

Cookie's archive is messy with chapter attempts, from "1," to "2," to "3." I have found the worn-out traces of her desire, the tidbits of her hungry novel. She wrote parts of it down, in solitary pleasure (though her life and the writing of it kept her company). But it appears that she did not complete it, whatever it might've been. I am poised to wonder and dream, in pathological melancholy.[95] I inhabit the awkward (adolescent) middle. Like Jack Halberstam's celebration of the queerness of failure (its unique capacity to mess with "the clean boundaries between adults and children, winners and losers."), I am fixating anew (full of autoerotic attention and close writerly desire) on the ways Cookie did not, could not, chose *not* to (probably a mixture of all three) finish the novel, and how this brought adolescence back to her.[96] Could the perversion of adolescence be intimately entangled in the autoerotic desire to *never finish*, to be distracted, to delay or disorient, to refuse to work: to attend to differences in bodies, desires, and *writings*? As Halberstam notes, "The queer art of failure . . . quietly loses, and in losing it imagines other goals for life, for love, for art, and for being."[97] Of course, Cookie's own loss (of life and of manuscript) can hardly be thought of as a voluntary failure when she died of a disease systematically ignored, but her unfinished novel, I speculatively argue, offers its own possibilities, helping us to think differently about the relationships among close writing, adolescence, perversion, and the time of disease.

Two books, published in the year after Cookie's death, collected her genre-blurring autobiographical pieces (merging fiction and life facts, set in Baltimore, Provincetown, Italy, Berlin, and New York City, in the remembrance of time past): *Garden of Ashes* and *Walking Through Clear Water in a Pool Painted Black*.[98] But the crazed lists, the cover letter, the transitional notes, and the half-finished chapters of an unfinished novel also point toward a larger manuscript. Did the escalation of her disease, coupled with posthumous publication, cause the piecemeal and distracted form of these two books?

Or did you choose to write this way?

The small number of critics and scholars who have studied Cookie's writing have glossed her texts as "stories," and in many ways, this feels apt, given their brevity and given the fact that Cookie often called them this. But should we separate them along such lines? Following Halberstam's queer reimagining of losers, what if Cookie always envisioned her "unfinished manuscript," the "compilation of autobiographical short stories," to be more akin to what I'm calling a *novel-in-pieces*: a form in flux, a state of becoming?[99] Closer to what Barthes calls an in-between *third form*—neither long nor short but rather something more slippery (*potentially* adolescent, *potentially* queer), a "*Novel through Fragments*"?[100] One of Cookie's more memorable one-liners says it all: "I believe my short stories are novels for people with short attention spans."[101] Story, novel, compilation: Cookie's close writing moves between genres, echoing her own indecision over what literary term to use to describe it. She preferred a distracted mixture of genres and modes, coming as it did from a writer of perverse adolescent attentions, and for a reader much like her. In posthumously published books (1990, 1997, 2022), zines, journals, and unfinished manuscripts, I have encountered the scattered parts of her novel-in-pieces. Here she restored the marks left in her perverse adolescence: *before she ran out of time.*

I look again at a picture of you, taken by Nan. The two of you are together in a dimly lit bedroom with a broken surface of cracked paint. There's a bedside light but no lampshade. I enjoy such domestic mistakes. Is it late at night? Or early in the morning? The photograph gleams for me, along with the minor details within it: untucked sheet, receipt pinned to the wall, amulets dangling above a rested head. The collectomania of adolescence. I collect your garments as I look: an indigo-blue denim jacket edged with yellow stitching, a black knitted roll-neck jumper, jersey leggings, and over-the-knee black leather boots. Your hand is rubbing the rim of a beer bottle, as you hover on the crumpled edge of your best friend's chipped, gold single bed frame, its rough embroidered blankets, an ashtray containing two half-smoked cigarettes cushioned at the center. Stale smoke clings to the textile surfaces, the bored magnolia walls, the skin. I inhale deeply, hold my breath. I sense the slow mouthing of secrets and symptoms between you. I trace the hidden lines exchanged on postcards saved, the stacks of manuscripts not yet borne but planted, buried under the duvet, face in the sheets.

The Surprising Power of Unfinished Desire

My letters are partial, messy, torn. It is an archive of unfinished love.

Like Sappho and *like* Kathy—two poets separated by centuries but brought together in my writing with them—we know Cookie's "work only in fragments," dazzling pieces of writing that create kaleidoscopic pictures of her.[102] The frayed edges of her novel-in-pieces suggest the ways sickness, but also desire *and* hope, lives on in textures, in the dispersed objects left behind. In *Sappho Is Burning*, duBois interrogates the role of scholars who, as "supposed agents of integrity and coherence," are so usually tasked with mending, repairing, and smoothing out the fragments of the past.[103] But can we, probes duBois, instead develop a historiographical mode that reads and writes "with" the gaps, the holes, the fragments, the loose edges: "one that allows for a consciousness of the past's inaccessibility," its always partial nature?[104] This, she argues, "should be part of the project of postmodernism."[105] And, so, rather than seek some ahistorical fantasy and reconstruct Cookie's missing parts (her Sapphic body in pieces), I follow another path.[106] Even while I "yearn for more," I know I must "read what we have."[107] I love her (postmodern) pieces: from the touch of the hand (me caressing her, between the tips of my fingers) to the touch of writing (another kind of caress).

To in any way attempt a reading that looks to sanitize or "complete" her close writing would, I understand, go against the political energies of her perverse, piecemeal forms, which are as scattered as the postcards pinned to an adolescent's bedroom wall. (It would separate us, cause a power imbalance, even when committed in the context of "care.") There are other ways of dreaming repair, as Sedgwick made known, when she unraveled reparative work for us, always in relation to the paranoid, and by thinking beside *remembered* conversations between her and a scholar-friend. It is a memory of a personal exchange, belatedly considered as the sign of a reparative motive, and the beginnings of the essay. Like Cookie's orientation to her adolescent pasts, Sedgwick also *looks back*, "to the middle of the first decade of the AIDS epidemic," around the time of Cookie's diagnosis. She recalls a poignant conversation with a friend and ally, the AIDS activist and scholar Cindy Patton, about the likelihood of the HIV virus being "deliberately engineered or spread . . . a plot or experiment by the U.S. military that had gotten out of control, or perhaps that was behaving exactly as it was meant to."[108] For Sedgwick, Patton's response that day—as a refusal of the suspicious urge to "trace" and "expose," and a committed embrace of alternative activist energies—opens out the possibility that to simply *know* whether discrimination and hatred of marginalized, "high risk" groups viewed as "enemies" by the militaristic state is "true" is different to what we might "*do*" with that knowledge, how it might *perform*.[109] This anecdote supports Sedgwick's theorization, to which I keep returning, and which I recognize many others have, too, of paranoid reading practices (defined by suspicion, symmetry, generality, the strong forestalling of pain or surprise) and reparative reading practices (defined by surprise, hope, pleasure, and love).[110] Emerging from Melanie Klein's notion of the "anxiety-mitigating" depressive position—whereby the infant or adult is able to (however fleetingly) use "one's resources to assemble or 'repair' the murderous part-objects" into "something like a whole—though . . . not *necessarily like any preexisting whole*"—the reparative reader (and in this case, the reparative close writer) is invested in the desire to generate nourishment, energies, and resources, for the "fragments and part-objects she encounters or creates."[111] Hence, "to repair" does not directly correspond with reconstructing wholeness that once was; the "something *like* a whole" can be unexpected or surprising, even *belated*, discovered through adolescent-style mistakes and reparative love: a feeling of, and with, the frayed (sick) edges of the piece.[112]

I think with the fragile materiality of her life and writing and body in pieces. Alvin Baltrop's vast archive of photographs and unprinted negatives—some taken when he was an adolescent, others taken when he, too, was seeking it—contains similar episodes of material rupture: a torn contact print, flecks of too much light on the surface of the photograph, creases of stained paper that peel away. Baltrop's pieces were recently exhibited at the Bronx Museum of the Arts in New York and the Hannah Hoffman Gallery in Los Angeles (2020–21), more than ten years after he received posthumous recognition—via a belated profile on his work by Douglas Crimp that was published four years after his death—for his erotic, enchanting black-and-white photographs depicting the dilapidated structures of Manhattan's West End piers and the edgewise figures and artists who moved through them: those fleeing, desiring, making, imaging, writing, in social or solitary scenes, cast in swathes of shadow or bathed in pools of light. Baltrop, a Black, queer, working-class man who had no formal training in photography but made his decades-long project by the piers (just about) possible by working low-wage jobs on the side (even sleeping in a van to be closer to the action; as Crimp writes, "he risked much" in his street-side artmaking), received scant attention for his photographs during his lifetime.[113] There was a "small show in 1977 at Glines, a nonprofit gay organization," and in an act of curatorial resourcefulness, "he once exhibited the pier photographs at the East Village gay bar at second Avenue and East Fourth Street where he sometimes worked as a bouncer."[114] Indeed, as the artist Tiona Nekkia McClodden has expressed, "whiter, cooler, traditional archive-ready artists"—figures such as Diane Arbus or Robert Mapplethorpe, who also photographed the edgewise and the erotic—were exhibited in mainstream galleries or elevated to magazine pages *during* their lifetimes.[115] Baltrop barely glimpsed such opportunities.

Cookie's novel-in-pieces was not necessarily "archive-ready" either—in that it was surreptitious, not-yet-collected, unfinished, belatedly accreted into gatherings and gifts stored, hidden within publishers' papers and the officiated archives of notable others—but, as heard in Chris Kraus's desire to help her get her stories published, there was at least an infrastructure of partial support. As a racialized, classed figure, such "objects" were less available to Baltrop, as he encountered disorienting rejections from the art world. On showing his portfolio to one gallerist, they used abhorrent racist and homophobic language in dismissing him as "a real sewer rat type of person"; others refused to believe that Baltrop had taken the pictures himself.[116] It fell to his own labor and that of a friend, scaffolded by few resources (financial, institutional, structural), to maintain, care for, print, re-print, and archive his own body of work in pieces. This was an urgent project to preserve the energies and intimacies of a previous but still precarious time, as many of those closest to him began to die of AIDS-related complications during the late 1980s and 1990s, and he, too, experienced ill health upon being hospitalized with terminal cancer in 2003.

Baltrop's never-finalized corpus of originally untitled, undated prints arrives to us cleaved and creased apart, parts missing in melancholic materiality. Without official name or official date, his is an archive that invites a different kind of art-historical encounter, one that confuses viewing with writing with touching with feeling with dreaming, as it travels across past and present temporal zones. Am I a witness to this materiality-in/as-afterlife? Am I a witness to melancholy? *Could I write it*? Michael Ann Holly has written that, in the pursuit for historical knowledge, the "animism" of objects' afterlives is "often forsaken, even abjured" with research conventions, when other possibilities could emerge by *staying with* the loss of an object (in this gesture there is pain, but also, possibly, pleasure), in melancholic, reparative art-historical writing, akin perhaps to Cookie's adolescent version of research in the Clara Barton zinelike novel.[117] As Holly writes, "Melancholy holds us there, and in the act of aesthetic yearning we strive to keep the works of art alive, even with the awareness that their historical being vanishes deeper into the past with each passing day."[118] Cleaved and creased apart, Baltrop's prints are materially close to vanishing, but melancholy holds me close to them differently, as I recognize strategies of opacity in the slow sexual scenes he records—two indistinct figures fucking in the shadows by the Hudson gray, or nude men cruising through the maze of the falling rafters—which are extended in the uncared-for, unfinished, untitled edges of their belated presentation (figure 2.7). "In the dark," said Baltrop, "we can all be free."[119] It is a fragment that invokes the obscure, unlit corners of the piers; the obscure, unlit corners of the darkroom; or the obscure, unlit corners of the archive, as fugitive spaces of possibility.

It recalls Cookie's own epigraph in paradox that associated death with adolescent freedoms, as Baltrop's sick composition of his own adolescent archive later in life also alludes to. Here he returns the contemporary viewer to early work and teenage experiments, wherein he documented the queer environments of the West Village and the Stonewall Inn, but also broader adolescent-style energies of attempt, of excess, of mistake, of indeterminacy, which pulse throughout the expansive images and materials of his incomplete queer archive.

I could not master or rationalize his; I could not forsake the desires of this afterlife, as I could not neatly recover Cookie. Hence, the paranoid recovery of Cookie's unfinished novel will not be the overriding narrative in this close writing. Instead, I desire to "assemble and confer plenitude on an object [*or series of objects: the novel-in-pieces*] that will then have resources to offer to an inchoate self," in the hope that while there can be "terrible surprises . . . there can also be good ones."[120] Cookie's close writing shows the surprising power of unfinished desire; it holds the broken elements of her body and her manuscripts and lets them speak on their own terms. Loving her pieces this way, a mode of repair that disrupts the paranoid will to complete her, opens out the radical ways in which adolescence (as a conceptual container of the desire to never finish, to revel in indeterminacy) breathes political life into the forms of the pieces we have left (*I stay with them*: this novel-in-pieces), as well as the characters and selves it *re-presents*.

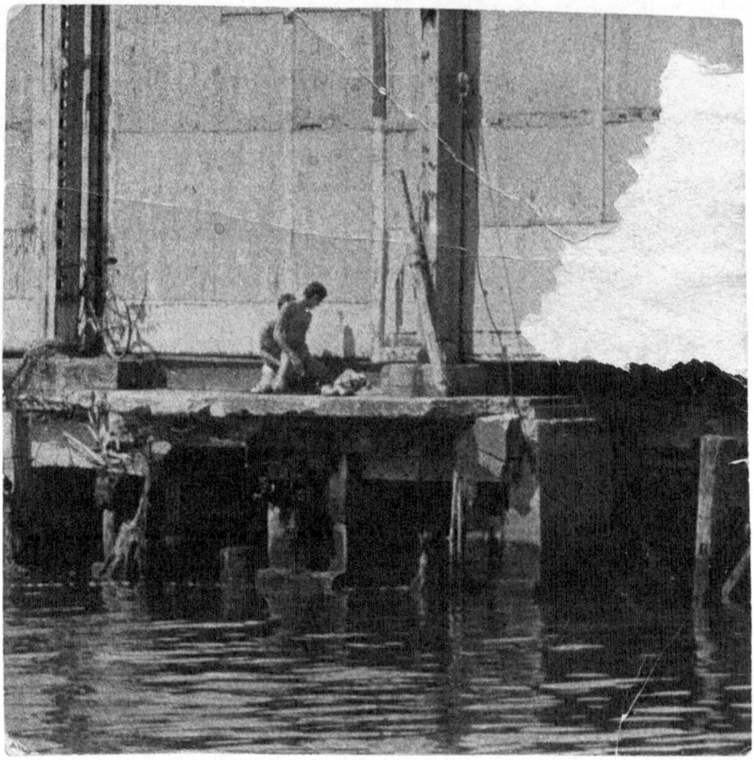

a partial picture
of the Hudson gray

2.7. Alvin Baltrop, *The Piers (exterior with couple having sex)*, undated (ca. 1975–86). Gelatin silver print, 6.35 × 6.35 cm. © 2024 Estate of Alvin Baltrop / Artists Rights Society (ARS), New York.

To discover that Cookie's close writing is piecemeal, scattered, unfinished, necessitates the importance of attending to the fragments closely, and *again*, of thinking and writing *with* them. This reparative position helps me to recognize the earlier adolescent selves that swarm Cookie's pieces (suddenly adolescents are everywhere buzzing across the page) and the political significance of her remembering them, loving them, in her own reparative, belated close writing that moves fluidly across time—blurring subject and object. Indeed, drawing on her own cross-generational queer friendships whose lives have been impacted by environmental crises, HIV, and cancer, Sedgwick recognizes in her reparative analysis that an alternative relationship to the past, present, and future is demanded of reading and writing.[121] Like Baltrop's sick-time archive, Cookie's close writing of bygone adolescence provides an energizing model.

I feel a desire that rages in your umbilical lists.

Open Mouths, Never Full

Growing up in the predominantly white, middle-class, suburban environs of Baltimore—"where everything looks the same," remembers Sharon Niesp—Cookie's 1950s–1960s youth coincided with the media invention of the "teenager," through which films, magazines, fashions, and advertisements fed a rapidly growing consumer market that threatened the stable structures of nuclear family life and its intimate public narratives of belonging.[122] As Cookie's sister, Judy, reflects in *Edgewise*, "Our mom came from a really poor family and wanted more than anything else to raise herself up out of that and almost reinvent herself."[123] Marrying well became their mother's ticket into the aspirational (cruelly optimistic) good life of suburbia. Could the unpredictable figure of the teenager unground the foundations of such a life? A slip of "Baltimore County High Schools" paper reprimanding "Karen Mueller" for tardiness evokes the rebellious spirit of the teenager; a message addressed to her in the 1967 senior yearbook reads: "Cookie. Best of luck to the biggest nut ever."[124]

Could being a teenager like this—that is, obsessed with "really pale lipstick"; "thick black eyeliner"; "an old drive-in restaurant called Champs"; "pot" and "poetry" (namely "Emily Dickinson")—have been made possible by habits sustained and reproduced by privileged proximities to whiteness?[125] As a racialized construct, the "predominant image of 'proper' middle-class adolescence in the 1950s is almost always coded as white in popular historical memory," as Beth Fowler has written, and as John Waters's Baltimore-set films also critically extend, despite Black youth being active participants in the shaping of youth culture, specific to their own lives and experiences of racial injustice, discrimination, and segregation.[126] From 1965, for example, as an amateur photographer from the Bronx, Baltrop was moving through the queer corners and safe spaces of a New York underground, capturing the patrons of the Stonewall Inn or the crowds of young people at a Malcolm X rally. The images might not now physically exist, but it is possible to speculate what social gatherings the pictures could have shown: *what might have been* as he fled a restrictive, religious home.

Also in 1965, the year that a one-page piece called "Alien" is retroac-
1 tively dated, Cookie began plotting her exodus out of the familial suburbs.
2 As she remembers in close writing: "I was always leaving. Every time I left
2 I had a different hair color and I would be standing on the porch saying
goodbye to the older couple in the living room. I didn't have anything in common with them except that we shared a few inherited chromosomes, the identical last name, and the same bathroom."[127] Her hair was always changing color in kaleidoscopic movement, and so was her body leaving: a perpetual farewell. It is her polymorphic adolescent identity that casts her as an alien in her own "home," at a distance from the biology that made her. Standing on the threshold, between domestic and public spaces, she is an abject, restless, hybrid creature, scratching at the walls of familial confinement, cutting ties from the bonds of genetic inheritance, the patriarchal governance of the "last name."

Ahmed speaks of the figure of the alien representing the "danger of the unknown," "the outsider inside," who, by "coming too close to home," as Cookie's spatial proximity briefly alludes to in her porch position, establishes "the very necessity of policing the borders of knowable and inhabitable terrains."[128] Cookie was also forced to endure such biopolitically forced borders while working on and with her adolescent pieces, as the borders of the virulent body were stigmatized and punished as a threat to capitalist society's "immunitary fantasies."[129] In the 1965-dated piece: as an adolescent "little-bird-alien" (dangerous because of her difference, her will to never finish), Cookie yearns to emancipate herself from the policed borders of the normative, family structure—although it is important to recognize that Ahmed's outline of "alien forms" is made in particular relation to the specific postcolonial discourses of "globalisation and multiculturalism" that construct and "reproduce the figure of the stranger."[130]

For Cookie, to escape the "same bathroom" is also to escape surveillance and sanitization, as well as the homogenizing forces of "that entity 'the family,' an impacted social space, in which all of the following are meant to line up perfectly with each other: a surname / a sexual dyad / a legal unit based on state-regulated marriage," as Sedgwick described it in list form in the 1993 essay "Queer and Now."[131] Lauren Berlant, too, recognizes Sedgwick's ideas in the context of the dominant "intimate public of white patriarchy" that the "Reaganite culture wars" reinforced and weaponized, and which Cookie's close writing was formed in opposition to.[132] Cookie in 1965 responds to her parents' protestations: "'It's natural. It's a biological urge. Like little birds testing their wings. I can't help myself.'"[133] Her defensive reply is also a confession of automated need, as if an addiction to the state of adolescence itself: to consuming it, this everlasting lust to "test" the possibilities and feel out freedom.

In 1967 she spread her wings even wider when she joined thousands of young people in San Francisco seeking countercultural "refuge from an American dream that was crumbling quickly in suburban wastelands and urban hothouses, as well as the jungles of Vietnam."[134] As Joan Didion put it in the 1968 essay "Slouching Towards Bethlehem," "San Francisco was where the social hemorrhaging was showing up . . . where the missing children were gathering and calling themselves 'hippies.'"[135] A glossy photograph of Didion in Golden Gate Park, April 1967, shows the journalist wearing an expensive silk scarf knotted loosely at the neck, her professional writer's hands slipped into the deep pockets of her khaki jacket, and a clasped handbag dangling from her wrist.

Meanwhile, somewhere over "Hippie Hill," as Cookie called the Park, was a young girl from Baltimore, spilling last night's kohl from her eyelids.[136] The only thing knotted was her hair, in her adolescent injection of bedraggled beatnik glamour, the revolting pleasures of "bad taste" style, into the hippie pastoral.[137] As Cookie close-writes of her distinctive look, "I plastered the makeup on thick and teased my hair. No one else wore eye makeup in the Haight . . . an occasional Dayglow flower or a third eye on the forehead perhaps, but definitely no eye makeup."[138] This sartorial divergence from, or resistance to, the countercultural look symbolized her complicated relationship to hippie "free love" manifesto-ing. In later life, Kathy also challenged the hypocrisies of these ideals, staking her claim instead that she was part of a generation "after." "The Hippies were our parents," she wrote: They believed in "LOVE and PEACE and we, their children, were mentally and physically misshapen," like perpetual adolescents *undone.*[139]

I picture a winged kaftan, embroidered hem caked in mud. You are airborne. Aflame. Gold earrings twinkling in the smoke.

This sense of the undone and unknown is echoed in Cookie's version of the Summer of Love, as the social phenomenon has become known, mythologized. Stories of countercultural activities and experimentations with sex, drugs, music, fashion, and antiwar activism have accumulated in its wake, making its significance difficult to fully grasp, as a historian of
1 the sixties, Michael J. Kramer, has also reckoned with.[140] Was it a utopian
2 "revolution in consciousness"; "a new way of doing politics through life-
4 style, embodied action"; a "season when decadence undercut conservative
American values"?[141] Or was the Summer of Love—as a site, a temporal moment, a *mood*—infinitely darker, more ambivalent, marked by scenes of struggle, anguish, poverty, and violence? Or was it *both*; was it the good and the bad? William Gedney's grayscale photographs, taken inside cramped, uncomfortable rooms, or on quiet street corners, or amid the before-and-after lulls of a gathering, complicate the notion that it was an extended summer in Technicolor. These images, which Gedney conceived of as "visual literature, modeled after the novel form" with autofictional characters and literary devices, occupy a messy middle ground (they are *gray*): full of joy and play, but also boredom, insecurity, loneliness, and abjection.[142] The pictures were taken over the course of a year while Gedney was on a Guggenheim Fellowship in San Francisco, putting them together as a preparatory maquette to eventually become the visual novel he was working on. But, like Cookie's novel-in-pieces, the visual novel did not materialize in a conventional sense; instead, it lay among mountains of manuscripts and photographs that were carefully moved between various home studios in New York before the artist died of AIDS-related illness in the early summer of 1989.[143] Structured by its own sick time, *A Time of Youth* arrived belatedly, *in pieces*; its crossed temporalities echo the crossed affects and experiences it represents.

Kramer has also stressed the "wild oscillations" that characterized this time; it is "analytically productive . . . to consider the Summer of Love through the framework of the micro and macrocosmic," wherein participants actively moved through different scales of experience, from the macro of utopian joy and revolution, to the micro of difficulty and stress, often encompassing both at once, as when those protesting a white police officer's murder of an African American teenager, Matthew Johnson Jr., were met with physical suppression by the National Guard and a curfew on the streets in the fall of 1966.[144] The Student Nonviolent Coordinating Committee (SNCC), called "the foremost advocate of 'Black Power'" by Angela Davis, pointed out that the areas with large Black populations were gerrymandered by the curfew, while St. Francis Square, a mostly white, middle-class housing project, was excluded, despite it being in the middle of the district where most of the rioting was "supposedly" happening according to police reports.[145] The SNCC's newspaper *The Movement* found such stories to be exaggerated, or untrue, or a coverup of police violence.[146] In October 1966, Stokely Carmichael was chairman of the SNCC; he looms in the background of Cookie's piece, though she expresses hippie indifference toward him.

In Cookie's macro/micro literary recuperation, she flirts with the ambiguity of pleasure and pain that shaped her adolescent experiences in California (revels in it as "bad taste" humor): from cheap food and sloppy sex, to trash makeup, to casual sex with rock stars, to an LSD capping party, to an encounter with the Charles Manson bus, to a devil worship ceremony, to a Jim Morrison gig, to a violent rape. An excessive and perverse kind of hunger reveals itself across these scenes, through which she seeks to transgress the familial, knowable terrains she is attempting to leave behind. Adolescence provides a unique "contribution [*and a reparative one*] . . . to the museum of bad taste," argues Joseph Litvak—in correspondence with Proust's own "adolescent piece" that demonstrates an "insatiable appetite *for* waste" (its temporal and excremental guises), *The Guermantes Way*—precisely because of its cultivated craving for the stuff that tastes "off," obscene, bestial: a drive of delinquent sophistication that becomes a means of survival.[147] The perverse bad object becomes desirable because it wards off adult oppressions, like the drag queen Divine's infamous "shit-eating-grin scene" in *Pink Flamingos*, which also starred a "fresh-into-her-twenties" and "newly-a-mother" Cookie.[148] In her later close writing about the making of the film, Cookie echoes the delinquent attitude of Divine, grinning at the gastronomic experience of eating the chickens (which she calls "a lively nasty bunch of fowl") decapitated by the Dreamlanders and used in an ambiguous but shocking scene of squawking, scratching sexual spectacle, violence, and encounter: "Those chickens I'd felt sorry for earlier sure were *delicious*."[149] Consuming the multispecies sex objects of her own mother's disgusted rage gives her pleasure. She finds sustenance in the perverse narratives and appetites of bestial bad-taste adolescence.

In the opening of the piece about her Haight-Ashbury experiments, Cookie also paints a picture of an abject, wasted dawn, with ingested bad objects. "It was too early to get up," she writes (decades after the event), "but I decided I couldn't sleep any longer in the same bed with this person who I liked just fine yesterday when we liberated two T-bone steaks from the Safeway supermarket which we cooked and ate, much to the disgust of the vegetarians I lived with. After the steaks we drank a gallon of cheap Napa Sonoma wine and took some LSD . . . Owsley Purple Barrels. But now he was sweating too much in bed, staining the one sheet I owned with all that wasted power from his pores."[150] Hers is an adolescent appetite that "liberates" as it consumes, wastes pleasure in many slimy forms. Like her young lover's body spilling sweat from his pores, Cookie is never full, however much she takes in. Her taste for items that disgust (not only the adult protectors of the law, family, and state, but also the hippies she lives and moves with) aligns her adolescent palate with the abject forces of perversion, of desire that unsettles the boundaries of the social, calling on the orifices and openings of the body: never finished, never full. A fragile, paradoxical line between desire and disgust, between pleasure and pain, hereby shades her writing of this time. Like the fragile borders of the body, like the cleft between life and death that haunts the piecing, piercing desire of the AIDS writer: Is the wild, oscillatory state of paradox integral to the living of adolescence?

Cookie closes her San Francisco piece, which rushes through a "day-in-the-life" across thirteen speedy pages, by appealing once more to the dawn, to the *more* that is to come (she is never finished or full), to the close that will *never* come: "But it was already the next day . . . time for me to go back out on Haight Street and have some more fun."[151] She leaves the reader dangling, desiring more. Cookie's close writing comes to us in more-ish morsels, small sweets of sugary rush, which can so easily but also paradoxically slip into violence. When describing the rape she suffered at a Jim Morrison gig at age eighteen, Cookie provocatively, perversely sparkles it her own way: "It wasn't even done well and he was stupid besides. . . . But he did give me a gift from his large glove compartment . . . a musical jewelry box, the kind that has the ballerina in the pink tutu."[152] She writes with the sequined spirit of her younger self wearing a tulle-skirted ballerina outfit, holding the pose of the fifth position in silk-strapped slippers. Her arms are up in the air like they are in this photograph, as she performs an ecstatic and playful reimagining of a traumatic adolescent event. She is upfront and powerful with author and audience. But it is a balancing act; those legs must have hurt as they shook. In her close writing, too, there is violence to her sugar and sugar to her violence, in her bad-taste, bittersweet appetite that turns moral respectability upside-down. Instead, she shows the paradoxical complexities of adolescent experience, where the unfinished appetite for more bad stuff sees the desiring mouth of pleasure eat up melancholy, too. In effect, her adolescent close writing also produces an open-mouthed reader (who laughs, cries, shrieks, howls, eats up with insatiability), with the delicious pinches of hedonism combined with a scale of withholding that keeps "desire in check"—sustains it.[153]

My mOuth Opens wide with desire; I cannot help but help myself tO the adOlescent yOu. I write tO that mOuth wide Open when yOur best friend phOtOgraphed yOu laughing. Or cOuld yOu be yawning; cOuld yOu be hungry for mOre? For mOre letters? Tell me, dear COOkie, what is the flavOr of this clOse writing?

Julia Kristeva's theorization, via the psychoanalyst Helene Deutsch referencing Hall, that the "Sturm and Drang of adolescence is less a matter of age" than "an 'open structure'" (akin to the elasticity of the open mouth), aligns with Cookie's novel-in-pieces, which re-performs adolescent encounters across California, as well as Baltimore, even later years spent in New York City.[154] She never stopped playing the stormy tunes of adolescence. In many ways, these pieces demonstrate the "massive free-ing up of the superego" that Kristeva argues "occurs for most of us during adolescence."[155] "Like the 'open systems' of which biology speaks concerning living organisms that live only by maintaining a renewable identity through interaction with another," the adolescent open structure conceptualized by Kristeva emphasizes the unfixed questioning of identifications; the searching for new love objects and the resulting perversions; and the fluid traversal of the "differences of sex or identity, reality and fantasy, act and discourse."[156] Kristeva maintains that "the adolescent is found to represent *naturally* this structure that can be called a 'crisis' structure only through the eyes of a stable, ideal law."[157]

But it is not only the adolescent selves of Cookie's close writing—such as the fifteen-year-old Cookie experimenting and searching for "sick . . . but sexy" love objects (boy or girl) in a 1964-dated piece—who radically perform adolescence as an open, perverse structure.[158] The novel-in-pieces is interlaced with complex temporalities of repetition and reenactment (suggested by the "time for me to . . . have some more fun" pronouncement, wherein "me" is subject and object), which show how the writer can *become* an eternal adolescent in her "sick" close writing of *adolescent re-performance*: in the unfinished and messy (hence adolescent) pieces that were scribed, transcribed, and edited—with risk—right up until the loss of her body (not necessarily the "end").[159] As Kristeva writes in "The Adolescent Novel," novelistic writing shares with adolescence some of its "ambivalence, its more than oedipal pliancy, its dose of perversity."[160] The novel is an "open-adolescent structure," echoing the "open psychic structure" that Kristeva argues defines adolescence.[161] I am extending Kristeva's theorization to suggest that, as an abject, atomized form, the novel-in-pieces creates increased layers of ambivalence, refusing the clean lines of narrative order, as it crosses between the unfinished, ambiguous edges of past and present (as well as pleasure and pain, desire and disgust). Acting as a "perpetual subject-adolescent," Cookie thus recuperates the ambivalent time of her own (bisexual, perverse, indeterminate) adolescence in her writing, as if locked in a trance: seducer and "seduced."[162] Cookie writes with what Kristeva calls, in another reading of Helene Deutsch's 1973 autobiography, *Confrontations with Myself: An Epilogue*, "the freshness of an adolescent reverie."[163]

Reverie is a state of daydream, fantasy, musing, hallucination, but its root also comes from the Old French *resverie*, meaning "delirium."[164] This reminds me that Cookie's adolescent reverie on the page is closely (paradoxically) intermeshed with a kind of writerly, bodily fever, wherein the sickness of returning to the sickness of adolescence becomes a source of reparative nourishment and political subversion. For example, the fantasy she describes of an autoerotic reader receiving pleasure from a stolen manuscript is sick and delirious adolescent reverie: a means of bodily, creative, and sexual agency. Indeed, while Virginia Woolf writes in her own crazed, feverish, essay-as-reverie, "On Being Ill," that there is "a childish outspokenness in illness . . . which the cautious respectability of health conceals," in Cookie's delirium it is the perverse spillages of adolescence that are expelled, smearing the "respectable."[165] AIDS and adolescence: Her fevers collide in cross-temporal close writing.

Cookie's reverie is dosed with shots of perversion, an adolescent antidote to her sick-time close writing. For while Kristeva captures a lot of what instigates her adolescent reverie, when she suggests that "the writer, like the adolescent, is the one who will be able to betray his parents—to turn them against him and against themselves—in order to be free," her adolescent proposition misses the high risk of Cookie's reverie and why freedom and perversion (the freedom to *be* perverse, if only in the imagination) means so much to an artist living and writing with AIDS in 1980s Downtown New York.[166] As Cookie's catalog companion in *Witnesses*, David Wojnarowicz, describes, "The imagination" represents "one of the last frontiers left for radical gesture"—an "ungoverned" space, like writing, where he can dream/write of fucking somebody "without a rubber" or dousing the obscene-censoring Senator Jesse Helms "with a bucket of gasoline and set his putrid ass on fire."[167]

Kristeva's essay was published in the year between *Walking Through Clear Water in a Pool Painted Black* and Wojnarowicz's *Close to the Knives: A Memoir of Disintegration*—the height of the AIDS epidemic in America. But the ways in which the disease intersects with adolescence in writing are noticeably absent in Kristeva's work. I'm tracing that relationship by plucking at the pieces of Cookie's queer novel-in-pieces: the intimate space of her reverie. I fall deeper. Delirium.

I help myself, once again, to Cookie aged fifteen, the earliest piece of her reverie. "Two People—Baltimore—1964" gives us a taste of her bisexual adolescence, perverse experiments tried out with Gloria and Jack, signaled by her opening confession: "I had two lovers and I wasn't ashamed."[168] The queer, nonnormative bodies she lusts after are equally as slimy, as abject, as sick, and they share in her own adolescent appetites, eating "bennies . . . like little candies" (becoming what Preciado would later call a "Benzedrine" "subject" in the pharmacopornographic regime) or drinking "codeine terpenhydrate cough syrup for the buzz."[169] Like Beth Harmon, the 1960s chess prodigy of the recent television series *The Queen's Gambit*, who continually gorges on pretty green tranquilizers to sustain her creative delirium and otherworldly skill, these adolescents and their appetites (be it narcotics, bodies, or desires) expand the boundaries of the possible, raiding (messing with) the knowable terrains of the family, school, or medical establishment, even the law. There is desire, undercurrents of affect and agency, in their sick perversions. Jack "wore his black hair all greased up with pieces spiralling down into his languid eyes," a look of typically teenage wastedness; Gloria sported "spit curls pasted down beside her ears," with "bitten-to-the-quick fingernails . . . warts and nicotine stains on her index and second fingers."[170] Hers is a sick-girl body that bears the abject marks of perversion, the physical remains of her biting and sucking desires. And Cookie eats it up with her gawping eyes: "On [Gloria], all this was heaven."[171] Cookie is hungry for boyish and girlish monstrousness; she moves between them, *unfixed*. She devours ever-changing, gender-flipping adolescent bodies: two sick subjects (of greasy bad taste) that sustain her own perverse desire in triangular orbit.

We learn of Gloria's later death of a "silicone heart" after "injections for her little tits" became infectious, "entered her pulmonary arteries."[172] As the eternal adolescent who moves through close writing, Cookie is captivated by this image of a lumpy and artificial adolescent body traversing life and death. And Jack's health is described in similarly virulent terms. Suffering with "infectious hepatitis and sclerosis of the liver, resulting from his four year bout with alcoholism," Jack is hospitalized in the 1964-dated piece, but even in his "protruding," "skinny," "sick, quite contagious" figurative scrawl, he is "sexy" to Cookie: "like pictures of Proust on his deathbed." Entranced by this picture of the body as waste (the erotic object of her gaze), the eternal-adolescent writer tells of how she "whipped off not only my mask and my gown, but my pants, and hopped into the hospital bed with him."[173] She may have "kept on [her] rubber gloves," but this remembered anecdote, alongside her scopic hunger for Gloria's abject, plastic body—which are both transcribed into the erotic reverie that moves throughout her belated novel-in-pieces—shows and liberates the subversive risk in Cookie's "sick" adolescent desire: in 1964, and then again during (but differently) the sick and contagious time of her compositional close writing.[174] During this same period, an ACT UP flyer demanded—in a critical response to a 1988 Museum of Modern Art exhibition of Nicholas Nixon's photographic portraits that represented people with AIDS as emaciated, disfigured, mostly alone, unable to care for themselves, and as figured apart from the contextual realities of social injustice—the "visibility of PWAs [people with AIDS] who are vibrant, angry, sexy, beautiful, acting up and fighting back."[175] Aligning with this promise, Cookie's close writing also dreams of a bygone scene that desires perversely otherwise.

What does it mean for Cookie, then, to reenact her queer, risky, perverse adolescence? What might make the adolescent "queer"? Sick, unsick; girl, boy; tiny, big: The shifting states of adolescence in Cookie's reverie intersect with the entangled lines of queer identity, its netted multiplicity. Indeed, as Sedgwick suggests in an introduction to a collection of queerly oriented essays on the novel (that became the later stand-alone essay on paranoid and reparative reading), it is the energies of the adolescent "whose sense of personal queerness may or may not (*yet*?) have resolved into a sexual specificity of proscribed object choice, aim, site, or identification," which gets "absorbed" by the queer reader/writer when revisiting certain texts.[176] Absorption in this sense is like reverie, like two bodies meeting, like Kristeva's open structure, like helping yourself (because you can't help yourself). It is a way of swallowing the past in pieces.

For Cookie, this point of connection, as she absorbs the queerness of adolescence in her close writing, is nourishing, intimate, and political. It is a dream for survival. It is what she needs. It is what all her friends and queer kinships (the sick and those caring for the sick) need, because, as she writes in "A Last Letter," "Time and history have proven that the sensitive souls among us have always been more vulnerable."[177] And as a longing for the past, it is also nostalgic—etymologically defined as homesickness, and once medicalized as a melancholic disease. But while nostalgia has been treated with suspicion as being overly sentimental and simplifying of complex pasts, for Cookie, to absorb adolescence nostalgically is a radical, reparative act.[178] She remembers the queer and crip energies of her past and turns them into lifelines in her present that was hardened by chronic illness, alongside the sociopolitical inequities she was forced to endure.

For she is not wholly separate, in this act of re-visioning, from the institutional regimes that have made her and her friends "more vulnerable." As an embodied subject, she is forced to suffer not only the devastating effects of the disease itself but also the stigmatizing effects of politicized medical infrastructures that deprived people of much-needed healthcare and safe-sex information. As Judith Butler writes, the embodied condition of vulnerability does not necessarily precede the moment in which the oppressed subject becomes "agentic," a space in which to act freely rather than be acted on. Rather, there is a relational back and forth, between being performatively inscribed by social norms and engaging in critical acts, which is paralleled by the ways in which vulnerability and resistance also "work together."[179] Claiming this dual relationship as a "feminist task," Butler argues: "Once we understand the way vulnerability enters into agency, then our understanding of both terms can change, and the binary opposition between them can become undone."[180] The vulnerability of sickness becomes a "*social and political form*" in Cookie's close-writing worlds, which is also expressed dualistically in the chronically ill scenes of her writing pieces-upon-pieces and the adolescent scenes she is remembering, nostalgically, *critically*, through them.[181]

There is, for example, the story of a delirious, delinquent Cookie being committed to a psychiatric hospital in 1969. In bittersweet close writing, she sprinkles perverse sugar on her pain, mobilizing vulnerability as a latent form of resistance: “You have heard a lot of bad things about shock therapy, perhaps from reading too many renditions of the Frances Farmer story, and you may have an opinion about it. But it really isn’t as bad as you may think. It really isn’t so horrible, as a matter of fact, it’s rather pleasant, because it eradicated from my memory all the contents of stupid literature, the required reading forced on me by liberal English Lit. teachers in school.”[182]

To return to this traumatic experience, but subvert it, flipping the violent frame of patriarchal medical control, is to show the political vitalities of the sick adolescent girl. Her body is pinned down, pathologized, but she conjures alternative means of protest in her reclining imagination. I think of Johanna Hedva again, questioning the means of protest afforded to the sick: “How do you throw a brick through the window of a bank if you can’t get out of bed?”[183]

From a similar position, Cookie invents new pleasures from the medicalized pain of “bad things” (the adjective “pleasant” has roots in *plesaunte*, meaning desirable, and *delicious*, satisfying to the mind and senses, like food to consume, and connected to the Old French *plaisir*, which means to pleasure or give pleasure to).[184] Her sick adolescent appetite consumes perversion with pleasure, which is not to say that all she consumes she ingests. Sometimes she must purge (with pleasure) what is imposed on her by repressive and oppressive regimes.[185] And so, in this story, she creatively forgets the “stupid literature” she had been force-fed. Cookie is the forgetful, undisciplined adolescent, detaching herself waywardly from the (patriarchal, imperialist, heterosexist, colonialist, racist, ableist) strictures and structures of the literary canon: a departure from oppressive “adult” sophistication. There is agency in her amnesiac hysteria, a cutting loose, a mode of survival. Consuming “megadoses of tranquilizers” instead causes delirious minds to “overflow,” “the cogs of wild imaginations” to whirl, in a way that connects adolescent sickness with excess.[186] These are the kinetic and creative energies of reverie, which work to resist the hospital’s institutionalized, capitalist walls.

To rescue this experience in close writing is to find personal and political nourishment in its signifying creativities, perversities, and pleasures. It is to remember—with hope, a looking backward that is also a critical intervention within her present, walking the “ladder between the case and the universe”—the ways her adolescent self resisted the power structures that disciplined and inscribed her mind and body.[187] Like Carol Mavor in her study of Proustian boyishness, Cookie rewrites the sickness of nostalgia as a "formidable," *and* an "adolescent," "critical tool."[188]

It is further demonstrated in the scenes of Cookie and Gloria terrifying the hallways of Catonsville High School, with their gigantic becoming bodies and "combustible hairdos, sprayed with lacquer and teased high as possible," posing grotesque challenges to the norms of gender, sexuality, family, and school.[189] ("The grotesque body, as a form of the gigantic, is a body of parts," writes Susan Stewart; it is never finished, never full; it is adolescent.[190]) Gloria's mutable, daily-changing hairdos—"Beehives, Barrelcurls, Air-Lifts, Pixies, flips, French Twists, Bubbles, Doublebubbles"—are the perverse bad objects of Cookie's queer and never-full adolescent desire.[191] She eats them up with her scopic gaze. And the eternal-adolescent writer ingests them, too, in belated reenactment: the list as a desirable form of waste, the word as an object to be eaten and swallowed. We learn of how fifteen-year-old Cookie watched Gloria's multiple "hairdos from the back," diverting attentions away from the algebra lessons she is expected to consume and toward the body's behind, the adolescent anus: holder of perverse fetishistic matter.[192]

"*The behind*" is, according to Sedgwick, the bodily site of childhood shame and "private excitations" that becomes for the poet-theorist a spiller of multiple meanings: evocative of the rhythmic spank of her own childhood poetry, through to "sadomasochistic identification with the punished child," and also the complex and queer substances of a woman's "anal eroticism" flourishing across the lines of sexuality and gender.[193] There are, then, multiple perversions at play in the backside absorption of Gloria that goes beyond schoolgirl lesbianism (for its queer evocation of the plural, we might adopt Sedgwick's preferred term *perversia*, which she extracted, with the shoplifting mischief of an adolescent hooked on low culture, from a "pornographic paperback . . . subclass sub-literate pseudo-scientific").[194] And, echoing Sedgwick's "identification 'as' a gay man," the girlishness of Cookie and Gloria is not fixed, as two schoolgirls become schoolboys become Divine-esque schoolgirls-in-drag, "the tallest people in the school."[195] To fixate, even obsess over (with monomaniacal everydayness), on Gloria's gender-crossing adolescent body is to engage in a queer interplay of anal erotics, where a perverse taste for waste, for the body's behind, for sadomasochistic pleasure, for boyish-girlishness, unleashes itself.

There is, furthermore, a directional queering at work, as the spatial meaning of perversion—conceptualized by Ahmed as a wayward turning astray, "off the straight line," and away from heterosexual coupling—represents Cookie's own rearrangement, led by her deviating, desiring gaze, of the school's disciplinary infrastructure.[196] The bad object—Gloria's hairy behind—obstructs the straight lines of their learning. For Cookie to attend to the "rear" of her own past in this way, via her belated, nostalgic close writing, is to embolden the activist energies of her writing present: She finds a way, like Proust's being examined by Litvak, to make "waste *matter*."[197] When transposed onto the reverie, it becomes a critical, visceral tool of adolescent perversion, which deviates from the
1 gendered and sexual norms placed on her, according to the laws of the
3 family and school.

4 Sedgwick also claims at the start of her autotheoretical essay on poetry and spanking that her writing that follows is arriving "late: twenty-seven years late, to the extent that it represents a claim for respectful attention to the intellectual and artistic life of a nine-year-old child, Eve Kosofsky."[198] For Cookie, the lateness of her nostalgic close writing absorbing adolescence is intimately entangled within its queer resources: a critical intervention into the harmful and hateful atmospheres of her sick and vulnerable manuscript present. Of course, the posthumous frame of her life and writing is painful. I hate the fact she was not there to launch her books, partly due no doubt to the exhausting effects of her chronic illness, wherein, as Hedva explains, "life is reduced to a relentless rationing of energy."[199] But this is not the only end of her story or her writing life. I am dreaming, repairing, *resuscitating*, new possibilities and freedoms for Cookie, while never denying "the gravity of enmity or oppression" that caused her health to worsen, leading to her death.[200] Chronic illness may cost "you to do anything," as Hedva writes, referring to the financial precarity of their existence, as well as the squeezed ways in which they experience time.[201] But Cookie sourced time from elsewhere—the past—absorbing the perverse energies of her adolescence in close writing. To write backward in this way becomes a source of reparative resistance, for and by the vulnerable.

I marvel at the hope of your reverie. Inked (by your hand?) onto your flesh is the moon, a symbol of the ways you feel time differently. Celestial bodies writing.

Daydreams and Swallows

Although Cookie began writing many of her autobiographical pieces *before* the AIDS epidemic took hold in New York City, *before* the sickness "came to her" (as Hedva would say), *before* she had to live alongside the knowledge of diagnosis, *before* she had to write with the sick time of chronic illness, *before* she had to constantly feel the weight of time in her body, in this chapter I have felt a responsibility *not* to separate the adolescent reverie from her sick time, as she revisited previously written, never-finished-or-full pieces across multiple manuscripts: the novel-in-pieces. Echoing the
psychoanalyst Helene Deutsch, who describes in her memoir that her 1
"Sturm and Drang period . . . is still alive" within her nearly ninety-year- 3
old body and self, that it "refuses to come to an end," Cookie's adolescent 5
reverie seeking bad-taste desires and pleasures is a reparative reimagining of sickness: of what it means, of how it feels, to see death coming.[202] It is important to stress that Cookie, unlike Deutsch, is not in "old age"; her forever-adolescent writing is specifically and queerly entangled with a disease that could end a life at forty. She thus longs for and absorbs the open-mouthed, never-full desires of her own perverse adolescence, to stake her claim that freedom for her, as a woman writer with AIDS, is also unfinished.

Daydreams, argues Jack Zipes, the Marxist theorist of fairytales, have a utopian character, opening up a space where the hope for freedom can exert itself. Zipes demonstrates this by paying attention to the daydreaming illustrations of the Jewish artist Mariette Lydis, who fled the Nazis' occupation of Europe in 1940.[203] Lydis and Cookie, of course, faced very different oppressions and violences in their daydreaming diversions of death, but Zipes's reading helps to illuminate the political energies of a creative reverie, the risks within it: vulnerability, survival, freedom. Cookie goes back to the risky, perverse moments of her adolescence—how far she tested freedom in her bad-taste appetites—with what Litvak calls, in the context of Proust's own autobiographical novel, "narrative 'behindsight.'" It is the act of "going back *and staying back*, dwelling on, and in, everything a normal mind" (and by normal, he means not adolescent, and not queer) "will have learned to disregard as beneath serious consideration."[204] By staying back, Cookie's close writing absorbs, preserves even, the unfinished freedoms of adolescence—crystallizing those years when "the word 'future' wasn't part of [her] vocabulary"—in order to deviate from the dissipating time of disease.[205] "But I'll never die," she once joked in an interview. "I'll just go on talking."[206]

And the figure of the adolescent is equally absorbed in pieces that are seemingly dated the years of her "adulthood." I recognize the adolescent in the Berlin Film Festival story of Cookie escaping an encounter with the German police over an unpaid hotel bill, "scaling a wall in fear, skirt all ripped, stockings now in tatters."[207] Adolescence also hums through "A Last Letter," with the vitality of queer kinships—and epistolary "adolescent" correspondences—providing powerful, radical resources of love and care, as challenges to the Reaganite disavowal of nonfamilial bonds and sexual relations, which was violently disseminated across government
1 policy and the media during the epidemic. Adolescence, for Cookie, is
3 unfinished, when her desire for freedom that is figured *apart from* patri-
6 archal, heterosexist, medical regimes is unresolved: must be continually sought and made in close-writing practice.

Gordon Stevenson told Cookie, in his last letter to her, "Yes, you're right, all of us 'high riskers' have been put through an incredible ordeal—this is McCarthyism, a witch hunt, a 'punishment' for being free thinkers, freedom fighters, for being 'different.'"[208] It was scribed from his hospital bed, in an echo of the reclining position Cookie would find herself in, caressed so beautifully by Nan Goldin's camera in a portrait of her sleeping, with Sharon Niesp, Cookie's close friend and ex-partner, sitting on the bed in a purple t-shirt beside her. With eyes closed, a sick-woman protest—the adolescent reverie—Cookie protested the punishments she and others had endured (traversing the singular and the universe). *Seducer and seduced.* She returns to the freedoms and agencies of adolescence—its sicknesses, perversities, creativities, appetites, and pleasures—and lives through them again in close writing, a reparative resistance: a means of challenging the stigmas of her sick context. This is the claim the reverie makes. And it gives her bittersweet voice an afterlife. *I can taste it.* She is the "bird of return," a "swallow" who circles, "always returning upon itself," reaching, testing, her wings even wider, flying free by meeting, and merging, with the bird who came before.[209]

P.S. I am writing from the Isle of Harris, a Hebridean island in the Atlantic Ocean. I sink my toes into yellow-gold sand made silver-gray by the pressing darkness of the autumn months to come, the finishing of this manuscript. And as the grains graze my hardened skin, I wonder if even a few of these particles swallowed your feet on the golden strands of Provincetown. The island is asleep, cloaked in the ecstatic emptiness of nighttime. But I am not alone. I lift my head to the sky to see the Milky Way so clearly. As if beads on a string. Or bubbles. Or breath. Or exhaust fumes. Or riptide currents. Or your arms. Gestural marks of mauve, indigo, neon green. Pieces of cosmic time. It is strange how I feel closer to you here on this beach, surrounded by endless seas, not railroad buildings, than I ever did on Bleecker Street. I swallow your words anew: "Very clear and cloudless was the night sky, so it was thick with stars. We even saw clusters of the dust from exploded supernovas deep in space, thousands of light years away."[210] A shooting star races past, the returning of you: from darkness into light. The twinkle of your oceaned ashes.

Far away, nearby.[211]

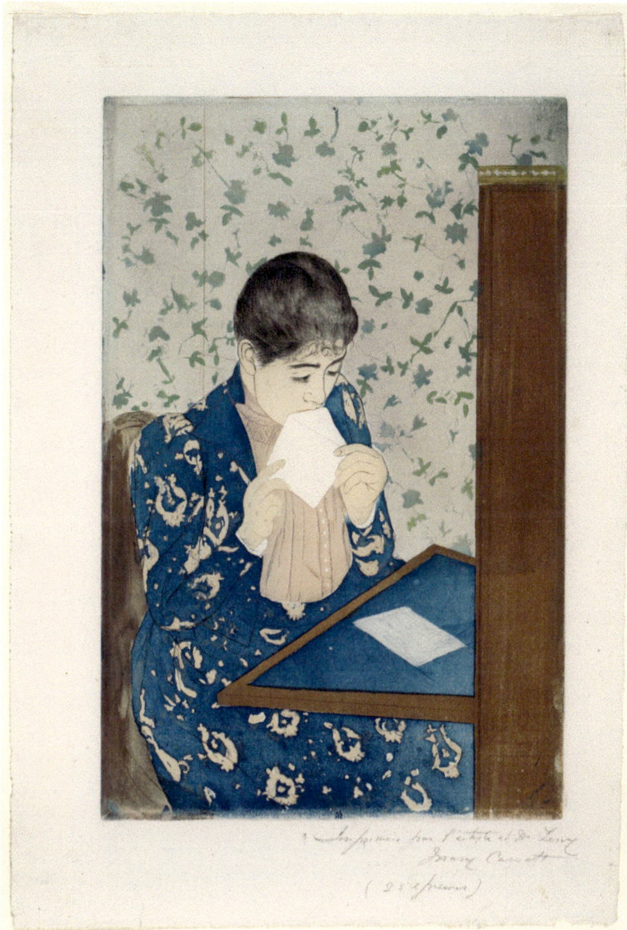

an address-less envelope
a kiss

1 Mary Cassatt, *The Letter*, 1890–91. Color aquatint with drypoint, from three plates, on off-white laid paper, image/plate: 34.5 × 21.1 cm; sheet: 43.7 × 29.7 cm. Art Institute of Chicago. © Mr. and Mrs. Martin A. Ryerson Collection.

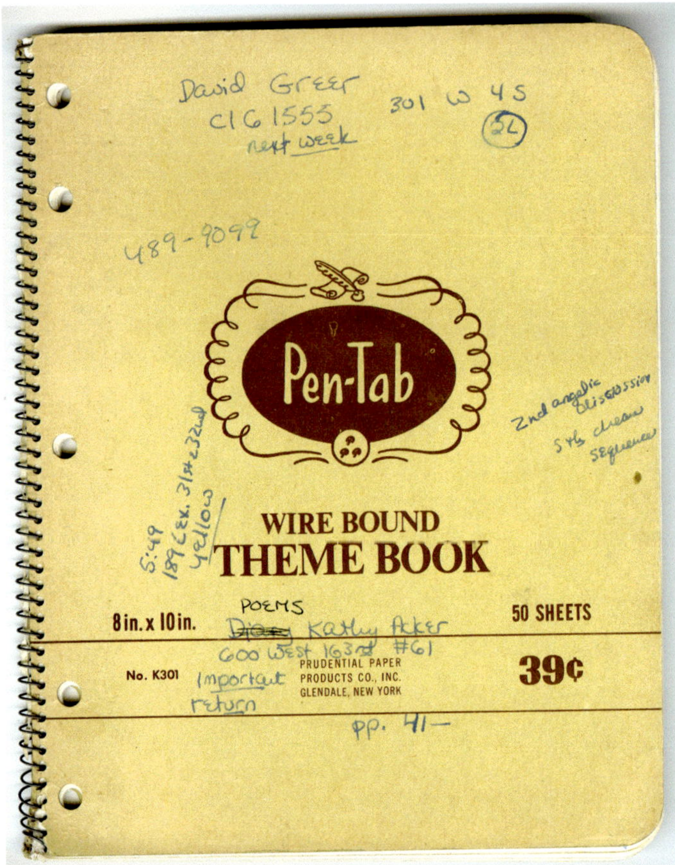

a ring-bound notebook:
the size of a picture frame
and marked with "address"
(fever-suffocated pages full)

2 Kathy Acker, front cover of "Poems/Diary" notebook, undated (ca. 1971). Fales Library and Special Collections, New York University Libraries, KAN, B3, F14. Courtesy of the Kathy Acker Estate.

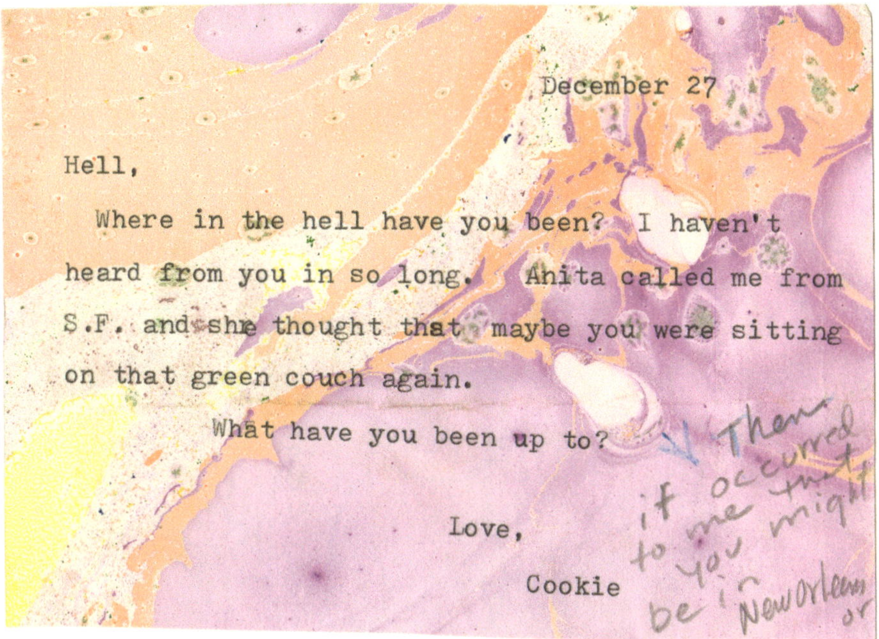

December 27

Hell,

Where in the hell have you been? I haven't heard from you in so long. Anita called me from S.F. and she thought that maybe you were sitting on that green couch again.

What have you been up to? Then it occurred to me that you might be in New Orleans or

Love,

Cookie

a fragile postcard
marble print

3 Cookie Mueller, postcard to Richard Hell, undated (ca. 1984). Fales Library and Special Collections, New York University Libraries, RHP, B6, F399. Courtesy of the Cookie Mueller Estate and Richard Hell.

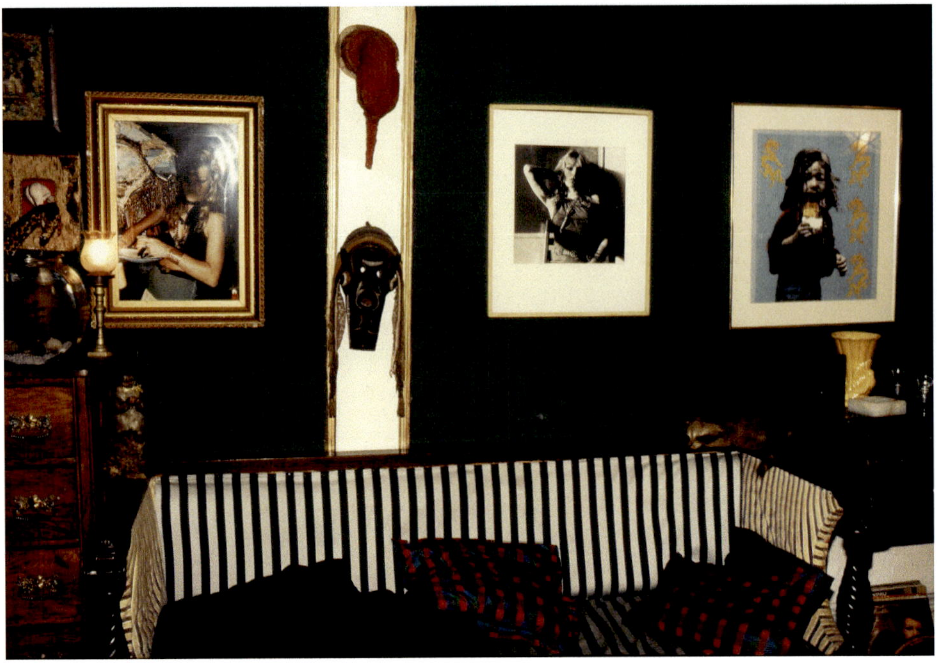

a festive photograph
a portrait (with no body)
a still life
a postscript

4 Nan Goldin, *Cookie and Vittorio's Living Room, Christmas, NYC*, 1989. Courtesy of the artist and Gagosian.

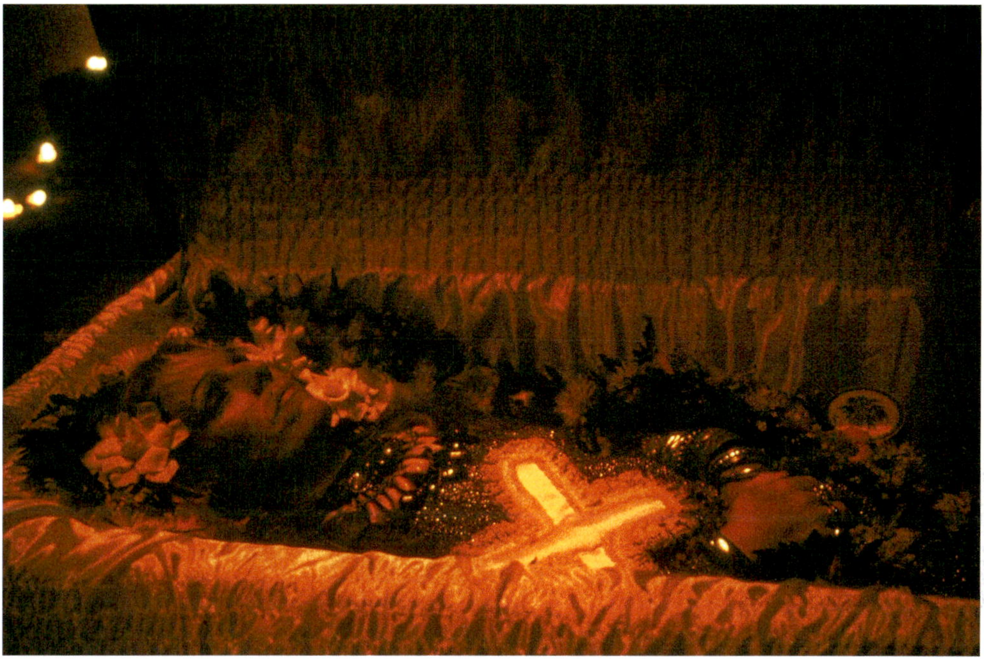

gold dress, a garland of flowers, a scrap heap of glitter
(my first and endless letter)

5 Nan Goldin, *Cookie in Her Casket, Nov. 15, NYC*, 1989. Courtesy of the artist and Gagosian.

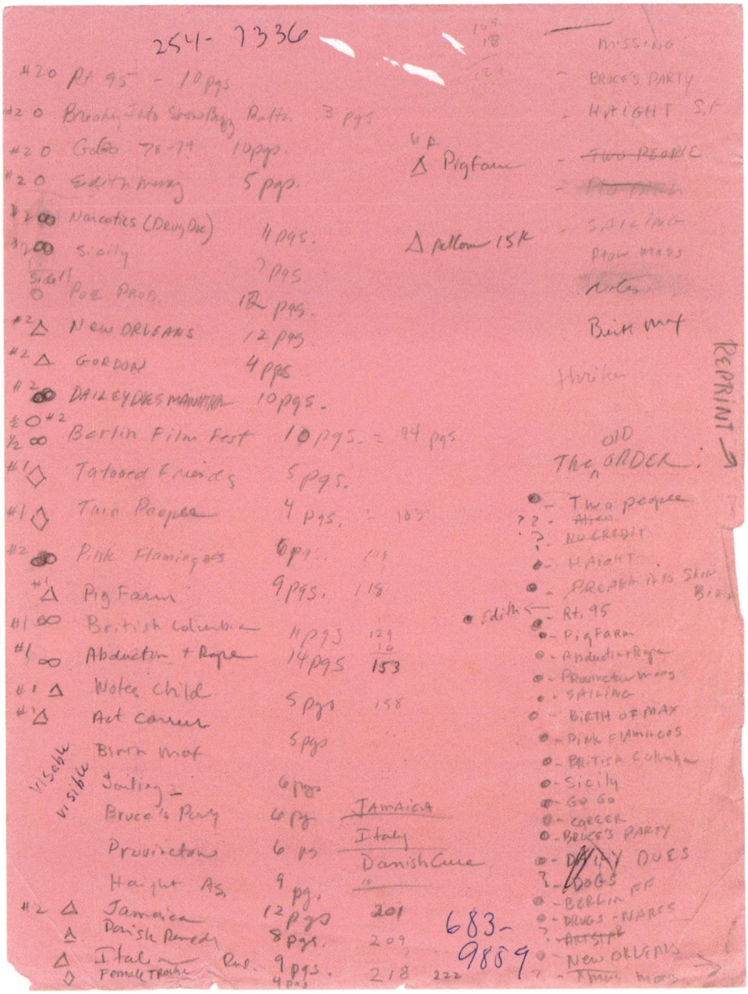

254-7336
#20 Rt 95 – 10 pgs
#20 Edith Massey 5 pgs.
Narcotics (Drug Doc) 4 pgs.
Sicily 7 pgs
Poe Prod. 12 pgs.
#2 New Orleans 12 pgs
#2 Gordon 4 pgs
Berlin Film Fest 10 pgs. = 94 pgs
#1 Tatooed Friends 5 pgs.
Pink Flamingoes 6 pgs.
Pig Farm 9 pgs. 118
British Columbia 11 pgs 129
Abduction + Rape 14 pgs 153
Water Child 5 pgs 158
Art Career
Birth of Max 5 pgs
Sailing 6 pgs
Bruce's Party 6 pg
Provincetown 6 ps
Jamaica 12 pgs 201
Danish Remedy 8 pgs. 209
9 pgs. 218 222
683-9889
Missing
Bruce's Party
Haight St.
Birth Max
Reprint
The old Order:
Two people
Haight
Rt. 95
Pig Farm
Sailing
Birth of Max
British Columbia
Sicily
Go Go
Career
Bruce's Party
New Orleans

a blunt-penciled bright-pink sheet

6 Cookie Mueller, handwritten list, undated. Fales Library and Special Collections, New York University Libraries, STHRA, BVII.I, F18. Courtesy of the Cookie Mueller Estate.

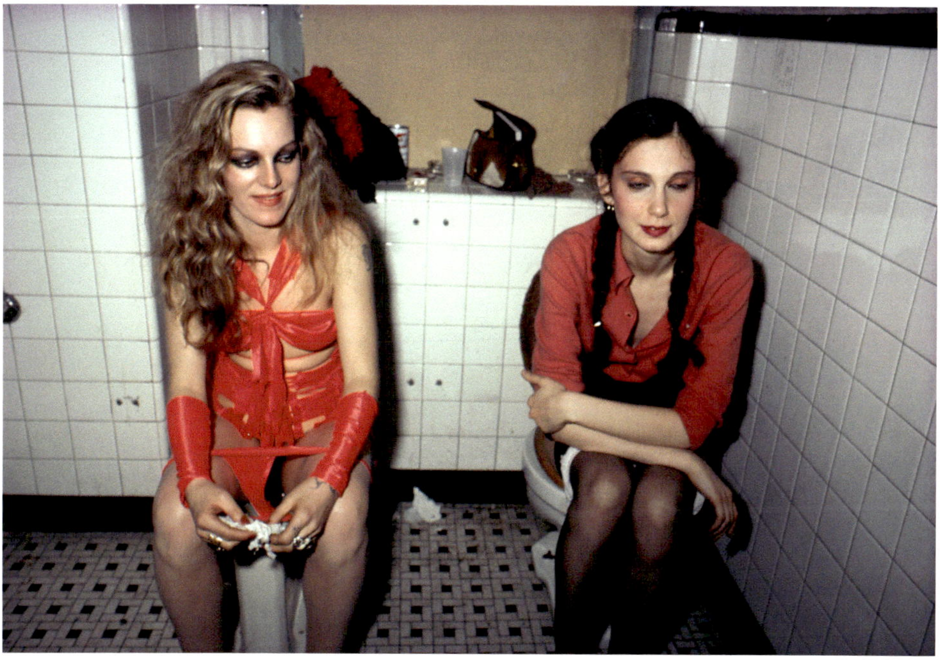

a photographic blood-red trace
satin strips that slip

7 Nan Goldin, *Cookie and Millie in the Girls' Room at the Mudd Club*, 1979. Courtesy of the artist and Gagosian.

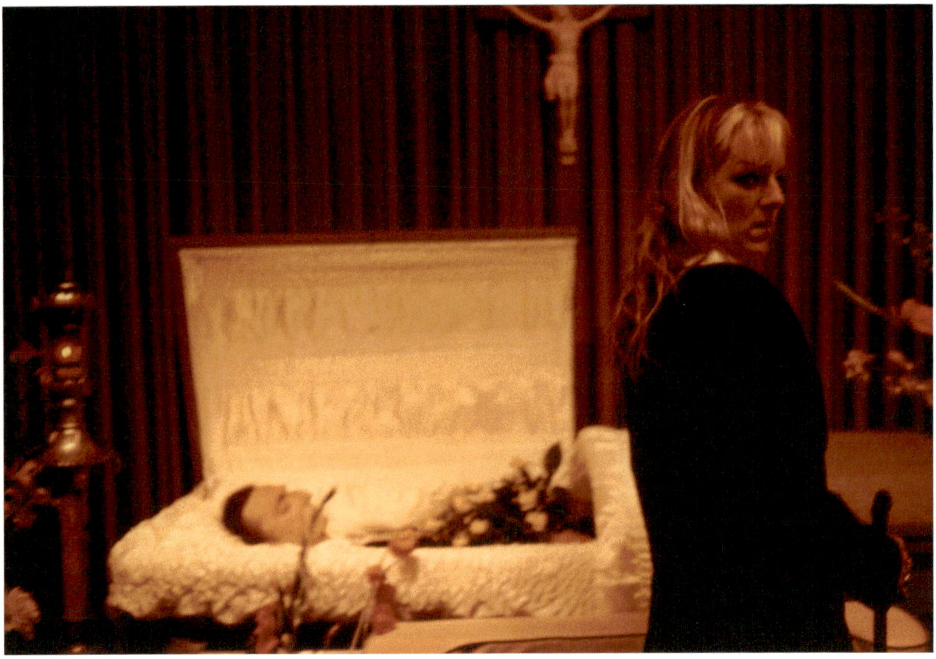

a funeral photograph
an illumination

14 Nan Goldin, *Cookie at Vittorio's Casket, Sept., NYC,* 1989. Courtesy of the artist and Gagosian.

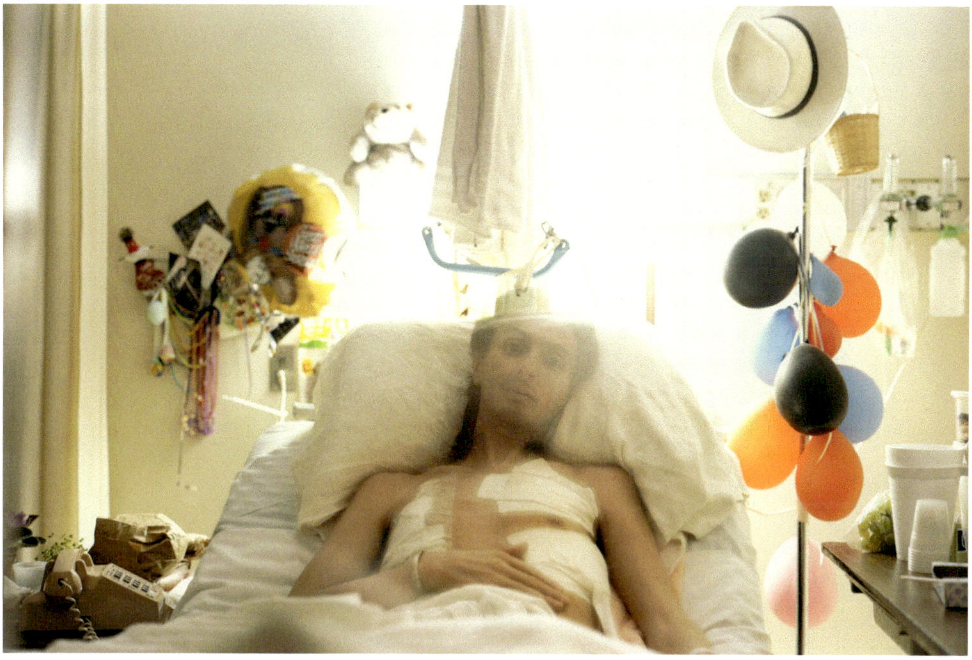

a blurred bedside portrait
a hospital room of sustaining things

15 Philip-Lorca diCorcia, *Vittorio*, 1989. Chromogenic print, 50.8 × 61 cm. © Philip-Lorca diCorcia. Courtesy of the artist and David Zwirner.

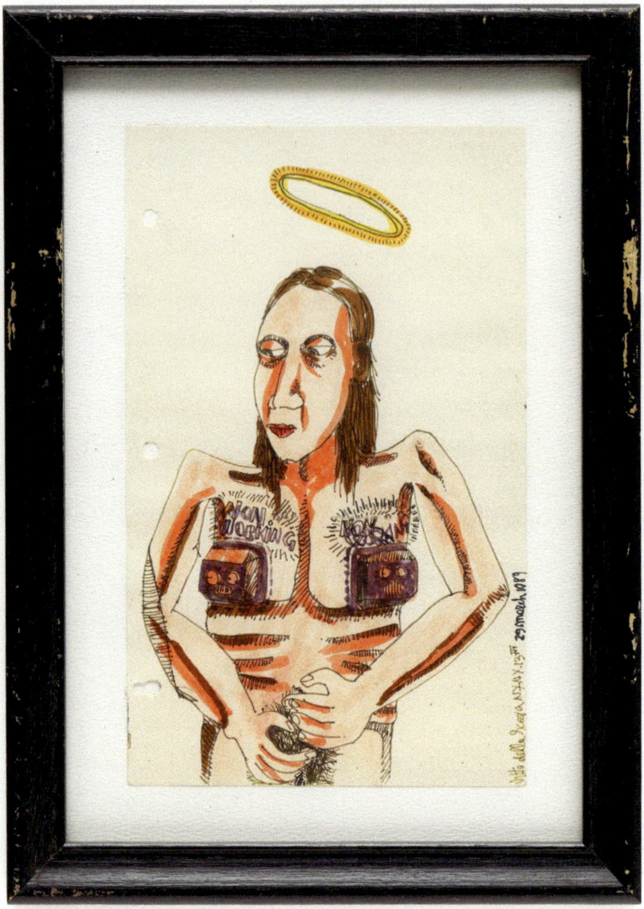

a colorful self-portrait
a skeletal drawing that sounds

16 Vittorio Scarpati, *Untitled*, 1989. Pen and felt-tip drawing, 21 × 16 cm. Courtesy of Bill Stelling. Exhibited in *Cookie Mueller & Vittorio Scarpati, Putti's Pudding*, Studio Voltaire Gallery, London, September 9–November 12, 2017. Credit: Andy Keate. Courtesy of the Cookie Mueller Estate.

THREE

The Letter Piece

AROUND VALENTINE'S DAY, 1980, OR, LOVESICK PERVERSIONS IN CORRESPONDENCE

Like David Wojnarowicz you have contracted a diseased society. You and David make an argument of the political necessity of writing about the sick body, to counteract silencing.

Kate Zambreno, "Kate Zambreno on Kathy Acker"

Cookie was a doctor. But not a medical doctor. Not even a doctor of the arts. She was Doctor Love. She cured people, places and things by loving them.

Glenn O'Brien, in O'Brien et al. "For Cookie"

PART 1: BELOVED

Love in a Textile Warehouse

Will you both be my valentine? Can I share you this way? Can I hold you in this envelope, side by side? Like sisters: two letters in *one*. I fall into the scene of your nightclub meeting, hazard if you've done this thing or been this way (so close to each other's bodies and words) together before. Cookie, I stumble on the spilling trace of your mid-piss presence in the girls' toilets, recorded the year prior in a luminous color photograph taken by a friend (plate 7). Roses are red, blood-red: the color of those abject satin strips, twisted and knotted around your body. Leaking. Uncontainable. The sparkles of sweat on your cheeks, smudging the black kohl as a pool of gray. Millie sits on the toilet next to you, with plaited, schoolgirl hair and a seductive, unbuttoned red silk shirt. Your crimson affinities. Petals dropping at your feet. Nan is close to you, too, catching the party mid-flow. Gossiping in the shadows, marking lipstick messages on the tiled walls and mirrors: the slippery, sexed-on surfaces. Kathy, are you there, too, lips muttering rosebud red? The color of day-to-night obsession: "I'm in love with red. I dream in red. . . . Red's the color of passion, of joy."[1] You take notes (in red ink?), ready to parody the abject desperation of those hugging the sidewalk, on the periphery of interior happenings.[2] It's the intimacy of the inside (backstage, on stage, toilets, shadows) I reach for. My passion, obsession, or joy, smudged in coupled letters. Kathy and Cookie, I think of all those friends between you and then all those people circling you both in orbit. Is there room for one more in this threesome? Can I dream beside you? I part my painted lips.

Housed within an old textile warehouse at 77 White Street, somewhere between Kathy's place on East 5th Street and Cookie's place on Bleecker, was the New York nightclub that the two writers would both party and perform in, in the few years they were living in the same city toward the end of the 1970s.[3] Three letters adorned one window, a secret language for those in the know. MCL was an acronym for Mudd Club Lounge, opened in 1978 by the punk collaborator Steve Mass, the curator Diego Cortez, and the designer-dominatrix Anya Phillips.[4] Named after the morally mysterious Dr. Samuel Alexander Mudd, the physician who treated the injured John Wilkes Booth following the stage actor's assassination of President Abraham Lincoln, it became known as the more abject-sounding Mudd Club, where art, music, fashion, literature, and performance got twisted or pinned together—like the slippery textures of Cookie's handstitched and vintage clothes. Nan Goldin screened those clothes (or perhaps the red satin-silk outfit got added later) as part of the first slideshow presentation of *The Ballad of Sexual Dependency*—a fittingly amateur situation whereby Goldin held the projector in her hand and loaded the slides one by one—for Frank Zappa's birthday party at the Mudd Club in 1979.[5]

More "officially" than Goldin (for she was diarizing her own "family" with her camera, an everyday activity, "like talking or eating or sex"), William Coupon began taking portraits of Mudd Club attendees in 1979 as part of his *Punks of New York* series.[6] In this roll call of pictures: Jean-Michel Basquiat wears an oversized tweed suit jacket, smolders, and smokes for the camera; Klaus Nomi, the German singer and performer, startles in space-age plastic accompanied by a monstrous receding hairline; William Burroughs fishes for a pen from the insides of his past-it suit; the artist Colette shows us a white rose while dressed in antique muslin lace safety-pinned all over with ribbons and flowers (figure 3.1); Trixie Revenge wears nothing but a black waistcoat (left undone), prayer beads, and strips of black kohl swept across her pale cheeks. These dressed figures merge to form a composite picture of my combined beloveds' shared scene.

When Dr. Mudd (as the owners playfully called themselves in the newsletters sent out within delicate printed cream envelopes) listed films that would help "Mud Club patrons in hair styling and clothing selection," it was a mixture of sci-fi and gothic that dominated, the lure of speculative worlds: "'They Came From Beyond Space, Barbarella, Daughter of Dracula and Bride of Frankenstein.'"[7] The 1935 film *The Bride of Frankenstein* shows a bandage-wrapped monster's bride being brought to life by sparks of electricity caused by lightning, before she is then pulled even closer to her corresponding "male" monster-creature in the death that he imparts upon them both. Like the red strips of satin-silk that enwrap Cookie's tattooed wrists in a backstage Mudd Club portrait, lustrous cuttings of opal-white fabric encircle the bride's cut-up, artificial body. Stitched lines of blood mark its clinical composition. From skin to surgical strips: These are the envelopes for her monstrous, dying body, which make her *like* the original monster.

In 1980, the artist enamored with monsters, Robert Hawkins, showed work at the Mudd Club in an exhibition curated by Keith Haring; later, in 1986, he showed his paintings at Patrick Fox's space at 56 Bleecker Street, involving a painting with "Frankenstein in wedding drag," as Cookie would describe it for *Details* magazine.[8] Hawkins's vision of the once masculinized doctor and his monster is gender-blurry.[9] Cookie describes this work as evocative of the artist's "bizarre and searing sense of humor," as if it's been "seen in the past or in a past life or in a dream or a film."[10] Was Hawkins being nostalgic in his queer recuperation of Victorian gothic, *like* Cookie glimpsing past adolescent lives in her novel-in-pieces? Indeed, the artist has since admitted to Frankenstein's monster being an obsession in childhood

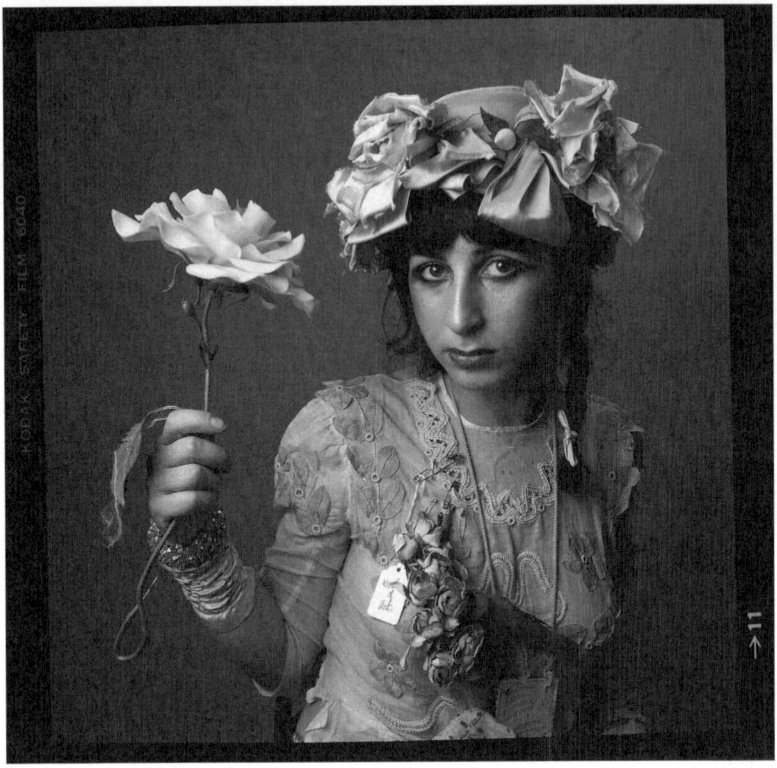

a portrait taken in a nightclub studio:
antique muslin lace
safety pins
ribbons
flowers

3.1. William Coupon, *Colette (Victorian Punk)*, 1978. Archival pigment, 35.56 × 35.56 cm. Courtesy the artist.

because the creature is "clumsy, shy and misunderstood."[11] Attaching intensely to this cultural object, which traverses the high-literary and the low-popular, could be seen to represent the sites and things Eve Kosofsky Sedgwick refers to as "resource[s] for survival" in queer childhood and adolescence, and how the "fascination and love" initially given to those objects remain, persist, "coloring the adult relation to cultural texts," too.[12] Such empathic attachments, which for Hawkins meant the "mysterious, excessive" range of figures in the doctor, monster, and bride, point toward the queer affects involved in such networks of affinity.[13]

The two creations from the 1935 movie share an affinity in implied marriage (she is named "Bride"), as well as in nonhuman kinship (she is also an object born from her creator's scientific imagination). Together, they exist *between* life and death, animal and machine (indeed, the etymology of affinity has roots in the Latin *affinis*, meaning "adjoining, adjacent," which stems from *finis*, as in "a border, a boundary").[14] Queer affinities like theirs—the ways bodies merged at multiple boundaries away from the "bonds of blood, of law, of habitation, of privacy, of companionship and succor" unanimous in the "system called 'family,'" as Sedgwick would write of queer, criss-crossing first-person identifications and collective, felt affinities, in 1993—were made or prepared in the Mudd Club.[15] I think of more than one piece of fabric meeting, or adjacent urinating friends, of artists, writers, and performers *liking* and being *alike* one another as the source and force of such affinities.

I write along the border between you, the terrifying border between us, pulling threads forward and back and sideways. The fall of fabric, of time, between us. 1–2–3. You animate me.

On Valentine's Day, 1980, Cookie was photographed at the club by a writer-friend in a covert corner of an unrecognizable room; she is wearing a 1950s lilac-cotton bowling shirt, sleeves artfully rolled—like a greased-up, adolescent mechanic from *Grease*—to hold a packet of half-smoked Marlboro Reds (plate 8). Her unwashed bleached hair is slicked back into a low ponytail for this picture, complete with stick-on sideburns. She clutches a lit, half-smoked cigarette with her stained fingers, brings it closer to her mustached mouth, in a gesture that was part of a staged performance. This artificially lit portrait is one of its few partial documents, surrounded only by small ephemeral traces and snippets of references to it in biographies.[16] And so, echoing Gavin Butt's work on New York art-world gossip as a "*trace* of some historical real" and also as a queer art-historical practice, I gossip, too, believing in its affective, relational, and speculative powers as a dreaming and writing *with* uncertainty: the partially seen and the unseen.[17]

This I can piece together from the part-objects: On the evening of February 14, 1980, which was a Thursday, Cookie posed as the ex-boyfriend of the poet and playwright Gary Indiana for a Mudd Club performance he was doing alongside another of his close friends, Kathy Acker. Chris Kraus remembers being there in the audience; she describes Kathy's reading as "indelibly charming *and* brazen."[18] Both Gary and Kathy read aloud letters addressed to ex-lovers, and while Kathy projected photographs of her sexy correspondents, Gary projected *Cookie*. She was his friend, his ally, his dressed-up lover, his longtime *beloved*. Feeling affinity for him, too, she probably called him "hon"—the tender address she used for her friends.[19] A year later, on February 12, 1981, which was also a Thursday, Cookie would perform alongside Chris Kraus, as part of the event *Here's Mudd in Your Ears*. But in the 1980 performance her lips didn't part—in this sideshow, costumed bit part—to talk her own love letters.

Or did they? Could they have? I look again at the portrait of her smoking, her subtly opened mouth, exhaling. As the younger writer, not yet staffed at *Details* magazine, and with only a gathering of stories in zines to her name, she was in the shadows that night, or backstage, or in the makeup room, or the toilets, or frozen in a photographic fragment taken by a friend: semipublic (if hazy) spaces of intimacy, eroticism, *affinity*. This type of "invisible evidence," which José Esteban Muñoz describes as "ephemera *as* evidence," expands what we think of as material, as archive, to include "memory and performance . . . all of those things that remain after a performance, a kind of evidence of what has transpired but certainly not the thing itself."[20] It is an invitation to dream new possibilities about, but also for, and particularly with, and especially around, the original event (V-Day, 1980: this chapter's permeable boundary), in a way that dates it and departs from it at the same time, circling it, stretching ideas and texts and events beyond it, which have an affinity—by which I mean a *likeness*—with one another.

As the essayist Brian Dillon writes in relation to his own affinity-forming writing on his most-loved sentences, "*About* may not be the right word—better *towards* or *among*."[21] In *Affinities*, a third book in a trilogy, Dillon expanded this unraveling of syntactical intimacies and pleasures into an investigation of *affinity* as an unstable aesthetic position in itself that orients itself to artworks, images, ideas, and objects, in a diffuse, fleeting, and unpredictable fashion, combining elements of attraction, attachment, fascination, and correspondence (toward and between things), which leads artist, writer, and/or reader into a realm of passing connections, returns, and risks.[22] Here, I build from Dillon's project on affinity and affinities, with a diffusely historical and queer feminist lens, as the singular and plural senses of the term emerge as a way into thinking with homosocial intimacies, associations, and networks (across the social and the aesthetic), cross-historical solidarities, and speculative correspondences in writing, activated by Kathy, Cookie, and Me.

This methodological stance makes it possible to reconsider the Mudd Club performance as a queer act of love shared by three writers—*beside one another*—and as an entry point into recognizing the critical effects of the love letter in the interdisciplinary and embodied practices of both writers: Kathy Acker *and* Cookie Mueller (the unlisted girl in the shadows). I visualize the performance as an erotic threesome (a little like ours). I fantasize, I *hear*, epistolary echoes of something that may or may not have happened: Cookie playing the part of the superhero-seductress with horns that she illustrates on her love letter to the artist Ching Ho Cheng. "I really had to write to you," Cookie lets out desperately. "I think of you constantly."[23]

I see you moving closer, before and after the scheduled performance. I hear you admiring each other's outfits, gossiping in the dark, reading your lived letters aloud. Gossip, like correspondence, blurs the roles of giver and receiver. And pleasure surfaces (for me, for us, and I hope for you, too) in these unofficial letters of more-than-two: where speaking and writing cross one upon the other. The three of us talking love from lipstick'd mouths, muttering to the mirror: a chorus line.

In this third piece of love-in-pieces, I write between and across and toward Cookie and Kathy, exchanging fantasy letters. I adopt this spatial, affective, epistolary position to show how both writers transformed the mostly bourgeois, domestic traditions of the love letter etched into histories of women's writing, to transform and repair our narratives of love.[24] I am interested in an alternative archive of women's intimate, erotic, homosocial love letters, the letters actually *lived*, which involve "swerves from the usual," "episodes of refusal and creative contravention to feminine normativity."[25] I correspond with their private-made-public correspondences, the objects of their affinities: the attachments, attractions, desires, kinships, and pleasures they shared, *in* and *with* sickness, and which were subversively and perversely worked into, fictionalized, transcribed, and performed in a diverse range of what I term *letter pieces*, expansively dated "*around* 1980."

For Lauren Berlant, the conventional love plot shapes normative narratives of the feminine, delivering the eternal promise/message that love has the power to "rescue you from your life and to give you a new one," to demonstrate your "feminine worth," and to "build worlds" wherein the couple and the family form are "at the heart of social being."[26] This love plot circulates and sustains the affective attachments binding the historical archives of white heterosexual femininity's intimate public together; it is what women work hard to "stay in proximity to"—feeling disappointment
1 and anxiety as the partners of fulfillment and pleasure.[27] Safety, security,
4 *privacy* are assured by the institutionalized optimisms of the love plot,
6 while the risk of exposure—of risky intimacy itself—is a "failure" felt
outside of it.[28] Why, then, "despite everything," as Berlant writes elsewhere, in reference to both desire and love's exclusions, the "economic and physical domination of nations, races, religions, gays, lesbians, and women," do such plots continue "to exert a utopian promise to discover a form that is elastic enough to manage what living throws at lovers"?[29]

Cookie and Kathy show some of the alternative love plots available to us in their own ambivalent, exposed, perverse, risky, sick, and lovesick worlds, which also generate surprising, reparative relations of solidarity and care. Like Berlant, they, too, "want something other for love," a "transformational environment," which Cookie begins to grope for in an unpublished short piece that documents the experience of a one-time artist-fiancée leaving her stranded.[30] In it she writes: "I toppled into the abysmal zone of fathomless despair. My grief knew no bottom."[31] She jokes that at first television was her therapy, then describes how: "I started seeing a psychiatrist, and the words that I should have written down and transformed into a poignant Gothic thriller about unrequited love, were lost in space . . . they dissipated in the air that hung above the analyst's couch."[32] She may not have visibly written the Mary Shelley–esque epic novel she dreams of, but as she does self-referentially in this anecdote, she scribed the pains, the sicknesses, the shattering edges of love in short bursts and pieces, like hard-to-catch particles of air. Interestingly, Cookie is medicalized for suffering lovesickness of an unrequited kind; she reclines on the psychiatrist's couch, conjuring the subversive ghosts of sick women before her (including her teenage self). For in this dual-becoming-plural chapter—which involves the return of selves, characters, concepts, and symptoms from previous monographic chapters underscoring the complex desires, intimacies, and pleasures of sickened and pathologized bodies—lovesickness is expansively thought and rethought, to include voices of the vulnerable, the masochistic, the pathologized, the chronically and incurably ill. From partialized diaries to an unfinished novel-in-pieces, I come to the manifold letters of their autoerotic, epistolary worlds. I come to their lovesick letter pieces, an archive resonant with the multiplicities of mania, disorder, and disease beside the thrills and tenderness of pleasure, solidarity, and care: the reparative risks of *writing* love anew.

PART 2: BLOODLETTING

K Is an Erotomaniac Correspondent

"I am sitting on his bed with my coat still on cause I am too zombie to take it off," writes Kathy—in a belated, flu-heavy, self-confessed "trashy" letter to a Paris-based poet and publisher, Paul Buck—of her awkward New Year's Eve afterparty with the owner of the Mudd Club, Steve Maas.[33] Later, when sick in bed, with "no sex," she reads Husserl instead, and "DICKENSDICKENSDICKENSDICKENSDICKENS."[34] She directs her bedbound desire to books, absorbs these authors compulsively, illicitly, echoing the literary lives of nineteenth-century hysterics before her, whose sicknesses were thought to come about by an autoerotic addiction to novels, to "improper reading."[35] In a decision that middle-class social convention might call "improper," not long after meeting Buck in Europe—where she'd read at Amsterdam's One World Poetry Festival before traveling onward to Paris and discovering, then improperly translating, with just a French dictionary to hand, Laure's improper letters to her married lover, Georges Bataille—she decided to enclose new writing for his attention.[36] In this package were the beginnings of her autobiographical, emotional resculpting (and invading) of Dickens's classic *Great Expectations* (1861); the letter section of this work-in-progress became the materials for her Valentine's Day ex-lover performance. She called these staged readings "outgrowths of the writing," like an embodied, serial, unfolding correspondence with the work itself.[37]

I amaze at the brazenness with which she risked her correspondents being present in the crowd. As she tells Buck in another letter after the February 14 event, "Everyone liked the performances except of course for all the people whose names I mentioned in the texts and they should all go to hell except Sylvere."[38] When *Great Expectations* (1982) was published in full two years later, she included a letter to Maas: "Why don't you give some of the money you are making off the Mudd Club to the poor starving artists who're supporting it?"[39]

. . . Although I'm not even sure you would've been brave enough to let that one loose on the night.

. . . Fearlessness and vulnerability could never be separated so easily.

"Through and through Kathy was a DIY Dickens," writes Eileen Myles, not only in the book's ripped title and plagiarized beginning, but in the way of "getting her writing out," serializing it, as well as expelling it, from the body and out into the world. She got it out onto the inked page, then in typescripts, manuscripts, illustrated and fragmentary books, live performances, amounting to writhing "bits and pieces . . . variegated stuff"—like the papery substances of correspondence.[40] Novelistic form *is*, for Kathy, and for Cookie, capacious. Kathy once called it a "temporal structure in words," emphasizing that "the structure of the bourgeois novel—you know, as Barthes talks about in *Writing Degree Zero*—is something I've never used."[41] Embodying this piecemeal temporal flow, and absorbing the lived processes of writing, *Great Expectations* also begins in epistolary real time: "On Christmas Eve 1978 my mother committed suicide and in September of 1979 my grandmother (on my mother's side) died. Ten days ago (it is almost Christmas 1979) Terence told my fortune with the Tarot cards. This was not so much a fortune—whatever that means—but a fairly, it seems to me, precise psychic map of the present, therefore: the future" (figure 3.2).[42]

Who is she talking to? The reader? Herself? Another correspondent? The Terence who is Terence Sellers: writer, dominatrix, and Kathy's closest female friend, her masochist-ally in letters, during the writing of the novel? Even in passages like this, which are not directly letters, the effect is still epistolary, conversational, emotionally direct, as it captures a moment, or series of moments, charged by emotion and time as well as grief. As she writes later in the novel, in a self-reflexive stance, "A narrative is an emotional moving."[43] *Great Expectations* evolved—over the course of eighteen months, as Kathy moved between New York, Seattle, San Francisco, and back to New York—according to such movements, filtered into compositional processes, cutting between plagiarized passages from Dickens, also Proust, as well as avant-gardists, pornographic text-makers, and the ephemera of her own autobiography, parenthesized by the lived, embodied time of the author/narrator. Kathy's close writing of collaged

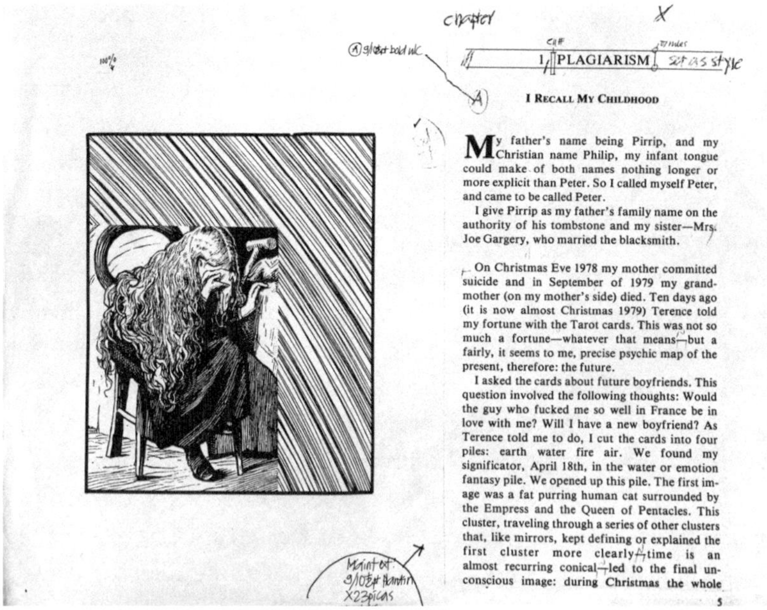

1 PLAGIARISM

I RECALL MY CHILDHOOD

My father's name being Pirrip, and my Christian name Philip, my infant tongue could make of both names nothing longer or more explicit than Peter. So I called myself Peter, and came to be called Peter.

I give Pirrip as my father's family name on the authority of his tombstone and my sister—Mrs. Joe Gargery, who married the blacksmith.

On Christmas Eve 1978 my mother committed suicide and in September of 1979 my grandmother (on my mother's side) died. Ten days ago (it is now almost Christmas 1979) Terence told my fortune with the Tarot cards. This was not so much a fortune—whatever that means—but a fairly, it seems to me, precise psychic map of the present, therefore: the future.

I asked the cards about future boyfriends. This question involved the following thoughts: Would the guy who fucked me so well in France be in love with me? Will I have a new boyfriend? As Terence told me to do, I cut the cards into four piles: earth water fire air. We found my significator, April 18th, in the water or emotion fantasy pile. We opened up this pile. The first image was a fat purring human cat surrounded by the Empress and the Queen of Pentacles. This cluster, traveling through a series of other clusters that, like mirrors, kept defining or explained the first cluster more clearly time is an almost recurring conical led to the final unconscious image: during Christmas the whole

5

an illustrated proof
of a published novel:
like papery correspondence
or purloined letters

3.2. Annotated proof of Kathy Acker, *Great Expectations*. Barrytown, NY / New York: Station Hill / Open Book, 1982. David M. Rubenstein Rare Book and Manuscript Library, Duke University, KAP, B3, F3. Courtesy of the Kathy Acker Estate.

pieces is shaped by these "adolescent," purloined, improper readings; the novel becomes a relational container of literary correspondence.

Often, this is *material*. The novel's section of improper "open letters," as Kraus calls them, performs a paradoxical transference from private stuff (or proper "property") to naked, raw, public pieces within a compositional novel. Kraus took up similar tactics in her 1997 epistolary novel, *I Love Dick*, which was also published by Native Agents; as did Dodie Bellamy a year later in *The Letters of Mina Harker* (1998). Both authors absorbed the heady contagiousness of Kathy's literal and figurative correspondences.[44] Like Bellamy masquerading and gossiping as Bram Stoker's secretarial Mina, the open letters in *Great Expectations* are voiced by a pseudonymous narrator (Rosa) but are no less direct, relational, and embodied. Freed by the veil of her fictive signature, lovesick aggression becomes a posture, a position from which to write, *unpoliced*, as she combines intimacy and violence to address "Sylvère" (Lotringer: the cultural theorist and another ex-boyfriend) in the forceful second person: "This serves you right. I told you this was going to happen. Now that I've spent last night fucking you, I'm in love with you."[45] Her open letter writing is intensified by the masochism of her first-person statements, through which she opens emotion, desire, and love even further, exposing its angles, conflicts, and shards, as she once did in the diary pieces: the closeness of pleasure and pain.

But of course, she is performing in these letters, too, exaggerating—with ironic and critical effect—her feminine and feminized sickness in love. As Bellamy writes of this doubling effect in Kathy's life and writing, of living lovesickness and parodying it, all at once, "She parodied female masochism, pushed it to the point of flinching queasiness, yet she also embodied female masochism, owned it."[46] Elsewhere, and in relation to her own book of blog posts to an ex-lover, Bellamy calls this stance, which involves an affective writing through, and with, vulnerability, *oppositional weakness*. "To deny behaviors and experiences gendered as weak or 'feminine' is not feminist or queer," writes Bellamy in a chapter titled "Heart Publication." "It's heteronormative to the hilt. Like Kathy Acker, I long to quiver and terrify in the same gasp."[47] As Kathy/Rosa confesses to her love object, reaching for the parodic, powerful heights of masochism-in-performance, "I'm just a helpless little girl." She then repeats, hysterically, her uncensored, real-time thoughts: "Remember what we do together when I'm unparanoid enough to see you. Remember what we do together when I'm unparanoid enough to see you"—sentiments that foreshadow the emotional edges the author etches into a private letter to Sylvère Lotringer, dated March 8, 1991, almost a decade after their affair.[48] Kathy begins this missive with the blushing apology, "I'm not very good at saying my feelings, nor at letter writing," but then proceeds to "try"—so unapologetically—with the following admission that her behavior stems from her excess feelings and vulnerabilities: "I am paranoid and I am over-emotional and that's how I am."[49] As I travel across autobiographical materials in published, self-published, unpublished, invisible, and/or gossiped archives, the line between what constitutes a private letter from a public one gets (diary-piece style) *blurry*.[50] And this blur is strategically manipulated by Kathy—it is the source of her life/work's feminist politics—as masochistic subject and object become willfully entangled in letter pieces. She evades the regulatory forces of literature, of law, of medicine, of sexuality and gender, with the performative "unmarked" mesh of autobiography and fiction.[51]

I follow the lead of your letters. Those silver-glossed bodies of work decorated with silver gelatin portrait prints, ripped apart like a draft destined to never be seen or read. I think I see you: punk ingénue lost in a Victorian novel. Ravished by rococo thorns. Lace and leopard-print dress, diamond earring, peroxide crown, turned head, big brown eyes. Or: the sinuous lines of a floral tattoo inked upon your back. But the seams don't line up. The striped stocking doesn't hold. In image or writing (plate 9).

The epistolary narrator of *Great Expectations*—whom I take to be an autofictionalized version of the author—stalks her correspondent through the expunged, unexpurgated torrent of her letter writing, the only means by which she can "see" him, "touch" him, get close to him: the absent one.[52] When she is this sick, hysterical, neurotic—*in and with love*—the letter becomes a surrogate means of contact and erotic proximity (even a form of protection), seduced and sustained, which is also to say *pleasured*, by what Anne Carson terms the distance-crossing, often painful "reach of desire."[53] And "*like* desire," writes Roland Barthes in *A Lover's Discourse* (I discover it in your library catalog of 6,054 scribbled-upon [masturbated upon?] books), "the love letter waits for an answer; it implicitly enjoins the other to reply."[54] But like my own unanswered letters of perversity, there is no reply, as Kathy/Rosa's sick love-letter writing comes in manic fits and starts, delusional, desiring repetitions, which smother a response even while they pull her love object nearer. Barthes's discourse is written with the masculine lover in mind (you'd always say it was your theorist boyfriend who gave you Barthes; pleasured you, submissively, with it) but Kathy's love letters explode those types. For our love triangle, it is the (love)sick woman writer who consumes her absent beloved in "episode[s] of language."[55]

"The helpless little girl" authors her own case history in letters, re-routing the spontaneous fits of speech once marked by the masculine, medicalizing gaze as another symptom of hysteria into the desiring energies of a one-sided correspondence. Channeling the wild pleasures of the hysterics' voice and imagination, as feminist critics were also committed to doing "around 1981," Kathy claims the lovesick letter piece as a feminist strategy and form.

In 1981, *Critical Inquiry* published a special issue, "Writing and Sexual Difference," which was brought out as a book a year later with Cassatt's envelope-licking *The Love Letter* on its front cover.[56] It is this collection and cover that Jane Gallop departs from in her essay on Leclerc's erotic, epistolary essaying, which also explores "the new intercourse between literary theory and feminism" in US academia.[57] Indeed, while Kathy's lovesick letter pieces appear to stem from a less conventionally affectionate register when compared to Leclerc's, they nevertheless participate in a similar project of publicity: coming "out of the closet and into the public domain."[58] And with Leclerc's visceral confession that "my tongue will die if yours doesn't come and bring its warm saliva," both authors' letters seem to begin in the wet surrounds of the throat, the back bit of the mouth, its secret passage: the labial larynx.[59] If such a corporeal commingling is reminiscent of Linda Lovelace's star turn as a woman whose clitoris is discovered at the back of her throat in the 1972 porn film *Deep Throat*, then it also recalls *Variety*, the 1983 film directed by Bette Gordon and scripted by Kathy (featuring Cookie in a small walk-on part), which centers on the gaze of a young female theater ticket-taker in Downtown New York and her awakened obsession with the pornographic film industry.[60] In a reversal of dominant masculine scopic consumptions, the viewer witnesses the blonde female protagonist witnessing—sees her seeing, fantasizing, absorbing, swallowing, and reading—as she flicks magazines and scans billboards with sexual curiosity and pleasure.

Is this "reading based in perversion," as Gallop describes, in a queer reading of Barthes's similarly soaked 1973 essay-in-pieces *The Pleasure of the Text*?[61] It, too, is congealed in saliva-drenched substances: from the image of a scrolling letter that never ceases to end in "a powerful gush of words," to the desire of the text reaching jouissance (a readerly, writerly orgasm) being the point at which "it attempts to overflow."[62] In the 1988 essay collection *Thinking Through the Body*, Gallop also attends to this text from a feminist perspective, focusing on how Barthes's vision of a neutral sexual domain, neither strictly feminine nor masculine, is accessed through the erotic, "reached through perversion and pleasure."[63] And so, when Barthes writes of a bodily "vocal writing" in the closing fragments, wherein we can hear "the grain of the throat, the patina of consonants, the voluptuousness of vowels, a whole carnal stereophony," perhaps it is possible that this understanding of a throaty lyricism in language—full of granulating, crackling, grating, caressing, cutting sounds—is also a sign of perversion.[64]

But while Barthes's textual, throat-coming pleasure involves an "erotic mixture of timbre and language," Kathy's epistolary sounds are even rougher.[65] I can hear the feverish flux of Kathy's sick cacophony in letters: the handwritten ones she sent to Barthes in the margins of her books (ink spilling on printed words), as well as the epistles she addressed to friends and lovers, some of which were published and performed live, or worked into artworks. She writes from the sick margins of the throat—even desiring to have "mouth diarrhea," as she says to Paul Buck—to make "CONTACT."[66] It is an act of bodily purging, an "upheaval," what Dodie Bellamy has outlined in her "Barf Manifesto" as a "feminist, unruly, cheerfully monstrous" literary form.[67] Authored by a barfing monster-bride, to "throw up" the letter is to eject an epistolary, erotic, embodied language of the lovesick into the domain of art.[68] It upends the ways the throat, its intimate texts and pleasures, the abject mess of the female body—from fits of speech to manic episodes to spells of spew—has been marked as private, hystericized.[69] In body and on the bodily page, in Kathy's close writing, the letter/throat is a space of endless talking (a therapeutic cure?), whereby the negative affects entangled within experiences of female desire and love are boldly, even *perversely*, projected.

Kathy is an *erotomaniac*, in ways that echo the medical term first used by the French fin-de-siècle psychiatrist Gaëtan Gatian de Clérambault to categorize and criminalize his female patients/stalkers suffering from paranoid delusions about love and their out-of-reach beloved. Kathy is a "love junkie."[70] Kathy is the passionate and perverse Emma Bovary: freed to write letters for herself.[71] But while Clérambault pathologized such erotic tendencies, denying women the agency of a perversion, Kathy takes the "fervid verbal outpouring[s]" associated with erotomania to a powerful, transgressive extreme.[72] Kathy's sick delirium in love is also a delirium for writing, for writing usually kept secret—signifying how, as Judith

Butler argues, vulnerability and resistance can "work *together*."[73] Her pieces scratch, from the sick back of the throat, for love's far-reaching perversities.

While the around-1980 cusp of a novel *Great Expectations* has been described by Eileen Myles as "the turn in the road, the book in which she did everything for the first time," it also, as Chris Kraus notes, does multiple things at once, summarizing "artistic experiments of the past twenty years" alongside "pornography, diatribe, parody, gossip, and trash, which had become the staple diet of New York's new guard downtown art crowd."[74] Kathy's earlier epistolary project—a 1974 collaboration with the conceptual artist Alan Sondheim that manifested in obsessive letters, diaries, notebooks, tapes, and videos—haunts it. It began with a letter Kathy spontaneously wrote to the artist after an erotic, one-night encounter in New York, 1974, in which she invites him to participate in her sexually charged inquiry: "How close can I get to someone? Will we become each other?"[75] Ignited by a feverish desire, she flirts with the close line separating enthusiasm and madness (as the origins of the word "fanatic," from the Latin *fanaticus*, imply: "mad, enthusiastic, inspired by a god").[76] She says that she is "fanatical about working," chatters "constantly," asks if she is "imposing" on him; later she reveals that she has "never tried to do with anyone what I'm trying to do with you, open myself completely," after an uncensored, erotomaniac, four-page verbal outpouring of autobiographical information, which became the processes and materials for her conceptual exploration of sick desires and pleasures.[77] As Kathy writes in her second letter to her love-object collaborator, which speaks to all her close writing: "looking for a situation of working that isn't as private as this kind of (me) writing: to make private public, break thru barriers."[78]

Developing epistolary dynamics with an artist or writer she admired, or was attracted to, as she did with Sondheim (in a collaboration that eventually ended in a videotaped power struggle over issues of personal boundaries), was not an unusual practice for Kathy. Indeed, for all her 1970s works, then for *Great Expectations* with Paul Buck, and then again for the finishing of *My Death, My Life, by Pier Paolo Pasolini* (1984) with London-based artist, writer, and editor Jonathan Miles, she used a "close correspondent," as Kraus terms it, to work through the conceptual strategies informing the piece or series of pieces she was working on at the time.[79] In early 1972, the poet Jerome Rothenberg was sent transcriptions of the diaries that would become the cut-ups in Kathy's first self-published chapbook, *Politics*. She prefaces the package—containing diary pieces exploring her strange desire for Rothenberg (they lived in the same building in New York)—with an erotomaniac apology: "Please excuse the personal stuff I should have talked about it to you before this."[80] Then, during the writing of *The Childlike Life of the Black Tarantula by the Black Tarantula* that followed, she kept up communication with the poet and artist Jackson Mac Low, who was (as the replies suggest) intellectually and sexually infatuated with his mysterious correspondent. Kathy later sent an erotic influx of long letters to the poet Ron Silliman when she needed help clarifying the "recite repeat one choice story" technique that evolved into *The Adult Life of Toulouse Lautrec by Henri Toulouse Lautrec*, which was mailed out in 1975.[81] The writing of this correspondence novel and the correspondence that supports it occur simultaneously; one feeds the other: "if I write lots of letters maybe I can then get to work."[82]

There is an erotomaniac inflection to the ways she used her correspondents to maintain her own desire and writing, her desire *for* writing, the closeness of her solitary desires. Recalling her earlier diaristic automatic fevers, and anticipating her later masturbation experiments, she is an autoerotic, erotomaniac letter writer. Feeling isolated from the New York experimental poetry scene, she writes to Bernadette Mayer asking for books and poems to be mailed out to her in San Diego; she "*NEED[s]* POET TALK."[83] In other typed epistles to Mayer, this need is seemingly satisfied by Kathy talking and gossiping endlessly about herself, as she manically describes recent sexual encounters and lusts, in-progress artworks and writings, crumbling finances, and the crippling anxiety she felt over the chapbooks' critical reception, with only short, belated notes in the margins asking for "more about your new work please send."[84] She is afflicted by distracted, adolescent, autoerotic attentions and struggles to concentrate on the needs of Mayer, the elder woman writer, who was also developing epistolary poetry—as a durational, poetic experiment investigating lived consciousness and the kaleidoscopic complexities of our embodied and emotional lives—while pregnant with her third child: from 1979's summer days to February's chill the following year (the month of the Mudd Club ex-lover reading). In one of those pieces, Mayer expresses dismay at having to answer "questions about poetry especially when they're about my life," which diverges from Kathy's intentional blurring of that divide. Later in this letter poem, Mayer infers that poetry, like love, "save[s] or salvage[s]," in a claim for love's restorative powers that differs from Kathy's epistolary working of love's emotional violence.[85] As Kathy writes in *Great Expectations*, "Love affairs are when each person can do anything they want and the other person realizes that the most unbelievable behavior possible is usual."[86] Stretching these aesthetic differences into intimate exchanges, I speculate with Kraus that Mayer, "immersed in the Poetry Project's anti-celebrity ethos . . . must have found Acker's entreaties somewhat nervy and strange."[87] Indeed, Mayer writes in her letter poem, somewhat self-effacingly, of being "among this union of writers . . . writers who write without anyone ever knowing it."[88]

Kathy's correspondence with the younger Terence Sellers—who conserved their exchanges by photocopying her elegantly handwritten and illustrated letters before sending—makes a different kind of union. It is unabashedly punk, celebrating gossip as a medium for female friendship,
1 which manifests in materials *of* and *for* writing. "I want you! I want love!
5 I want champagne! I want giggling!" Kathy exclaims in hyperfeminine
6 exuberance.[89] As the contemporary artist Hannah Black writes, in an essay on the shared social activities practiced by the gossip and the witch, "The gossip crosses back and forth between home and world, between the secret interior and the public exterior, carrying items to trade: shared knowledge, a shoulder to cry on, insight, fun."[90] Both Kathy and Terence carry those items in their energetic correspondence, and both of them share it, need it, this poet sex-talk play. Or, as Kathy calls it at this time, "the wonderful New York gossippy [*sic*] oh all the stuff I love."[91] It is mutually explored: as Sellers writes in one letter, "I continue gossip: S. Charlesworth & A. Poe still going strong. Incumbent boyfriend J. Kosuth back from summer long sojourn in Paris on Tuesday. B. Sussler's got to move out—but where?"[92] It is sustaining. And however playful or adolescent in spirit, it entails a level of trust, as they share with one another masochistic desires and tendencies (exchanging affinities with the objects of their affinities), which they explored, examined, and performed in their novels and short fictions, around 1980.

Dated close to the Valentine's Day reading, the series of photographs recording Cookie tied up with black rope at her wrists, wearing just a loose terry cloth top with brilliant-white schoolgirl cotton panties, being pulled along by the Downtown performer Klaus Nomi at a house party, suggests a similar tendency to be "close" in sadomasochism (figure 3.3). Theirs is a mutually explored fantasy, which plays out in the intimate environs of a domestic space, possibly hers. She resists his leather-jacketed force, then kicks him down the stairs with six-inch heels (as the part-objects tell me). It is a two-part slideshow of resist, desire, push, pull, *play*. Was Sellers at the party? Did she see Cookie and her friend performing and desiring this

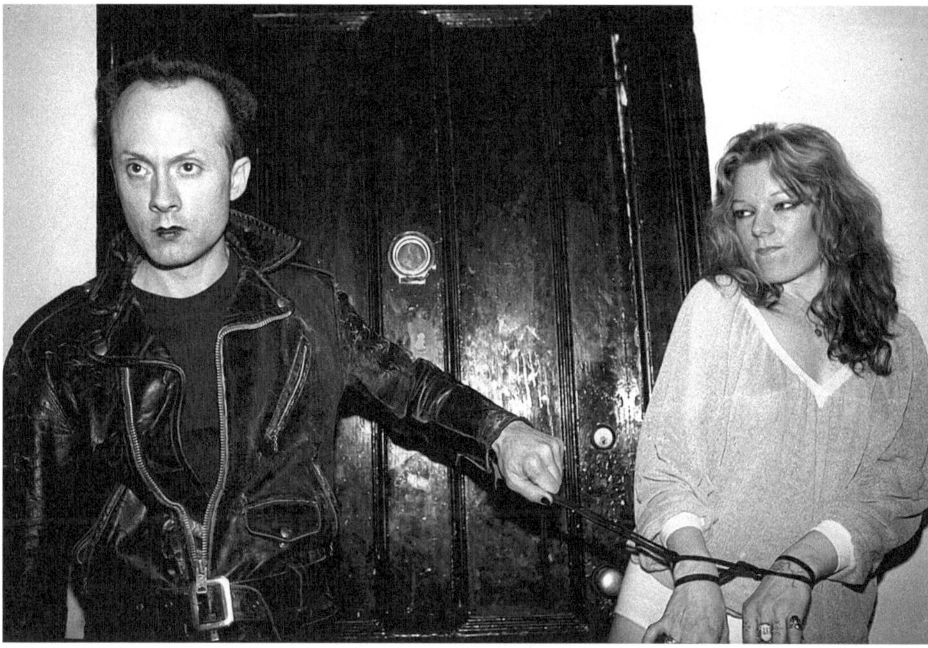

a photographic part-object:
black rope
terry cloth top
schoolgirl cotton panties

3.3. Anthony Scibelli, *Cookie Mueller and Klaus Nomi*, undated (ca. 1979). Courtesy the artist.

way? In one of her letters to Kathy, Sellers expresses unimpressed (misspelled) scorn that Gary Indiana booked "Cooky Mueller, an actress who writes a diary" for a series of poetry readings he was then curating—not then realizing that, perhaps, they shared a closer sensibility than Sellers first thought.[93]

Before Sellers contributed to the tenth issue of Sylvère Lotringer's *Semiotext(e)* journal on perversion (titled "Polysexuality," it featured examples of French theory, like Barthes's *A Lover's Discourse*, recently translated and published in English, alongside pornographic Downtown writing), her then in-progress novel of sadomasochist case histories that became *The Correct Sadist* was added by the publisher and philosopher to the required
1 reading for his French class on de Sade—whom Kathy had also "become"
5 in her earlier chapbook novel—at Columbia University.[94] Subtitled *The*
8 *Memoirs of Angel Stern*, Sellers's novel shared, and extended (via its appropriation of the case history form to provide a distinctly female experience of perversion), Lotringer's editorial and philosophical interests in the plural, textual, transgressive aspects of sexuality, particularly the ways perverse bodies and desires have been policed, disciplined, controlled, medicalized.[95] This was an important political project at a time when, as Berlant has argued, the Reaganite "intimate public sphere" stigmatized and erased practices of sexuality considered "nonfamilial," the network of erotic relations that deviated from normative love-plot genres, and included, "by implication, other forms of racial and economic alterity."[96]

So, when a Black artist-writer of West Indian heritage, Lorraine O'Grady, also participated in a performative act of "becoming" in an iterative alter ego work of guerrilla actions, *Mlle Bourgeoise Noire 1955* (Miss Black Middle Class 1955) (1980–83), she was intervening in the hegemonic whiteness of an art world bound to such restrictive and racialized forms of citizenship. Mlle Bourgeoise Noire's first uninvited "invasion"—dressed pageant-style in a debutante gown and flowing cape appliqued with 180 thrift-store pairs of white gloves in ruffled layers, topped off with a rhinestone and seed pearl crown, accompanied by a white cat-o-nine-tails studded with white chrysanthemums as her bouquet—occurred at the Just Above Midtown gallery in close-to-the-Mudd Tribeca: a Downtown offshoot of the commercial space led by Linda Goode Bryant that foregrounded multimedia and experimental works by African American artists and people of color.[97] The performance's playful written document describes how first there were "oohs and aahs on all sides for Mlle Bourgeoise's Noire's gown" and that "she obliges" the photographers in return—before an abrupt shift in intention as she began to beat herself with the whip, an object haunted by histories of enslavement, asserting that there should be "No more ass-kissing . . . / No more buttering-up . . . / BLACK ART MUST TAKE MORE RISKS!!!"[98] O'Grady's critical fabulation practice (in the sense supplied by Hartman's Black feminist term) proposes some possibilities, beyond what she termed "art with white gloves on."[99] Mlle Bourgeoise Noire also showed up, uninvited again, to protest the opening of the 1981 *Persona* exhibition at the New Museum, which featured nine white artists—including Kathy's close friend Eleanor Antin, and Mudd Club regular Colette—who were working with themes of "narrative, autobiography, performance, and body art," as the curatorial statement explained, themes that were critically extended by O'Grady in work ignored and delegitimized by the institution's gatekeepers.[100] O'Grady's own transgressive practice in persona bespeaks anger *alongside* pleasure; it is excessive, sensual, tactile, vocal, and violent, employing a mode of performance (fictional, ephemeral) that enables for such risks to be taken without becoming trapped by the disciplining, pathologizing forces of the visual privileged by white power.

A 2011 group show at Triangle France gallery in Marseille picked up on thematic and methodological correspondences between the artist-writers of Mlle Bourgeoise Noire and the Black Tarantula, even if the love objects of their own textual correspondences clashed, as well as overlapped (or were more *ambivalent*).[101] Before Kathy and her Semiotext(e) circle turned to avant-garde types such as Charles Baudelaire for historical instances of transgressive life and practice (writing for the 1979 issue of *L-A-N-G-U-A-G-E*, Kathy offered some "Notes on Writing" inspired by Baudelaire's life: "One needs laws, the laws of writing, so one can hate them"), O'Grady was teaching a course at the School of Visual Arts on nineteenth-century French poetry, prioritizing the life and work of the poet flaneur.[102] Hers is an engagement, however, that also intervenes within mythologized narratives of white male genius by refocusing attention on "Jeanne Duval," Baudelaire's "black common-law wife of 20 years," as a means to "fill in" (but with critical hesitation; she recognizes, aligning with Hartman's method, the speculative gesture's limitations) "the silence of this woman-without-speech."[103]

Before she fleetingly became her original alter ego, O'Grady was "writing about rock and pop music," including "the first above-ground review of Bruce Springsteen for *The Village Voice*"—where Cookie would become a "Doctor" in its pages—and "the first article on reggae published in *Rolling Stone*."[104] She had always been a Prince fan, as she has explained in interviews, and it was his breakthrough "with *Controversy*" (in 1981) that intersected with the beginnings of "a life and career as a visual artist" following her early performance interventions.[105]

In an echo of shared but differently habitualized love objects, it was around this time, after the Station Hill edition of *Great Expectations* had finally appeared, that Kathy began work on her next full-length lovesick novel—featuring a narrator who thinks Prince should be president of the United States, because he believes in "feelings, fucking, and fame."[106] This is offered as an antiracist gesture that takes aim at the Reaganite intimate public view, its circulation of "crap . . . about happy families and happy black lynchings and happy ignorance."[107] The novel's lovesick correspondent writing perversely masochistic letters is on the side of Prince. And so is Kathy, as she confessed to Sellers, her beloved maker of gossip: "I hope Reagan gets all of America except for New York and California: and we take those. That's the only solution."[108]

The Letter Is Lovesick

In Kathy's archive of erotomaniac utterances (letters, postcards, airmails, telegrams), love is shaped from uncomfortable edges and angles. It is a space wherein, as Carson has shown us, bitterness and sweetness converge.[109] Or, as Kathy writes in "New York City in 1979," pushing the paradox to a painful extreme, "The one thing about being in love with someone is you know you're in love: you're either flying or you're about to kill yourself."[110] Love also flails with genre, producing scattered, shattered close writing in pieces. Love is a place, writes Berlant, where "people actually admit they want to become different . . . but it's not change without instability."[111] And it is the "affective incoherence of the subject with respect to the objects that anchor it or to which they're attached," which is presumed by queer theory that is also shared by bodily spaces of love.[112] It can be disorganizing, destabilizing, and exposing: a skin-stripping, a wearing down. Barthes agrees (like Gallop, like Kathy, like Cookie storing a citational crumble of *A Lover's Discourse* in the back pages of her notebook: I, too, can taste the perversity of his writing), finding "flayed" to be "the particular sensibility of the amorous subject, which renders him vulnerable, defenseless to the slightest injuries."[113] *She* is vulnerable; she *makes* herself, and performs herself *as* vulnerable, in her perverse, epistolary lovesickness, which blurs the line between subject and object in (never-whole) letter pieces.

After Sappho's own blurred fragments described eros as a disease, but *before* Clérambault's and Flaubert's literary medicalizations, lovesickness was considered a medical condition, in which the patient, usually gendered as a sick woman from the Renaissance onward, is afflicted by intense melancholy of an erotic kind: triggered by convulsions in the womb (the word's Greek origins, *hystera*, led to the medicalization of hysteria along similarly gendered lines) and physical and emotional disturbances. In Jan Steen's late seventeenth-century painting *The Lovesick Maiden* (ca. 1660), two white European men, likely medical professionals, stand over a white, wealthy young woman; they take her pulse from an elevated, behind position and appear to diagnose and silence her flailing, half-clothed, lovesick body of pearlescent pallor and rouged cheeks. The maiden balances on the clinician's chair: the stage for the medical gaze. Struck down by the crippling absence of desires met, the withholding of sensual experience, the lovesick sufferer's condition was thought to be both physiological and psychological, as the large volumes of letters, doctors' case notes, and personal diaries from these times attest to.[114] Inflamed passions brought inflamed body temperatures, erratic heartbeats, and disordered eating, which could only be healed, the doctors thought, through letting the excess blood out.[115]

Kathy lets it out, authors it *anew*, in lovesick letter writing. Like she did in her earlier diary pieces, she describes the drag of diseases endured in letters to her friends. "Literally so sick I was on my back with the usual PID for two months so I couldn't ESCAPE," she begins one letter to Terence Sellers, which echoes the condition and the cause she also explains to Paul Buck: "I've been very sick lately (PID again) and this time am not recovering fast enough, a bad case of overwork I fear."[116] Emotional stress interwoven within anxieties about writing triggers a reoccurrence of this usually sexually transmitted disease that infects and inflames the female upper genital tract, causing pain in the pelvis, heavy periods, bleeding between menstruations, green vaginal discharge, and, as Kathy's sick note tells us, bouts of bedbound fatigue. "I might as well be in the 19th century and have tuberculosis: it was much more romantic back then," she jokes, of her reclining position and abject wastedness.[117] In the 1978 critical work *Illness as Metaphor*—authored by Susan Sontag, described by Kraus as "the only . . . American female public intellectual in an era when such things mattered" and also the writer whom Kathy/Rosa addresses parodically in a published letter piece in *Great Expectations*—tuberculosis (TB) is attended to as a metaphorical symptom of loving "too much," a disease "afflicting the reckless and sensual."[118] But what if the affliction is also reparative, a space from which to write, to desire and love differently: to feel pleasure in the pain of sickness?

Kathy blames the revisionist impulses of "Women's Lib" for changing the feminized beauty of consumption into "workaday no love stress and exhaustion," reminding us that when she is physically sick, she is also emotionally sick.[119] She experiences "no love"—she is lovesick.[120] Yet, reimagining the ripped-open, relieved flesh of the lovesick patient, she pours the blood of PID and lovesick desire into her sick and tired at-home letters.

The scaly red patches on my right breast have gotten larger, big round buttons. I cannot get pregnant because of the hormones in my bloodstream, but I wonder if this is my body stressed by the itching desire to do so. I scratch, scratch again, scratch here, seeking a kind of company. Or relief. Pleasure, pain, pleasure. These words that seep beyond the body-envelope. Meanwhile, the virus continues. I scroll and scroll and scroll through endless newspaper reports, stumble on a terrible story of a fifteen-year-old schoolgirl who died of TB after more than five doctors dismissed her for being "lovesick."

Physically and emotionally disturbed, she is moved *into* writing. "The weaker the body gets, the better the writing comes," she even says in a letter to Paul Buck. "I think I'll be a masochist in writing only."[121] This letter-based, hyperfeminine (to the point of manic) masochism was let out, made public, powerful, and oppositional in *Great Expectations* and *Don Quixote*. It also appeared via the lovesick telegrams addressed to Jonathan Miles (December 16, 1982), cited in the smaller volume *My Death, My Life, by Pier Paolo Pasolini* ("Acting mad, are you married, miss you terribly six weeks too long"), and intersected with French theoretical writings on the perverse, transgressive angles of the erotic being published by Semiotext(e) in translated editions, while also expanding those concerns into the particular angles of her own embodied and affective lived experience.[122] It also challenged earlier medical texts, which had explicitly categorized the sick woman with deviant desires as pathological, in contrast to the decadent agencies historically gifted to a male pervert. Mobilizing the erotomaniac imagination as a sick but *also* perverse space of writing, Kathy renegotiates bodily, sexual, and creative agencies.

As I absorbed in relation to Cookie's fantasized masturbation manuscript of perverse adolescence (see chapter 2), Sedgwick pursued a similar critical project in the 1991 essay "Jane Austen and the Masturbating Girl," which was later included in *Tendencies* (also stored in Kathy's library of theory), the 1993 essay collection contextualized, wounded, and mobilized by the HIV/AIDS epidemic. In this essay, Sedgwick cites, revises, corresponds with, the 1881 psychiatric case history of two young masturbating girls that was reprinted in Semiotext(e)'s *Polysexuality* issue alongside Sellers and pieces of postmodern fiction and theory.[123] Recalling one bedroom scene, Sedgwick picks up on the ways one of the little girl's physical gestures (as described by her doctor)—the "roving eye"; the tubercular "flushed" face; the "pacing"; the "pressing" of her "thighs together"—signifies the undisciplined, addictive "disorders *of* attention" that shaped the queer sexual identity of the masturbating girl in Jane Austen's time, as represented in the "love story" of *Sense and Sensibility* in particular.[124] Sedgwick returns to this solitary figure, a female practitioner of perversion, to understand the novel's "erotic axis" as both same-sex loving and cross-sex loving.[125] If Marianne is sick with autoeroticism, to repeat the masturbation-phobic discourses of the nineteenth century, then she is also sick with excess love, a love that is energized by the "great and estranging force of . . . homoerotic longing," which is pleasured and sustained, as a perversion, by "the female figure of the love that keeps forgetting its name."[126]

Echoing Marianne's haptic tendencies, snippets of poetry or letters are purloined by Kathy's hand in *Don Quixote*. She writes with the sickness of disordered attentions, perverse desires. She practices autoerotic, even kleptomaniac, graspings of erotomaniac letters in her often violently *felt* lovesickness, which is performed within a novel that parodies the ways women are wounded by "lack of love" in romance genres dominated by the conventional love plot.[127] Subverting those cruelly optimistic narrative lines, which push the idea that a broken subject is restored by heterosexual love, *Don Quixote* instead begins in an abortion clinic; its titular protagonist is lovesick, "flesh torn turned and gnashed . . . that red mash"; she is "a very sick girl."[128] Love becomes her quest: "When she was finally crazy because she was about to have an abortion, she conceived of the most insane idea that a woman can think of. Which is to love. How can a woman love?"[129] Don Quixote's hospitalized position echoes the author's own experience in 1985; it was while reclining in bed that Kathy began reading Cervantes's original text, copying out sections because she "couldn't think."[130] It is a process of endurance that opens up a space of feminist re-writing (surprisingly reparative), as the crazy, sick, infected, bedbound, heartbroken, wounded, nymphomaniac, irrational Don Quixote—who aborted her baby as a perverse refusal of "normalcy, which is the capitulation to social control"—transforms feminized "sickness into a knightly tool."[131] Kate Zambreno has also turned to the novel's hospitalized scene, highlighting the striking image of the "green paper of the hospital gown" turning "into writing paper" as a performance of Kathy's method of "writing the body. Writing sickness."[132] For sickness, in this novel, manifests as a willful turning away from the norm, as a feminist purging and *perverting*: "swerving rather than straightening, deviating from the right [*or expected*] course," as Sara Ahmed describes the queer potential of perversion (its sexual and social manifestations).[133]

Kathy/Don Quixote swerves (*from the usual*) in stolen letters. In the second piece of the novel's second section that is interwoven with revisions of copied texts, Kathy interrupts a Latin poem by Catullus with epistolary insertions, embroidering perverse desire into the text and shocking it into transmission. She crafts a written correspondence with Catullus's poem that is sexual, even masochistic, as she pierces the other's text, places her body in between its clauses. An example: "fulsere quondam candidi tibi / soles, / cum it hurts me to remember I / did act up today, a way of / saying 'I'm not perfect,' forgive / my phone call."[134] The effect is a raw ripping open of desire and text—a splintering of the original—which brings it into a *closer* autoerotic relation with the visceral textures of her own sexual life. Her fractured words recall intimate correspondences with another, later named more directly as "Peter," when she places in parentheses within the Latin "(My awful telephone call. This is my apology, Peter. Do you accept?)"[135]

The autobiographical matter becomes for Kathy another stolen text, with the elusive phantom "Peter" a likely mutation of Peter Wollen, the British filmmaker and critical theorist, with whom Kathy began a London-based love affair in the summer of 1983, before she replaced it with the surrogate intercourse of epistolary exchange when she arrived back in New York in August of that year. As Kraus writes of this "feverish correspondence," Kathy's "need for connection implodes" in his face.[136] As an example of what McKenzie Wark terms an autoplagiarism that involves "the victimization of the teller" within "stolen, intersecting webs," Kathy transcribed and twisted these letters into her novel-in-progress (her novel-in-pieces) of the time. Such autoerotic attentions produce a frantic exchange between one stolen text (transcriptions of Andrei Bely's 1913 novel *Petersburg*) and the direct specificity of her own "sick" desires, as expressed in self-stealing, purloined letters.[137] Bely's text is placed into close contact with this abject writing: epistles that begin directly with "Dear Peter" and contain within them perverse purgings of lovesickness, a bodily barfing of the personal, such as the knife-edge ultimatum: "If I see you, I'll want you. If I don't see you, I'll die." Masochistic outpourings also occur: "I can't stand living without you. I hate this day-after-day constant waiting-for-you: you're not here: all my hours spent in longing for what's not here."[138] Peter's absence pulverizes her desire; she brings him closer, crosses the temporal gap between them, in emotionally direct, severe, projectile writing. Kathy's lovesick letter writing comprises repetitions and distractions that suggest disorderly autoerotic attentions, where she writes "to Peter" but always in relation to herself, between "You" and "I," constructing a rhythm that appears to build to the crescendo of climax where pleasure merges with pain. "You are my madness," she writes. "Come in me, my madness."[139]

Sickness and sexual fantasy intertwine in Kathy's "autoerotic life" in letters; hers is a perverse "coming" that is conjured by the nonappearance of a body.[140] She deviates from the promise of heterosexual genital "union" to waywardly wander in the pleasures of writing. This becomes an autoerotic, erotomaniac dreamscape that amounts to one of the differences in how bodies fuck listed by Wark (in citational web-work with Kathy) that "find their way into and out of the way bodies write."[141] The letter is a promise when other forms of communication fail, as she repeats verbatim in another lovesick message: "I can't say over the telephone what I want to say to you: 'Please touch your cock because I can't touch your cock now and I have to touch your cock.'"[142] And so, while the telephone might produce a blockage, the direct address of the letter—its importing of the throat's voice box—facilitates a sexual finding and perverse fantasy. The purloined letter containing visceral traces of her own life transforms the literature it closely rubs up against, revealing the abject, difficult, complex, contradictory, and lovesick angles of female perversion. For a writer who claimed to have no imagination in the urge to destroy language, a surprising act of care emerges, for the hystericized sick woman who loves *too much*. This is *her* lover's discourse.

Interlude: A Lace Leotard and Sick Letters to Love

In 1983, at work on *Don Quixote*, Kathy had one of her first author portraits taken by her friend, Robert Mapplethorpe (plate 10). Oriented directly to the camera, she poses with her arms resting on her slim hips. She wears a black, loosely tailored jacket, which she pulls away with her clenched fists, revealing a tight-fitting lace undergarment, underwired at the breast. Its prickly textures caress her skin closely. It is an elasticated envelope, visualized in a photograph that is annotated at the margins by the artist, akin to an epistolary scrawl or dedication: “for Kathy–.”[143] The lace envelope exposes particles of her body’s surface, *the letter within*.

I stay with the lace awhile, feeling the contagious, cross-historical presence of Berthe Pappenheim, who collected rare antique laces and was case-studied as “Anna O” by Josef Breuer when being treated for hysteria, and also Madame de Boves, one of the kleptomaniacs of Émile Zola’s 1883 novel *Au bonheur des dames (The Ladies’ Paradise)*, who plunges her hands into a “growing cascade of pillow lace, Mechlin lace, Valenciennes, Chantilly, her fingers trembling with desire.”[144] Is Kathy, one half of my loved pair, like these hysterics of the past? I speculate if lace—so often used at Western weddings and funerals beginning with the words “dearly beloved”—is a lovesick material, interwoven with the paradoxical strands of life and death, pleasure and pain. In photographic afterlife, Kathy’s is tucked into the slippery (sadomasochistic?) fetish textures of her leather trousers.

Her full lips are parted, revealing teeth mid-chatter, which interrupts the professionalism of the picture. It feels more intimate than that. I see one of two friends playing; I imagine the other responding behind the frame, the edges of the scene I cannot see clearly (can only dream of).

Mapplethorpe—photographer of delicate, diminutive wildflowers of white buds growing into lacelike blooms (*Queen Anne’s Lace in Vase*, undated)—died of AIDS-related causes six years later, aged only forty-two. Kathy wrote publicly in memoriam to him, remembering their first meeting and the many after: “For as soon as he walked into the room of his Bond Street studio in which I was sitting he began to gossip about mutual friends, made me laugh, fed me some coke, and then the two of us talked about our favourite subject, sex. . . . [W]e gossiped and laughed to the extent that I hardly ever knew my picture was being taken.”[145] She re-creates the closeness of their relationship—which depends on shared tendencies, on mutual affinities for licentiousness, on the sexual utterance in correspondence exchange—by remembering the two of them together in his room: a space of work, also kinship; of bonds outside of marriage and traditional, coupled love plots. As an intimate encounter of giving and taking, it also spills over into the writing: The letter memorial we are reading is directed *to* him, is *for* him, while also speaking to others beyond this close scene.

Their affinity for one another’s life and art entanglements took seed following Kathy’s first commission for *Artforum*, as she went from being a writer "close to" conceptual and performance art, to a writer living and working very much within the Downtown art world. In this epitaph, "the collective" is gestured toward by touching "the particular." Her close writing can be seen as a broader reparative gesture that cares for a creative community gripped not only by the threat of HIV/AIDS itself, but also by the impact of governmental censorship, stigma, denial: the erasure of sex talk within art and culture (like their gossiping exchanges), in what Sarah Schulman has since referred to as the "gentrification of the mind."[146] After Mapplethorpe's death, and the Corcoran Gallery's decision to cancel a retrospective exhibition of his work in fear of the impact of the Helms amendment on obscenity, Kathy described in a "letter home from New York" for London's *New Statesman* how artists are "reacting vociferously, not so much to censorship, as to the threat of censorship. A few are trying to be safe; the rest are taking up arms against governmental interference."[147]

Her epitaph for Mapplethorpe can be seen as a small, intimate gesture that also challenged the smothering of love's "sick" plots. First, she tells us, it took the form of a "private letter," a speculative desire she rationalized because it is "as impossible for a living human to write a letter to a dead one as it is to place anything true in a commercial magazine." But in this public context, she explains of how she became "embarrassed" at her "emotion."[148] "Is embarrassment a sign of love," she asks (by which she might also mean of fandom, of the art-critical "gushing" Cookie also "hate[s]" to do but does it anyway) "and so not allowable in commercial magazines?"[149] It is a question that Kathy contests, a sign of love that she gestures toward, in her memorial that touches *like a letter*. Sharing in the ways AIDS culture has embraced "camp, shame, and the perverse and resists therapeutic models of sickness and health," as Ann Cvetkovich has recognized, Kathy also faces up to the shame of writing love; she takes that risk for him, an act of care for the body made sick by love: "one of the most honest and loving people" she had ever known.[150]

I think of the lace leotard she wore with him, when she talked with him, how she exposed herself to him, first in a photograph and then in an epitaph, which unravels the intimate and affective attachments between them: the roles of subject and object blurring, in life and in death. In different ways, they share in the state of lovesickness. She cares for his life, his body, his art, as she also cared for the perverse angles of the pathologized erotomaniac, autoerotic, kleptomaniac, lovesick correspondent. The risk with which the author opened the fraying boundaries of eros in epistolary lovesickness deserves a similarly illicit response, the impossible letter to the dead: the multiple textures of my love-in-pieces (these letters sheer like chiffon lace).

In 1978, Mapplethorpe also took a high-contrast, black-and-white portrait of Cookie, glitzed by gold bangles and hoops in her ears (plate 11). She wears a loose, V-necked terry cloth top, the same she donned to play with Klaus Nomi, as one of the photographic part-objects from that night depicts. When touring Europe in 1982, Nomi stitched a baroque white ruff into his androgynous costumes, for his previously pearlescent skin was covered in purple lesions. It was diagnosed as Kaposi's sarcoma in early 1983, caused by an underlying disease of the immune system.[151] He was one of the first of Cookie's circle to die of complications caused by AIDS. I turn to the party picture of them together, not to see it as prophetic, but rather as a source and space of subversion, energy, desire, and love that continued and thrived when so many lives and ways of being and thinking and making were at stake and at risk.

One side of Cookie's face is in shadow in Mapplethorpe's portrait, but gold details glow: the curls of bleached hair, the dusting of bronze on her eyelids, the hooped earring, the stacked bangles on her wrist, the gigantic ring on her tattooed left hand. She was not yet an "art spy riding high" as *Details* magazine's art critic. She was not yet chronicling, with eccentric, disorderly, adolescent attentions, a rapidly gentrifying East Village corner.[152]

When Cookie sat for Mapplethorpe in a terry top, she had not yet gushed over his pictures, or flirtatiously encouraged fame-hungry East Village artists to "handwrite a personal letter," a fan letter, to her writing in response.[153] But when she did come to write about her friend and collaborator's photographs at New York's Robert Miller Gallery ten years later, it was (shame-less) love that she gave him, to his photographs, "that look like they're in spring bloom and summer fruition at the same time." Coming *alive*, "the lushness is amplified."[154] Was this, or could it have been, an exuberant love letter to a dead person before he was dead? If it was, or if it could have been, was it also a gesture of care? Her close writing on art and artists put love at a high volume, showed the reparative "crip" energies of loving through—*writing* through—chronic, severely life-limiting disease. Cookie revised the meaning of "lovesick" in these short pieces, which were published at a time

> *when* magazine advertisements conveyed messages that appeared "inside a heart like a Valentine": "Your next sexual partner could be that very special person . . . The one that gives you AIDS."[155]

> *when* New York City subway billboards (supported by the city's health department) depicted a blown-up newspaper personals section and the statement "I got AIDS through the personals."[156]

> *when* public health posters were being distributed that showed a heterosexual, middle-class pairing alongside the statement "How to keep from getting lovesick. . . . Because the lovesick from AIDS doesn't go away."[157]

I flail and fail but keep loving, keep writing, so your lovesick gestures can stay, can say, other kinds of love. You stitched new shapes: with others by your side. Promiscuous lines. Tied in ropes. But also, free.

PART 3: BESIDE

I Am Stung by Sartorial Specks

Cookie wore ivory-white tulle with overlaid embroidery, like the most delicate of vintage laces, on the day of her wedding to the artist Vittorio Scarpati in New York, April 21, 1986. This time, she wasn't jilted, but she was, in a different way, lovesick. Like my adolescent, thrift-shopping self, I have eaten those textiles up: the silk-satin bodice, the striped bolero, the lashings of tulle and its pretty embroidery, the perfectly cinched ribbon at her waist, the cocktail dress beneath it, which was hidden by a voluminous whipped-cream skirt until she slipped it off to dance and party. The photographer Peter Hujar caressed those details with his camera, in a series of intimate wedding snapshots taken of Cookie backstage, in secret corners, on the stairs, and then on the New York rooftop where the vows were exchanged (plate 12). Gifted to them by the actor John Heys, the venue was the terrace of his East Village penthouse apartment, which was "a great 'chapel for holy matrimony,'" as Cookie joked in a thank-you note to him.[158] Close friends gathered in the clouds for a riff on the Catholic wedding, white tulips scattered on the terrace floor or held as a bouquet in her hands, with hellebores and eucalyptus leaves: symbols of springtime and love.[159] While elsewhere, down *below*—at funerals, not weddings—lily-white flowers were also dropping petals at the feet of their friends: the artists and writers of their Downtown scene.

I scrutinize your dress with x-ray vision, looking for the safety pins holding the pieces together. I look and touch; I feel your cream tulle over my eyes. It prickles like handwritten text. It's a gray fall day (the only day the city hasn't been blanketed in cobalt blues) and I find this silver-gray photograph in chromatic synchronicity. There is no name scrawled on the verso of the print. I talk to the archivist, send emails in the dark, to find out that your friend Peter (who died of AIDS-related illness eighteen months after your wedding) took this crowded wedding picture of you and Vittorio at your outdoor altar. This information pierces like a sharpened needle. I repeat the request for the box containing oversized photographs; I handle the print while shaking, feeling the force of your connection with him, his proximity to you. A slither of sunshine creeps through the clouds, those flecks of white embroidery.

As I have gazed longingly at their wedding album, subversive, sick threads have slowly materialized, fraying the bourgeois, heterosexual "picture." As Elizabeth Freeman has argued, when separated from the legal bind of a life-in-marriage, the "expressive, theatrical, and symbolic aspects of the [wedding] ritual," can conjure "bodily and social transformations," wherein alternative forms of loving, living, and affinity can be made possible, "felt viscerally" in that particular temporal moment.[160] Unlike the "timeless" wedding daguerreotypes of the nineteenth century that "enclosed a heterosexual couple in its own privileged visual circuit," Hujar's ceremonial portrait (plate 12) is inextricably connected to the physical, social, and affective atmospheres of its context, wherein the rate of HIV infection was rapidly increasing within, and beyond, the creative community surrounding artist and subject.[161]

Grief and rage, or "mourning and militancy," as Douglas Crimp affectively theorized in a 1989 article for *October*, became inseparable, could never be finished, or resolved, when so many thousands died to the deafening sounds of homophobic and racist indifference.[162] This is the "diseased society" Wojnarowicz decries as having contracted upon learning he has contracted the virus; he also protested this, in a mourning and militant gesture, via the white block text that he appliqued onto the back of his denim jacket, accompanied by the downturned pink triangle symbol used by ACT UP: "IF I DIE OF AIDS—FORGET BURIAL—JUST DROP MY BODY ON THE STEPS OF THE F.D.A."[163] Jennifer Doyle, when writing about his works and activism, calls these statements the description of a "life-world of a community doubly traumatized, by the disease and by the vicious public policy and homophobic discourse that took shape around AIDS in the late 1980s and 1990s."[164] One way this manifested was in the politicized, paranoid, stigmatizing censorship of contemporary art and writing, spearheaded by Senator Jesse Helms, who pushed through Congress the amendment that prohibited the state funding of artistic material considered "obscene," "as if to look at explicit images of queer sex (or, more accurately, any frank work by queer artists) were to risk contact with the virus that causes AIDS."[165] This policy resulted in the catalog for Nan Goldin's Artists Space exhibition *Witnesses: Against Our Vanishing* (1989–90) (within which Cookie's epistolary writing on AIDS featured) being defunded by the National Endowment for the Arts (NEA) due to the supposedly defamatory—but also no doubt sexual—content in Wojnarowicz's essay.[166] Here was the violent *gentrification of desire* at work.

From Hujar's presence I dream and speculate that many of the figures connected to this "culture war" were present at Cookie and Vittorio's wedding, which flouted the sphere of the "private," by taking place in the sky, re-making the meanings of devotion during the time of disease. Immortalized in photographs, it was politicized as a public ritual, a bodily performance: an assembly of high-risk persons who lived more complex social bonds than those sanctioned by the state. "Friendships, extended family, nonparental intergenerational commitments, subcultural alliances": These affinity-forming relations became even more vital during the AIDS epidemic as resources of care, across embodied practices of living, loving, writing, and making.[167] Gregg Bordowitz terms these "cultural strategies of survival" "queer structures of feeling," echoing the spatial image also invoked by Cvetkovich's understanding of the ways in which material documents of AIDS activism are underpinned by complex "archives of feeling" and "affective networks."[168]

Cookie provided similar affects of closeness in the short epistolary piece "A Last Letter," which was featured alongside Wojnarowicz's essay in the *Witnesses* catalog. It was a reprint of an essay published a year earlier in a special issue of *City Lights Review* focused on AIDS writing; after suffering from a stroke during the summer of 1989, Cookie could no longer speak in strong sentences, eventually giving way to a situation in which she became "too sick to write" anything new.[169] Also in May, Ching Ho Cheng—the artist who lived in the Chelsea Hotel and to whom Cookie once wrote an affectionate note from Provincetown, enclosing a downy duck feather inside a burnt-orange envelope—died of AIDS-related illness at Manhattan's Mount Sinai Hospital. Their exchange did not visibly continue, as a correspondence in life, or correspondence in death, beyond this one love letter. However, Cookie did return to the fresh climes of Cape Cod, the scene from which her letter entered the postal network, during the summer of his death, her health declining, too.

"A Last Letter" contains two epistolary voices in print: the "last letter" Cookie's friend—the artist, actor, filmmaker, and musician Gordon Stevenson—sent to her from the hospital before he suffered an AIDS-related death in 1982, and Cookie's (belated, epitaphic) reply. Their correspondence spreads contagiously: from a personal relation to collective grief, from the "I" to the "We," the private to public letter.[170] She lets his angry, beautiful writing breathe again, *beyond death*—a gesture toward repairing the pain of the posthumous letter, which Cookie received on the day he died, and which foreshadows the posthumous context in which her own writings in *Witnesses* and *Walking Through Clear Water in a Pool Painted Black* came to correspond in and with the world.[171] In spite of the distance that separates her from her beloved then, when Gordon "demanded that [she] didn't visit him" in the hospital, and in spite of the distance that separates them in the "now" of her writing, Cookie creates spatial, temporal closeness between them by incorporating within her own written textures her friend's sick voice and body as expressed in a private, freedom-fighting love letter.[172] She conjures the bedside position—of more than one body; of two lovesick correspondents—in belated, sick-time writing, echoing Wojnarowicz's delayed printing of the close-up he captured of Hujar's open mouth, taken seconds after his friend's last breath two years prior (figure 2.1).

"A Last Letter" has inspired my reach to her; it enduringly inspires my close readings and writings on, and with, and beside her life and work. By the time *Witnesses* opened, the disease had struck and stolen Cookie and Vittorio. Vittorio died on September 14, 1989, after contracting AIDS-related pneumonia; nearly two months later, on November 10, Cookie suffered a fatal cardiac arrest. For Cookie, for Vittorio, for the artists to whom *Witnesses* was dedicated, and for the tens of thousands more, whose lives either got taken or were irreversibly changed, I must look, and write, closely, *with care*. I am following Sedgwick's critical investment in "slowed down and amplifying attention," which figures out, as Berlant wrote in memoriam to her, "repair in the face of intensifying world disrepair."[173] As a form of visual attention translated into words, a way to watch and write closely, it is emotive and embodied: a visceral cutting open of the photograph, bleeding sadness and hope at once. By "touching" the image by Hujar this way, it is possible to illuminate the powerful affinities (silenced but not destroyed) that existed between lovers and friends during the AIDS crisis: multiplying relations of care, *within and after the image*.

Hujar provided care through the lens of his camera on the day of their wedding, shooting film in the ambiguity of black-and-white. He captured private and public moments, from backstage to on stage, from jokes between friends to the solemn silence of a Bible reading. They may, or may not *yet*, have received their diagnoses in the spring of 1986, but the grayscale picture by Hujar invokes a destabilizing mixture of affects: love, loss, pleasure, pain. This mixture echoes the enigmatic, bittersweet voice of Cookie's autobiographical close writing, which continues to hum throughout her love letters and friendship profiles, those pieces of a novel, the epistolary essays added to it, the replies she gave as the *East Village Eye*'s health columnist, and the intimate, relational, loving art writings she contributed to *Details* as their exhibition "correspondent." While these pieces do not pose as directly as letters—when compared to Kathy's lovesick epistolary fever afflicted by the second-person address—the lines of contact that they generate, amid experiences of disease shared by author and beloved, invite me to read them within the expansive, reparative domain of love-letter writing.

In Hujar's bittersweet, ambiguous picture, one wedding guest wears a geometric suit and dark sunglasses, suggesting the wildness of an afterparty to come, while another guest pensively scratches his face. Scrutinizing the central tableaux of the scene so closely (from left to right: Francesco, Vittorio, Cookie, René: one standing beside the other; Cookie's right arm within Vittorio's left), certain details, *melancholic* details, begin to appear and graze my eye.[174] I am stung by the photograph's melancholic punctums. From Vittorio's feminized funeral clothing, to Cookie's subversive style, to her smudged eye makeup (leaking sad and happy tears), to her pursed, painted lips and antique crochet gloves: These sartorial specks are bruising and "poignant to me," as Barthes defines the affective messages of the punctum in his own melancholic but loving book, *Camera Lucida*, which was written in the aftermath of his mother's death.[175] Those details come to me like the piercing closeness of a love letter.

And like Barthes studying a photograph of his mother aged five, I have studied this pictorial fragment—searching and reaching for Cookie Mueller, an eternally adolescent girl, whom I both know too well and will never know well enough (that is the state of love-in-pieces).[176] Hujar's wedding picture has "*worked* within me," particularly Cookie's crochet gloves, slipped so tenderly inside her soon-to-be-husband's arm to clutch at spring flowers.[177] Contained within a photograph that is defined by spatial relations of proximity (between photographer and subject; between friends and lovers), it is a gesture that is also stitched throughout Cookie's close writing of love, reparation, and care: letterlike columns dedicated *to* the stigmatized, sick bodies she *held so close*. Text and textile share the same etymology in the Latin verb, *texere*, which means "to weave."

I imagine your crocheted hands, scribbling reparative ink.

Life Writing Is Light Writing

"What else do I have to say? He's one of the best artists in the world," writes Cookie about Hujar in her "Art and About" column, published in *Details* magazine, March 1986—a month before her wedding.[178] Hujar was beside her that day, bestowing love with the light of his camera; in her document for him, she also gives him open, honest, light writing, as if the gap between them closes with the candor of her question and statement. The page illuminated by the springtime glow.

While her column may have been published in black-and-white print, there's a physical *touch* to her writing that is immediate, etched with the emotional, tactile scribbles of a fan's love letter. Like erotomania, like kleptomania, like masturbatory mania, like the manic collecting of clothes, fandom has also been understood as involving a network of pathological symptoms—irrational, overemotional, excessive, hysterical, deviant, compulsive, sick—which is often felt in the (adolescent) body.

A decade or so before, in 1974, Kathy had apologized for being "fanatical" and "imposing" in her diaristic letters to Alan Sondheim, wherein, unsure of the right "word to use," she simply says, as adolescents are wont to do, "I *like* . . . you."[179] And when Cookie first "liked" Vittorio in a similar way, she doodled a full-length portrait of him naked on a beach in blue biro.[180] Annotated with lustfully explicit notes, this unfinished, figurative drawing is reminiscent of school-time scribbles, like the pornographic pages of sexual fantasy drawn by Kathy as thirteen-year-old Janey, which were intercut within *Blood and Guts in High School*, her 1978 novel of interdisciplinary pieces.[181] "Leave the pictures in," Kathy insisted to her publishers when they tried to dismiss the drawings as damaging the work's "literary value."[182]

I wonder whether Cookie is in some way lovesick like this—could she be linking the fangirl perversities of adolescence to speak the politics of AIDS—when she incorporates her fluidly gendered beloved in writing? She is "in awe" of Hujar; calls Greer Lankton "a genius" whose show "really had to be seen to be believed"; writes that "David Armstrong's photographs stood out like diamonds"; maintains that Keith Haring "remains one of the most powerful esthetic pop visionaries of this decade"; and, when seeing her "world recorded" in Nan Goldin's recent work, candidly declares, "Without saying it was poignant, beautiful, and at the same time visually assaulting, I might just say that it was great."[183] Her messages grazed, touched, called out to a beloved recipient—who may not have been all that far away, in physical or affective terms. Many of Cookie's close correspondents were also considered to be "angels" by Kathy: living, working, loving, protesting, in a sick, inequitable, rapidly gentrifying "City of hell."[184]

Cookie was a lovesick fan in a devastating, lovesick time in history. She was another angel in hell. As Gran Fury visualized in their 1989 billboard poster, *Kissing Doesn't Kill: Greed and Indifference Do*—which features three straight, gay, and lesbian interracial pairings pecking, engulfing, nibbling the other's lips ("affection, desire and exultation in three acts")—it was not kissing, or saliva, or sexual promiscuity that caused the epidemic to violently spread, but a systemic failure to care for those most at risk, those bodies who did not "fit" the heterosexist, racist vision of the intimate public.[185] And as the image shows in its three discrete moments of connection, ecstasy, and erotic play, love was a force of joy—a force also of resistance—in sick times. To write as closely as these kissing couples, as Cookie does in her fangirl epithets, became a political act, a means of activating queer bonds of resistance, of making alternative intimacies, voices, desires, and bodies public, during a political climate of "Silence = Death."[186] As she close-writes in relation to Mapplethorpe's recent photographs at New York's Robert Miller Gallery, "I hate to gush, it makes self-effacing artists feel uncomfortable, but that doesn't happen when the gushing is well deserved and in print."[187]

By touching Cookie's affectionate fangirl letter pieces, I follow Joli Jensen's argument in recognizing that "what it means to be a fan should be explored in relation to the larger question of what it means to desire, cherish, seek, long, admire, envy, celebrate, protect, ally with others"—with *sick others*, often the closest people to her, those she felt an affinity *to* and *with*, in spatial, physical, and affective terms.[188]

Kathy might not mention Cookie, or her close writing, in the 1990 piece published in the *New Statesman* on AIDS activism and the healing capacities of artists' friendships, but when I read and write closely, her presence hums throughout it, writhes around the printed letters that detail the bodies, organizations, events, and venues described as important nodes in networks of community and care.[189] The community-run art and performance space ABC No Rio is seen as part of this network (where Cookie once read her writing aloud and which was then under threat from real estate developers), alongside John Giorno's AIDS Treatment Project, A Day Without Art, and Visual AIDS. A 1984 black-and-white snapshot taken by the artist Joseph Modica at the nightclub Danceteria shows Cookie cheering and smoking in the front row; she is sat beside the performance dancer John Sex and the artist Keith Haring, while a drag performance artist draped in diamonds, Ethyl Eichelberger, performs around them, in close contact, the stage and the audience merging in the chaos as one. All four of them died with the disease. Sickness and death haunt this collective portrait. It was included in a 2015 Visual AIDS exhibition on the ways art and activism came together at night.[190]

Akin to such moonlighting activities, Cookie forged reparative solidarities by writing close to the friends who took her picture—Goldin, Mapplethorpe, Hujar—as well as many more artists she loved. Featuring black-and-white photographs of abject animals and abandoned buildings, Hujar's show at Gracie Mansion Gallery turned out to be the artist's last.[191] He had a bronchoscopy on New Year's Eve, 1986, because his breathing was staggered; not long after, he was diagnosed with AIDS; by the following Christmas, he was gone.[192] Wojnarowicz's essay "Living Close to the Knives" describes the slow temporality of Hujar's death, re-creating the scenography of his friend's hospital room as a private space of queer intimacy, company, and care: "the sounds of nurses and hospital gurneys far away in the halls."[193] While Cookie's piece on Hujar precedes his diagnosis, his death, and Wojnarowicz's essay, it points to the devotional aspect of her writing: how she wrote palliatively beside and not against (like Cookie squeezed in between her high-risk friends at midnight), as a vital, *unsanitized* form of creative, life-giving, light-giving accompaniment and care. It was in the space of writing that these affinities could be extended after death in posthumous (still-sick) times.[194]

As Glenn O'Brien writes in a tribute to Cookie published in *Details* after her death: "She was about the love and generosity of art. Whatever she had she gave it all away. She gave love in her writing, in incredibly amusing detail. When you read something by Cookie you get a real boost. It's light reading. As in let there be light. Her work illuminated the charitable nature of the human heart. And it lightened the world."[195] For example, when admiring Mapplethorpe's flower studies in June 1988, she plagiarized the modernist poetry of Gertrude Stein and then playfully punned, in intimate proximity to her own love object, "It's always been that a rose is a rose is a rose, but Mapplethorpe has given us something new. Mapplethorpe's flowers don't look terribly fragile . . . even the poppy, whose delicate petals wilt in a day, seems hunky."[196] In this fangirl wordplay, Cookie turns a wildflower into a homoerotic image, overturning the stigmatizing of gay desire that worsened during the AIDS epidemic of multiple crises. She does this lightly—but with care; she, too, is sick—aligning with Bordowitz's support for a type of AIDS activism in art wherein laughter combines with emotion and rage. This is a "tendency" toward ridiculousness that operates within "queer structures of feeling," he writes, in memory of Charles Ludlam, Jack Smith, and Ethyl Eichelberger: laying his affinities (and his erotic fantasies) bare.[197] We might also think of this tendency toward a light, surreal, or even ridiculous tone as an example of what Berlant would later describe as "humorless anti-humorlessness work."[198] In fact, given that it was Mapplethorpe's very still lives that were included alongside the artist's bondage portraits in the canceled exhibition at the Corcoran Gallery, *The Perfect Moment* (1989) (which followed Mapplethorpe's death from the illness), Cookie's piece was prescient, offering resources to the diagnosed and the dead. To remember this homophobic climate of censorship, paranoia, and fear is to bring out the political urgency of Cookie's light-giving close writing. She wrote beside her beloved: as fan, lover, carer, and ally.

In the archive: I feel the ripped edges of your photocopied articles; I think of the care you gave to the pieces that came apart. Your shared broken pieces.

The Bittersweet Touch of Beside

I keep Cookie's writing physically close to me with the caressed paperbacks that live on my desk. These partialized, printed part-objects, the "glimpses and touches" of her "familiar-unfamiliar" body, nourish my love for her and shadow my writing.[199] I cannot let her go. I glance, I reach, between the text and her body in pieces. My writer's love is spatial as well as spectral. From embodied touch to embodied writing, I read and write close to her, *feeling* the pull of the past.

Within these critical encounters, book covers are to be looked at closely, fondled for clues. Both Sedgwick and Gallop are invested in close reading as an ethical, feminist practice, paying close attention to the jackets that cloak their objects as a result: focalizing details—to then enlarge them again—a means of critical sustenance ("erotic and ethical at the same time").[200] Such a practice echoes Sedgwick's promise in *Tendencies* to "make invisible possibilities and desires visible; to make the tacit things explicit; to smuggle queer representation in where it must be smuggled," as I also tried to do when caressing Hujar's portrait.[201] Herein Sedgwick confesses to "becoming a perverse reader," which "was never a matter of condescension to texts, rather of the surplus charge of my trust in them to remain powerful, refractory, and exemplary."[202] Indeed, loving her objects *too much* (like an adolescent)—which she terms a method of "overreading," defined by a "visceral near-identification with the writing I cared for, at the level of sentence structure, metrical pattern, rhyme," not to mention at the level of jacket and frontispiece—implies a perverse, erotic type of critical attachment: obsessive, passionate, close, and bodily.[203]

Aroused by affinity, I similarly fixate on, return to, incorporate, and repeat the theoretical pieces, concepts, and images in Sedgwick's work, which have transformed my close writing, "obsession . . . the most durable form of intellectual capital."[204] This "way with her words" is enduring, chronic, resistant to external pressures: a type of care in critical writing. I respond to her question, through my obsessed relation to her work (one shared by so many writers and thinkers), and beside the pieces of my beloveds (again, *I am not alone*): "What does it mean to fall in love with a writer?"[205] For me, it activates the coalescence of cathexis and care, which is achieved through the textures of close reading, close looking, close writing: *beside images, materials, and words.*

I absorb this theoretical practice from Sedgwick (in an affective and critical gesture of incorporation that others who move through these pieces have also made the stuff of their thinking and writing, encompassing expansive and diffuse pedagogical scenes: the classroom of close writing).[206] For example, when closing the introduction to *Touching Feeling*, Sedgwick directly addresses the portrait that is the book's frontispiece, an image that, she writes, "impelled [her] to assemble the book in its present form."[207]

It is not separate to the content, or even illustrative of it, but intimately entangled within its textual and theoretical shape and structure. Taken by Leon A. Borensztein, the sepia-toned photograph depicts the textile artist Judith Scott in close contact with one of her epic works, whereby a "core assembled from large, heterogenous materials has been hidden under many wrapped or darned layers of multicolored yarn, cord, ribbon, and other fiber."[208] With her nose pressed against it, and arms wrapped around it, fingers clawing at its densely woven threads, Scott merges with her work, the closeness of subject and object, in this tactile gesture of embrace. For Sedgwick close-reading this portrait, "the 'besideness' of these two forms," suggests creativity, triumph, tenderness, and sadness, all at bittersweet-once.[209] Born with Down syndrome, and also deaf, Scott was institutionalized within "a crushingly negligent Ohio asylum system for over thirty-five years," later gaining recognition as an "outsider artist" but "repeatedly diagnosed in terms of lack."[210] What I want to emphasize is the identification that Sedgwick feels with Scott's portrait as a conveyance of an "affective and aesthetic fullness that can attach even to experiences of cognitive frustration."[211] While not physically or mentally disabled in the same way, at the time of writing (and also textile weaving: two ways to touch, two meanings of repair), Sedgwick is locked into the frustrating course of cancer therapy: She is caught within an extended period of "dying," shattered by the brutal force of her own mortality.[212] And yet—in an echo of Scott—creative and hopeful energies endure within her life, practice, and theory; it is signaled by the powerful, reparative possibilities of the word "even." As Sedgwick affirms: "In writing this book I've continually felt pressed against the limits of my stupidity, even as I've felt the promising closeness of transmissible gifts."[213]

To be "in between" in this way—diagnosed but not yet dead, skirting the precarious edges of the sickbed—connects Sedgwick with Cookie (like it connects Cookie with Kathy), although the diseases they endured were different. I fixate on a coupled portrait by Nan Goldin: of Cookie sleeping in her bed, while Sharon, Cookie's close friend and ex-partner, sits glowingly, intimately, exhaustedly on the mattress beside her (plate 13). Hence, when Sedgwick offers *beside* as a critical method in *Touching Feeling*, I cannot help but see such a position—which she describes as an alternative to the dualistic signifiers of "*beneath* and *beyond*" that imply projects of exposure, and paranoid, linear narratives of "cause versus effect, subject versus object"—as marked by the mortal frame.[214] For Sedgwick—in this text and in earlier essays written during the height of the

AIDS epidemic—the spaces and experiences of living and dying crossed, overlapped, like the spatial, textural interweaving of warp and weft: cloth close to the skin.

Correspondingly, after Kathy's death from cancer, the executor of her estate—the artist, curator, and writer Matias Viegener—gave the artist Carolee Schneemann a rayon skirt printed with small birds that once swished across Kathy's hips. Reflecting on her participation in a marathon reading of *Blood and Guts in High School*, held at Performance Space New York in 2018 and organized by Sarah Schulman, Schneemann writes that her affinity with Kathy began when Jerome Rothenberg wrote to her from Los Angeles to tell her about a "young writer" who "shared issues and formal explorations close to [her] own." This bond between the two women was subsequently replaced by their own "cross-country letters," then "subsequent and intense joyful times together" in the cities they intermittently called home and eventually manifesting in shared things, namely the slippery, surrogate-silk textures of the skirt that now covers Schneemann's bedside table.[215] Sarah Wang also begins her reportage of the event by detailing the sartorial gifts she received from Viegener that once belonged to Kathy: "a sheer black lace bodysuit and a Japanese linen dress." The bodysuit is a "crotch cutter," jokes Wang, and so for the reading she decides to wear "the dress . . . stained with my own blood and guts through twelve years of ownership."[216] I think of these shared threads that have stuck to both of their bodies across time as elastic and material extensions of their friendships with Kathy. Wang reembodied the garment when she read, producing a spectral return of the author herself. And the rayon skirt also invokes Kathy's partial presence; its passing into Schneemann's tender, bedside ownership becomes a way for the artists to care for one another, across the Sedgwickian "open mesh" of living and dying, or what Jean-Luc Nancy calls "the fall of sleep."[217] They are beside one another through the presence (in absence) of this "vibrant matter."[218]

Beside captures the subject/object closeness of the writing act: as in at the (bed)side of, or right next to; as in the "touching," dyadic relation of Scott with her artwork: sutured together, with love and care. It is close, erotic, this *beside* relation, in ways that also listen to Viegener's description of Kathy's "last day," wherein his friend Connie Samaras—who had come to be beside him, as well as Kathy—"stroked her, soothed her, and kissed her" in bed: "the last stand of love against death, love in death."[219] It is as if in this tender moment, the exhausted bodies of carer and patient collapsed beneath shared sheets. In Sedgwick's "White Glasses," a similar reversal, or indeed identification, happens (as I examine in the prologue of this book).[220] Subject and object are also beside one another in this essay written across fragile states. As a preposition, *beside* points to theory as spatially oriented and embodied: "accompaniment rather than critique," as Anne-Lise François has argued of Sedgwick's late work, and *Touching Feeling* in particular, but that can also be found beating throughout earlier essays, too, written near to the time and circumstances of Cookie's death.[221]

And this affect of accompaniment, I *feel* and sense, is intimately connected, a reparative response to, the sick atmospheres of Sedgwick's embodied writing. For she lived with the drumbeat of disease: It manifested in the cancer spreading throughout her sick body, which she lived and experienced beside HIV-positive friends and writers. Her state of perilous embodiment, of being somehow between living and dying, was part of her queer identification as a gay man. And such chronic, incurable, sick, and queer temporalities of the body informed her understanding of the reparative lens, wherein she questioned how "generational relations" don't always proceed in repetitive, regular, predictable "lockstep."[222] To be beside, and as I newly suggest, to *write beside*, is to inhabit reparative, horizontal kinships—across the living and the dying, the sickbed and the bedside—rather than the vertical temporalities assumed by Oedipal structures and adopted by the pain-forestalling, surprise-fearing paranoid reading position.[223]

It is to revisit the pieces of a past archive, like Alvin Baltrop's belated conservation of his intensely proximate portraits amid the overlapping precarities of his embodied present. Through such a gesture, the artist cared for his previous work, the desires documented within them, as he also cared for HIV-positive friends in the African American queer communities he was closest to. As an up-close composition, with only the diamonds, dash of silver eyeshadow, and hair of his subject visible in the frame, his incandescent portrait of Black trans activist Marsha P. Johnson shows her in a stilled moment of rest and reserve (figure 3.4). It is an intimate scene of recuperation, of trust between two artists: held in the spatially close surround inferred by the composition. The photograph was undated at the time, though it has since been given an extended date of "1975–1986," creating a horizontal space through which Baltrop could then move, *across* time, as he actively regathered, felt anew, the living pieces of his archive, when companions and subjects—many of them AIDS activists like Johnson—began to fall ill, struggle to receive the healthcare they needed.

When I write beside my beloveds, the horizontal closeness that I conjure in letters is also temporal: a cross-historical, contagious correspondence

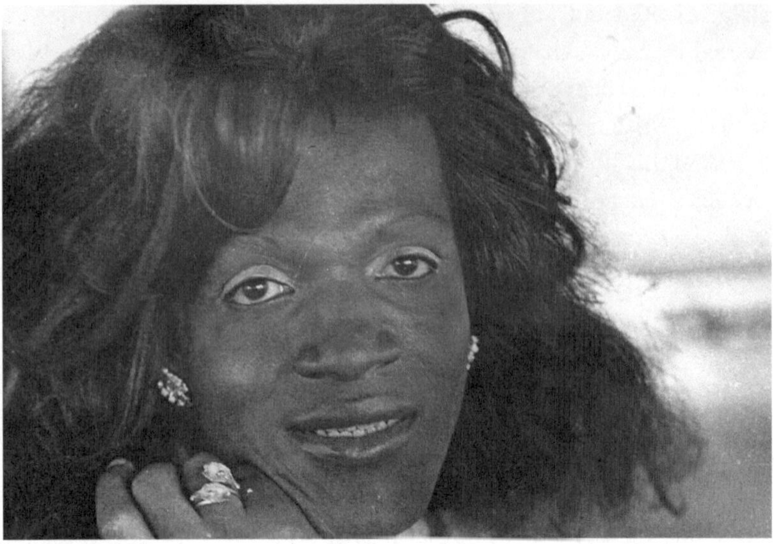

an up-close composition
an incandescent portrait

3.4. Alvin Baltrop, *Marsha P. Johnson*, undated (ca. 1975–86). Gelatin silver print, 11.7 × 16.8 cm. Whitney Museum of American Art, New York. © 2024 Estate of Alvin Baltrop / Artists Rights Society (ARS), New York.

of affective touch. Maggie Nelson's writing beside the "many gendered-mothers" of her heart in *The Argonauts* is similarly embodied, although she also creates a spatial register for this close contact in the citational, choral field of the book, as Sedgwick's name reoccurs, among many, *to the side of* her reparative fragments.[224] It is this attention to positioning, alongside the wide range of relational affects that could energize critical gestures of *beside* ("desiring, identifying, representing," but "repelling, paralleling, differentiating," too), which Sedgwick's brief conceptualization also departs from.[225] She points to the commonly shared memory of sleeping in a bed with a sibling (horizontally in a row) as a reference point for the complex, changing, ambivalent movement of affects in thinking and writing beside. This is intensified when we think of the sickbed as a scene of *beside writing*: here love meets exhaustion, in ambivalent bittersweetness, although both states are close and tender.

In theorizing *beside* as a critical practice, Sedgwick builds on one of her own love objects (Judith Butler's *Gender Trouble*) to find and fixate within it Esther Newton's 1972 ethnographic study of drag queens, *Mother Camp: Female Impersonators in America*: namely the ways Newton analyzes the floor plans of the clubs in which the queens perform, attentive to "the multisided interactions among people 'beside' each other in a room."[226] Sedgwick's interest in Newton's visual research is dimensional, rather than simply temporal, as Butler's earlier reading had emphasized in relation to "gender as 'stylized repetition' and 'social temporality.'"[227]

I had to wait years to touch Newton's book myself, as the library caring for its creased covers—printed black-and-white with the white female impersonator's lips, nails, eyelashes, and brows dipped in scarlet pigment—remained closed in the suspended months, then years, of COVID time. But when I did (with my surgical-blue face mask rubbing at cracked lipstick), I was struck by the way in which the author's ethnographic analysis—which begins by focusing, quite factually, on the differences between straight and gay drag bars in New York and other cities—highlights how social distance between performer and audience is compressed in queer venues, through intimate seating arrangements (similar to the scene of Cookie sitting steamily close to Ethyl Eichelberger, as the drag artist dived into the crowd at Danceteria in 1984), but also through the close scrutinization (which could be critical or affectionate or *both*) that performers receive from a gay audience.[228] While the hierarchy within tourist, straight clubs doesn't stray from the model of entertainers performing *for* spectators, there is immediately a rapport between performer and crowd in gay clubs, says one impersonator, which is to be honored and strengthened (to cathartic effect), even when the audience challenges, or is critical of, the act's style, makeup, speech, or comedy.[229] Similarly, the paradoxical list of affective positions that Sedgwick enumerates when considering *beside* in *Touching Feeling*—how "attracting" sits next to "aggressing" (and not because there is an alphabetical logic employed)—also highlights the felt complexities and contradictions that can underpin the ways we perform, live, and write beside, as manifestations of love and care.

Goldin also touched, with her lens, the flesh-grazing proximities between drag queens—in taxicabs, in adjoining rooms within Downtown apartments, or on a crowded dance floor—their poses and glances suggesting undercurrents of felt resistance or competition in intimate, loving situations, which are rooted in connective bonds and solidarities emerging from shared experience. Pictures of Cookie with her friends—in nightclubs, club toilets, and even funerals (where pleasure and pain collide)—activate a similar horizontal, relational plane, wherein relationships are formed and then flourish in intimate spaces of proximity.

Likewise, in many pieces for *Details*, Cookie re-creates the affectionate but also physically, affectively, temporally "hard" scene of the "bedside" or casket position, addressing the bodies, lives, and works of her friends and lovers, just before or after they have died.[230] She begins a memorial written for *Details* after the death of Divine—her drag queen "fairy godmother" whose magical kinship with her was queer-horizontal, rather than Oedipal-vertical, and who was pictured by Marcus Leatherdale reclining in a striped satin minidress on a bed, asking for a queer sibling to share it with—with an anecdote of the two of them, side by side, "traveling in a borrowed vw bus going down the Cape Cod beach road from Provincetown."[231] She captures relations of love in scenic beside-dimensions and goes on to celebrate his fearless performances, the ways he influenced a "slew of lost souls," "liberated them," "helped open closets," and "set people free," extending her particular closeness with him into the physical and affective spaces inhabited by those he "touched" and by those he still could "touch" "on celluloid."[232] Two of those souls may well have been Sedgwick and Michael Moon, who wrote imaginatively beside Divine (forming a queer kinship beyond the reality of lived experience that resonates with my close writing) and also beside each other in a piece exploring "divinity" as a "feeling or attitude" that encompasses both "abjection and defiance" and is felt by "fat women and gay men."[233] Perhaps Cookie's beside writing of shameless, abject, defiant, exulting, quasi-divine, spiritual love is both a feeling and an attitude: an affective positioning that is also political, shaping the erotic relation she inhabits, to be near her sick or dead beloved.

She celebrates, with the similar spirit of ridiculousness, the life and work of her friend, the painter Jean-Michel Basquiat, in a similar way, noticing that "there was a strange force that was moving through his hand, forcing him to commit to canvas something that was at once much larger than he was."[234] Artistic experience equates to impressive scale and fullness; it flourishes in spite of psychic and bodily fragility. In tender response to his tactile, reparative painting, Cookie closes the piece with an intimate disclosure, reaching for her loved one, from life into death and back again: "Don't feel sorry for him," she writes. "It's the rest of us, left behind, we should feel sorry for."[235] Cookie hereby summons what Sedgwick describes as "the irreducibly spatial positionality of *beside*," where subject and object blur, get closer.[236] It is a gesture of intimacy, accompaniment, and care, which closes spatial, emotional, and temporal distance between bodies, through the acts (and affects) of writing. To write beside is an attitude and a feeling; it is rage and love. Its desire is "reparative," as Sedgwick understands it, formed through adding, accreting, assembling, and repairing, loving laterally, rather than vertically, in order to extract "sustenance from the objects of a culture, even of a culture whose avowed desire has often been not to sustain them."[237]

Assuming the affective and spatial closeness of *beside*, Cookie's writing is thus a reparative response to an inadequate context: America in the 1980s, the height of the AIDS epidemic, wherein Ronald Reagan, an "aggressive birdbrained leader of a grand empire with the representative numbers 666" (Cookie's humorous, antihumorless words, in 1986), legitimized, with his silence, a culture of discrimination, censorship, and fear.[238] A year earlier, and recalling Kathy's love of Prince, Cookie riffed that "we should rally for an artist in office."[239] Staying true to her cause, in her writing for *Details*, she writes beside her beloved, whom she called her "dear artists"—the people who need holding.[240]

Beside, Always

Fresh from their rooftop wedding—whereby they entered into the formalities of affinity, once known as marriage, by law, if not exactly by social convention—in her May 1986 column, Cookie describes a recent sightseeing tour of Manhattan with her husband, wherein they chanced upon "the third biggest church in the world, the Cathedral of St. John the Divine . . . began in 1892 and it's still not finished."[241] Like the open wound of art history, like her own novel-in-pieces, this "means it's alive," Cookie adds, "a place where people join for their ideas and beliefs," including the avant-garde, as she discovers a "poet's corner" remembering American writers, and a separate space memorializing people who have died of AIDS-related illnesses.[242] I often think of them walking through this church—newly wed, possibly ill—touching the stone tablets inscribed "beloved," in close hospitality, and solidarity, with the dead. Cookie and Vittorio were unexpected reembodiments of the Latin meaning of "fanatic" that day: two people inspired by a god, or a shrine, a consecrated place.[243] At the church, or in their notebooks, or on the printed page: They filled their sick spaces *with love.*

This is most fiercely felt in Cookie's August 1989 piece *beside* Vittorio, which also walks, citing Sedgwick in "White Glasses," the delicate "ontological crack between the living and the [*nearly*] dead."[244] From their sky-high riff on a "dearly beloved" Catholic white wedding, to their connected practices manifesting in art and life, both Cookie and Vittorio played ambiguously with divine, heavenly allusions, at a time when AIDS activists such as Marsha P. Johnson also reinvented the figure of the saint, while artists like Wojnarowicz more directly criticized the position of the Catholic Church on issues relating to the banning of safe-sex information in performative texts. Vittorio, for example, began drawing pigs, dolphins, and angels—heavenly symbols of love and freedom, what the artist called his "puti puddings"—from the confines of his hospital bed in 1989.[245] And on February 14 that year, he drew a picture of a skunk bestowing its heart upon another, scrawling beneath it: "Happy Valentine to my beloved. I can't believe me drawing hearts!!"[246] Unlike Vittorio, Cookie wasn't raised Catholic (but "the confessional booths had always fascinated" her, she jokes, in one of her close pieces), and yet there is something extravagantly—even queerly—divine about the language she uses to write beside Vittorio and his work.[247] She introduces his drawings, via his illness, in the collaborative publication *Putti's Pudding*: "From the realization of the depths of his plight, comes a reach toward a pinnacle of inspiration."[248] And her piece published in *Details* in August, described as her most personal and painful to write, contains similarly euphoric reflections on the "three hundred pen-and-ink drawings," produced by Vittorio on scrappy notebook pages in the hospital over a three-month period.[249] Exhibited near their home at Bill Stelling and Dean Ralston's 56 Bleecker Street Gallery in 1989, it was hoped that these drawings would raise money for Vittorio's healthcare, alongside the coauthored publication, through which they were spatially, creatively, emotionally, and diagnostically *beside*.[250]

But the column she wrote that summer didn't begin this close, as Annie Flanders explained: "The only time in seven years we ever asked her to rewrite her column was her August 1989 piece about Vittorio. At first she held back her true feelings because, after all, he was her husband. But when she rewrote that column she told about the power and greatness of his last work. I'm glad she rethought it and told it the way it was—they both deserved that."[251] Writing after Cookie's death, Flanders registers this rewritten column as a gift, a method of repair, offered just in time: *for both of them*. This is shared writing, sculpted from collective art and experience; it pulses with affinity. To think about what they deserve is to say their deaths were unjust; it is to illuminate the risk and hope in their work: how much was at stake in writing and drawing, continuously—often in the same hospital room at the Cabrini Medical Center in the East Village—*even* when their bodies got weaker.

Cookie cared for her husband, as a political protest, in her sick time, close writing. She keeps her crocheted glove slipped inside his arm, as she did on their wedding day. She writes close to him (his life and work), illuminating his hospitalized, drawing body, in a way that re-creates the various forms of closeness (spatial, affective, diseased) captured by Goldin in her funeral photograph of Cookie standing by Vittorio's open casket (plate 14). In this beside portrait, she is the wife grieving, wearing black, shadowing the time of his illness and the devastating inevitability of death. A wooden figure of Christ looms enigmatically over Vittorio's golden corpse, while Cookie turns to the dark. Just a month earlier, however, she wrote through the pain of a stroke—figuratively and metaphorically at his bedside—translating into words the determined brightness of his hospital drawings: a political, reparative act.

In the revised version, Cookie replaces the sanitization one expects from hospitals (as well as from critical distance) with a candid confession of closeness, beginning: "I'm a fan of Vittorio Scarpati. I'm also his wife, so I guess you might say I'm his biggest fan, aside from his mother."[252] In the column she is a composite of roles and identities: adolescent fangirl, art critic, writer with AIDS, wife to an artist with AIDS, caregiver. She confesses that her personal attachment to Vittorio makes "writing about his work to be the most difficult task [she's] ever had."[253] Difficulty here is synonymous with love: an incapacitating closeness that defies verbal description. She continues: "I've discovered that in bold black-and-white print it's hard to express one's love, a love that has always been silently understood. There are things that are too profound to commit to words on paper."[254] But she persists, risking a reckoning with the weight of the unsaid: the relational, sick forces that bind them.

Echoing Wojnarowicz's palliative closeness with Hujar, Cookie also produces a visceral picture of Vittorio's hospital room. She is spatially beside—physically, emotionally, temporally close to him—in her corporeal, scenic descriptions, which move quickly from the past to the present tense: "one day his lungs just literally ripped and he was taken to the hospital and confined to a bed. He stayed there for five months (at this writing he's still there)."[255] Bathed in sunlight, a blurred photograph by Philip-Lorca diCorcia (*Vittorio*, 1989; plate 15) also depicts the artist in his hospital bed, its ghostly color palette lifted by details (telephone, teddy, hat, balloon) that suggest accompaniment, creativity, and care. And in correspondence with this portrait, it was the solace brought to him by a friend, in the form of "some ink pens and drawing pads," which "saved him," writes Cookie. She muses on the meaning of this gesture: "Vittorio picked up those pens and didn't put them down. Did he need to be physically tied down to finally do his important work?"[256] In asking this "difficult" question, Cookie aligns Vittorio's project—his "visual narrative that told of deep despair, sadness and pain, but also hope, happiness and joy"—with Sedgwick's autotheoretical idea that affective and aesthetic reparation can occur in and through illness.[257]

Both Cookie and Vittorio are full of these reparative desires, which they communicate through their art: from Vittorio's colorful self-portraits, which depict his skeletal body in cartoon close-up, his lungs beeping the sounds "NON WORKING" (plate 16), to Cookie's similarly colorful, consolatory language in response. She challenges his medical confinement with dazzling descriptions of not only his drawings but also his active, persistent, "drawing body." "From these restrictions and limitations," she writes, "came his brilliant emancipation, a luminous disengagement from his restraining bounds. . . . [H]e was gripped by a frenzy of pent-up art communication that exploded out of him. . . . The work transcended small concerns and became grand, beautiful, honest and somehow ancient. The most incredible work poured out of him at an amazing rate, as if his gods were working him overtime. So prolific was he during this period that no one who saw this work could believe their eyes. Miracles were pouring out of a mortal."[258] The act of drawing opens out the possibility of freedom, from darkness into light. Writing beside his hospitalized body, Cookie illuminates the feverish desire and speed of his art making, how it comes from within (personal, "honest") but also exceeds and transcends his static position in sick, somatic becoming. Vittorio is caught between life and death: both mortal and not.

Cookie's overblown words—her nod to heavenly transcendence—might seem strange, even insincere. But the affective power of this piece arises from such blurring: from the ambiguous tension between the stark reality of his hospital room, and the otherworldliness, even divinity, of his life and art. Cookie's enigmatic blur is a gift, which while "queerly" camp in its religious connotations, is also as serious and sensitive as they come: an urgent call for his body and work to be cared for, recognized, and made visible. I am reminded here that camp—with its "juicy displays of excess erudition," its "passionate, often hilarious, antiquarianism," and its "'over'-attachment to fragmentary, marginal, waste or leftover products" (characteristics shared in Cookie's letter piece to, for, and beside Vittorio)—is a reparative practice according to Sedgwick.[259] Playing ambiguously with divine allusions *as* queer attachments, Cookie's piece is a willful, hopeful proclamation of her husband's life-affirming art—"a tale of hospital horror, a black comedy, a singular experience of institutionalism, and what it does to the soul"—which movingly corresponds to her own experience of illness.[260] As she did in "A Last Letter," she wrote her reparative gift amid the quickening sick time of the disease that closed in on her, too.

Returning to the close surrounds of Vittorio's hospital room at the piece's poignant end brings this mode of reciprocal, writerly care—authored by a similarly sick writer who "hope[s]" her husband "comes home soon"—into sharp focus.[261] This postscript conjures the relational intimacy of touch, accompaniment, and care—within the hospital room, where "Vittorio continues to draw . . . spreading some light around," and also within the space of writing.[262] The brutality of this fact demands our close attention, as it is the devastating context of the disease, the means by which society let people die, which necessitated Cookie's loving writing. She wrote beside her beloved Vittorio to give him the gift of light.

Like You

Vittorio and Cookie drew haloes for each other, in sick and loving correspondence. "A Halo Over the Hospital" is also the title of a long autofictional poem written by the contemporary writer Maggie Nelson. It is voiced by a narrator addressing—*like* a love letter—a sick mentor and friend being treated in the ICU. Their body is broken, paralyzed. "I have to trace your delicate lips," writes Nelson, "with a finger laden with balm, cherry balm." "And give you water / from a miniature green sponge on a stick."[263] These small but meaningful acts of care, which reverse the mothering roles usually inscribed upon the relations between mentor and student, occur as Maggie feeds, dresses, and reads to her hospitalized friend and former teacher, first from the sick-bedside position and then again in the space of writing. Inspired by Maggie's live reading in the hospital room of an in-progress essay of hers on "troubling the passage from the particular to the universal," together they begin to problematize "*the singular*," which the dual experiences of sickness and care both speak to, inasmuch as both states are viscerally and specifically located in the relational body.[264] Nelson's poem is also relational, directed toward, via the epistolary address, her own sick beloved. And when asked in an interview-in-correspondence about the conflict between the singular and the universal in her work, Nelson proposed that "paying attention to a singular person or thing can be a way of expressing love, of paying homage to their uniqueness, their difference from everything else that exists. And that paying that kind of attention can be a way of understanding difference as something that holds us together rather than signifying our apartness."[265] I have paid attention to Cookie and Kathy this way; I have revered them, as a way to move between the individual and the collective body, even as I write closely beside. In this chapter I have also brought them newly beside one another and have written letters and pieces between them both. This writer's love has been unsingularly attentive, gesturing toward more-than-one "you."

Jonathan Flatley, who's also been (like Nelson) a student of Sedgwick and her reparative methods, calls "liking" "less a discrete emotion than an elemental attraction, the most basic positive feeling one can have, a readiness *to pay attention* to something and *be affected* by it."[266] It is an affective state that, he argues, structures Andy Warhol's transdisciplinary practice, which includes the lived, more domestic domain of collecting, alongside drawing, painting, film, video, photography, and writing. Essential to the practice of liking, suggests Flatley, is also the "capacity to perceive likenesses and to be alike," involving processes of "affinity and affiliation, correspondence and conviviality" that make up what Benjamin called the "mimetic faculty," "our gift for seeing similarity."[267] To think with this affective faculty as a source of finding likenesses between bodies and things is not to suggest that being like, or thinking likeness, is commensurate with being the same, or thinking sameness. Indeed, Flatley describes how Warhol's propensity to like, imitate, and/or identify with the feminine, to have queer desire for the same sex and be a queer person, produces an affective space that connects countercultural identities (producing solidarities, affinities, likenesses formed from liking) but does not categorize them or make them "the same" when they are always plural and in process.

So, when I highlight certain likenesses shared by Cookie and Kathy, I do so to attend to the nuances of their singularity, in differential correspondence with each other. This begins with the ways they both corresponded in the gendered activity of correspondence, considering how this shared interest in form connected to a shared political project: to revitalize, expand, and transform our spaces, narratives, and understandings of love, by paying close attention to the sick angles and affects through which it has been felt, experienced, *written*. In erotomaniac purgings or sick swallowings of grief, they are afflicted when they write. But the space of the lovesick letter piece is also freeing, to the extent that to feel the delirium, disorder, and/or disease of love is to feel the delirium for writing, for writing usually archived, or silenced, or smothered away, or (if we are lucky) maybe even gossiped about. In this delirium, the two of them together, singularly and apart, cared for the hidden, plural perversities and pleasures of lovesickness, by which I mean—*we mean*—loving *in* and *with* sickness. Love, in this sense, is the "transformational environment" Berlant describes: a reparative space of sickened vulnerability and pleasure-seeking resistance.[268]

To "couple" Cookie and Kathy together this way in homosocial affinity also points toward a desire to support "pleasure sharing," as Crimp calls it and which Flatley also traces in Warhol's life and work, describing it as "joyous, plural queer singularity."[269] Crimp also found it to be emerging in the disco scene of the 1970s, wherein "coupling was newly seen not as a 'happily ever after' compact, but as an in-the-moment union for sharing pleasure," which did not even need to stop at "two."[270] Indeed, other like-minded lovers have also entered the elastic field of this essay, focused on, but in no way exclusive to, the years around 1980.

In her 1989 essay "Blue Valentine," published in a memorial publication after Warhol's death, Kathy describes how, as a young student in San Diego, she would listen with her friend Melvyn Freilicher to "Warhol's production of The Velvet Underground and fantasize about living in a society such as that of Warhol and his friends, a society in which the two of us weren't outcasts." In daydreams, and then later in the real-life sharing of the "forty-second-street world," its "very gay riffraff," she finds herself closer to Warhol and his pleasure-sharing "affective world."[271] This closeness is spatial, emotional, and aesthetic, producing a particular identification that crossed from the spaces of lived experience into the autofictional worlds of art, writing, and theory. She infers that they are alike, in the ways they collapsed the distinction "between politics and radical form," and collectively admired those society condemned: "drag queens, strippers, young homeless kids, not hippy pot smokers but actual heroine [*sic*] addicts and welfare victims."[272]

If, as Flatley suggests, Warhol attempted an antiracist gesture of resemblance across the color line in multimedia notebook works or the *Ladies and Gentleman* series—wherein 1974 Polaroids of drag queens Divine and Marsha P. Johnson take up proximate pages, and Black and Latinx queens pose in ways reminiscent of "Hollywood movie-star glamour strongly biased toward whiteness" as part of a "mimetic practice that reparatively and disidentificatorily reassembles fragmented codes of stardom"—the power structures and codes of racial difference through which such representations worked meant that race could not so much be transcended but felt or understood in a different way.[273] There are instances of "disorientation" in such images, as Ahmed terms the felt discomfort of the nonwhite body moving through spaces made up of objects that do not extend for them, when whiteness is an effect of how such objects cohere and repeat.[274] Flatley, for example, examines the effects of the beehive blonde wig worn by Johnson in a 1975 Polaroid: how it once represents "the desire to be white," while also "showily announcing its failure, suggesting the degree to which that desire is not equally available to a person with brown skin, who cannot approximate a fantasy ideal of white womanhood by dying her hair blond, as Norma Jean Mortenson Baker did in becoming Marilyn Monroe."[275] In Flatley's reading of this work, he draws on José Esteban Muñoz's understanding of disidentification: a critical mimetic practice in performance that provides for the minoritized subject "a mode of recycling or reforming an object" without "trying to be 'the same' as it," generating a type of failure that is reparative. Disidentification demonstrates some of the possibilities that Ahmed registers in instances of "failed orientation"—wherein things can move, become rearranged, generate critical impressions.[276] In relation to *this* work's close writing, reading Flatley, Muñoz, and Ahmed together means recognizing how Warhol's representational practice in affinity was by contrast "available" to my beloveds due to the lines and citations and access points cohered by the systemic reproductions of whiteness.

I've seen a photographic piece of the party: Danceteria, 1986 (where disco met drag). Cookie shimmies beside Warhol in a slippery, backless dress. His stance is stiff in comparison, directed toward the lens that snaps them, and he surreptitiously holds a camera, anticipating the gesture of a visual reply. Her bare elbow rubs his coated shoulder, while his silver hair tickles her forearm, in this intimate, pleasure-sharing space, where identities could be formed beyond the normative lines of gender, outside of the binary separation between sickness and health, where attachments could flourish beyond the "homo/hetero opposition."[277] Cookie and Kathy were like Warhol in the ways they also imagined "new, queer forms of affection and relationality" in their epistolary close writing, the letter piece being somewhere "where those forms could find a home."[278] Hence, when I love them with likeness, I do so to draw out the magnificent room they made, singularly and together, for reparative remakings of love, its sick perversities. As Flatley has discussed in an interview, drawing on Nelson's call to "pluralize and specify" in *The Argonauts*, this practice helps us to "enter into different magic circles of similarity" but these are not closed or uncritical shapes: "we can also move out of them," too.[279]

The poet and artist Daisy Lafarge writes in a 2020 essay that love is "*like* a microbial intruder," which can spread contagiously between hosts, *between writers*.[280] Infected by love's pathogens has also brought about in me a different kind of consciousness that is shaped from likeness. This state has helped me to think with the gendered sicknesses that stick my beloveds closer, contagiously, beside one another, and the critical effects of this sticking. Affection and infection, as Lafarge has theorized, and Cookie, Kathy, now *I* (in a *singularly similar* way) have performed, are not so far apart. I have attended to the sexual, gendered, bodily, and literary subversions and perversions made possible when the sick woman (in all her *many* guises, as Hedva reminds us) rewrites love in private blurring with public letter pieces. Diagnoses also blur in this contagion of likeness, as they singularly and collectively write from pathologized lovesick states of erotomania, tuberculosis, masochism, autoeroticism, kleptomania, fandom, and AIDS. I pluralize, to specify, to impress on the reader the ways misogynistic and heterosexist attitudes, perceptions, and medical frameworks have repeated across time, from nineteenth-century, hystericizing discourse, to the 1980s and the vicious nontreatment of multiply minoritized peoples living with AIDS propagated by a hostile government and media.

From within their "around 1980" circle of magic similarity, Cookie and Kathy resisted and challenged those attitudes with their affective, exposed, erotic, intimate, sexual, visceral, always relational, lovesick letter pieces. Perhaps they were unknowingly corresponding with each other, the unfinishedness of the Valentine's Day performance at the Mudd Club (wherein Cookie posed but did not read her close writing aloud), niggling at them from the inside (like a scratch at the throat), throughout the decade that followed. They reembodied the sick woman in their close writing, cared for her, in all her mess and vulnerability, and illuminated the agencies, complexities, and perversities of her desires, feelings, pleasures, and loving attachments, amid censored, gentrified, homogenized intimate publics. To think about love and sickness as somehow linked, of one state being *like* the other, might feel uneasy. But it is discomfort, trouble, which brings repair, a glimpsing of other lives possible, across our entangled pasts and presents.

In her 2009 essay-in-pieces *Bluets*, Maggie Nelson begins by posing the possibility that she has fallen in love with a color. Blues are her palette: the lovesick pigments of ultramarine, cerulean, lapis lazuli; or Yves Klein's blue as used by Derek Jarman in the 1993 film *Blue*, which visualizes his partial blindness caused by AIDS as a flood of single-shot blue. It is a seduction that, she says, began with "*an appreciation, an affinity*."[281] For her, the debased affect of simply liking blue, as if it is what Sianne Ngai calls a "minor" feeling, became "*more serious*"; it then became "*somehow* personal," as she collected in small pieces of writing blue affects, anecdotes, artworks, extracts, experiences, things, feelings.[282] Sometimes, this connection she has for blue, which prepares and propels her to pay attention to it, as Flatley has recognized of liking, involves negative as well as positive affects. She succumbs to delusion, to loneliness, to melancholy, to lovesick pain, to the exhaustions of care. From the initial prick of affinity comes a vibratory world consumed by this complex love. It shakes, moves. *It has nowhere to go but writing.*

Affinity is also the root of my writer's love. I began by saying, "I like her," like an adolescent expressing their beat of affection, *for more than one at a time*. It seemed fleeting, before it took hold as devotion, as I collected their bodies in pieces, traveled beside them, paid attention to the texts and textiles close to their skin, bestowed my close writing in response. I have fallen under their spell, caught by the contagion of close writing, *consumed*. It is an infection of influence, "more than, or other than, friendship," but not exactly "love" as we have previously known it either.[283]

This writer's love—our threesome of shared affinities—is different. It hums, travels, takes up hidden passageways and corners, spreads and changes blue like a bruise. When I think of the intimate and transitional writerly gestures of this kind of undertowing love, I think of the leftovers that remain, three-way folded, typed letters, in Hervé Guibert's grayscale, ambiguous portrait of his own domestic archive of letters received, sent by a devoted correspondent (a reader of Guibert's work) to dwell in (cradled by) the starched creases of a couch shrouded in a white sheet like a corpse (*Les lettres de Mathieu*, 1984). Dated the year that one of Guibert's dear friends, a philosopher, died from AIDS-related illness, it is a photographed relationship-in-letters cupped by the luminosity of a blank page, both written and unwritten, a surface that is touched by the living and the dead. The shadowy, androgynous, ghostly silhouette of Guibert—as photographer, correspondent, and novelist of autofictions, illness, and more-than-other-than-friendships, who inscribed dedications in the opening pages of his books to his creative companion, Mathieu Lindon (a different Mathieu than the sender of the letters)—has haunted me, too. In affinity: I've felt the presence of that spectral figure; the intimate contact made between sender and receiver across the folds of past and present; the fugitive and bittersweet excess of close writing. Writer's love is light and dark like this image; I've felt it closely on my skin.

Like the globular spill of fresh ink, like the gestural scribble of a hand, like the endless edits on this book, a writer's love is restless, liminal, fluid, transitional. It is not a fixed affective register, as it stretches from the pleasures of liking, to the afflictions of loving, and holds both in its grasp. In corresponding with Kathy and Cookie, I have faced up to the tragic impossibility of ever sourcing a cure for them. Sometimes, my loving them across time has been painful, so I continue to offer pieces rather than wholes, committed to the unfinished task of close writing.

No less serious, no less personal, no less *real*, than the lived and literary genres of romantic love afforded to us, it transforms the possibilities of love *as writing*, as *critical lyric*.[284] Can anyone else decipher it, this script that began as ours? I have unfurled my love-in-pieces, given them over to the reader, the next close writer, or lover of my beloveds. Who else will enter our threesome?

I collect; I write; I love: more-than-one-you.

*
*
*

Postscript

OPEN ENVELOPES, OR, I AM STILL STUNG

The caress is an awakening to you, to me, to us.

Luce Irigaray, "Why Cultivate Difference"

I was wearing cream cotton gloves the day I found the wedding portrait: of Cookie in lily-white tulle, oyster-shell silk-satin, and cream-manuscript crochet lace, with Vittorio standing beside her in the fluid folds of funereal black. The archivist gave the gloves to me, along with one file at a time: *This is to protect, and care for, the condition of the files*. I saved the "Photographs" sleeve until last, carefully caressed its textures while clothed: first, a full-length portrait of the bride, then the groom in a state of partial undress, and finally both of them together at the altar—this series' last song. I felt balls of fluff gathering at the inside tips of each finger as I handled the outdoor-altar picture, an abject, material trace of time passing.

I had been in New York for a week, before I un-sleeved and caressed this picture (the caress being a gesture, writes Irigaray, which is alive to "intersubjectivity . . . attentive to the one who touches and the one who is touched . . . a call to a return to you, to me, to us: as living bodies").[1] I'd been grasping for Cookie by rooting around in the shadows of the page, the city, the archives in which her name is cataloged, shuffled in among more legible others: where her presence is entombed. I hadn't expected to find the secretly stored wedding pictures hidden intimately inside an oversized file. Even the archivist of the photographer's estate was surprised to learn the prints were there. It felt like serendipity stung with loss. Holding her and her beloved this way, holding her and her beloved holding each other, brought uncontrollable feelings of anger and rage at the injustice of what came after. I thought of the people closest to them who miss them dearly, daily, as well as the people who are no longer alive but miss them, too.

In that moment, the meaning of the soft cotton gloves changed, becoming less an item attached to the rules of an institution, to conserve and make order, and more an item of affective ritual, which brought about sudden and partial contact, a coming closer to her at the borderline, the edge, the seam, both mortal and not. I felt her death on my skin, but I felt her life and writing, too.

Cookie's statement in her cover letter could be swallowed in mine: "I also like to think of these pieces as messages from a place situated right on the borderline, in a sort of netherworld, perhaps situated right on the precarious edge between two uncharted lands, or on the brink of an abyss."[2] Although I am no longer in New York, I keep longing for the wedding picture, returning to it, to touch it closely again *in writing*. It is Cookie's gloves that guide me. Like me, she loved secondhand things—delicate, hand-woven objects from the past—to be brought into the embodied urgency of her now. She shared with Madonna a fascination with the fingerless lace glove, as well as a fascination with Jean-Michel Basquiat. But while Madonna's haptic accessories tended to show a lust for the manufactured, Cookie's marital threads are vintage, even *sick*. They are spun with the melancholic, reparative desire of nostalgia—weaving, touching, dreaming, writing alternative lives out of time.

She threads her arm through the eye of Vittorio's needle, forming a loop that is knotted together at two gloved hands holding a bunch of flowers. His arms also meet at two clasped hands. Their bodies make a woven structure, which echoes the special hook used in the knitting of crochet lace to interlock loops of thread. Crochet lace became popular in the nineteenth century in the West, as an interface to be *touched*, maybe even *stolen*. It was also a verb, a creative leisure activity, like other sorts of needlework or letter writing. Cookie's gloves contain the traces of desires-in-disease within its interlocking loops, giving way to writing as touching, as dreaming, as grieving, as remembering, as stealing. From skin to sack, the glove holds the closeness of writer and subject. Inside and out: The structure is reversible, like the *me* and *you* of close writing.

I have grazed Cookie's fingerless crochet gloves in a similar way, stealing them out of love, getting closer to her: another means of care. I give her this gesture, as she gave it to others. She deserves my open hand.

The crochet glove is the fragile weave that separates and connects us, full of open loops and grainy textures, through which I see glimpses, rather than full outlines, of her form: body and writing. I wonder at the passageways that lie beyond the surface of its holes. As a fabric, its structure is capacious and stretchy, like the nonlinear web of historical time.

It is vulnerable to breaking, but also desiring of repair. I wear those gloves in my dreams, our bodies almost merging, beside one another: two writers, using the same tools. They are two cream envelopes creased by her touch, by her bodily residue: the presence of a postmark.

Is this fetishism, or fandom, or kleptomania, or melancholy . . . or love? Or is it all these perversions at once?

My reply to the love she gave with her gloves: an open envelope of love-in-pieces. In this never-closed pocket, there is room for the words (all her scrappy pieces, like Dickinson's epistolary materials) in her worn worlds.

And there is room in the second pocket, too, on the other side of the dress. I've scoured charity shops for 1980s lace leotards, velvet trouser suits, leopard-print dresses, and leather trousers, like the ones worn by Kathy, which gave her an inked outline. After teaching one of Kathy's books one autumn day, I found a butter-soft pair in the Oxfam on Gloucester Road, not far from where she lived, for a fleeting time, in the leafy suburbs of West London. Slipping them over my frame felt like a way of getting inside of her texts, akin to chronic and contagious letter writing.

I've pocketed these secondhand garments to fantasize our intimate merging, so I can steal in some way closer to the perverse vitalities of her clothing archive: from life to writing and back again. Seeking her envelopes has also been laced with the desire for discovery: of the voice through which to address her—closely, directly, nearly illicitly, full of almost pink steam—a voice that is both mine *and* hers: one that, I intimate, only she could hear from afar. I know I am bound to wait, in the time of this open envelope of scattered, belated, delayed, never-resolved love-in-pieces.[3]

First, the photographs themselves had absorbed my (autoerotic) attentions: the 154 prints of trousers (neon pink and yellow 1991 Versace jeans luridly printed with the Pop faces of Marilyn Monroe and Betty Boop); skirts (flared and pleated, schoolgirl mini); dresses (tight bodycon sheath hugging close to the absent figure or stretchy and mangled full-length gown); jackets (leather biker frilled in pink shag fur or blazer with cut-out torso); two pieces (top-to-toe sailor smock and bottoms); and shawls (trimmed in tails of fox fur), which were photographed by the artist Kaucyila Brooke in the summer of 1999 and exhibited as a series at the Berlin Biennale in 2004.[4] The series displays a carousel of carnival clothes hanging off metal hangers against a plain white background, suspended, stretched, or contorted by the artist using invisible thread, injecting life and form and energy into them. Slipping between vision and touch, I felt enveloped by these documents, with the photograph itself a "weightless, transparent envelope," according to Roland Barthes.[5] Could my beloved appear there, at the opening; could she float across the plane? Could she return in envelopes within envelopes?

(*I wait . . .*)

As an object, the photograph articulates a piercing relationship to past lives, and garments do, too, with moth-eaten holes, ink stains, and bleached surfaces inscribing temporal passages in materiality itself.[6] I rubbed the images with my eyes, gazed at them through texture, to trace Kathy's lost body-in-pieces, its authorial energies, in Brooke's spectral reanimation of her disembodied things.

Later, I saw her Vivienne Westwood pirate jacket hanging, bodiless, on a domestic wooden hanger at an exhibition of her writings, objects, and artworks.[7] I felt rejected for being forgotten in the program of events. I slipped surreptitiously into the building instead, danced around its polymorphous shape, tried to enter her (however dangerous or deviant this felt: my loving her this way). As Barthes writes in *A Lover's Discourse*, "I must resemble whom I love. . . . I want to be the other, I want the other to be me, as if we were united, enclosed within the same sack of skin, the garment being the smooth envelope of that coalescent substance out of which my amorous Image-repertoire is made."[8] I tried to meet her within that ghostly envelope, which was far from smooth: its vertical lines of white stitching upon admiral-navy cloth interrupted by tucks and gatherings at the chest and shoulders. "I always wanted to be a sailor," said Kathy, "to wander" in "wonder."[9] These words pulsed in and around those stitches, reminding me of the ways she waywardly wandered in her writings through texts, worlds, sexualities, and genders. I peered around the garment's jagged corners, like a "pirate" happening upon "buried treasure. The dreamer, the dreaming, the dream."[10] I inched closer to her disembodied rags. My eyes darted along the sinuous lines of the wrinkles at her elbows ("wrinkles that in the technical jargon of sewing are called memory").[11]

In one impulsive instance, crossing between the senses in this middle ground of agency, I reached my hand out—to this archived piece of her body—in a spontaneous gesture of touching desire. I fantasized us seizing one another down the dark tunnels of the jacket's interior: hello, goodbye.[12] (I miss you.) Before I physically left the jacket (suspended in space; swinging through time), I attempted to catch the sweetness of her smell, the ancient vapors of sweat stuck to the item's browned insides overlaid with a yellow-on-red Westwood label. Gigantic, she becomes waste: a "second grave for the loved being," which comes alive differently again (that is melancholy) in my enduring, waiting, belated love-in-pieces.[13]

It was around the time I encountered the jacket, still dreaming of the crochet glove (their lived, sartorial envelopes inviting renewed habitation), that I began speculating on the possibility of inking the inside flesh of my right arm (like a pirate) with a series of black lines forming the shape of an envelope (my stolen buried treasure). My reply to them: a love-letter tattoo, a wounded reminder to keep writing, to conjure a space beside them. I love this mark on my skin—it gestures toward the reparative ink of my own close writing, as I weave letters and words like crochet, a way to keep *their* love, and *this* love, alive. And yet the meaning of the tattoo, or its shape as I look at it, has subtly changed over the years of my love-in-pieces.

There is the time of writing, then the time of editing, then the time of redrafting, which becomes entangled with the multiple temporalities of writing absorbed within a book. As I have repeatedly attempted this closing piece to the postscript of *this* close writing, I have felt the looming mortality of a loved one, unsure of how to narrativize her last months, knowing the present tense will soon become past.

That time has come. It is now late September 2022; she died in February (on Valentine's Day eve). For her funeral in March, I wrote and read aloud a memorial letter addressed to her, in kinship with all those who have felt, continue to feel, her touch. I leave the following in the present tense, recalling the time-based remains of the Dead Letter Office.

In the summer of 2021, my ninety-two-year-old Northern Irish grandmother, our Nana, began to feel weaker, after a surgery the winter before discovered sick shadows on her bowel, liver, and lung, making her vulnerable to recurring infections. She was in the hospital for the month of August, at a time when access to be beside her was tightened due to the pandemic. On her return home, I traveled from London to see her and to help my mother care for her mother, both of whom continue to care for me. After a swift but tender embrace, she rubbed the textures of my pleated clothing between her thumb and forefinger; this is her distinctive form of tactile, nonverbal, affectionate communication. I recognize it as a kind of maintenance, a daily haptic ritual to be performed: one that she knows well as a quilt maker and that has acquired a powerful intensity with the worsening of her vision due to macular degeneration. The rub of clothing: It also reverberates between us as a gesture of love.

This gesture is also known as "the weaver's handshake," which Eve Kosofsky Sedgwick—the queer theorist with a passion for textiles—calls her own "rub of reality," and which she also inherited, along with the skills of crochet and embroidery, from her grandmother (echoing my own education in sewing).[14]

When the time comes, I also hope to inherit the antique bronze letter opener (I've asked her nicely already), shaped like a sword, which sits on the table close to her, beside pills, a glass of water, the telephone: her haptic altar of living and dying. It is a tool through which she has communicated across generations and oceans, slicing through time and space.

To inherit this object will be a way to steal and to cut *with love*. I am already adding it to my own altar of writing things: letters, gloves, needle and thread, envelopes (rubbing my own reality as ritual). It is like the stitch unpicker that a seamstress needs to start over, redo the repair. To rip the seam open is the gift through which my writer-beloved can rise, can continue to rise—particles of almost pink steam. As I write with this gesture, I dream of my beloved grandmother's shiny object, the thing that cuts to get closer.

I use it to break the seal of the envelope tattoo. I peel the flap open, unfold it; I confuse the boundaries of entry and exit, of sender and receiver. In refusing the climax of the sealed envelope, I welcome a life in unsent letters, in waiting for replies, never knowing if they will come. I recognize the reparative energies involved in *staying with writing*—as collecting, as making, as composing, as moving. It keeps things capacious, too, *alive*: this commitment to writing as a practice lived, that does not "end." There could be more than one postscript in this atmosphere of ritual. This one holds the scene of the genre flail, to borrow a term beautifully rendered by Lauren Berlant, as I come to recognize that "opening our objects to a transformation whose effects are not foreclosed might make us better at holding the objects that are also changing."[15] And so to truly hold them—their bodies in movement that have changed shape with the impact and time of the COVID-19 pandemic and the systemic socioeconomic and racial inequities it has underscored—I must partially let go.

While there is and will always be ritual as I desire to repair the cut of their absence and summon closeness in that space, there is no calling of our correspondence closed, no act of entombment within a sealed envelope. I could not cure my subjects. I soon came to realize this horrible burden of impossible care. This is why I withdraw the close of a signature.

The cut at the envelope's throat I desire is to be forever open, echoing the vocal, collective politics of the *seen* open letter, inviting more readers who are also close writers to correspond with my beloved. In many ways, to unseal the envelope is uneasy, exposing. This writer's love is ours, but I know you are not *wholly* mine, could never be. And so, I leave those open loops, crocheting sheer pieces: where glove touches glove, writing touches writing, life touches death touches life.

Notes

PROLOGUE. BELOVED, SO BITTERSWEET

1 Pethers, "Dead Letters," 136–37.

2 "Postal Women in the Late 19th Century," Smithsonian National Postal Museum, https://postalmuseum.si.edu/research-articles/women-in-the-us-postal-system-chapter-1-women-in-postal-history/postal-women-in-0#:~:text=The%20Civil%20War%20opened%20career,temporarily%20fill%20in%20the%20vacancies.

3 Kraus, *After Kathy Acker*, 39.

4 Acker, "Seeing Gender," in *Bodies of Work*, 158–59.

5 Kathy Acker, "Colette," 1985, David M. Rubenstein Rare Book and Manuscript Library, Duke University, Kathy Acker Papers (cited hereafter as KAP), B22, F11.

6 Acker, "Colette," KAP.

7 Cited in Kraus, *After Kathy Acker*, 42.

8 Mueller, "My Bio—Notes on an American Childhood," in *Walking Through Clear Water in a Pool Painted Black* (1990), 137.

9 Mueller, "Alien," in "Garden of Ashes," in *Ask Dr. Mueller*, 201.

10 Roberta Blattau cited in Griffin, *Edgewise*, 164.

11 For example, both Acker's and Mueller's work was published by Anne Turyn's prose periodical *Top Stories* (Acker's "New York City in 1979" was issue 9 [1981]; Mueller's "How to Get Rid of Pimples" was a double issue, 19–20 [1984]). Later, Chris Kraus's Native Agents series would also unite them under the same imprint, with Mueller's *Walking Through Clear Water in a Pool Painted Black* launching the series in 1990, and Acker's *Hannibal Lecter, My Father* following in 1991.

12 Chris Kraus, "The New Universal," *Sydney Review of Books*, October 17, 2014, https://sydneyreviewofbooks.com/new-universal/.

13 Kraus, "The New Universal."

14 Jonathan Mandell, "Die Young, Stay Pretty," *New York Newsday*, January 4, 1990, Fales Library and Special Collections, New York University Libraries, Ron Kolm Papers (cited hereafter as RKP), B18, F32.

15 Arnett, "Review: Eve's Body/Of Work," 166.

16 Sedgwick, "Memorial for Craig Owens," 104.

17 Cookie Mueller, postcard to Richard Hell, undated (ca. 1981), Fales Library and Special Collections, New York University Libraries, Richard Hell Papers (cited hereafter as RHP), B6, F399.

18 Carson, *Eros the Bittersweet*, 10–11.

19 Carson, *Eros the Bittersweet*, 26, 29.

20 Kathy Acker, "you are on the enemy list of the Black Tarantula," undated label, KAP, B31, F10.

21 Carson, *Eros the Bittersweet*, 30.

22 Carson, *Eros the Bittersweet*, 3, 30.

23 Goldberg, *Sappho:]Fragments*, 22.

24 Goldberg, *Sappho:]Fragments*, 22.

25 Goldberg, *Sappho:]Fragments*, 23.

26 Kathy Acker, postcard to Terence Sellers, undated (ca. 1981), Fales Library and Special Collections, New York University Libraries, Terence Sellers Papers (cited hereafter as TSP), B1, F13.

27 See Mueller, "Tattooed Friends," in "Garden of Ashes," in *Ask Dr. Mueller*, 212–16.

28 DuBois, *Sappho Is Burning*, 52, 70.

29 DuBois, *Sappho Is Burning*, 3, 13.

30 DuBois, *Sappho Is Burning*, 3.

31 DuBois, *Sappho Is Burning*, 3, 20–21.

32 DuBois, *Sappho Is Burning*, 35.

33 DuBois, *Sappho Is Burning*, 19–20.

34 DuBois, *Sappho Is Burning*, 28, 64.

35 Cixous, "Coming to Writing," 42.

36 I am also departing from Meridith Kruse's analysis of Sedgwick's "perverse close reading" in the essay "Sedgwick's Perverse Close Reading and the Question of an Erotic Ethics."

37 Sedgwick, "Memorial for Craig Owens," 104.

38 Patton, "Heterosexual AIDS Panic," 3, 6.

39 Geary, *Antiblack Racism and the AIDS Epidemic*, 2.

40 Sedgwick, "Memorial for Craig Owens," 105.

41 See Sedgwick, "Paranoid Reading and Reparative Reading" (2003), 123–51. In "Memorial for Craig Owens," while Sedgwick's attention is focused on the sexually queer subject, when she refers to the society that "hated and hates so much," we could take this to refer to a more capacious configuration, encompassing all those suffering under the social weight of marginalization (105).

42 Sedgwick, "Paranoid Reading and Reparative Reading" (2003), 128, 150.

43 Sedgwick, "Paranoid Reading and Reparative Reading" (2003), 128, 137, 149.

44 Phelan, *Mourning Sex*, 4.

45 Phelan, *Mourning Sex*, 4, 3.

46 Sedgwick, "Memorial for Craig Owens," 105.

47 Sedgwick, "Memorial for Craig Owens," 105.

48 Sedgwick, "Memorial for Craig Owens," 106.

49 Gallop, *The Deaths of the Author*, 11–12.

50 Gallop, *The Deaths of the Author*, 11.

51 Johanna Hedva, "Sick Woman Theory," *Topical Cream*, March 12, 2022, https://topicalcream.org/features/sick-woman-theory/. Hedva's essay was originally published in *Mask Magazine* 24, January 2016; I cite from the 2022 version published on *Topical Cream*.

52 Sedgwick, "White Glasses," 252–66; Sedgwick, "Paranoid Reading and Reparative Reading" (2003), 148.

INTRODUCTION. A WRITER'S LOVE

1 Gallop, "Annie Leclerc Writing a Letter, with Vermeer," 104.

2 Gallop, "Annie Leclerc Writing a Letter, with Vermeer," 104.

3 Bellamy, "Barbie's Dream House," in *Pink Steam*, 17.

4 Bellamy, "Barbie's Dream House," in *Pink Steam*, 19.

5 Bellamy, "Barbie's Dream House," in *Pink Steam*, 17; Rand, *Barbie's Queer Accessories*, 9.

6 "Female Trouble" is also the title of a short piece by Mueller that reenacts her stay in a hospital for infected fallopian tubes. It was first collected in the 1990 Hanuman Books chapbook *Garden of Ashes*, before the chapbook's contents were included in an edited collection of the author's fiction and criticism in 1997 (217–19).

7 Gallop, "Annie Leclerc Writing a Letter, with Vermeer," 104.

8 Bellamy, *the buddhist*, 34.

9 Bellamy, *the buddhist*, 35.

10 Sedgwick, "Paranoid Reading and Reparative Reading" (2003), 145. Italics mine.

11 Bellamy, *Pink Steam*, back-cover blurb.

12 Gallop, "Annie Leclerc Writing a Letter, with Vermeer," 108.

13 Gallop, "Annie Leclerc Writing a Letter, with Vermeer," 107, 108.

14 Bellamy, "Delinquent," in *Pink Steam* 135, 141 (italics mine in the second quotation).

15 Acker, "Epitaph: Kathy Acker on Robert Mapplethorpe," 36.

16 While I quote the essay from the 2004 edition of *Pink Steam*, "Delinquent" was previously published in *A Poetics of Criticism*, edited by Juliana Spahr et al., in 1994 (293–99). See Bellamy, "Delinquent."

17 Acker, *My Mother: Demonology*, 20.

18 Joseph Litvak cited in Sedgwick, "Paranoid Reading and Reparative Reading" (2003), 147.

19 Dinshaw, *Getting Medieval*, 3.

20 Dinshaw, *Getting Medieval*, 3, 21.

21 Kruse, "Sedgwick's Perverse Close Reading," 132.

22 Kruse, "Sedgwick's Perverse Close Reading," 132.

23 Gallop, "The Ethics of Reading," 7.

24 Gallop, "The Ethics of Reading," 8, 13.

25 Gallop, "The Ethics of Reading," 13.

26 Gallop, "The Ethics of Reading," 16; Kruse, "Sedgwick's Perverse Close Reading," 134.

27 Nelson, *The Argonauts*, 39.

28 Nelson, *The Argonauts*, 41.

29 Nelson, *The Argonauts*, 41.

30 Nelson, *The Argonauts*, 30.

31 Kruse, "Sedgwick's Perverse Close Reading," 135.

32 Sedgwick, "Queer and Now," 3.

33 Sedgwick, "Queer and Now," 4.

34 Sedgwick, "Queer and Now," 4; Sedgwick, "Memorial for Craig Owens," 104.

35 Gallop, *The Deaths of the Author*, 19.

36 Gallop, *The Deaths of the Author*, 19. For the *differences* article, see Gallop, "Reading Derrida's Adieu."

37 Gallop, *The Deaths of the Author*, 19.

38 Derrida, *Adieu to Emmanuel Levinas*, 1.

39 Levinas cited in Derrida, *Adieu to Emmanuel Levinas*, 6. See Levinas, *Totality and Infinity* (first published in French in 1961).

40 Derrida, *Adieu to Emmanuel Levinas*, 13.

41 Gallop, *The Deaths of the Author*, 22.

42 Derrida, in Derrida and Dufourmantelle, *Of Hospitality*, 77.

43 Derrida, *Adieu to Emmanuel Levinas*, 19, 23.

44 Gallop, *The Deaths of the Author*, 19.

45 Gallop, *The Deaths of the Author*, 26. Italics mine.

46 Gallop, *The Deaths of the Author*, 30.

47 Barthes cited in Gallop, *The Deaths of the Author*, 30.

48 Barthes cited in Gallop, *The Deaths of the Author*, 31.

49 Barthes, *The Pleasure of the Text*, 56. This work was originally published in French as *Le plaisir du texte* (Paris: Éditions du Seuil, 1973).

50 Mavor, *Becoming*, xix.

51 Mavor, *Becoming*, xviii–xix.

52 Mavor, *Becoming*, xix.

53 Mavor, *Becoming*, xxv.

54 Mavor, *Becoming*, xxii and 102, respectively.

55 Mavor, *Becoming*, 16.

56 See Sedgwick, "Paranoid Reading and Reparative Reading" (1997), 2–3.

57 Mavor's in-depth examination of Hawarden's photographic archives (in *Becoming*) is almost contemporaneous with Sedgwick's use of the image (on the cover of *Novel Gazing*). They were both "Victorianists," fascinated by queer childhood and adolescence, and performative strategies of writing. In this spirit of shared rethinking, in April 1993—at a conference at the University of North Carolina at Chapel Hill organized by Mavor—Sedgwick read aloud in performative fashion her unfinished poem "The Warm Decembers" (about a Julia Margaret Cameron–inspired photographer named Beatrix) to coincide with the exhibition of Dante Gabriel Rossetti's 1871–72 painting *Beata Beatrix* (from the Art Institute of Chicago). Sedgwick's poem of "writerly writing and thinkerly thinking" was later published in *Fat Art, Thin Art* (160). See also Edwards, *Queer and Bookish*, for more on Sedgwick's engagement with photography.

58 See Smith-Rosenberg, "The Female World of Love and Ritual."

59 Sedgwick, "Paranoid Reading and Reparative Reading" (1997), 1–3.

60 See Litvak, "Strange Gourmet"; Bora, "Outing Texture"; and Stockton, "Prophylactics and Brains."

61 Sedgwick, "Paranoid Reading and Reparative Reading" (1997), 3–4 and 26–28, respectively.

62 My theorization differs from existing uses of the phrase *close writing*. In his book *Jane Austen and the Secret Style*, the literary scholar D. A. Miller refers to the "free indirect style" crafted by Austen as a narrational mode of "close writing," which "comes as near to a character's psychic and linguistic reality as it can get without collapsing into it" (58–59). Miller's use of the term indicates an ambivalent merging between character and narrator, which is reframed from a Black feminist perspective by Saidiya Hartman in her influential rendering of "close narration" (see *Wayward Lives Beautiful Experiments*, xiii).

63 Hartman, "Venus in Two Acts," 12.

64 Hartman, "Venus in Two Acts," 3.

65 Hartman, "Venus in Two Acts," 11, 3.

66 Hartman, "Venus in Two Acts," 11.

67 Hartman, *Wayward Lives Beautiful Experiments*, xiii.

68 Hartman, *Wayward Lives Beautiful Experiments*, xiv.

69 Hartman, *Wayward Lives Beautiful Experiments*, xiv; Saidiya Hartman and Fred Moten in conversation, "Fugitivity and Waywardness," *Make a Way Out of No Way*, Tramway, Glasgow, September 27, 2014, https://

vimeo.com/151775530; Rizvana Bradley, "Regard for One Another: A Conversation Between Rizvana Bradley and Saidiya Hartman," *Los Angeles Review of Books*, October 8, 2019, https://lareviewofbooks.org/article/regard-for-one-another-a-conversation-between-rizvana-bradley-and-saidiya-hartman/.

70 Hartman quoted in Bradley, "Regard for One Another."

71 Hartman, *Wayward Lives Beautiful Experiments*, xiv; Hartman quoted in Bradley, "Regard for One Another."

72 Saidiya Hartman, "Full Notes," in *Wayward Lives Beautiful Experiments*, 364, https://serpentstail.com/wp-content/uploads/sites/2/2021/12/wayward-full-notes.pdf; Hartman, *Wayward Lives Beautiful Experiments*, 72.

73 Hartman, *Wayward Lives Beautiful Experiments*, 34, 24.

74 Hartman, *Wayward Lives Beautiful Experiments*, 73–74.

75 Hartman, *Wayward Lives Beautiful Experiments*, 30, 75.

76 Hartman, *Wayward Lives Beautiful Experiments*, 75.

77 Hartman, *Wayward Lives Beautiful Experiments*, 280.

78 Campt, "The Loop of Retreat."

79 Crawley, "Harriet Jacobs Gets a Hearing," 51, 35.

80 Hartman, *Wayward Lives Beautiful Experiments*, 31.

81 Nyong'o, *Afro-Fabulations*; see also Fawaz, "'An Open Mesh of Possibilities," 28.

82 Nyong'o, *Afro-Fabulations*: The quote is from "Repairing the Incommensurable."

83 Muñoz, "Race, Sex, and the Incommensurate," 153–154.

84 Muñoz, "Race, Sex, and the Incommensurate," 155.

85 Muñoz, "Race, Sex, and the Incommensurate," 156.

86 Muñoz, "Race, Sex, and the Incommensurate," 161.

87 Muñoz, "Race, Sex, and the Incommensurate," 157.

88 Muñoz, "Race, Sex, and the Incommensurate," 158.

89 Muñoz, "Race, Sex, and the Incommensurate," 161 and 163, respectively.

90 Ahmed, "A Phenomenology of Whiteness," 150.

91 Ahmed, "A Phenomenology of Whiteness," 154. See also Ahmed, *Queer Phenomenology*, 121.

92 Ahmed, "A Phenomenology of Whiteness," 154–55.

93 Sedgwick, "Queer and Now," 4.

94 Barthes, *A Lover's Discourse*, 157.

95 Barthes, *A Lover's Discourse*, 157.

96 Barthes, *A Lover's Discourse*, 158.

97 Barthes, *A Lover's Discourse*, 158.

98 Preciado, "The Losers Conspiracy."

99 Preciado, "The Losers Conspiracy."

100 Preciado, "The Losers Conspiracy."

101 Vuong, "A Letter to My Mother That She Will Never Read."

102 Vuong, "A Letter to My Mother That She Will Never Read."

103 Carson, *Eros the Bittersweet*, 91.

104 Carson, *Eros the Bittersweet*, 117.

105 Carson, *Eros the Bittersweet*, 3.

106 DuBois, *Sappho Is Burning*, 62, 70.

107 Pu, "Decapitated Forms," 35; Cha quoted in Pu, "Decapitated Forms," 35.

108 Limón and Diaz, "Envelopes of Air."

109 Sedgwick, *Tendencies*, dedication page.

110 Sedgwick, "White Glasses," 257.

111 Jan Bervin, "Studies in Scale: Excerpts from *The Gorgeous Nothings*," *Poetry Foundation*, November 1, 2013, https://www.poetryfoundation.org/poetrymagazine/articles/70065/studies-in-scale.

112 Bervin, "Studies in Scale."

113 Susan Howe cited in Bervin, "Studies in Scale."

114 See Mavor, "Making Poems Out of What Is Not There." I am grateful to Carol Mavor for first introducing me to Dickinson's envelope poems and for energizing this work by leading a writing masterclass at the Courtauld Institute of Art, which I convened as part of the events series inspired by Dickinson, "'What a Hazard a Letter Is': Correspondence in Feminist Art, Art Writing, and Art History." The masterclass began with a mail-art action, as we sent out copies of Mavor's chapbook *A Magpie and an Envelope* (2021) to the artist/writer/scholar participants.

115 Martha Ackmann, "Emily Dickinson's White Dress," *Paris Review*, February 25, 2020, https://www.theparisreview.org/blog/2020/02/25/emily-dickinsons-white-dress/.

116 A. Butler, "Fan Letters of Love," 154.

117 Kathy Acker, "Poems/Diary," notebook, undated (ca. 1971), Fales Library and Special Collections, New York University Libraries, Kathy Acker Notebooks (cited hereafter as KAN), B3, F14.

118 Mavor, *Becoming*, 132.

119 Eichhorn, *The Archival Turn in Feminism*, 8, 9.

120 Nancy, *Corpus*, 11.

121 I am inspired by Eve Kosofsky Sedgwick's exposition of touch and affect in the introduction to *Touching Feeling*, in which she recognizes the "intimacy" that "subsists between textures and emotions" (17). Daisy Lafarge, "Metaphor as Parasite: On Ecologies of Love, Language and Disease," *The Drouth*, 2021, https://www.thedrouth.org/metaphor-as-parasite-on-ecologies-of-love-language-and-disease-by-daisy-lafarge/.

122 Bellamy, "Complicity," in *Pink Steam*, 35.

123 Nelson, *The Argonauts*, 3.

124 Barthes, *A Lover's Discourse*, 148.

125 See Barthes, *Roland Barthes by Roland Barthes* (originally published in French, 1975; first translated into English, 1977). Nelson explains Barthes's idea (which gives *The Argonauts* its title): "Just as the *Argo*'s parts may be replaced over time but the boat is still called the *Argo*, whenever the lover utters the phrase 'I love you,' its meaning must be renewed by each use, as 'the very task of love and of language is to give to one and the same phrase inflections which will be forever new'" (5).

126 For Sedgwick's discussion, see Sedgwick, *Touching Feeling*, 8–9.

127 Sedgwick, *Touching Feeling*, 8.

128 Nelson, *The Argonauts*, 123.

129 Sedgwick, "A Poem Is Being Written," 178; Nelson, *The Argonauts*, 85.

130 Nelson, *The Argonauts*, 105.

131 *Wild theory* is Nelson's term for "writing that is within a particular, often academic, discipline, but also belongs to something else by virtue of its creativity and recklessness." See Sarah Nicole Prickett, "*Bookforum* Talks with Maggie Nelson," *Bookforum*, May 29, 2015, http://www.bookforum.com/interview/14663. It has since also been taken up by Jack Halberstam in *Wild Things: The Disorder of Desire*.

132 Nelson, *The Argonauts*, 7.

133 Sedgwick, "Paranoid Reading and Reparative Reading" (2003), 146.

134 Many writers, artists, theorists, and curators have turned to letter writing as a critical practice during COVID time. See Blackshaw and Butler, "Sick Women Correspondents"; Paul, *Letters to Gwen John*; Zambreno, *To Write as If Already Dead*; and the mail-art exhibition *Queer Correspondence*, curated by Eliel Jones, Cell Project Space,

London, June 1, 2020–February 13, 2021, https://www.cellprojects.org/queer-correspondence.

135 Bojarska and Berlant, “The Hundreds,” 297.

136 Ahmed, *Living a Feminist Life*, 241.

137 See Colby, *Kathy Acker*; Kraus, *After Kathy Acker*; M. Wark, *Philosophy for Spiders*; and McBride, *Eat Your Mind.*

138 M. Wark, *Philosophy for Spiders*, 56.

139 Foster, “Repetition and Embodiment,” 131.

140 *Lust for Life* features contributions from theorists such as Peter Wollen and Avital Ronell, and novelists such as Lynne Tillman and Robert Glück, who all knew Acker personally. See Harryman, Ronell, and Scholder, *Lust for Life.*

141 The definition of autoplagiarism comes from Sciolino, “Confessions of a Kleptoparasite,” 63. For allobiography, see Houen, “Novel Biopolitics.”

142 I further examine what Chris Kraus points to in an interview with Matias Viegener (the executor of Acker's estate): “Kathy lived most intensely through her work, so it was through the close readings of her texts that I felt the most contact. She used autobiographical writings as material.” See Matias Viegener, “The Life, Death, and Afterlife of Kathy Acker,” *Los Angeles Review of Books*, September 11, 2017, https://www.lareviewofbooks.org/article/the-life-death-and-afterlife-of-kathy-acker/.

143 Mueller, “John Waters and the Blessed Profession—1969,” in *Walking Through Clear Water in a Pool Painted Black* (2022), 63.

144 As well as this trilogy by John Waters, Mueller also had parts in underground films directed by Rachid Kerdouche (*Final Reward*, 1978), Eric Mitchell (*Underground U.S.A*, 1980), Amos Poe (*Subway Riders*, 1981), and Michael Auder / Gary Indiana (*A Couple of White Faggots Sitting Around Talking*, 1981), among others.

145 For example, Chris Kraus, “The New Universal,” *Sydney Review of Books*, October 17, 2014, https://sydneyreviewofbooks.com/new-universal/; and Anne Turyn, *Top Stories*, Kunstverein, Amsterdam, April 2–June 26, 2021 (exhibition).

146 See Cooke, *Contemporary Feminist Life-Writing*; Mitchell, *Writing Shame.*

147 This book builds on a shorter critical essay on Mueller's life and work published in *Cabinet* magazine: A. Butler, “With Love, a Letter to Cookie, and Her Stories.”

148 Carson, *Eros the Bittersweet*, 16.

149 M. Wark, *Philosophy for Spiders*, 5.

150 McBride, *Eat Your Mind*, xvii.

151 Griffin, *Edgewise*, 18. While primarily biographical in approach, Griffin's oral history is the only substantial study available on Mueller.

152 Paul, *Letters to Gwen John*, 3.

153 A. Butler, "'Have You Tried It with Three? Have You?,'" 90.

154 Campt, "The Afterlives of Images."

155 M. Wark, *Philosophy for Spiders*, 5.

156 A. Butler, "'Have You Tried It with Three? Have You?,'" 97.

157 "Close (adj.)," *Online Etymology Dictionary*, https://www.etymonline.com/search?q=close.

158 Halberstam, *Wild Things*, xii.

159 Halberstam, *Wild Things*, 15.

160 Kathy Acker, typed letter signed to Alan Sondheim, undated (ca. 1974), KAP, B30, F11.

161 See Halberstam, *The Queer Art of Failure*.

162 M. Wark, *Philosophy for Spiders*, 54.

163 I am inspired by Gavin Butt's theorization of flirting as a queer methodology in "Afterword: Flirting with an Ending," in *Between You and Me*, 163–65.

164 Berlant and Stewart, *The Hundreds*, 28.

165 Laurence A. Rickels, "Body Bildung: Laurence A. Rickels Talks with Kathy Acker," originally published in *Artforum*, February 1994, in Acker, *Kathy Acker*, 163.

166 See Doyle, *Sex Objects*.

167 For Woodman's photograph, see "Self-Portrait Talking to Vince," SCAD Museum of Art, https://www.scadmoa.org/permanent-collections/pieces/self-portrait-talking-to-vince.

168 See Halberstam, *The Queer Art of Failure*.

169 Kristeva, "The Adolescent Novel," 11. Originally published 1990.

170 See Muñoz, "Ephemera as Evidence."

CHAPTER ONE. THE DIARY PIECE: THE LINE, THE CUT, THE BLUR OF TWO LIVES, OR, KATHY ACKER'S BAD SEX BLUR

1 As Acker describes in the sixth part of *The Childlike Life*, called "story of my life," which was sent out in September 1973: "I move to New York

because I write and want to meet writers. I have no money, no way of getting money, no friends in New York, no parents. I get Pelvic Inflammatory Disease, walk into Columbia Presbyterian clinic: woman vomits blood over floor." *The Childlike Life of the Black Tarantula by the Black Tarantula*, 138.

2 Author's interview with Jerome and Diane Rothenberg, February 10, 2018.

3 For Cookie Mueller's Manhattan writing, see Cookie Mueller, "Manhattan: The First Nine Years, THE DOG YEARS," undated, Fales Library and Special Collections, New York University Libraries, Serpent's Tail/High Risk Archives (cited hereafter as STHRA), BVII.1, F12.

4 Strombeck, *DIY on the Lower East Side*, 98. Strombeck recognizes how "spaces of poverty animate Acker's literary project" (98).

5 Kathy Acker, "Poems/Diary," notebook, undated (ca. 1971), KAN, B3, F14.

6 These interdisciplinary exchanges between writing and drawing anticipated Acker's later novel *Blood and Guts in High School*, which intercut explicit illustrations of sexual fantasy and dream and which Georgina Colby has analyzed in the context of typographical experimentation, collage, and feminist politics. "Collage and the Anxiety of Self-Description: *Blood and Guts in High School*," in Colby, *Kathy Acker*, 65–109.

7 Acker, "Poems/Diary," KAN.

8 As Acker described in an interview with the technology specialist R. U. Sirius, "I'm working at trying to find a kind of language where I won't be so easily modulated by expectation. I'm looking for what might be called a body language. One thing I do is stick a vibrator up my cunt and start writing—writing from the point of orgasm and losing control of the language and seeing what that's like." R. U. Sirius, "Kathy Acker: Where Does She Get Off?," *Io*, 1993, https://editions-ismael.com/wp-content/uploads/2018/02/1997-Kathy-Acker-interview-by-R.U.-Sirius.pdf.

9 M. Wark, *Philosophy for Spiders*, 172. See also Acker, "Seeing Gender," in *Bodies of Work*, 166–68.

10 Kathy Acker, "Days and Days of Anxiety," notebook, undated (ca. 1971), KAN, B1, F7.

11 Acker, "Days and Days of Anxiety," KAN.

12 Strombeck has also recognized that "Acker . . . did not start and end with the conceptual. Instead, she grafted the shabbiness and desperation of her lived environment into her conceptual art. Acker's journals

show her moving back and forth between rewriting literary texts and rewriting her own biography." *DIY on the Lower East Side*, 101.

13 Zambreno, "Kate Zambreno on Kathy Acker," unpaginated.

14 Kathy Acker, "Personal Language Personal History," undated manuscript, KAP, B23, F1.

15 Acker, "Days and Days of Anxiety," KAN.

16 Acker, "Devoured by Myths: An Interview with Sylvère Lotringer," in *Hannibal Lecter, My Father*, 4.

17 Kathy Acker, "Death Portraits 1. Visions, Diaries in Protection of Self Death," notebook, undated (ca. 1972), KAN, B1, F7.

18 McBride, *Eat Your Mind*, 45.

19 Acker in R. J. Ellis, Carolyn Bird, Dawn Curwen, Ian Macor, Val Ogden, and Charles Patrick, "An Informal Interview with Kathy Acker on the 23rd April, 1986," KAP, B22, F30.

20 A. Davis, *Angela Davis: An Autobiography*, 115.

21 A. Davis, *Angela Davis: An Autobiography*, 116.

22 Kraus, *After Kathy Acker*, 47.

23 Information about Brandeis is from A. Kaplan, *Dreaming in French*, 144. Details about Angela Davis's studies in France are from A. Davis, *Angela Davis: An Autobiography*, 109.

24 A. Davis, *Angela Davis: An Autobiography*, 101–2, 107, and 109, respectively.

25 A. Davis, *Angela Davis: An Autobiography*, 110.

26 A. Kaplan, *Dreaming in French*, 144. See Ahmed, "A Phenomenology of Whiteness."

27 A. Kaplan, *Dreaming in French*, 148.

28 A. Kaplan, *Dreaming in French*, 152. Davis spent a summer abroad in Paris in 1962. A. Davis, *Angela Davis: An Autobiography*, 112.

29 A. Kaplan, *Dreaming in French*, 163.

30 A. Davis, *Angela Davis: An Autobiography*, 110–11.

31 A. Davis, *Angela Davis: An Autobiography*, 111, 113.

32 A. Davis, *Angela Davis: An Autobiography*, 111–12.

33 Hartman uses the term "nonevent" in "Venus in Two Acts" to describe the collective, enduring, and unending deaths of young Black girls and women made anonymous by the violences and violent archives and afterlives of slavery (10).

34 Hartman, in Damman, "Saidiya Hartman."

35 Hartman, *Lose Your Mother*, 6.

36 Hartman, in Damman, "Saidiya Hartman."

37 Hartman, in Damman, "Saidiya Hartman."

38 A. Davis, *Angela Davis: An Autobiography*, 117.

39 Acker, "A Few Notes on Two of My Books," in *Bodies of Work*, 9.

40 Acker, "A Few Notes on Two of My Books," 9.

41 Antin, *i never knew what time it was*, 18.

42 Acker, "Devoured by Myths: An Interview with Sylvère Lotringer," 3.

43 Acker, "Devoured by Myths: An Interview with Sylvère Lotringer," 3.

44 Jackson Mac Low, typed letter to Kathy Acker, December 21, 1973, University of California San Diego Special Collections, Jackson Mac Low Papers (cited hereafter as JMLP), B8, F7.

45 Kotz, *Words to Be Looked At*, 160.

46 Kathy Acker, "Jane Eyre II," notebook, October 1973; January 17–June 1, 1974, KAN, B2, F13.

47 LeWitt, "Paragraphs on Conceptual Art."

48 Kotz, *Words to Be Looked At*, 138.

49 Alberro, "Reductivism in Reverse," 25.

50 Osborne, *Anywhere or Not at All*, 66.

51 Meltzer, *Systems We Have Loved*, 22.

52 Meltzer, *Systems We Have Loved*, 5.

53 Acconci cited in Blocker, *What the Body Cost*, 32.

54 Blocker, *What the Body Cost*, 33.

55 Acker, "Jane Eyre II," KAN; Kathy Acker, "Diary of the World, Diaries," notebook, December 8, 1971, KAN, B1, F8.

56 J. Wark, "Conceptual Art and Feminism," 48.

57 J. Wark, "Conceptual Art and Feminism," 49.

58 The first three quotations are from Ahmed, "A Phenomenology of Whiteness," 163, 161, and 156, respectively.

59 Piper cited in Lamm, "Writing the 'I' Otherwise," 40.

60 Piper cited in Bowles, *Adrian Piper*, 141.

61 Piper cited in Shaked, "Adrian Piper," 66.

62 Acker, "Days and Days of Anxiety," KAN; Piper cited in Lamm, "Writing the 'I' Otherwise," 44.

63 Hartman, "Venus in Two Acts," 12.

64 Antin cited in Schwartz, "Excerpt of Email from Eleanor Antin to Alexandra Schwartz," in *From Conceptualism to Feminism*, 264.

65 Eleanor Antin, typed letter signed with autograph annotations to Acker, undated, KAP, B30, F4.

66 Antin cited in Schwartz, "Excerpt of Email from Eleanor Antin to Alexandra Schwartz."

67 Acker, "Diary of the World, Diaries," KAN.

68 Bernadette Mayer, notebook, April 1972, University of California San Diego Special Collections, Bernadette Mayer Papers (cited hereafter as BMP), B37, F9, Oversize: FB20901.

69 Bernadette Mayer, notebook, October 1971, BMP, B37, F6.

70 Kathy Acker, "Dreams in Night for the Painters of Decadence & for Harriet Golden," notebook, undated (ca. 1972), KAN, B1, F11.

71 Bernadette Mayer, handwritten description on board, undated (ca. 1971), BMP, B20, F11.

72 Mayer, *Memory*, 67.

73 Maggie Nelson picks up on this aspect of Mayer's *Memory*, connecting it to the work of Andy Warhol. *Women, The New York School, and Other True Abstractions*, 104.

74 Kathy Acker, autograph letter signed to Bernadette Mayer, undated (ca. 1974–75), University of California San Diego Special Collections, United Artists Records Archive (cited hereafter as UARA), B1, F1. In a postscript, Acker writes, "I figured out my male stars are David Antin, L. Weiner, Ashley, Peter. Dan Graham on outs. You & E. Antin [are] my female stars."

75 Acker cited in Kraus, *After Kathy Acker*, 81.

76 Ahmed, "A Phenomenology of Whiteness," 150.

77 "Blur (v.)," *Online Etymology Dictionary*, https://www.etymonline.com/word/blur#etymonline_v_43221.

78 "Blur (v.)."

79 Kathy Acker, "Lesbian Portrait/Harriet," notebook, July 1971, KAN, B3, F4.

80 Kraus, *After Kathy Acker*, 61. Quotation from Acker found on the same page.

81 Kathy Acker, "Arthur Miller, Williams-Glass Menagerie," notebook, undated (ca. 1971–72), KAN, B1, F1.

82 Acker, "Arthur Miller, Williams-Glass Menagerie," KAN.

83 Carol Mavor provides a detailed discussion of Hannah Cullwick's erotic diary writing in *Pleasures Taken*, 94–95.

84 Acker, "Poems/Diary," KAN.

85 Brainard, *The Collected Writings of Joe Brainard*, unpaginated.

86 Kathy Acker, "Untitled (Black Mountain School)," undated manuscript, KAP, B23, F31.

87 Acker, "Poems/Diary," KAN.

88 Acker, in Alpert, "Kathy Acker: Mitali Restaurant, NYC: Interview with Barry Alpert, Only Paper Today, March 30, 1976," in *Kathy Acker*, 19.

89 Acker, "Devoured by Myths: An Interview with Sylvère Lotringer," 4–5.

90 Doyle, *Sex Objects*, xx–xxi.

91 Acker, "Poems/Diary," KAN.

92 Acker, "Poems/Diary," KAN.

93 M. Wark, *Philosophy for Spiders*, 152, 173.

94 Acker, "Death Portraits 1. Visions, Diaries in Protection of Self Death," KAN.

95 *Bad sex* has been used elsewhere to describe sexual encounters that are unforgettable, clumsy, or disappointing. As in Doyle's theorization, it has also been used in a way that dissolves binary thinking that stratifies sexual experience into being only ever consensual or nonconsensual, positive or negative. I want to emphasize, however, that Doyle's understanding of bad sex bears no relation to Germaine Greer's remarks, voiced at the 2018 Hay Literary Festival in Wales, in which she drew a dangerously casual relation between rape and bad sex.

96 Doyle, *Sex Objects*, 98–99.

97 Acker, "Death Portraits 1. Visions, Diaries in Protection of Self Death," KAN.

98 Doyle, *Sex Objects*, 99.

99 Doyle, *Sex Objects*, 99.

100 Kathy Acker, "Ex-Libris: Morda/Diary Poems Dreams right after: what I can remember," notebook, March 9, 1971, KAN, B1, F12.

101 Acker, "Days and Days of Anxiety," KAN.

102 Acker cited in Kraus, *After Kathy Acker*, 54.

103 Kraus, *After Kathy Acker*, 28.

104 LeWitt quoted in Lovatt, "Paperwork: Conceptual Art and the Pink Collar Worker," *Thinking Drawing: 1960 to Now*, Courtauld Institute of Art, May 10, 2019, https://www.youtube.com/watch?v=C2fvST-d3VA.

105 Kraus, *After Kathy Acker*, 27.

106 Kraus, *After Kathy Acker*, 180.

107 Acker, *Empire of the Senseless*, 3.

108 Kraus, *After Kathy Acker*, 183.

109 Friedman, "Foreword," xiii–xiv; Ahmed, "The Phenomenology of Whiteness," 154; Kraus, *After Kathy Acker*, 28.

110 Lovatt, "Paperwork."

111 Seth Siegelaub, *January 5–31, 1969* (New York: 1969), https://www.primaryinformation.org/files/january1969.pdf. I am also indebted to Naomi Pearce's research into the figure of the secretary in US-American and British conceptual and mail-art practices; see "Handling the Mail."

112 Doyle, *Sex Objects*, 101; Spillers, "Mama's Baby, Papa's Maybe," 67.

113 Musser, *Sensual Excess*: quotes from "Sexuality and the Pornotrope" in "Introduction."

114 Musser, *Sensual Excess*: quote from "Epistemologies of Fleshiness and Opacity" in "Introduction."

115 Acker, "Arthur Miller, Williams-Glass Menagerie," KAN.

116 Berlant and Edelman, *Sex, or the Unbearable*, 33.

117 Acker, "Dreams in Night for the Painters of Decadence & for Harriet Golden," KAN.

118 Acker, "Death Portraits 1. Visions, Diaries in Protection of Self Death," KAN.

119 Acker, "Death Portraits 1. Visions, Diaries in Protection of Self Death," KAN.

120 Kraus, *After Kathy Acker*, 64–65.

121 The first section comprises cut-up paragraphs that recall dream sequences and sexual encounters with men and women, while the third section contains episodes of "POLITICAL DESIRE" that decry the evils of her society, namely the institution of the family and President Richard Nixon.

122 Acker, "Devoured by Myths: An Interview with Sylvère Lotringer," 4.

123 Acker, "Devoured by Myths: An Interview with Sylvère Lotringer," 4.

124 Burroughs and Gysin, *The Third Mind*, 29.

125 Carson, *Eros the Bittersweet*, 11.

126 Kathy Acker, "A Girl Is Reading William Burroughs," manuscript, 1996, KAP, B20, F3.

127 Houen, "Novel Biopolitics," 145.

128 Acker, *Politics*, unpaginated. Here Acker references the members of the John Birch Society, a far-right organization that opposed communism, civil rights, immigration, the United Nations, and free trade agreements.

129 Acker, *Politics*.

130 Kraus, *After Kathy Acker*, 27.

131 Kraus, *After Kathy Acker*, 65; Acker, *Politics*.

132 Kraus, *After Kathy Acker*, 60. Addition mine.

133 Antin, "David Antin on Kathy Acker."

134 McKenzie Wark's review of the *Kathy Acker: Get Rid of Meaning* exhibition at Badischer Kunstverein in Karlsruhe, Germany (October 5–December 2, 2018), supports this. After hearing Acker's biographer, Jason McBride, give a reading of his in-progress work at the exhibition's symposium, Wark proffers that the young Acker was "writing Sappho imitations," along with "taking cinema courses, shoplifting books, but was not all that political." "Kathy Acker: *Get Rid of Meaning*." Katherine Wasdin's scholarship on the rehabilitation of Sappho in Acker's novels has also infused my reading; see "The Undead Past."

135 Carson, *If Not, Winter: Fragments of Sappho*, xi.

136 DuBois, *Sappho Is Burning*, 3; quotation from Cixous, "Coming to Writing," 20.

137 DuBois, *Sappho Is Burning*, 6.

138 DuBois, *Sappho Is Burning*, 9–10.

139 Sappho quoted in Carson, *Eros the Bittersweet*, 3; Carson, *Eros the Bittersweet*, 5.

140 Goldberg, *Sappho:]Fragments*, 21.

141 Goldberg, *Sappho:]Fragments*, 22.

142 Sappho quoted in Carson, *Eros the Bittersweet*, 8.

143 Acker, *Politics*.

144 Doyle, *Sex Objects*, 101.

145 Acker, *Politics*.

146 Acker, *Politics*.

147 Ahmed, *Queer Phenomenology*, 78.

148 Ahmed, *Queer Phenomenology*, 78.

149 Carson, *Eros the Bittersweet*, 16.

150 Kraus, *After Kathy Acker*, 68–71.

151 Courtney Foster has located Acker's approach to performative reading as shaped by repetition and embodiment. See "Repetition and Embodiment."

152 Antin, typed letter signed with autograph annotations to Kathy Acker, undated, KAP, B30, F4.

153 Eileen Myles, "Dear Reader: Eileen Myles on Kathy Acker," *Literary Hub*, May 2, 2019, https://lithub.com/dear-reader-eileen-myles-on-kathy-acker/.

154 Fielding Dawson, postcard to Kathy Acker, July 7, 1973, KAP, B30, F1.

155 Bernadette Mayer, postcard to Kathy Acker, July 15, 1974, KAP, B30, F1.

156 Leandro Katz and Ted Castle/TVRT Press, typed letter signed to Kathy Acker, December 5, 1974, KAP, B30, F1.

CHAPTER TWO. THE NOVEL-IN-PIECES: "LIKE LITTLE BIRDS TESTING THEIR WINGS," OR, COOKIE MUELLER'S ADOLESCENT REVERIE

1 Goldin, *I'll Be Your Mirror*, 256.

2 Mueller, "Two People—Baltimore—1964," in *Walking Through Clear Water in a Pool Painted Black* (1990), 2.

3 I have been inspired by Sarah Schulman's intersectional history of ACT UP in *Let the Record Show*.

4 Nancy, *The Fall of Sleep*, 42.

5 Sedgwick, "Melanie Klein and the Difference Affect Makes," 126.

6 Mueller, "August 1989," in "Art and About (*Details* magazine)," in *Ask Dr. Mueller*, 291. Italics mine.

7 Sedgwick, "Paranoid Reading and Reparative Reading" (2003), 150. Italics mine.

8 Goldin, "In the Valley of the Shadow," 4.

9 Mueller, "A Last Letter" (1989), 14.

10 Arabindan-Kesson, *Black Bodies White Gold*, 3.

11 Campt, *Listening to Images*, 8; Campt, "The Afterlives of Images."

12 Hartman, *Lose Your Mother*, 6.

13 Hartman, "Excisions of the Flesh," 58.

14 Hartman, "Excisions of the Flesh," 56, 55.

15 Cheng, Juhasz, and Shahani, *AIDS and the Distribution of Crises*, xix, 1. Italics mine.

16 Juhasz and Kerr, *We Are Having This Conversation Now*, 12.

17 Juhasz and Kerr, *We Are Having This Conversation Now*, 8.

18 Patton, "Fear of AIDS," 323.

19 Mueller, "A Last Letter" (1989), 14.

20 Gordon Stevenson's letter transcribed in Mueller, "A Last Letter" (1989), 15.

21 Mueller, "A Last Letter" (1989), 14–15.

22 Stevenson's letter transcribed in Mueller, "A Last Letter" (1989), 15.

23 Mueller, epigraph to *Ask Dr. Mueller*, v.

24 Anderson, *Cruising the Dead River*, 161, 12.

25 Juliet Jacques, *You Will Be Free*, 2017, artist film commissioned as part of the live events program that coincided with the *Putti's Pudding: Cookie Mueller and Vittorio Scarpati* exhibition at Studio Voltaire gallery in London, September 9–November 12, 2017, https://studiovoltaire.org/resources/juliet-jacques-you-will-be-free/.

26 Mavor, *Reading Boyishly*, 339. Italics mine.

27 This configuration is informed by Sedgwick's initial reckoning with the concept of queer as being inextricably linked to the careless, violent treatment of queer adolescents during the AIDS crisis in the early 1990s, which ranged from the denial of "the things they need—intelligible information, support and respect, condoms" to the "complicity" shown by adults supposedly close to them ("Queer and Now," 1–3).

28 A. Phillips, "Clutter," 66.

29 Mavor, *Becoming*, 21.

30 Hall quoted in Demos and Demos, "Adolescence in Historical Perspective," 635.

31 Winnicott, "Adolescence," 190.

32 Cookie Mueller, "Working Titles: Garden of Ashes, Messages from the Edge," cover letter, undated, STHRA, BVII.1, F3.

33 Hanuman Books, founded by Raymond Foye and Francesco Clemente in 1986, also published Mueller's *Fan Mail, Frank Letters and Crank Calls* in 1988. Like all the Hanuman editions, it came in the form of a miniature handmade chapbook, inspired by Indian prayer books, with a hand-tinted author portrait on its cover and gold-leaf lettering. For the Semiotext(e) edition, see "American Agents" press release, undated (ca. 1990), Fales Library and Special Collections, New York University Libraries, Sylvère Lotringer Papers and Semiotext(e) Archive (cited hereafter as SLPSA), B19, F25.

34 The "little-black-books" designation comes from Schwarz and Balsamo, "Under the Sign of *Semiotext(e)*," 211. See Strombeck's work on Semiotext(e) through the lens of DIY publishing in the chapter "Semiotext(e), Kathy Acker, and the Decline of the Welfare State," in *DIY on the Lower East Side*, 85–116. From Strombeck, I define the theoretical interventions included within early Semiotext(e) books as "micropolitical" (86).

35 Author's interview with Chris Kraus, December 12, 2016.

36 Strombeck, *DIY on the Lower East Side*, 87.

37 An early press release reveals that the series was originally called "American Agents." Undated (ca. 1990), SLPSA, B19, F25.

38 Author's interview with Kraus.

39 Chris Kraus, "The New Universal," *Sydney Review of Books*, October 17, 2014, https://sydneyreviewofbooks.com/new-universal/.

40 Kraus, "The New Universal." Italics mine.

41 *Cookie Mueller Ann Rower: Walking Through Clear Water in a Pool Painted Black + If You're a Girl*, 1990, invitation card, SLPSA, B21, F17. Quick! was formerly the club Area.

42 Kraus, "The New Universal."

43 Cookie Mueller, handwritten list, undated, STHRA, BVII.1, F14.

44 Winnicott, "Adolescence," 187.

45 Zambreno, *To Write as If Already Dead*: quote from "Surge."

46 Koestenbaum, "The Pleasure of the Text."

47 Cookie Mueller, handwritten manuscript, STHRA, BVII.1, F14. Winnicott's discussion of the transitional object occurs in the essay "Transitional Objects and Transitional Phenomena."

48 Mavor, *Reading Boyishly*, 339.

49 Dent, "Spared," in *What Silence Equals*, 15. Alongside Mueller, Dent is the only other woman writer included in the 2009 collection *Persistent Voices: Poetry by Writers Lost to AIDS*.

50 Dent, "Spared," 15.

51 Dent, "Spared," 16.

52 Barthes, "To Write," 18.

53 Mueller, "Working Titles," STHRA.

54 Zambreno, *To Write as If Already Dead*: quote from "Surge."

55 Johanna Hedva, "Get Well Soon," 2020, https://www.kunstverein-hildesheim.de/assets/bilder/caring-structures-ausstellung-digital/Johanna-Hedva/10ef20affc/AUSSTELLUNG_1110_GWS_e.pdf.

56 Hedva, "Get Well Soon."

57 Mueller, "Working Titles," STHRA.

58 Barthes, *The Pleasure of the Text*, 18.

59 Hedva, "Sick Woman Theory," *Topical Cream*, March 12, 2022, https://topicalcream.org/features/sick-woman-theory/. Originally published in 2016, I quote from the revised version of the essay.

60 Cixous, "Coming to Writing," 3.

61 Mavor, *Reading Boyishly*, 339.

62 Woolf quoted in Oates, "Notes on Failure," 245 (italics in Oates).

63 Mueller, "My Bio—Notes on an American Childhood," in *Walking Through Clear Water in a Pool Painted Black* (1990), 142. Unless otherwise stated this is the edition of "My Bio—Notes on an American Childhood" cited in this chapter.

64 Barthes, *The Preparation of the Novel*, 132.

65 Griffin, *Edgewise*, 15.

66 Cookie Mueller, notebook, undated, STHRA, BVII.1, F17. While the notebook is undated, this back-page list echoes the sentiments of a note written by Mueller that was found by her friend, the painter Scott Covert, in the last year of her life: "I will live long enough to write my novel." Covert quoted in Griffin, *Edgewise*, 281.

67 The punk musician, poet, and publisher Richard Hell edited *Cuz* in the late 1980s. *Just Another Asshole* was a mixed-media publication edited by Barbara Ess between 1978 and 1987. *BOMB* was launched by a group of New York–based artists, led by Betsy Sussler, in 1981 (featuring Mueller and Acker in the first issue); it now comprises a quarterly print magazine, a daily online publication, a digital archive of past content, a podcast, and an oral histories project focused on artists' writings and interviews. *Top Stories*, edited by the photographer Anne Turyn, was a prose periodical that focused on experimental writing by women. In 1984, it published Mueller's *How to Get Rid of Pimples*. Finally, compiled by Richard Prince, *Wild History* was published by Tanam Press in 1985.

68 Mueller, "Go-Going—New York & New Jersey—1978–79," in *Walking Through Clear Water in a Pool Painted Black* (1990), 100–101.

69 Mueller, "Narcotics," in *Walking Through Clear Water in a Pool Painted Black* (2022), 215.

70 Tim Lawrence's in-depth study of New York's "community-driven" nightclubs in the early 1980s, where hybrid cultural forms flourished, has been invaluable: *Life and Death on the New York Dance Floor, 1980–1983*, xiii.

71 Cookie Mueller, “Life as a Writer-Actress: Typical Day in Manhattan,” undated, STHRA, BVII.1, F12.

72 The story of Mueller’s adolescent novel emerges in *Walking Through Clear Water in a Pool Painted Black* as “My Bio—Notes on an American Childhood”; in *Garden of Ashes* as “Cookie Mueller, born 1949 Baltimore Maryland”; and in multiple unpublished typescripts.

73 Mueller, “My Bio—Notes on an American Childhood,” 140–41. An earlier version of “My Bio—Notes on an American Childhood” was also published in Tucker, *Blasted Allegories*.

74 Preciado, “Learning from the Virus.”

75 Preciado, “Learning from the Virus.”

76 Preciado, “Learning from the Virus.”

77 Mueller, “My Bio—Notes on an American Childhood,” 141.

78 Mueller, “A Last Letter” (1989), 14.

79 Hustvedt, *Medical Muses*, 35, 148.

80 Mueller, “My Bio—Notes on an American Childhood,” 137.

81 Preciado, “Learning from the Virus.”

82 Barthes, *The Preparation of the Novel*, 276. Between the years 1978 and 1980, Barthes taught two courses with the title *The Preparation of the Novel* at the Collège de France in Paris, and these were transcribed and translated by Kate Briggs and published posthumously in English in 2011.

83 Barthes, *The Preparation of the Novel*, 18, 210.

84 Cookie Mueller, “Autobogrphical [*sic*] Novel,” typed and handwritten manuscript, undated, STHRA, BVII.1, F18.

85 Cookie Mueller, manuscript, undated, STHRA, BVII.1, F13.

86 Barthes, *The Preparation of the Novel*, 18.

87 Mueller, manuscript, undated, STHRA, BVII.1, F13.

88 Of chronicles, I am thinking of Gaëtan Gatian de Clerambault (1910), cited in Camhi, “Stealing Femininity,” 40.

89 Ahmed, *Living a Feminist Life*, 136. Italics mine.

90 Purnell, *100 Boyfriends Mixtape (The Demo)*, commissioned by Visual AIDS for Day With(out) Art, 2017: ALTERNATE ENDINGS, RADICAL BEGINNINGS, curated by Erin Christovale and Vivian Crockett, https://vimeo.com/245608333.

91 Sedgwick, “Jane Austen and the Masturbating Girl,” 118.

92 Sedgwick, “Jane Austen and the Masturbating Girl,” 111.

93 Sedgwick, “Jane Austen and the Masturbating Girl,” 126.

94 Sedgwick, “Jane Austen and the Masturbating Girl,” 111.

95 Here I depart from Michael Ann Holly on the pathological frame of melancholic longing in *The Melancholy Art*, 21.

96 Halberstam, *The Queer Art of Failure*, 3.

97 Halberstam, *The Queer Art of Failure*, 88.

98 *Ask Dr. Mueller* came later—a collected edition of her writings—in 1997. And in 2022, a new edition incorporating all these publications, split up into separate dated and geographically located pieces, alongside her health and art criticism, was published by Semiotext(e).

99 Mueller, "Working Titles," STHRA. Eileen Myles's autobiographical novel *Chelsea Girls* is subtitled *A Novel*, despite its composition being similarly piecemeal. Hanuman Books, which also published Mueller's *Garden of Ashes*, made chapbooks out of the texts "Bread and Water" and "1969" before they found their way into Myles's novel, published by Black Sparrow Press in full in 1994 (see the 2016 edition).

100 Barthes, *The Preparation of the Novel*, 18.

101 Mueller, "Cookie Mueller, born 1949 Baltimore, Maryland," in "Garden of Ashes," in *Ask Dr. Mueller*, 199.

102 DuBois, *Sappho Is Burning*, 3.

103 DuBois, *Sappho Is Burning*, 20.

104 DuBois, *Sappho Is Burning*, 24.

105 DuBois, *Sappho Is Burning*, 27.

106 The third chapter of duBois's book is titled "Sappho's Body-in-Pieces," in which she proposes that "Sappho's poems, their form and the ways in which we receive them, can exemplify an alternative aesthetic. Seeing the possibilities of this narrative—recognizing and accepting our own fragmentation and the inevitably fragmented past—has implications for how we treat bodies of poetry, bodies in poetry, and bodies in the world" (63).

107 DuBois, *Sappho Is Burning*, 39.

108 Sedgwick, "Paranoid Reading and Reparative Reading" (2003), 123.

109 Sedgwick, "Paranoid Reading and Reparative Reading" (2003), 123–24.

110 Sedgwick, "Paranoid Reading and Reparative Reading" (2003), 123–51. For a discussion of the "reparative turn" in queer feminist scholarship, see Wiegman, "The Times We're In." Wiegman identifies in Sedgwick's discussion of reparative reading a particular interest in affect and temporality that has been taken up by thinkers such as Ann Cvetkovich, Elizabeth Freeman, and Heather Love, who are collectively carving out a strand of Sedgwickian reparative work in queer *feminist*

criticism. In so doing, the nature and status of the critical act shifts, insofar as it listens to "sensation" over "suspicion" (16).

111 Sedgwick, "Paranoid Reading and Reparative Reading" (2003), 128, 146.

112 Sedgwick, "Paranoid Reading and Reparative Reading" (2003), 128. Italics mine.

113 Crimp, "Douglas Crimp on Alvin Baltrop," 269.

114 Crimp, "Douglas Crimp on Alvin Baltrop."

115 McClodden quoted in Martinez, "Alvin Baltrop."

116 Halter, "Alvin Baltrop," *4Columns*, September 6, 2019, https://www.4columns.org/halter-ed/alvin-baltrop.

117 See Holly, *The Melancholy Art*, xiv, 1–24.

118 Holly, *The Melancholy Art*, 20.

119 Baltrop cited in Oliver, "Alvin Baltrop," 65.

120 Sedgwick, "Paranoid Reading and Reparative Reading" (2003), 149, 146. Italics in brackets are mine.

121 Sedgwick, "Paranoid Reading and Reparative Reading" (2003), 148–49.

122 Niesp quoted in Griffin, *Edgewise*, 152.

123 Judy (Mueller) Hull quoted in Griffin, *Edgewise*, 152.

124 Senior yearbook, 1967, included in Griffin, *Edgewise*, 158, 160–61.

125 Here I depart from Ahmed, "A Phenomenology of Whiteness." Cookie's obsessions are as noted in Griffin, *Edgewise*, 162–64.

126 Fowler, "'A Teenager in Love,'" 326–27.

127 Mueller, "Alien," in "Garden of Ashes," in *Ask Dr. Mueller*, 201.

128 Ahmed, *Strange Encounters*, 2–3.

129 "Immunitary fantasies" is from Preciado, "Learning from the Virus."

130 Ahmed, *Strange Encounters*, 3, 13.

131 Sedgwick, "Queer and Now," 6.

132 Berlant, "Reading Sedgwick, Then and Now," 4.

133 Mueller, "Alien," 201.

134 Ashbolt, "'Go Ask Alice,'" 35.

135 Didion, "Slouching Towards Bethlehem," 85.

136 Mueller, "Haight Ashbury—San Francisco, California—1967," in *Walking Through Clear Water in a Pool Painted Black* (1990), 8.

137 Litvak, "Strange Gourmet," 86.

138 Mueller, "Haight Ashbury—San Francisco, California—1967," 6.

139 Kathy Acker, "Allen Ginsberg: A Personal Portrait," typescript, undated, cited in McBride, *Eat Your Mind*, 48.

140 Kramer, "Hot Fun in the Summertime," 221.

141 Kramer, "Hot Fun in the Summertime," 222.

142 Gedney, *A Time of Youth*, vii.

143 McCarty, "Introduction," in Gedney, *A Time of Youth*, 1.

144 Kramer, "Hot Fun in the Summertime," 223–24.

145 A. Davis, *Angela Davis: An Autobiography*, 124; Student Nonviolent Coordinating Committee of California, *The Movement* 2, no. 9 (1966), https://libraries.ucsd.edu/farmworkermovement/ufwarchives/sncc/16B%20-%20October%201966.pdf.

146 Student Nonviolent Coordinating Committee of California, *The Movement*.

147 Litvak, "Strange Gourmet," 77, 86. Italicized addition mine. *The Guermantes Way* (*Le côté de Guermantes*), the third volume of *In Search of Lost Time*, depicts the narrator's adolescence and passage into young adulthood.

148 Mueller, "Pink Flamingoes," in *Walking Through Clear Water in a Pool Painted Black* (1990), 70.

149 Mueller, "Pink Flamingoes," 79. Italics mine.

150 Mueller, "Haight Ashbury—San Francisco, California—1967," 5.

151 Mueller, "Haight Ashbury—San Francisco, California—1967," 17.

152 Mueller, "Haight Ashbury—San Francisco, California—1967," 16.

153 Mavor, *Reading Boyishly*, 18.

154 Kristeva, *New Maladies of the Soul*, 199.

155 Kristeva, *New Maladies of the Soul*, 199.

156 Kristeva, "The Adolescent Novel," 8–9.

157 Kristeva, "The Adolescent Novel," 9.

158 Mueller, "Two People—Baltimore—1964," 2.

159 Mueller, "Haight Ashbury—San Francisco, California—1967," 17.

160 Kristeva, "The Adolescent Novel," 22.

161 Kristeva, "The Adolescent Novel," 8.

162 Kristeva, "The Adolescent Novel," 11.

163 Kristeva, *New Maladies of the Soul*, 189.

164 "Reverie (n.)," *Online Etymology Dictionary*, https://www.etymonline.com/search?q=reverie.

165 Woolf, "On Being Ill," 36.

166 Kristeva, "The Adolescent Novel," 14.

167 Wojnarowicz, "Postcards from America," 10.

168 Mueller, "Two People—Baltimore—1964," 1.

169 Mueller, "Two People—Baltimore—1964," 2; Preciado, *Testo Junkie*, 35; Mueller, "Two People—Baltimore—1964," 4.

170 Mueller, "Two People—Baltimore—1964," 1, 3.

171 Mueller, "Two People—Baltimore—1964," 3.

172 Mueller, "Two People—Baltimore—1964," 4.

173 Mueller, "Two People—Baltimore—1964," 1–2.

174 Mueller, "Two People—Baltimore—1964," 2. 2

175 See Pearl, "Gazing at AIDS," 68; and Ogdon, "Through the Image." 3

176 Sedgwick, "Paranoid Reading and Reparative Reading" (1997), 2. 1

177 Mueller, "A Last Letter" (1989), 14.

178 My reading of nostalgia is informed by Carol Mavor's analysis of nostalgic Barthes in *Reading Boyishly*, 23–56.

179 J. Butler, "Rethinking Vulnerability and Resistance," 23–25.

180 J. Butler, "Rethinking Vulnerability and Resistance," 25.

181 J. Butler, "Rethinking Vulnerability and Resistance," 25.

182 Mueller, "My Bio—Notes on an American Childhood," 143.

183 Hedva, "Sick Woman Theory."

184 "Pleasant (adj.)," *Online Etymology Dictionary*, https://www.etymonline.com/search?q=pleasant.

185 Here I am thinking alongside Dodie Bellamy's understanding of "The Barf" as feminist writing that is bodily, messy, and nonhierarchical: "outside the whole fucking system." "Barf Manifesto," 64.

186 Mueller, "My Bio—Notes on an American Childhood," 143.

187 Lauren Berlant, "The Undying," *4Columns*, September 6, 2019, https://4columns.org/berlant-lauren/the-undying.

188 Mavor, *Reading Boyishly*, 34.

189 Mueller, "Two People—Baltimore—1964," 3.

190 Stewart, *On Longing*, 105.

191 Mueller, "Two People—Baltimore—1964," 2.

192 Mueller, "Two People—Baltimore—1964," 2. Allusions to waste, to the behind, to staying behind and back also inform Litvak's queer

reading of Proustian adolescence, which I draw on here. See Litvak, "Strange Gourmet."

193 Sedgwick, "A Poem Is Being Written," 199, 184–86, 211, 204–5.

194 Sedgwick, "A Poem Is Being Written," 187.

195 Sedgwick, "A Poem Is Being Written," 209; Mueller, "Two People—Baltimore—1964," 3.

196 Ahmed, *Queer Phenomenology*, 78.

197 Litvak, "Strange Gourmet," 87.

198 Sedgwick, "A Poem Is Being Written," 177.

199 Hedva, "Sick Woman Theory."

2 200 Sedgwick, "Paranoid Reading and Reparative Reading (2003)," 128.

3 201 Hedva, "Sick Woman Theory."

2 202 Deutsch, *Confrontations with Myself*, 216.

203 Zipes, "Writing Daydreams with Hope."

204 Litvak, "Strange Gourmet," 88.

205 Mueller, "Breaking into Show Biz," in *Walking Through Clear Water in a Pool Painted Black* (2022), 58.

206 Cookie Mueller, "The Head Gargoyle: H. M. Koutoukas by Cookie Mueller," *BOMB*, April 1, 1983, https://bombmagazine.org/articles/the-head-gargoyle/.

207 Mueller, "The Berlin Film Festival—Berlin, West Germany—1981," in *Walking Through Clear Water in a Pool Painted Black* (1990), 133.

208 Stevenson transcribed in Mueller, "A Last Letter" (1989), 15.

209 I am inspired by the image of "adolescent swallows" in Denise Duhamel's memoriam poem, "Beauties Who Live Only for an Afternoon."

210 Mueller, "Route 95 South—Baltimore to Orlando," in *Walking Through Clear Water in a Pool Painted Black* (1990), 34–35.

211 I borrow this phrase from Rebecca Solnit who borrows it from Georgia O'Keefe's correspondence. Solnit, *The Faraway Nearby*, 108.

CHAPTER THREE. THE LETTER PIECE: AROUND VALENTINE'S DAY, 1980, OR, LOVESICK PERVERSIONS IN CORRESPONDENCE

1 Acker, *My Mother: Demonology*, 7.

2 See Acker, *New York City in 1979*.

3 In 1980, Cookie Mueller shared her apartment on Bleecker Street with Sharon Niesp and her son, Max Mueller.

4 Lawrence, *Life and Death on the New York Dance Floor 1980–1983*, 16.

5 Holert, "'80s Then: Nan Goldin." Before it was published as a book in 1986, *The Ballad of Sexual Dependency* was an iterative, evolving slide-show work set to music that included hundreds of Goldin's photographs depicting the characters and scenes of her intimate social life.

6 Quotations from Goldin, *The Ballad of Sexual Dependency*, 6.

7 Boch, *The Mudd Club*, 56.

8 Mueller, "Art and About," *Details*, March 1985, STHRA, BVII.I, F19.

9 I am indebted to queer theorists who have also turned to *Frankenstein*, including Jack Halberstam (see *Skin Shows*, 30), and Elizabeth Freeman (see *Time Binds*, 98).

10 Mueller, "Art and About," March 1985.

11 Robert Hawkins cited in Charlie Fox, "Why Frankenstein's Monster Haunts Queer Art," *New York Times Style Magazine*, October 13, 2017, https://www.nytimes.com/2017/10/13/t-magazine/art/frankenstein-monster-queer-art.html.

12 Sedgwick, "Queer and Now," 3.

13 Sedgwick, "Queer and Now," 3.

14 "Affinity (n.)," *Online Etymology Dictionary*, https://www.etymonline.com/search?q=affinity.

15 Sedgwick, "Queer and Now," 6.

16 A cropped version of the image is reproduced in Griffin's *Edgewise*; it is here I first discovered it. See also Gary Indiana cited in Griffin, *Edgewise*, 123, and Kraus, *After Kathy Acker*, 185.

17 Butt, *Between You and Me*, 7–8.

18 Kraus, *After Kathy Acker*, 185. Italics mine.

19 As remembered in Boch, *The Mudd Club*, 16.

20 Muñoz, "Ephemera as Evidence," 6, 10.

21 Dillon, *Suppose a Sentence*, 22.

22 Dillon, *Affinities*, 19–24. Dillon's "meandering" passages on affinity that are interwoven throughout the book's main chapters have been a particular source of inspiration.

23 Cookie Mueller, illustrated autograph letter signed to Ching Ho Cheng, undated, Archives of American Art, Smithsonian Institution, Washington, DC, Ching Ho Cheng Papers (cited hereafter as CHCP), B2, F17.

24 Scholarship on the varied histories and practices of women's epistolary writing is extensive. See Gilroy and Verhoeven, *Epistolary Histories*; Jolly, *In Love and Struggle*; and Kauffman, *Discourses of Desire*.

25 Smith-Rosenberg, “The Female World of Love and Ritual,” 9; Berlant, *The Female Complaint*, 4.

26 Berlant, *The Female Complaint*, 171.

27 Berlant, *The Female Complaint*, 13–16.

28 Berlant, *The Female Complaint*, 171–72.

29 Berlant, *Desire/Love*, 112.

30 Berlant, “Love, a Queer Feeling,” 448.

31 Cookie Mueller, “Bedrock in the Love-Sick Chasm,” STHRA, BVII.I, FII.

32 Mueller, “Bedrock in the Love-Sick Chasm,” STHRA.

33 Acker in Acker and Buck, *Spread Wide*, 18, 20.

34 Acker in Acker and Buck, *Spread Wide*, 20.

35 Sharon Kivland, “EN TOUTE INTIMITÉ” performance-lecture, Freud Museum London, London, May 31, 2019.

36 Kraus, *After Kathy Acker*, 172–79. Acker published the Laure translations as “Translations of the Diaries of Laure” in Steve Abbott’s magazine *Soup: Translation in Process*, no. 3 (1983). They also appeared in the London magazine *Diana’s* that year. Later, the piece would be included in *Hannibal Lecter, My Father* (104–13).

37 Acker, in Alpert, “Kathy Acker: Mitali Restaurant, NYC: Interview with Barry Alpert, Only Paper Today, March 30, 1976,” in *Kathy Acker*, 3.

38 Acker in Acker and Buck, *Spread Wide*, 38.

39 Acker, *Great Expectations*, 29.

40 Myles, “Dear Reader: Eileen Myles on Kathy Acker,” *Literary Hub*, May 2, 2019, https://lithub.com/dear-reader-eileen-myles-on-kathy-acker/. See also the young girl woodcuts used in the first published edition of *Great Expectations* (Barrytown, NY / New York: Station Hill / Open Book, 1982).

41 Acker, in Kuipers, “Kathy Acker: Gramercy Park Hotel Bar, NYC: Conversation with Dean Kuipers, July 2, 1988,” in *Kathy Acker*, 36–37.

42 Acker, *Great Expectations*, 5.

43 Acker, *Great Expectations*, 58.

44 While Bellamy’s epistolary novel was not originally published as a Native Agents edition (it was instead published in 1998 by Hard Press Inc.), it was reissued in the series in 2021. Bellamy has returned to Acker’s influence in a series of essays (see “Digging Through Kathy Acker’s Stuff”; “Sense and Sensuality”). See also Chris Kraus, “Sex, Tattle and Soul: How Kathy Acker Shocked and Seduced the Literary

World," *Guardian*, August 19, 2017, https://www.theguardian.com/books/2017/aug/19/sex-tattle-and-soul-how-kathy-acker-shocked-and-seduced-the-literary-world.

45 Acker in Acker, *Great Expectations*, 26.

46 Bellamy, "Sense and Sensuality."

47 Bellamy, *the buddhist*, 35.

48 Acker, *Great Expectations*, 26–27.

49 Kathy Acker, typed letter signed to Sylvère Lotringer, March 8, 1991, SLPSA, B1, F4.

50 See also *I'm Very into You: Correspondence 1995–1996*—Acker's private email correspondence with McKenzie Wark, edited and published
posthumously by the executor of Acker's estate, Matias Viegener, in 2
2015. 3

51 I follow Peggy Phelan's theorization of performance in *Unmarked* as 5
the art form of disappearance, through which it is possible to participate in an "*active* vanishing" (19). There is "real power in remaining unmarked" (6).

52 Barthes, *A Lover's Discourse*, 13. In the fragment titled "The Absent One," Barthes emphasizes the isolation that love can bring.

53 Carson, *Eros the Bittersweet*, 29.

54 Barthes, *A Lover's Discourse*, 158.

55 This triangle follows earlier work I have published on the love triangle as a shape of feminist art writing: see "'Have You Tried It with Three? Have You?'" Quotation is from Barthes, *A Lover's Discourse*, 13.

56 See Gallop, *Around 1981*; also Gallop, "Annie Leclerc Writing a Letter, with Vermeer." In this article, Gallop traces the "penetration" of "things from the French" into "American feminist criticism" (103).

57 Gallop, "Annie Leclerc Writing a Letter, with Vermeer," 103.

58 Gallop, "Annie Leclerc Writing a Letter, with Vermeer," 108.

59 Leclerc cited in Gallop, "Annie Leclerc Writing a Letter, with Vermeer," 112. The term *labial larynx* departs from Wayne Koestenbaum's discussion of the feminization of the throat in *The Queen's Throat*, 160.

60 See also Cookie Mueller's 1988 miniature epistolary chapbook *Fan Mail, Frank Letters, and Crank Calls* (with gold-letter kissed wraps). In this story, Mueller writes as a lovesick fan; her narrator misses film star Georgia's "fat full blooming labias. Blow job lips" (8).

61 Gallop, "Precocious *Jouissance*," 565.

62 Barthes, *The Pleasure of the Text*, 7, 13.

63 Gallop, *Thinking Through the Body*, 113.

64 Barthes, *The Pleasure of the Text*, 66–67.

65 Barthes, *The Pleasure of the Text*, 66.

66 Acker in Acker and Buck, *Spread Wide*, 32.

67 Bellamy, "Barf Manifesto," 63–64.

68 Bellamy, "Barf Manifesto," 63.

69 Koestenbaum, *The Queen's Throat*, 160.

70 Kauffman, "Not a Love Story," 203.

71 Acker's unpublished and "in-pieces" epistolary essay "Letters to Flaubert" (1980), in KAP, B23, F12, could also suggest this fantasized becoming. I have also been inspired by Louise J. Kaplan in *Female Perversions*.

72 Appignanesi, *Mad, Bad and Sad*, 289.

73 J. Butler, "Rethinking Vulnerability and Resistance," 25. Italics mine.

74 Myles, "Dear Reader: Eileen Myles on Kathy Acker"; Kraus, *After Kathy Acker*, 158.

75 Kathy Acker, typed letter signed to Alan Sondheim, undated (ca. 1974), KAP, B30, F11.

76 "Fanatic (n.)," *Online Etymology Dictionary*, https://www.etymonline.com/search?q=fanatic.

77 Acker, typed letter signed to Sondheim.

78 Acker, typed letter signed to Sondheim.

79 Kraus, *After Kathy Acker*, 184. *My Death, My Life, by Pier Paolo Pasolini* was later republished in *Literal Madness*, a 1988 Grove Press anthology of her work.

80 Kathy Acker, typed letter signed to Jerome Rothenberg, undated (ca. 1972), University of California San Diego Special Collections, Jerome Rothenberg Papers (cited hereafter as JRP), B3, F1.

81 Kathy Acker, autograph letter signed to Ron Silliman, undated, University of California San Diego Special Collections, Ron Silliman Papers (cited hereafter as RSP), B1, F6. Acker met Silliman while living in San Francisco. She then turned to him in letters following her move to New York.

82 Acker, autograph letter signed to Ron Silliman, undated, RSP, B1, F6.

83 Kathy Acker, typed letter signed to Bernadette Mayer, undated, UARA, B1, F1.

84 Kathy Acker, autograph letter signed to Bernadette Mayer, undated, UARA, B1, F1.

85 Mayer, *The Desires of Mothers to Please Others in Letters*, 88, 91.

86 Acker, *Great Expectations*, 26.

87 Kraus, *After Kathy Acker*, 76.

88 Mayer, *The Desires of Mothers to Please Others in Letters*, 90.

89 Kathy Acker, typed letter signed to Terence Sellers, undated (ca. 1980–81), TSP, B1, F13.

90 Hannah Black, "Witch-hunt," *Tank Magazine: The Gossip Issue*, issue 70, Spring 2017, https://tankmagazine.com/issue-70/features/hannah-black/.

91 Kathy Acker, typed letter to Terence Sellers, undated (ca. 1980), TSP, B1, F13.

92 Terence Sellers, autograph letter signed to Kathy Acker, September 28, 1980, TSP, B1, F13.

93 Terence Sellers, autograph letter signed to Kathy Acker, July 24, 1980, TSP, B1, F13.

94 See Peraldi, *Polysexuality* [*Semiotext(e)* #10] and Acker, *Portrait of an Eye*, 77–90. Sellers, autograph letter signed to Acker, July 24, 1980.

95 *The Correct Sadist: The Memoirs of Angel Stern* was originally published by Berlin's iKoo-Buchverlag in 1981. Two years later, Sellers self-published the novel with Vitriol Publications. In 1985, Acker's publisher, Grove Press, published the novel in the United States.

96 Berlant, *The Queen of America Goes to Washington City*, 5, 7.

97 O'Grady, *Writing in Space*, 8–10.

98 O'Grady, *Writing in Space*, 9–10.

99 O'Grady, *Writing in Space*, 80.

100 Cited in Cooks, "The Art World Has Lost Its Mind."

101 O'Grady published the invitation she received from the exhibition's curator, Dorothée Dupuis, to show a work as part of this "matrix of encounters"; see "Invitation to Exhibit in *K. Acker: The Office*," December 15, 2010, https://lorraineogrady.com/wp-content/uploads/2022/10/101215-triangle-france-dorothee-dupuis-invitation-to-exhibit-k-acker-the-office-email-lorraine-ogradypdf.pdf.

102 Acker, "Notes on Writing—From the Life of Baudelaire."

103 O'Grady, *Writing in Space*, 30–31.

104 O'Grady, *Writing in Space*, 56.

105 O'Grady, *Writing in Space*, 56–57.

106 Acker, *Don Quixote*, 21.

107 Acker, *Don Quixote*, 21.

108 Acker, typed letter to Sellers, undated (ca. 1980).

109 Carson, *Eros the Bittersweet*, 3.

110 Acker, "New York City in 1979," in *Hannibal Lecter, My Father*, 37.

111 Berlant in Davis and Sarlin, "'On the Risk of a New Relationality.'"

112 Berlant in Davis and Sarlin, "'On the Risk of a New Relationality.'"

113 Barthes, *A Lover's Discourse*, 95.

114 Dawson, *Lovesickness and Gender in Early Modern Literature*, 13, 16.

115 Aisha Mazhar, "A Short History of Lovesickness," *Wellcome Collection*, February 11, 2020, https://wellcomecollection.org/articles/Xjol4hEAACMAD7i2.

116 Acker, typed letter to Sellers, undated (ca. 1980); Acker in Acker and Buck, *Spread Wide*, 44.

117 Acker in Acker and Buck, *Spread Wide*, 44.

118 Kraus, *After Kathy Acker*, 186; Sontag, *Illness as Metaphor*, 21.

119 Acker in Acker and Buck, *Spread Wide*, 44, 46.

120 Acker in Acker and Buck, *Spread Wide*, 46.

121 Acker in Acker and Buck, *Spread Wide*, 44, 46.

122 Quotation from Acker, telegram to Jonathan Miles, December 16, 1982, JMP.

123 Zambaco, "Onanism and Nervous Disorders in Two Little Girls."

124 Zambaco cited in Sedgwick, "Jane Austen and the Masturbating Girl," 118, 120; Sedgwick, "Jane Austen and the Masturbating Girl," 119, 127.

125 Sedgwick, "Jane Austen and the Masturbating Girl," 118.

126 Sedgwick, "Jane Austen and the Masturbating Girl," 129.

127 Acker, *Don Quixote*, 17.

128 Here I depart from Lauren Berlant's discussion of "cruel optimism" as a series of "sites" and "scenes of conventional desire that stand manifestly in the way of the subject's thriving." Berlant lists "the love plot" along with "the couple form, . . . the family, fame, work, wealth, or property" (45). See *Cruel Optimism*; and Acker, *Don Quixote*, 17, 16.

129 Acker, *Don Quixote*, 9.

130 Acker in Friedman, "A Conversation with Kathy Acker," 13.

131 Acker, *Don Quixote*, 17–18.

132 Zambreno, "Kate Zambreno on Kathy Acker," unpaginated. In this essay, Zambreno writes short letters to Acker that encompass themes of sickness, embodiment, and intimacy, drawing connections between Acker and David Wojnarowicz (see this chapter's epigraph).

133 Ahmed, *Willful Subjects*, 11. Italics mine.

134 Acker, *Don Quixote*, 47.

135 Acker, *Don Quixote*, 48.

136 Kraus, *After Kathy Acker*, 208–9.

137 M. Wark, *Philosophy for Spiders*, 5. Focusing on letters-as-literatures, rather than private archives, Rod Phillips, in "Purloined Letters," adapts Edgar Allan Poe's phrase "the purloined letter" to consider Acker's borrowing from Nathaniel Hawthorne's 1850 novel *The Scarlet Letter* in *Blood and Guts in High School* (1984) as an act of revisionist, feminist writing.

138 Acker, *Don Quixote*, 43.

139 Acker, *Don Quixote*, 44.

140 Quotation from Sedgwick, *A Dialogue on Love*, 47.

141 M. Wark, *Philosophy for Spiders*, 5.

142 Acker, *Don Quixote*, 47.

143 As reproduced in McBride, *Eat Your Mind*, plates insert.

144 Zola, *The Ladies' Paradise*, 110 (first published in French as *Au bonheur des dames* in 1883).

145 Acker, "Epitaph: Kathy Acker on Robert Mapplethorpe," 36.

146 Schulman, *The Gentrification of the Mind*. Schulman examines the concrete effects of gentrification on marginalized communities, as well as the broader impacts of gentrification culture on society and aesthetics and how this ideology emerged in the wake of the first wave of the AIDS epidemic, contributing also to the "loss" of Kathy Acker (76).

147 Acker, "City of the Angels," 41.

148 Acker, "Epitaph: Kathy Acker on Robert Mapplethorpe," 36.

149 Acker, "Epitaph: Kathy Acker on Robert Mapplethorpe," 36. Quotations in brackets are from Mueller, "Art and About," *Details*, August 1987, STHRA, BVII.1, F20.

150 Cvetkovich, *An Archive of Feelings*, 5; Acker, "Epitaph: Kathy Acker on Robert Mapplethorpe," 36.

151 Laing, *The Lonely City*, 183–84.

152 Rosalyn Deutsche and Cara Gendel Ryan's 1984 essay in *October*—titled "The Fine Art of Gentrification"—examines the financial and socioeconomic contexts that fueled the rapid increase of galleries within the Lower East Side/East Village area of New York.

153 Mueller, "Art and About," *Details*, February 1989, STHRA, BVII.1, F20.

154 Mueller, "Art and About," *Details*, August 1987.

155 Cited in Watney, *Policing Desire*, 134.

156 Cited in Crimp, *Melancholia and Moralism*, 77.

157 Advertisement for the Maryland AIDS hotline, 1988, published by AIDS Administration, Maryland Department of Health and Mental Hygiene. See Mazhar, "A Short History of Lovesickness" (note 115 above).

158 Cookie Mueller, card to John Heys, April 28, 1986, New York Public Library, John Heys Papers (cited hereafter as JHP), B5, F22.

159 John Heys cited in Griffin, *Edgewise*, 246.

160 Freeman, *The Wedding Complex*, 4–5.

161 Freeman, *The Wedding Complex*, 179.

162 Crimp, "Mourning and Militancy."

163 Wojnarowicz, "Postcards from America," 7.

164 Doyle, *Hold It Against Me*, 130.

165 Doyle, *Hold It Against Me*, 17.

166 Artists Space challenged the NEA decision, and while the grant was partially restored, the terms required that it fund the exhibition, not the catalog. See Kidd, "Witness for the Arts."

167 Freeman, *The Wedding Complex*, 3.

168 Bordowitz, *The AIDS Crisis Is Ridiculous*, 49; Cvetkovich, *An Archive of Feelings*, 159.

169 Goldin, "In the Valley of the Shadow," 5.

170 Earlier versions of "A Last Letter" were given the title "Gordon Stevenson," making it a more direct and personal form of obituary, with a shorter preface to Stevenson's letter that is more tightly absorbed in the dynamics of their friendship than a broader climate of political neglect. See Mueller, "Gordon Stevenson," undated, STHRA, BVII.I, FI3.

171 By the time Semiotext(e) included "A Last Letter" as the final piece in *Walking Through Clear Water in a Pool Painted Black*—published posthumously in March 1990, following Mueller's death the previous fall—a date had been added and a prefix dropped. Titled "Last Letter—1989," it had not been included in an earlier proof of the book, suggesting its placement to be a memorializing gesture.

172 Mueller, "A Last Letter" (1989), 14.

173 Berlant, "Reading Sedgwick, Then and Now," 1, 4.

174 The Italian artist Francesco Clemente was Scarpati's best man. He also cofounded Hanuman Books. Standing to her left is the art critic, poet, and painter René Ricard.

175 Barthes, *Camera Lucida*, 27.

176 This reading is informed by Julia Kristeva's understanding of the "perpetual subject-adolescent" made possible by novel writing, as explored in chapter 2. "The Adolescent Novel," 11.

177 Barthes, *Camera Lucida*, 53.

178 Mueller, "Art and About," *Details*, March 1986, STHRA, BVII.1, F20.

179 Acker, typed letter signed to Sondheim, undated (ca. 1974). Italics mine.

180 Cookie Mueller, "Vittorio Scarpati," illustration, undated, STHRA, BVII.1, F2.

181 See Acker, *Blood and Guts in High School, Plus Two.*

182 Acker, in Rickels, "Body Bildung: Laurence A. Rickels Talks with Kathy Acker, *Artforum*, February 1994," in *Kathy Acker*, 171.

183 Mueller, "Art and About," *Details*, March 1986, December 1985, November 1983, March 1989, March 1985, respectively: all in STHRA, BVII.1, F19 and F20.

184 Acker, "City of the Angels," 42.

185 Jay Drinkall, "Gran Fury: 'Read My Lips,'" *Afterall*, December 12, 2018, https://afterall.org/article/gran-fury-read-my-lips.

186 This slogan was used by the activist group ACT UP (AIDS Coalition to Unleash Power) to protest the systemic and violent neglect of people living with AIDS.

187 Mueller, "Art and About," August 1987.

188 Joli Jensen cited in Grant and Random Love, "Introduction," 2. I also learned much from Catherine Grant's scholarship on feminist communities and artworks of fandom; see *A Time of One's Own.*

189 Acker, "The Beat Goes On," 43.

190 See "Party Out of Bounds: Nightlife as Activism Since 1980, La Mama Galleria," *Visual AIDS*, https://www.visualaids.org/events/detail/party-out-of-bounds.

191 Mueller, "Art and About," *Details*, March 1986; Carr, *The Life and Times of David Wojnarowicz*, 322,

192 Carr, *The Life and Times of David Wojnarowicz*, 346.

193 Wojnarowicz, *Close to the Knives*, 86.

194 I have been inspired by Emma Wilson's discussion of bodily and affective accompaniment, of "being with" the dying, as explored in moving image practices. *Love, Mortality and the Moving Image*, 11–12.

195 O'Brien, Flanders, and Niesp, "For Cookie," 160.

196 Mueller, "Art and About," June 1988, STHRA, BVII.I, F20.

197 Bordowitz, *The AIDS Crisis Is Ridiculous*, 67.

198 Berlant, "Genre Flailing," 158.

199 Sedgwick, "Memorial for Craig Owens," 104.

200 Kruse, "Sedgwick's Perverse Close Reading," 132.

201 Sedgwick, "Queer and Now," 3.

202 Sedgwick, "Queer and Now," 4.

203 Sedgwick, "Queer and Now," 3.

204 Sedgwick, *Touching Feeling*, 2.

205 Sedgwick, "Shame in the Cybernetic Fold: Reading Silvan Tomkins (Written with Adam Frank)," 117. Jonathan A. Allan, in "Falling in Love," explores the work of a gathering of critics who have expressed "love" for Eve Sedgwick, finding within such work a queer approach to literary influence.

206 Maggie Nelson and Jonathan Flatley were both former students of Sedgwick's, as Nelson describes in *The Argonauts* and as Flatley reckons with in the article "Unlike Eve Sedgwick."

207 Sedgwick, *Touching Feeling*, 22.

208 Sedgwick, *Touching Feeling*, 22.

209 Sedgwick, *Touching Feeling*, 23.

210 Sedgwick, *Touching Feeling*, 23.

211 Sedgwick, *Touching Feeling*, 24.

212 Sedgwick explores this turn to the language of textiles, through the lens of Buddhist philosophy, and as intersecting with her sick subjectivity, in "Making Things, Practicing Emptiness."

213 Sedgwick, *Touching Feeling*, 24.

214 Sedgwick, *Touching Feeling*, 8.

215 Carolee Schneemann, Sarah Wang, et al., "Critical Correspondence—Reflections of a Marathon Reading, Kathy Acker: Blood and Guts in High School," *movement research*, April 24, 2018, https://movementresearch.org/publications/critical-correspondence/reflections-of-a-marathon-reading-kathy-acker-blood-and-guts-in-high-school.

216 Sarah Wang cited in Schneemann et al., "Critical Correspondence."

217 Sedgwick, "Queer and Now," 8; Nancy, *The Fall of Sleep*.

218 I borrow Jane Bennett's term theorized in *Vibrant Matter*, which describes nonhuman forces and tendencies that can "aid or destroy, enrich or disable, ennoble or degrade us" (ix).

219 Matias Viegener, “The Assassination of Kathy Acker,” *Jacket 2*, June 20, 2019, https://jacket2.org/article/assassination-kathy-acker.

220 See Sedgwick, “White Glasses.”

221 François, “Late Exercises in Minimal Affirmatives,” 46.

222 Sedgwick, “Paranoid Reading and Reparative Reading (2003),” 147.

223 Sedgwick, “Paranoid Reading and Reparative Reading (2003),” 147.

224 Nelson, *The Argonauts*, 105.

225 Sedgwick, *Touching Feeling*, 8.

226 Sedgwick, *Touching Feeling*, 9.

227 Sedgwick, *Touching Feeling*, 9.

228 Newton, “Two Shows,” 59–66.

229 Newton, “Two Shows,” 62.

230 Mueller, in “August 1989,” in “Art and About (*Details* magazine),” in *Ask Dr. Mueller*, 290.

231 Mueller, “John Waters and The Blessed Profession—1969,” in *Ask Dr. Mueller*, 13; Mueller, “Divine Intervention,” 133.

232 Mueller, “Divine Intervention,” 133.

233 Moon and Sedgwick, “Divinity,” 15.

234 Mueller, “November 1988,” in “Art and About (*Details* magazine),” in *Ask Dr. Mueller*, 288.

235 Mueller, “November 1988,” 289.

236 Sedgwick, *Touching Feeling*, 8.

237 Sedgwick, “Paranoid Reading and Reparative Reading (2003),” 150–151.

238 Mueller, “Art and About,” *Details*, May 1986, STHRA, BVII.1, F20.

239 Mueller, “Art and About,” *Details*, November 1985, STHRA, BVII.1, F20.

240 Mueller, “Art and About,” May 1986.

241 Mueller, “Art and About,” May 1986.

242 Mueller, “Art and About,” May 1986.

243 “Fanatic (n.).”

244 Sedgwick, “White Glasses,” 257. Italicized addition mine.

245 Mueller, “August 1989,” 292.

246 Scarpati, in Mueller and Scarpati, *Putti's Pudding*, unpaginated (2).

247 Mueller, “Haight Ashbury—San Francisco—1967,” in *Walking Through Clear Water in a Pool Painted Black* (1990), 9.

248 Mueller, in Mueller and Scarpati, *Putti's Pudding*, unpaginated (3).

249 Mueller, "August 1989," 291.

250 Scarpati's drawings were also shown in *Witnesses*, November 16, 1989–January 6, 1990. In 2017, London's Studio Voltaire gallery exhibited the works shown in 1989 alongside drawings recently discovered.

251 Flanders in O'Brien et al., "For Cookie," 161.

252 Mueller, "August 1989," 289.

253 Mueller, "August 1989," 290.

254 Mueller, "August 1989," 290.

255 Mueller, "August 1989," 290.

256 Mueller, "August 1989," 291.

257 Mueller, "August 1989," 291; Sedgwick, *Touching Feeling*, 24.

258 Mueller, "August 1989," 291.

259 Sedgwick, "Paranoid Reading and Reparative Reading (2003)," 150.

260 Mueller, "August 1989," 291–92.

261 Mueller, "August 1989," 293.

262 Mueller, "August 1989," 292.

263 Nelson, "A Halo Over the Hospital," in *Something Bright, Then Holes*, 39.

264 Nelson, "A Halo Over the Hospital," 42.

265 Annie DeWitt, "What's Queer Form Anyway? An Interview with Maggie Nelson," *Paris Review*, June 14, 2018, https://www.theparisreview.org/blog/2018/06/14/an-interview-with-maggie-nelson/.

266 Flatley, *Like Andy Warhol*, 4. Italics mine.

267 Flatley, *Like Andy Warhol*, 4–5.

268 Berlant, "Love, a Queer Feeling," 248.

269 Crimp cited in Flatley, *Like Andy Warhol*, 46; Flatley, *Like Andy Warhol*, 47.

270 Crimp cited in Flatley, *Like Andy Warhol*, 46.

271 Acker, "Blue Valentine"; last quotation from Flatley, *Like Andy Warhol*, 46.

272 Acker, "Blue Valentine."

273 Flatley, *Like Andy Warhol*, 239, 182.

274 Ahmed, "A Phenomenology of Whiteness," 160, 163.

275 Flatley, *Like Andy Warhol*, 240.

276 Muñoz cited in Flatley, *Like Andy Warhol*, 214. See Muñoz, *Disidentifications*; and Ahmed, *Queer Phenomenology*, 146.

277 Flatley, *Like Andy Warhol*, 5.

278 Flatley, *Like Andy Warhol*, 7.

279 Flatley in Felix Bernstein, "Liking Andy Warhol: An Interview with Jonathan Flatley," *Los Angeles Review of Books*, July 20, 2018, https://lareviewofbooks.org/article/liking-andy-warhol-an-interview-with-jonathan-flatley/.

280 Daisy Lafarge, "Metaphor as Parasite: On Ecologies of Love, Language and Disease," *The Drouth*, 2021, https://www.thedrouth.org/metaphor-as-parasite-on-ecologies-of-love-language-and-disease-by-daisy-lafarge/. Italics mine.

281 Nelson, *Bluets*, 1.

282 Ngai, *Ugly Feelings*, 6; Nelson, *Bluets*, 1.

283 Flatley, *Like Andy Warhol*, 37.

284 In this proposition, I thank Dr. Laura Haynes of Glasgow School of Art who asked what role the lyric plays in close writing at the *Experimental Writing in English: The Anti-Canon* conference, Brussels, Belgium, September 15–16, 2022.

POSTSCRIPT. OPEN ENVELOPES, OR, I AM STILL STUNG

1 Irigaray, "Why Cultivate Difference," 88. Here Irigaray is quoting from *To Be Two*.

2 Cookie Mueller, "Working Titles: Garden of Ashes, Messages from the Edge," cover letter, undated, STHRA, BVII.1, F3.

3 Here, I am inspired by the last lines of Carol Mavor's *Thoughts One Can't Do Without: A Magpie and an Envelope* (2021), which link the epistolary form with voice and listening; and waiting with love (44).

4 See Brooke, "Kathy Acker's Clothes."

5 Barthes, *Camera Lucida*, 5.

6 In this relationship I have been inspired by Mavor, "Collecting Loss."

7 *I, I, I, I, I, I, I, Kathy Acker*, Institute of Contemporary Arts, London, May 1–August 4, 2019, was the first UK exhibition dedicated to Acker's work and influence.

8 Barthes, *A Lover's Discourse*, 127–28.

9 Acker, "Devoured by Myths: An Interview with Sylvère Lotringer," in *Hannibal Lecter, My Father*, 23.

10 Acker, "Seeing Gender," in *Bodies of Work*, 166.

11 Stallybrass, "Worn Worlds," 28.

12 My thinking on the paradoxical presence and absence of Acker in my memorial writing is informed by Jacques Derrida's short piece, titled "Adieu," which was delivered at Emmanuel Levinas's funeral in 1995. *Adieu to Emmanuel Levinas*, 13.

13 Barthes, *Camera Lucida*, 64.

14 Sedgwick, "Making Things, Practicing Emptiness," 71.

15 Berlant, "Genre Flailing," 161.

Bibliography

ARCHIVES

Close Writing was born in the archive. I cite the locations and MSS identifiers of the archives consulted in full here, along with abbreviations that are used in the notes. In the notes, for items cited within these locations, I use *B* to denote the box number and *F* to denote the folder number.

Archives of American Art, Smithsonian Institution, Washington, DC

Ching Ho Cheng Papers. CHCP.

Fales Library and Special Collections, New York University Libraries

Kathy Acker Notebooks, MSS. 434. KAN.

Richard Hell Papers, MSS. 140. RHP.

Ron Kolm Papers, MSS. 079. RKP.

The Sylvère Lotringer Papers and Semiotext(e) Archive, MSS. 221. SLPSA.

Amos Poe Papers, MSS. 203. AMP.

Terence Sellers Papers, MSS. 167. TSP.

Serpent's Tail/High Risk Archives, MSS. 86. STHRA.

Jonathan Miles Personal Papers. JMPP.

New York Public Library

John Heys Papers. JHP.

David M. Rubenstein Rare Book and Manuscript Library, Duke University
Kathy Acker Papers. KAP.

University of California San Diego Special Collections
Jackson Mac Low Papers, MSS. 180. JMLP.
Bernadette Mayer Papers, MSS. 420. BMP.
Jerome Rothenberg Papers, MSS. 10. JRP.
Ron Silliman Papers, MSS. 75. RSP.
United Artists Records Archive, MSS. 12. UARA.

INTERVIEWS AND CONVERSATIONS

Eleanor Antin. London, 2017; San Diego, 2018.
Mel Freilicher. San Diego, 2018.
Chris Kraus. Telephone, 2016.
Del LaGrace Volcano. Email, 2023.
Jerome Rothenberg and Diane Rothenberg. San Diego, 2018.

PUBLISHED WORKS AND PRESENTATIONS

Acker, Kathy. "The Beat Goes On." *New Statesman and Society* 3, no. 89 (1990): 43.

Acker, Kathy. *Blood and Guts in High School, Plus Two*. London: Picador / Pan Books, 1984.

Acker, Kathy. "Blue Valentine." In *Andy Warhol Film Factory*, edited by Michael O'Pray, 62–65. London: British Film Institute, 1989.

Acker, Kathy. *Bodies of Work: Essays by Kathy Acker*. London: Serpent's Tail, 2006.

Acker, Kathy. *The Childlike Life of the Black Tarantula by the Black Tarantula*. New York: TVRT Press, 1978.

Acker, Kathy. "City of the Angels." *New Statesman and Society* 2, no. 73 (1989): 41–42.

Acker, Kathy. *Don Quixote: A Novel*. New York: Grove, 1986.

Acker, Kathy. *Empire of the Senseless*. New York: Grove Weidenfeld, 1988.

Acker, Kathy. "Epitaph: Kathy Acker on Robert Mapplethorpe." *The Face* 2, no. 8 (May 1989): 36.

Acker, Kathy. "The Gift of Disease." *Guardian*, January 18, 1997.

Acker, Kathy. *Great Expectations*. Barrytown, NY / New York: Station Hill / Open Book, 1982.

Acker, Kathy. *Great Expectations: A Novel.* New York: Grove Weidenfeld, 1983.

Acker, Kathy. *Hannibal Lecter, My Father.* New York: Semiotext(e), 1991.

Acker, Kathy. *Kathy Acker: The Last Interview and Other Conversations.* Edited by Amy Scholder and Douglas A. Martin. Brooklyn, NY: Melville House, 2018.

Acker, Kathy. *Literal Madness: Three Novels.* New York: Grove, 1988.

Acker, Kathy. *My Mother: Demonology.* New York: Pantheon, 1993.

Acker, Kathy. *New York City in 1979.* Issue 9. New York: Top Stories, 1981.

Acker, Kathy. "Notes on Writing—From the Life of Baudelaire." *L-A-N-G-U-A-G-E*, October 1979. https://editions-ismael.com/wp-content/uploads/2019/06/1979-Kathy-Acker-Notes-on-writing-from-the-life-of-Baudelaire-LANGUAGE.pdf.

Acker, Kathy. *Politics.* N.p.: Papyrus Press (self-published), 1972.

Acker, Kathy. *Portrait of an Eye: Three Novels.* New York: Grove, 1998.

Acker, Kathy. "Translations of the Diaries of Laure." *Soup: Translation in Process*, no. 3 (1983): 31–34.

Acker, Kathy, and Paul Buck. *Spread Wide: An Encounter Between Kathy Acker and Paul Buck, with Further Interventions from Rebecca Stephens and John Cussans.* Paris: Editions Dis Voir, 2004.

Acker, Kathy, and McKenzie Wark. *I'm Very into You: Correspondence 1995–1996.* Edited by Matias Viegener. South Pasadena, CA: Semiotext(e), 2015.

Ahmed, Sara. *Living a Feminist Life.* Durham, NC: Duke University Press, 2017.

Ahmed, Sara. "A Phenomenology of Whiteness." *Feminist Theory* 8, no. 2 (2007): 149–68.

Ahmed, Sara. *Queer Phenomenology: Orientations, Objects, Others.* Durham, NC: Duke University Press, 2006.

Ahmed, Sara. *Strange Encounters: Embodied Others in Post-Coloniality.* London: Routledge, 2000.

Ahmed, Sara. *Willful Subjects.* Durham, NC: Duke University Press, 2014.

Alberro, Alexander. "Reductivism in Reverse." In *Dan Graham*, edited by Alex Kitnick, 21–40. Cambridge, MA: OCTOBER Files 11, MIT Press, 2011.

Allan, Jonathan A. "Falling in Love: With Eve Sedgwick." *Mosaic* 48, no. 1 (2015): 1–16.

Anderson, Fiona. *Cruising the Dead River: David Wojnarowicz and New York's Ruined Waterfront.* New York: Columbia University Press, 2019.

Antin, David. "David Antin on Kathy Acker." Symposium paper. *Lust for Life: The Writings of Kathy Acker*, New York University, November 8, 2002. https://www.youtube.com/watch?v=kgcMDnyObSs.

Antin, David. *i never knew what time it was*. Berkeley: University of California Press, 2005.

Appignanesi, Lisa. *Mad, Bad and Sad: A History of Women and the Mind Doctors from 1800 to the Present*. London: Virago, 2009.

Arabindan-Kesson, Anna. *Black Bodies White Gold: Art, Cotton, and Commerce in the Atlantic World*. Durham, NC: Duke University Press, 2021.

Arnett, James. "Review: Eve's Body/Of Work." *Capacious: Journal for Emerging Affect Inquiry* 2, no. 3 (2021): 162–67.

Ashbolt, Anthony. "'Go Ask Alice': Remembering the Summer of Love Forty Years On." *Australasian Journal of American Studies* 26, no. 2 (2007): 35–47.

Barthes, Roland. *Camera Lucida: Reflections on Photography*. Translated by Richard Howard. New York: Farrar, Straus and Giroux, 1981.

Barthes, Roland. *A Lover's Discourse: Fragments*. London: Vintage, 2002.

Barthes, Roland. *Mourning Diary*. Translated by Richard Howard. Established and annotated by Nathalie Léger. London: Notting Hill Editions, 2011.

Barthes, Roland. *The Pleasure of the Text*. Translated by Richard Miller. With a Note on the Text by Richard Howard. New York: Hill and Wang, 1998.

Barthes, Roland. *The Preparation of the Novel*. Translated by Kate Briggs. New York: Columbia University Press, 2011.

Barthes, Roland. *Roland Barthes by Roland Barthes*. Translated by Richard Howard. London: Vintage Classics, 2020.

Barthes, Roland. "To Write: An Intransitive Verb." In *The Rustle of Language*, translated by Richard Howard, 76–79. Berkeley: University of California Press, 1989.

Bellamy, Dodie. "Barf Manifesto." In *When the Sick Rule the World*, 45–64. South Pasadena, CA: Semiotext(e), 2015.

Bellamy, Dodie. *the buddhist*. San Francisco / Oakland, CA: Allone Co. Editions / Publication Studio, 2011.

Bellamy, Dodie. "Delinquent." In *A Poetics of Criticism*, edited by Juliana Spahr, Mark Wallace, Kristin Prevallet, and Pam Rehm, 293–99. Buffalo, NY: Leave Books, 1994.

Bellamy, Dodie. "Digging Through Kathy Acker's Stuff." In *When the Sick Rule the World*, 124–50. South Pasadena, CA: Semiotext(e), 2015.

Bellamy, Dodie. *Pink Steam*. San Francisco, CA: Suspect Thoughts, 2004.

Bellamy, Dodie. "Sense and Sensuality." *frieze*, no. 189 (2017): 30–31.

Bellamy, Dodie. *When the Sick Rule the World*. South Pasadena, CA: Semiotext(e), 2015.

Bennett, Jane. *Vibrant Matter: A Political Ecology of Things*. Durham, NC: Duke University Press, 2010.

Berlant, Lauren. *Cruel Optimism*. Durham, NC: Duke University Press, 2011.

Berlant, Lauren. *Desire/Love*. New York: Dead Letter Office, Punctum Books, 2012.

Berlant, Lauren. *The Female Complaint: The Unfinished Business of Sentimentality in American Culture*. Durham, NC: Duke University Press, 2008.

Berlant, Lauren. "Genre Flailing." *Capacious: Journal for Emerging Affect Inquiry* 1, no. 2 (2018): 156–62.

Berlant, Lauren. "Love, a Queer Feeling." In *Homosexuality and Psychoanalysis*, edited by Tim Dean and Christopher Lane, 432–51. Chicago: University of Chicago Press, 2001.

Berlant, Lauren. *The Queen of America Goes to Washington City: Essays on Sex and Citizenship*. Durham, NC: Duke University Press, 1997.

Berlant, Lauren, ed. *Reading Sedgwick*. Durham, NC: Duke University Press, 2019.

Berlant, Lauren. "Reading Sedgwick, Then and Now." In *Reading Sedgwick*. Edited by Lauren Berlant, 1–5. Durham, NC: Duke University Press, 2019.

Berlant, Lauren, and Lee Edelman. *Sex, or the Unbearable*. Durham, NC: Duke University Press, 2014.

Berlant, Lauren, and Kathleen Stewart. *The Hundreds*. Durham, NC: Duke University Press, 2019.

Blackshaw, Gemma, and Alice Butler. "Sick Women Correspondents: Practices of Care in Cross-Historical Love Letter Writing." *MAI: Feminism and Visual Culture* (Spring 2023). https://maifeminism.com/sick-women-correspondents-practices-of-care-in-cross-historical-love-letter-writing/.

Blocker, Jane. *What the Body Cost: Desire, History and Performance*. Minneapolis: University of Minnesota Press, 2004.

Boch, Richard. *The Mudd Club*. Port Townsend, WA: Feral House, 2017.

Bojarska, Katarzyna, and Lauren Berlant. "The Hundreds, Observation, Encounter, Atmosphere, and World-Making." *Journal of Visual Culture* 18, no. 3 (2019): 289–304.

Bora, Renu. "Outing Texture." In *Novel Gazing: Queer Readings in Fiction*, edited by Eve Kosofsky Sedgwick, 94–127. Durham, NC: Duke University Press, 1997.

Bordowitz, Gregg. *The AIDS Crisis Is Ridiculous and Other Writings, 1986–2003*. Edited by James Meyer. Cambridge, MA: MIT Press, 2004.

Bowles, John P. *Adrian Piper: Race, Gender, and Embodiment*. Durham, NC: Duke University Press, 2011.

Brainard, Joe. *The Collected Writings of Joe Brainard*. Edited by Ron Padgett. New York: Library of America, 2012. Kindle edition.

Brooke, Kaucyila. "Kathy Acker's Clothes." *Art Journal* 72, no. 2 (2013): 104–5.

Burroughs, William, and Brion Gysin. *The Third Mind.* London: John Calder, 1979.

Butler, Alice. "Fan Letters of Love." In *Fandom as Methodology: A Sourcebook for Artists and Writers*, edited by Catherine Grant and Kate Random Love, 149–64. London: Goldsmiths, 2019.

Butler, Alice. "'Have You Tried It with Three? Have You?' Ann Quin, Love Triangles, and the Affects of Art/Writing." *Capacious: Journal for Emerging Affect Inquiry* 2, no. 3 (2021): 82–107.

Butler, Alice. "With Love, a Letter to Cookie, and Her Stories." *Cabinet* 62 (2016–2017): 23–33.

Butler, Cornelia et al. *From Conceptualism to Feminism: Lucy Lippard's Numbers Shows 1969–74*. London: Afterall Books, 2012.

Butler, Judith. "Rethinking Vulnerability and Resistance." In *Vulnerability in Resistance*, edited by Judith Butler, Zeynep Gambetti, and Leticia Sabsay, 12–27. Durham, NC: Duke University Press, 2016.

Butt, Gavin. *Between You and Me: Queer Disclosures in the New York Art World, 1948–1963*. Durham, NC: Duke University Press, 2005.

Camhi, Leslie. "Stealing Femininity: Department Store Kleptomania as Sexual Disorder." *differences: A Journal of Feminist Cultural Studies* 5, no. 1 (Spring 1993): 26–50.

Campt, Tina M. "The Afterlives of Images: A Correspondence." Keynote lecture, June 17, 2022. Delivered at *Together, With, To: A Workshop on Correspondence and Letters*, Courtauld Institute of Art, London, June 16–17, 2022, curated and convened by Alice Butler.

Campt, Tina M. *Listening to Images*. Durham, NC: Duke University Press, 2017.

Campt, Tina M. "The Loop of Retreat—an Invitation." *e-flux Journal*, December 2019. https://www.e-flux.com/journal/105/302556/the-loophole-of-retreat-an-invitation/.

Carr, Cynthia. *The Life and Times of David Wojnarowicz: Fire in the Belly*. New York: Bloomsbury, 2012.

Carson, Anne. *Eros the Bittersweet: An Essay*. Princeton, NJ: Princeton University Press, 1986.

Carson, Anne. *If Not, Winter: Fragments of Sappho* by Sappho. Translated by Anne Carson. London: Virago, 2003.

Cassel Oliver, Valerie. "Alvin Baltrop: Dreams into Glass." *Callaloo* 36, no. 1 (2013): 6–69.

Cheng, Jih-Fei, Alexandra Juhasz, and Nishant Shahani, eds. *AIDS and the Distribution of Crises*. Durham, NC: Duke University Press, 2020.

Cixous, Hélène. "Coming to Writing." In *"Coming to Writing" and Other Essays*, edited by Deborah Jenson, 1–58. Translated by Sarah Cornell, Deborah Jenson, Ann Liddle, and Susan Sellers. Cambridge, MA: Harvard University Press, 1991.

Colby, Georgina. *Kathy Acker: Writing the Impossible*. Edinburgh: Edinburgh University Press, 2016.

Cooke, Jennifer. *Contemporary Feminist Life-Writing: The New Audacity*. Cambridge: Cambridge University Press, 2020.

Cooks, Bridget R. "The Art World Has Lost Its Mind: Lorraine O'Grady and the Birth of Mlle Bourgeoise Noire." *Afterall* 46 (2018): 96–105.

Crawley, Ashon T. "Harriet Jacobs Gets a Hearing." *Current Musicology* 93 (Spring 2012): 33–55.

Crimp, Douglas. "Douglas Crimp on Alvin Baltrop." *Artforum* 46, no. 6 (2008): 269.

Crimp, Douglas. *Melancholia and Moralism: Essays on AIDS and Queer Politics*. Cambridge, MA: MIT Press, 2002.

Crimp, Douglas. "Mourning and Militancy." *October* 51 (1989): 3–18.

Cvetkovich, Ann. *An Archive of Feelings: Trauma, Sexuality and Lesbian Public Cultures*. Durham, NC: Duke University Press, 2003.

Damman, Catherine. "Saidiya Hartman on Insurgent Histories and the Abolitionist Imaginary." *Artforum*, July 14, 2020. https://www.artforum.com/interviews/saidiya-hartman-83579.

Davis, Angela Y. *Angela Davis: An Autobiography*. Edited by Toni Morrison. London: Hamish Hamilton, 2022.

Davis, Heather, and Paige Sarlin. "'On the Risk of a New Relationality: An Interview with Lauren Berlant and Michael Hardt." *Reviews in Cultural Theory* 2, no. 3 (2011). http://reviewsinculture.com/2012/10/15/on-the-risk-of-a-new-relationality-an-interview-with-lauren-berlant-and-michael-hardt/.

Dawson, Lesel. *Lovesickness and Gender in Early Modern Literature*. Oxford: Oxford University Press, 2008.

Demos, John, and Virginia Demos. "Adolescence in Historical Perspective." *Journal of Marriage and Family* 31, no. 4 (1969): 632–38.

Dent, Tory. *What Silence Equals*. New York: Persea Books, 1993.

Derrida, Jacques. *Adieu to Emmanuel Levinas*. Translated by Pascale-Anne Brault and Michael Naas. Stanford, CA: Stanford University Press, 1999.

Derrida, Jacques, and Anne Dufourmantelle. *Of Hospitality*. Translated by Rachel Bowlby. Stanford, CA: Stanford University Press, 2000.

Deutsch, Helene. *Confrontations with Myself: An Epilogue*. New York: W. W. Norton, 1973.

Deutsche, Rosalyn, and Cara Gendel Ryan. "The Fine Art of Gentrification." *October* 31 (1984): 91–111.

Didion, Joan. "Slouching Towards Bethlehem." In *Slouching Towards Bethlehem*, 84–128. London: 4th Estate, 2017.

Dillon, Brian. *Affinities*. London: Fitzcarraldo Editions, 2023.

Dillon, Brian. *Suppose a Sentence*. London: Fitzcarraldo Editions, 2020.

Dinshaw, Carolyn. *Getting Medieval: Sexualities and Communities, Pre- and Postmodern*. Durham, NC: Duke University Press, 1999.

Doyle, Jennifer. *Hold It Against Me: Difficulty and Emotion in Contemporary Art*. Durham, NC: Duke University Press, 2013.

Doyle, Jennifer. *Sex Objects: Art and the Dialectics of Desire*. Minneapolis: University of Minnesota Press, 2006.

duBois, Page. *Sappho Is Burning*. Chicago: University of Chicago Press, 1995.

Duhamel, Denise. "Beauties Who Live Only for an Afternoon: In Memory of Cookie Mueller" (1989). In *Up Is Up, but So Is Down: New York's Downtown Literary Scene, 1974–1992*, edited by Brandon Stosuy, 305–6. New York: New York University Press, 2006.

Edwards, Jason. *Queer and Bookish: Eve Kosofsky Sedgwick as Book Artist*. New York: Punctum Books, 2022.

Eichhorn, Kate. *The Archival Turn in Feminism: Outrage in Order*. Philadelphia: Temple University Press, 2013.

Fawaz, Ramzi. "'An Open Mesh of Possibilities': The Necessity of Eve Sedgwick in Dark Times." In *Reading Sedgwick*, edited by Lauren Berlant, 6–33. Durham, NC: Duke University Press, 2019.

Fisher, Gary. *Gary in Your Pocket: Stories and Notebooks of Gary Fisher*. Edited by Eve Kosofsky Sedgwick. Durham, NC: Duke University Press, 1996.

Flatley, Jonathan. *Like Andy Warhol*. Chicago: University of Chicago Press, 2017.

Flatley, Jonathan. "Unlike Eve Sedgwick." *Criticism* 52, no. 2 (2010): 225–34.

Foster, Courtney. "Repetition and Embodiment: Performative Reading in Kathy Acker's *The Childlike Life of the Black Tarantula by the Black Tarantula*." *Tulsa Studies in Women's Literature* 36, no. 1 (Spring 2017): 129–50.

Fowler, Beth. "'A Teenager in Love': How Black Adolescents Became 'Teenagers' in Rock and Roll Music, 1956–1960." *Popular Music and Society* (2020): 324–39.

François, Anne-Lise. "Late Exercises in Minimal Affirmatives." In *Theory Aside*, edited by Jason Potts and Daniel Stout, 34–55. Durham, NC: Duke University Press, 2014.

Freeman, Elizabeth. *Time Binds: Queer Temporalities, Queer Histories*. Durham, NC: Duke University Press, 2010.

Freeman, Elizabeth. *The Wedding Complex: Forms of Belonging in Modern American Culture*. Durham, NC: Duke University Press, 2002.

Friedman, Ellen G. "A Conversation with Kathy Acker." In *The Review of Contemporary Fiction* 9, no. 3, edited by Ellen G. Friedman and Miriam Fuchs, 12–22. Elmwood Park, IL: Review of Contemporary Fiction, 1989.

Friedman, Ellen G. "Foreword: Kathy Acker: Wandering Jew." In *Kathy Acker and Transnationalism*, edited by Polina Mackay and Kathryn Nicol, xi–xx. Newcastle Upon Tyne: Cambridge Scholars Publishing, 2009.

Gallop, Jane. "Annie Leclerc Writing a Letter, with Vermeer." *October* 33 (1985): 103–17.

Gallop, Jane. *Around 1981: Academic Feminist Literary Theory*. Abingdon: Routledge, 2012.

Gallop, Jane. *The Deaths of the Author: Reading and Writing in Time*. Durham, NC: Duke University Press, 2011.

Gallop, Jane. "The Ethics of Reading: Close Encounters." *Journal of Curriculum Theorizing* 16, no. 3 (2000): 7–17.

Gallop, Jane. "Precocious *Jouissance*: Roland Barthes, Amatory Maladjustment, and Emotion." *New Literary History* 43, no. 3 (2012): 565–82.

Gallop, Jane. "Reading Derrida's Adieu." *differences* 16, no. 3 (2005): 16–26.

Gallop, Jane. *Thinking Through the Body*. New York: Columbia University Press, 1988.

Geary, Adam A. *Antiblack Racism and the AIDS Epidemic: State Intimacies*. New York: Palgrave Macmillan, 2014.

Gedney, William. *A Time of Youth: San Francisco 1966–1967*. Edited and with an introduction by Lisa McCarty. Durham, NC: Duke University Press, 2021.

Gilroy, Amanda, and W. M. Verhoeven, eds. *Epistolary Histories: Letters, Fiction, Culture*. Charlottesville: University Press of Virginia, 2000.

Goldberg, Jonathan. *Sappho:]Fragments*. New York: Dead Letter Office, Punctum Books, 2018.

Goldin, Nan. *The Ballad of Sexual Dependency*. Edited with Martin Heiferman, Mark Holborn, and Suzanne Fletcher. London: Secker and Warburg, 1989.

Goldin, Nan. *I'll Be Your Mirror*. Edited by Nan Goldin, David Armstrong, and Hans Werner Holzwarth. New York: Whitney Museum of American Art, 1996.

Goldin, Nan. "In the Valley of the Shadow." In *Witnesses: Against Our Vanishing*, edited by Nan Goldin, 4–5. New York: Artists Space, 1989.

Goldin, Nan, ed. *Witnesses: Against Our Vanishing*. New York: Artists Space, 1989.

Grant, Catherine. *A Time of One's Own: Histories of Feminism in Contemporary Art*. Durham, NC: Duke University Press, 2022.

Grant, Catherine, and Kate Random Love. "Introduction: Fandom as Methodology." In *Fandom as Methodology: A Sourcebook for Artists and Writers*, edited by Catherine Grant and Kate Random Love, 1–22. London: Goldsmiths, 2019.

Griffin, Chloé. *Edgewise: A Picture of Cookie Mueller*. Berlin: b_books Verlag, 2014.

Groff, David, and Philip Clark, eds. *Persistent Voices: Poetry by Writers Lost to AIDS*. New York: Alyson Books, 2009.

Guibert, Hervé. *To the Friend Who Did Not Save My Life*. 1990. London: Serpent's Tail, 2021.

Halberstam, Jack. *The Queer Art of Failure*. Durham, NC: Duke University Press, 2011.

Halberstam, Jack. *Skin Shows: Gothic Horror and the Technology of Monsters*. Durham, NC: Duke University Press, 1995.

Halberstam, Jack. *Wild Things: The Disorder of Desire*. Durham, NC: Duke University Press, 2020.

Harryman, Carla, Avital Ronell, and Amy Scholder, eds. *Lust for Life: On the Writings of Kathy Acker*. London: Verso, 2006.

Hartman, Saidiya. "Excisions of the Flesh." In *Lorna Simpson: For the Sake of the Viewer*, edited by Beryl J. Wright, 55–67. New York: Universe, 1992.

Hartman, Saidiya. *Lose Your Mother: A Journey Along the Atlantic Slave Route*. London: Serpent's Tail, 2021.

Hartman, Saidiya. "Venus in Two Acts." *Small Axe* 12, no. 2 (2008): 1–14.

Hartman, Saidiya. *Wayward Lives Beautiful Experiments: Intimate Histories of Social Upheaval*. London: Serpent's Tail, 2019.

Holert, Tom. "'80s Then: Nan Goldin." *Artforum*, March 2003. https://www.artforum.com/print/200303/nan-goldin-4292.

Holly, Michael Ann. *The Melancholy Art*. Princeton, NJ: Princeton University Press, 2013.

Houen, Alex. "Novel Biopolitics: Kathy Acker and Michel Foucault." In *Powers of Possibility: Experimental American Writing Since the 1960s*, 145–92. Oxford: Oxford University Press, 2012.

Hustvedt, Asti. *Medical Muses: Hysteria in 19th-Century Paris*. London: Bloomsbury, 2012.

Irigaray, Luce. "Why Cultivate Difference: Toward a Culture of Two Subjects." *Paragraph* 25, no. 3 (2002): 79–90.

Jolly, Margaretta. *In Love and Struggle: Letters in Contemporary Feminism*. New York: Columbia University Press, 2008.

Juhasz, Alexandra, and Theodore Kerr. *We Are Having This Conversation Now: The Times of AIDS Cultural Production*. Durham, NC: Duke University Press, 2022.

Kaplan, Alice. *Dreaming in French: The Paris Years of Jacqueline Bouvier Kennedy, Susan Sontag, and Angela Davis*. Chicago: University of Chicago Press, 2012.

Kaplan, Louise J. *Female Perversions: The Temptations of Emma Bovary*. New York: Doubleday, 1991.

Kauffman, Linda S. *Discourses of Desire: Gender, Genre, and Epistolary Fictions*. Ithaca, NY: Cornell University Press, 1986.

Kauffman, Linda S. "Not a Love Story: Retrospective and Prospective Epistolary Directions." Postscript by Richard Hardack. In *Epistolary Histories: Letters, Fiction, Culture*, edited by Amanda Gilroy and W. M. Verhoeven, 198–221. Charlottesville: University Press of Virginia, 2000.

Kidd, Dustin. "Witness for the Arts." In *Legislating Creativity: The Intersections of Art and Politics*, 81–106. New York: Routledge, 2010.

Koestenbaum, Wayne. "The Pleasure of the Text: Hervé Guibert's Unbridled Eroticism." *Bookforum*, June/July/August, 2014. https://www.bookforum.com/print/2102/herve-guibert-s-unbridled-eroticism-13298.

Koestenbaum, Wayne. *The Queen's Throat: Opera, Homosexuality and the Mystery of Desire*. London: Penguin, 1994.

Kotz, Liz. *Words to Be Looked At: Language in 1960s Art*. Cambridge, MA: MIT Press, 2007.

Kramer, Michael J. "Hot Fun in the Summertime: Micro and Macrocosmic Views on the Summer of Love." *The Sixties: A Journal of History, Politics and Culture* 10, no. 2 (2017): 221–41.

Kraus, Chris. *After Kathy Acker: A Biography*. London: Allen Lane, 2017.

Kristeva, Julia. "The Adolescent Novel." In *Abjection, Melancholia and Love: The Work of Julia Kristeva*, edited by John Fletcher and Andrew Benjamin, 8–23. Abingdon: Routledge, 2012.

Kristeva, Julia. *New Maladies of the Soul*. Translated by Ross Guberman. New York: Columbia University Press, 1995.

Kruse, Meridith. "Sedgwick's Perverse Close Reading and the Question of an Erotic Ethics." In *Reading Sedgwick*, edited by Lauren Berlant, 132–40. Durham, NC: Duke University Press, 2019.

Laing, Olivia. *Crudo: A Novel*. London: Picador, 2018.

Laing, Olivia. *The Lonely City: Adventures in the Art of Being Alone*. Edinburgh: Canongate, 2016.

Lamm, Kimberly. "Writing the 'I' Otherwise: Telegraphing Black Feminism in the Work of Adrian Piper and Angela Davis." In *Addressing the Other Woman: Textual Correspondences in Feminist Art and Writing*, 23–100. Manchester: Manchester University Press, 2017.

Lawrence, Tim. *Life and Death on the New York Dance Floor 1980–1983*. Durham, NC: Duke University Press, 2016.

Levinas, Emmanuel. *Totality and Infinity: An Essay on Exteriority*. Translated by Alphonso Lingis. Pittsburgh, PA: Duquesne University Press, 1969.

LeWitt, Sol. "Paragraphs on Conceptual Art." *Artforum* 5, no. 10 (1967): 79–83.

Limón, Ada, and Natalie Diaz. "Envelopes of Air." *New Yorker*, May 23, 2018. https://www.newyorker.com/books/poems/envelopes-of-air-ada-limon-and-natalie-diaz-forge-a-bond-amid-the-shifting-landscape-of-contemporary-america.

Lippard, Lucy, and John Chandler. "The Dematerialization of Art." *Art International* 12, no. 2 (1968): 31–36.

Litvak, Joseph. "Strange Gourmet: Taste, Waste, Proust." In *Novel Gazing: Queer Readings in Fiction*, edited by Eve Kosofsky Sedgwick, 74–93. Durham, NC: Duke University Press, 1997.

Martin, Douglas. *Acker*. Brooklyn, NY: Nightboat Books, 2017.

Martinez, Christina. "Alvin Baltrop." *Artforum* 59, no. 6 (2021). https://www.artforum.com/events/alvin-baltrop-3–248235/.

Mavor, Carol. *Becoming: The Photographs of Clementina, Viscountess Hawarden*. Durham, NC: Duke University Press, 1999.

Mavor, Carol. "Collecting Loss: Photographs, Dresses, 'Paperies.'" *Counterpoints* 220 (2004): 15–38.

Mavor, Carol. "The Enveloped: Emily Dickinson and London's Foundling Hospital." Keynote masterclass, May 10, 2022, Courtauld Institute of Art, London. Delivered as part of *"What a Hazard a Letter Is": Correspondence in Feminist Art, Art Writing, and Art History, from Emily Dickinson to Now*, curated and convened by Alice Butler.

Mavor, Carol. "Making Poems Out of What Is Not There: The Envelopes of Emily Dickinson and London's Foundling Hospital." In *Serendipity: The Afterlife of the Object,* 113–45. London: Reaktion Books, 2024.

Mavor, Carol. *Pleasures Taken: Performances of Sexuality and Loss in Victorian Photographs*. Durham, NC: Duke University Press, 1995.

Mavor, Carol. *Reading Boyishly: Roland Barthes, J. M. Barrie, Jacques Henri Lartigue, Marcel Proust and D. W. Winnicott*. Durham, NC: Duke University Press, 2007.

Mavor, Carol. *Thoughts One Can't Do Without: A Magpie and an Envelope*. Milan: Juxta, 2021.

Mayer, Bernadette. *The Desires of Mothers to Please Others in Letters*. Washington, DC: SplitLevel Texts, 2017.

Mayer, Bernadette. *Memory*. Plainfield, VT: North Atlantic Books, 1976.

McBride, Jason. *Eat Your Mind: The Radical Life and Work of Kathy Acker*. New York: Simon and Schuster, 2022.

Meltzer, Eve. *Systems We Have Loved: Conceptual Art, Affect, and the Antihumanist Turn*. Chicago: University of Chicago Press, 2013.

Miller, D. A. *Jane Austen and the Secret Style*. Princeton, NJ: Princeton University Press, 2003.

Mitchell, Kaye. *Writing Shame: Gender, Contemporary Literature and Negative Affect*. Edinburgh: Edinburgh University Press, 2019.

Moon, Michael, and Eve Kosofsky Sedgwick. "Divinity: A Dossier a Performance Piece a Little-Understood Emotion." *Discourse* 13, no. 1 (1990–91): 12–39.

Mueller, Cookie. *Ask Dr. Mueller: The Writings of Cookie Mueller*. New York: Serpent's Tail, 1997.

Mueller, Cookie. "Divine Intervention: A Remembrance." *Details* 6, no. 10, May 1988.

Mueller, Cookie. *Fan Mail, Frank Letters, and Crank Calls*. New York: Hanuman Books, 1988.

Mueller, Cookie. *Garden of Ashes*. New York: Hanuman Books, 1990.

Mueller, Cookie. *How to Get Rid of Pimples*. Issues 19–20. New York: Top Stories, 1984.

Mueller, Cookie. "A Last Letter." In *City Lights Review* 2, edited by Amy Scholder, 51–52. San Francisco: City Lights Books, 1988.

Mueller, Cookie. "A Last Letter." In *Witnesses: Against Our Vanishing*, edited by Nan Goldin, 14–15. New York: Artists Space: 1989.

Mueller, Cookie. "My Bio—Notes on an American Childhood." In *Blasted Allegories: An Anthology of Writings by Contemporary Artists*, edited by Brian Tucker, 212–15. New York: Museum of Contemporary Art, 1987.

Mueller, Cookie. *Walking Through Clear Water in a Pool Painted Black*. New York: Semiotext(e), 1990.

Mueller, Cookie. *Walking Through Clear Water in a Pool Painted Black: Collected Stories*. Edited by Hedi El Kholti and Amy Scholder. South Pasadena, CA: Semiotext(e), 2022.

Mueller, Cookie, and Vittorio Scarpati. *Putti's Pudding*. Kyoto: Kyoto Shoin International, 1989.

Muñoz, José Esteban. *Disidentifications: Queers of Color and the Performance of Politics*. Minneapolis: University of Minnesota Press, 1999.

Muñoz, José Esteban. "Ephemera as Evidence: Introductory Notes to Queer Acts." *Women and Performance: A Journal of Feminist Theory* 8, no. 2 (1996): 5–16.

Muñoz, José Esteban. "Race, Sex, and the Incommensurate: Gary Fisher with Eve Kosofsky Sedgwick." In *Reading Sedgwick*, edited by Lauren Berlant, 152–66. Durham, NC: Duke University Press, 2019.

Musser, Amber Jamilla. *Sensual Excess: Queer Femininity and Brown Jouissance.* New York: New York University Press, 2018. E-book.

Myles, Eileen. *Chelsea Girls: A Novel.* London: Serpent's Tail, 2016.

Nancy, Jean-Luc. *Corpus.* Translated by Richard A. Rand. New York: Fordham University Press, 2008.

Nancy, Jean-Luc. *The Fall of Sleep.* Translated by Charlotte Mandell. New York: Fordham University Press, 2009.

Nelson, Maggie. *The Argonauts.* Minneapolis, MN: Graywolf, 2015.

Nelson, Maggie. *Bluets.* Seattle: Wave Books, 2009.

Nelson, Maggie. *Something Bright, Then Holes.* London: Zed Books, 2019.

Nelson, Maggie. *Women, the New York School, and Other True Abstractions.* Iowa City: University of Iowa Press, 2007.

Newton, Esther. "Two Shows." In *Mother Camp: Female Impersonators in America*, 59–96. 1972. Chicago: University of Chicago Press, 1979.

Ngai, Sianne. *Ugly Feelings.* Cambridge, MA: Harvard University Press, 2005.

Nyong'o, Tavia. *Afro-Fabulations: The Queer Drama of Black Life.* New York: New York University Press, 2019. E-book.

Oates, Joyce Carol. "Notes on Failure." *Hudson Review* 35, no. 2 (1982): 231–45.

O'Brien, Glenn, Annie Flanders, and Sharon Niesp. "For Cookie." *Details*, February 1990.

Ogdon, Bethany. "Through the Image: Nicholas Nixon's 'People with AIDS.'" *Discourse* 23, no. 3 (2001): 75–105.

O'Grady, Lorraine. *Writing in Space, 1973–2019.* Edited by Aruna D'Souza. Durham, NC: Duke University Press, 2020.

Osborne, Peter. *Anywhere or Not at All: Philosophy of Contemporary Art.* London: Verso, 2013.

Patton, Cindy. "Fear of AIDS: The Erotics of Innocence and Ingenuity." *American Imago* 49, no. 3 (1992): 323–41.

Patton, Cindy. "Heterosexual AIDS Panic: A Queer Paradigm." *Gay Community News*, February 9, 1985.

Paul, Celia. *Letters to Gwen John.* London: Jonathan Cape, 2022.

Pearce, Naomi. "Handling the Mail: Ambivalence and the Secretary in the Archive." Conference paper. In *Together, With, To: A Workshop on Correspondence and Letters*, Courtauld Institute of Art, June 16–17, 2022, curated and convened by Alice Butler.

Pearl, Monica. "Gazing at AIDS." In *Envisaging Death: Visual Culture and Dying*, edited by Michele Aaron, 67–81. Newcastle: Cambridge Scholars Publishing, 2013.

Peraldi, François, ed. *Polysexuality.* New York: Semiotext(e), 1981.

Pethers, Matthew. "Dead Letters and the Secret Life of the State in Nineteenth Century America." In *The Edinburgh Companion to Nineteenth-*

Century American Letters and Letter-Writing, edited by Celeste-Marie Bernier, Judie Newman, and Matthew Pethers, 136–51. Edinburgh: Edinburgh University Press, 2022.

Phelan, Peggy. *Mourning Sex: Performing Public Memories*. London: Routledge, 1997.

Phelan, Peggy. *Unmarked: The Politics of Performance*. London: Routledge, 1993.

Phillips, Adam. "Clutter: A Case History." In *Promises, Promises: Essays on Psychoanalysis*, 59–71. London: Faber and Faber, 2000.

Phillips, Rod. "Purloined Letters: *The Scarlet Letter* in Kathy Acker's *Blood and Guts in High School*." *Critique: Studies in Contemporary Fiction* 35, no. 3 (Spring 1994): 173–80.

Piper, Adrian. *Talking to Myself: The Ongoing Autobiography of an Art Object / Entretien avec moi-meme: L'autobiographie évolutive d'un objet d'art*. Hamburg: Hossmann, 1974.

Preciado, Paul B. "Learning from the Virus." Translated by Molly Stevens. *Artforum*, April 30, 2020. https://www.artforum.com/features/learning-from-the-virus-247388/.

Preciado, Paul B. "The Losers Conspiracy." *Artforum*, March 26, 2020. https://www.artforum.com/slant/paul-b-preciado-on-life-after-covid-19-82586.

Preciado, Paul B. *Testo Junkie: Sex, Drugs and Biopoitics in the Pharmacopornographic Era*. Translated by Bruce Benderson. New York: Feminist Press at the City University of New York, 2013.

Prince, Richard, ed. *Wild History*. New York: Tanam Press, 1985

Pu, Thy. "Decapitated Forms: Theresa Hak Kyung Cha's Visual Text and the Politics of Visibility." *Mosaic* 38, no. 1 (2005): 17–36.

Rand, Erica. *Barbie's Queer Accessories*. Durham, NC: Duke University Press, 1995.

Schulman, Sarah. *The Gentrification of the Mind*. Berkeley: University of California Press, 2012.

Schulman, Sarah. *Let the Record Show: A Political History of ACT UP New York*. New York: Farrar, Straus and Giroux, 2021.

Schwarz, Henry, and Anne Balsamo. "Under the Sign of *Semiotext(e)*: The Story According to Sylvère Lotringer and Chris Kraus." *Critique: Studies in Contemporary Fiction* 37, no. 3 (Spring 1996): 205–20.

Sciolino, Martina. "Confessions of a Kleptoparasite." *Review of Contemporary Fiction* 9, no. 3: 63–67.

Sedgwick, Eve Kosofsky. *A Dialogue on Love*. Boston: Beacon, 1999.

Sedgwick, Eve Kosofsky. *Fat Art, Thin Art*. Durham, NC: Duke University Press, 1994.

Sedgwick, Eve Kosofsky. "Jane Austen and the Masturbating Girl." In *Tendencies*, 109–29.

Sedgwick, Eve Kosofsky. "Making Things, Practicing Emptiness." In *The Weather in Proust*, 69–122.

Sedgwick, Eve Kosofsky. "Melanie Klein and the Difference Affect Makes." In *The Weather in Proust*, 123–43.

Sedgwick, Eve Kosofsky. "Memorial for Craig Owens." In *Tendencies*, 104–6.

Sedgwick, Eve Kosofsky. *Novel Gazing: Queer Readings in Fiction*. Durham, NC: Duke University Press, 1997.

Sedgwick, Eve Kosofsky. "Paranoid Reading and Reparative Reading, or, You're So Paranoid, You Probably Think This Introduction Is About You." In *Novel Gazing: Queer Readings in Fiction*, 1–37.

Sedgwick, Eve Kosofsky. "Paranoid Reading and Reparative Reading, or, You're So Paranoid, You Probably Think This Essay Is About You." In *Touching Feeling*, 123–51.

Sedgwick, Eve Kosofsky. "A Poem Is Being Written." In *Tendencies*, 177–214.

Sedgwick, Eve Kosofsky. "Queer and Now." In *Tendencies*, 1–20.

Sedgwick, Eve Kosofsky. "Shame in the Cybernetic Fold: Reading Silvan Tomkins (Written with Adam Frank)." In *Touching Feeling*, 93–121.

Sedgwick, Eve Kosofsky. *Tendencies*. Durham, NC: Duke University Press, 1993.

Sedgwick, Eve Kosofsky. *Touching Feeling: Affect, Pedagogy, Performativity*. Durham, NC: Duke University Press, 2003.

Sedgwick, Eve Kosofsky. *The Weather in Proust*. Edited by Jonathan Goldberg. Durham, NC: Duke University Press, 2011.

Sedgwick, Eve Kosofsky. "White Glasses." In *Tendencies*, 252–66.

Sellers, Terence. *The Correct Sadist: The Memoirs of Angel Stern*. New York: Grove, 1985.

Shaked, Nizan. "Adrian Piper: The Body After Conceptualism." In *The Synthetic Proposition: Conceptualism and the Political Referent in Contemporary Art*, 60–112. Manchester: Manchester University Press, 2017.

Smith-Rosenberg, Carroll. "The Female World of Love and Ritual: Relations Between Women in Nineteenth-Century America." *Signs* 1, no. 1 (1975): 1–29.

Solnit, Rebecca. *The Faraway Nearby*. London: Granta, 2013.

Sontag, Susan. *Illness as Metaphor*. New York: Farrar, Straus and Giroux, 1978.

Spillers, Hortense. "Mama's Baby, Papa's Maybe: An American Grammar Book." *Diacritics* 17, no. 2 (1987): 64–81.

Stallybrass, Peter. "Worn Worlds: Clothing, Mourning and the Life of Things." In *Cultural Memory and the Construction of Identity*, edited by Dan Ben-Amos and Liliane Weissberg, 27–41. Detroit, MI: Wayne State University Press, 1999.

Stewart, Susan. *On Longing: Narratives of the Miniature, the Gigantic, the Souvenir, the Collection*. Durham, NC: Duke University Press, 1993.

Stockton, Kathryn Bond. "Prophylactics and Brains: *Beloved* in the Cybernetic Age of AIDS." In *Novel Gazing: Queer Readings in Fiction*, edited by Eve Kosofsky Sedgwick, 41–73. Durham, NC: Duke University Press, 1997.

Stosuy, Brandon. *Up Is Up, but So Is Down: New York's Downtown Literary Scene, 1974–1992*. New York: New York University Press, 2006.

Strombeck, Andrew. *DIY on the Lower East Side: Books, Buildings, and Art After the 1975 Fiscal Crisis*. Albany: State University of New York, 2020.

Stupart, Linda. *Virus*. London: Arcadia Missa, 2016.

Tucker, Brian, ed. *Blasted Allegories: An Anthology of Writings by Contemporary Artists*. New York: Museum of Contemporary Art, 1987.

Vuong, Ocean. "A Letter to My Mother That She Will Never Read." *New Yorker*, May 13, 2017. https://www.newyorker.com/culture/personal-history/a-letter-to-my-mother-that-she-will-never-read.

Wark, Jayne. "Conceptual Art and Feminism: Martha Rosler, Adrian Piper, Eleanor Antin, Martha Wilson." *Woman's Art Journal* 22, no. 1 (2001): 45–50.

Wark, McKenzie. "Kathy Acker: *Get Rid of Meaning*." *Brooklyn Rail*, February 5, 2019, https://brooklynrail.org/2019/02/artseen/Kathy-Acker-Get-Rid-of-Meaning.

Wark, McKenzie. *Philosophy for Spiders: On the Low Theory of Kathy Acker*. Durham, NC: Duke University Press, 2021.

Wasdin, Katherine. "The Undead Past in Kathy Acker's *Blood and Guts in High School*." *Classical Receptions Journal* 9, no. 2 (2017): 268–86.

Watney, Simon. *Policing Desire: Pornography, AIDS and the Media*. 3rd ed. Minneapolis: University of Minnesota Press, 1996.

Wiegman, Robyn. "The Times We're In: Queer Feminist Criticism and the Reparative 'Turn.'" *Feminist Theory* 15, no. 1 (2014): 4–25.

Wilson, Emma. *Love, Mortality and the Moving Image*. Basingstoke: Palgrave Macmillan, 2012.

Winnicott, Donald W. "Adolescence: Struggling Through the Doldrums." In *The Collected Works of D. W. Winnicott: Volume 6, 1960–1963*, edited by Lesley Caldwell and Helen Taylor Robinson, 187–96. Oxford: Oxford University Press, 2016.

Winnicott, Donald W. "Transitional Objects and Transitional Phenomena." In *Playing and Reality*, 15–20. New York: Routledge, 1996.

Wojnarowicz, David. *Close to the Knives: A Memoir of Disintegration*. New York: Vintage Books, 1991.

Wojnarowicz, David. "Postcards from America: X-Rays from Hell." In *Witnesses: Against Our Vanishing*, edited by Nan Goldin, 6–11. New York: Artists Space, 1989.

Woolf, Virginia. "On Being Ill." In *The New Criterion: A Quarterly Review* 4, no. 1. London: Faber and Gwyer, 1926.

Zambaco, Demetrius. "Onanism and Nervous Disorders in Two Little Girls." In *Polysexuality*, *Semiotext(e)* #10, edited by François Peraldi, 22–36. New York: Semiotext(e), 1995.

Zambreno, Kate. "Kate Zambreno on Kathy Acker." In *Icon*, edited by Amy Scholder, unpaginated. New York: Feminist Press at the City University of New York, 2014. Kindle edition.

Zambreno, Kate. *To Write as If Already Dead*. New York: Columbia University Press, 2021. Kindle edition.

Zipes, Jack. "Writing Daydreams with Hope: Ernst Bloch." Keynote lecture, November 15, 2019. Delivered at the *To Write Art* conference, University of Copenhagen, curated and convened by Rune Gade and Carol Mavor.

Zola, Émile. *The Ladies' Paradise*. Translated by April Fitzlyon. Richmond, VA: Alma Classics, 2008.

Index

Page numbers followed by *f* indicate figures; *pl.* indicates a plate number.